# Pacific Asia?

**Asia in World Politics**

Series Editor: Samuel S. Kim

# Pacific Asia?

## Prospects for Security
## and Cooperation in East Asia

Mel Gurtov

ROWMAN & LITTLEFIELD PUBLISHERS, INC.
*Lanham • Boulder • New York • Toronto • Plymouth, UK*

ROWMAN & LITTLEFIELD PUBLISHERS, INC.

Published in the United States of America
by Rowman & Littlefield Publishers, Inc.
A wholly owned subsidiary of The Rowman & Littlefield Publishing Group, Inc.
4501 Forbes Boulevard, Suite 200, Lanham, Maryland 20706
www.rowmanlittlefield.com

Estover Road
Plymouth PL6 7PY
United Kingdom

British Library Cataloguing in Publication Information Available

**Library of Congress Cataloging-in-Publication Data**

Gurtov, Melvin.
    Pacific Asia? : prospects for security and cooperation in East Asia / Mel Gurtov.
      p. cm. — (Asia in world politics)
    Includes bibliographical references and index.
    ISBN 0-7425-0850-1 (alk. paper) — ISBN 0-7425-0851-X (pbk. : alk. paper)
      1. East Asia—Relations—Foreign countries. 2. National security—East Asia. I. Title:
  Prospects for security and cooperation in East Asia. II. Title. III. Series.

DS518.1 .G87 2002
327'.095—dc21                                                         2001048803

Printed in the United States of America

⊖™ The paper used in this publication meets the minimum requirements of American
National Standard for Information Sciences—Permanence of Paper for Printed Library
Materials, ANSI/NISO Z.39.48-1992.

# Contents

# Abbreviations

| | |
|---|---|
| ADB | Asian Development Bank |
| AMF | Asian Monetary Fund |
| AFTA | ASEAN free trade area |
| APEC | Asia-Pacific Economic Cooperation |
| ARF | ASEAN Regional Forum |
| ASEAN | Association of Southeast Asian Nations |
| ASEAN-PMC | ASEAN Post-Ministerial Conference |
| ASEM | Asia-Europe Meetings |
| CBMs/CSBMs | confidence building measures/confidence security building measures |
| CMC | Central Military Commission (China) |
| COCOM | Coordinating Committee on Multilateral Export Controls |
| CSCAP | Council for Security Cooperation in the Asia Pacific |
| CTBT | Comprehensive Test Ban Treaty |
| CWC | Chemical Weapons Convention |
| DPRK | Democratic People's Republic of Korea |
| EEZ | Exclusive Economic Zone |
| ESCAP | (UN) Economic and Social Commission for Asia and the Pacific |
| EU | European Union |
| FDI | foreign direct investment |
| FPDA | Five Power Defence Arrangements |
| GATT | General Agreements on Tariffs and Trade |
| IAEA | International Atomic Energy Agency |
| IMF | International Monetary Fund |
| KEDO | Korean Peninsula Energy Development Organization |
| LDP | Liberal Democratic Party (Japan) |
| MTCR | Missile Technology Control Regime |

| | |
|---|---|
| NAEF | Northeast Asia Economic Forum |
| NAFTA | North America Free Trade Agreement |
| NATO | North Atlantic Treaty Organization |
| NEANPEF | North-East Asia and North Pacific Environmental Forum |
| NET | natural economic territories |
| NGOs | nongovernmental organizations |
| NICs/NIEs | newly industrialized countries/newly industrialized economies |
| NPT | Nuclear Non-Proliferation Treaty |
| NWFZ | nuclear weapon free zone |
| ODA | official development assistance |
| OECD | Organization for Economic Cooperation and Development |
| OSCE/CSCE | Organization for (Conference on) Security and Cooperation in Europe |
| PAP | People's Armed Police (China) |
| PBEC | Pacific Basin Economic Council |
| PECC | Pacific Economic Cooperation Council |
| PKOs | peacekeeping operations |
| PLA | People's Liberation Army (China) |
| PLAN | PLA Navy |
| PRC | People's Republic of China |
| ROK | Republic of Korea |
| SCS | South China Sea |
| SDF | Self-Defense Forces (Japan) |
| TAC | Treaty of Amity and Cooperation |
| TMD | theater missile defense |
| TNC | transnational corporation |
| TRA | Taiwan Relations Act (U.S.) |
| TRADP | Tumen River Area Development Program |
| UNDP | United Nations Development Program |
| UNCLOS | United Nations Convention on the Law of the Sea |
| WMD | weapons of mass destruction |
| WTO | World Trade Organization |
| ZOPFAN | Zone of Peace, Freedom and Neutrality |

# Preface

It is hazardous duty to write about foreign and security policy in East Asia. The changes come with such frequency and, often, unpredictability that one week's writing is next week's garbage. Nevertheless, some things must simply be attempted because they are important. The chief inspiration for me, as some readers will know from previous work, is my dissatisfaction with the usual discussions of national and international politics, which are dominated by values and visions associated either with power (Realism) or profit (Globalism). To the extent I can contribute to the debate, or to *creating* debate, it is by writing within a critical paradigm that I have elsewhere identified as global humanism.

Since I do not devote space in this book to a discussion of global humanism, a few words about the concept are in order. Global humanism maintains that "security" needs to be redefined in terms of advancing humane values and policies—those that foster peace, social justice, environmental protection and ecological balance, political liberties, and accountable institutions. It is a critical perspective: critical of governments that make a practice of antihuman, antienvironment, unlawful behavior; critical of global corporations that put profit and resource extraction ahead of community interests; and critical of all institutions that have no intention of fulfilling their noble-sounding declarations. No single country, specifically not the United States, should be regarded as the standard-bearer or standard maker of humane values and policies.

Unlike Realism and Globalism, global humanism eschews self-interested positions; it seeks to speak for the global majority, that proportion of the world's population that experiences acute deprivation on a daily basis. Those billions of people understand far better than we, the privileged of the world, the meaning of insecurity and denial of fundamental human rights. But except for a small number of such people who come in contact with a nongovernmental organization (NGO), they have no voice. This book is one small way to give them a voice, as well as to point out the usually unpublicized work of NGOs that makes a difference in their lives.

With specific respect to East Asia, this book is an attempt to treat the question of national and regional security differently from most other writings on the subject. In no way do I mean to negate the work of others; one look at the bibliography should make clear how indebted I am to the expertise of colleagues in Asian studies and international affairs. Still, I do take issue with the pessimism, power-politics orientation, and American centeredness that guides so much analysis of East Asian security. Hopefully, the approach here will contribute to rethinking the conventional wisdom.

I would like to thank Ma Jisen, Sam Kim, Martin Hart-Landsberg, and Masahide Shibusawa for reading and commenting on portions of the book. Thanks also go to a grant from the Asia Research Fund in Seoul, which funded a trip to various Asian countries in the summer of 1999; to the Graduate School of Asia-Pacific Studies and the Transnational Program in the Center for International Education of Waseda University in Tokyo, which provided facilities and support that enabled me to finish the manuscript while there on sabbatical leave in 2001; to Jordan Durbin, Sun Lee, and Peter Noordjik for research assistance, and to Alan Ely for other kinds of support, at Portland State University; and to Susan McEachern at Rowman & Littlefield and Sam Kim for encouraging me to tackle this project. Needless to add, any errors or omissions are mine alone.

# Chapter One

# The New Face of Security
# in Post–Cold War Asia

During the 1980s and into the 1990s, when many Asian countries were recording double-digit annual economic growth rates, commentators were generally celebrating the advent of the Pacific era. There seemed to be no stopping Japan and other emerging export leaders from conquering world markets and changing the global strategic picture from military to commercial competitiveness. Then came Japan's prolonged recession, which was precipitated by the bursting of its real-estate "bubble," concerns about China's rise and America's supposed retreat from Asia, the Asian financial crisis, the eleven Indian and Pakistani nuclear tests, and renewed attention to a host of unresolved disputes between Asia Pacific countries. Optimism, even a certain Asian hubris, gave way to deep gloom.

As the new century begins, the overall picture is more muddied than before. Clearly, the end of the Cold War held many positive consequences for regional security. Propelled largely by rapid economic changes, relations between countries that were once mortal enemies have significantly improved. The strategic landscape is in this sense more stable than it was during the Cold War. But it is also more complex and uncertain: New problems have arisen, some old rivalries have refused to go away, and the once-confident belief that economic progress would be enough to make peace break out has been shaken. Just how dangerous disputes in the region are, what the elements of regional stability are, which countries' actions should be treated as threats to security, and what forms of cooperation best safeguard security are among the divisive issues.

The present and future of security in East Asia[1] are the subjects of this study. Its chief purpose is to convey different ways of defining and promoting security—different, that is, from the traditional Cold War era balance of power and from the pessimistic assumptions about East Asia's security underlying balance-of-power thinking. Everyone is agreed on the need to promote regional security, but what kind of security most urgently needs attention? Though military and strategic concerns are addressed here, the study puts great emphasis on the generally neglected areas of human, environmental, and resource security, and issues of sustainable

1

development and social justice. As to the form this understanding of security should take, I introduce, not altogether uncritically, what has come to be called an "Asian way" of building security and resolving conflicts. And I elaborate a *common*-security agenda for East Asia that is already beginning to take shape. Asia Pacific is different from other regions in the particular manner and context in which post–Cold War era issues relevant to security are being addressed. Unlike Western Europe, neither the Asia Pacific region as a whole nor East Asia in particular has formalized arrangements for security cooperation. Yet the region's governments *have* embraced various other forms of cooperation, notably of the multilateral and nonmilitary variety, and these may amount to a new way of addressing some aspects of security. Whether or not the governing parties have gone far enough, however, needs investigating.

The study begins by raising a much debated question: *Is there an Asia Pacific or an East Asian identity?* The answer is pertinent to interpreting the political shifts and other changes in the region since the end of the Cold War, and the imposing problems, domestic and transnational as well as interstate, that remain on the regional agenda. Across East Asia, economic growth is the linchpin of security, and chapter 1 also looks at the contradictory ways that rapid growth has affected international relations and domestic security in the region.

In chapter 2, our examination turns to the range of domestic and external problems that complicate East Asia's security picture. The central question tackled here is whether or not the predominant analytical approaches to understanding security, namely Realism and Globalism, are satisfactory. In attempting to answer that question, the discussion focuses on the political economy of Northeast Asia and issues that ordinarily do not make it onto the agenda of security concerns—human development and environmental degradation—as well as those that do, such as territorial disputes and arms buildups. I stress the importance of domestic and transnational nonmilitary problems, which now and even more so in the long run are fundamentally more important to regional security than are concerns about external military threats.

Southeast Asia is the focus of chapter 3, where I explore the "Asian way" of dealing with security problems. The Asian way is characterized as a consultative model of multilateralism, founded on principles of noninterference and coexistence that go back to the 1950s. It is represented primarily in the work of two groups: the ten-member Association of Southeast Asian Nations (ASEAN)[2] founded in 1967, and the twenty-one-member Asia-Pacific Economic Cooperation (APEC) forum founded in 1989.[3] These groups may be seen as responses both to Cold War era bilateralism and to the need for consensus-building in a region of great national differences, historical vulnerability, and increasingly sophisticated armaments. The Asian way is appraised in several ways, including evaluations of criticisms that it is all talk and little action, or that it has failed to meet the challenges of social injustice and environmental neglect.

These background discussions are necessary to the consideration of the most immediate matters on East Asia's security agenda: China's ambitions, Japan's quest for "normalcy," and mutual security on the Korean peninsula. These are the subjects of chapters 4, 5, and 6. In each case I take issue with some prevailing interpretations and suggest alternative ideas that can turn our thinking to common-security ways of resolving inter-state problems. The "China threat" thesis, to instance, comes into criticism, and a new look is taken at the Taiwan problem in light of Chinese realities. A "normal Japan," looking to redefine its interests in terms of a global civilian power, is preferable to a Japan still tied to and contained by the United States. Enhancing the security of *both* Koreas, I suggest, best serves the cause of peace and security in Northeast Asia.

Needless to say, these alternatives require serious rethinking about U.S. policy in East Asia, particularly the long-held conviction in Washington and in many East Asian countries that a balance of power sustained by U.S. military commitments is the only sure guarantee of regional security. The argument in chapter 7, however, is that the balance of power, already an inherently ambiguous concept, reflects Cold War thinking that is out of step with the new realities of security in East Asia. U.S. policy, I suggest, is best characterized as hegemony, not balancing of power; as such, it undermines real security needs in a number of ways. There is an urgent need to reassess U.S. strategic planning, for example with respect to forward force deployments, and embrace a common-security approach.

Common security and related ideas, such as preventive diplomacy, are the themes of the concluding chapter. There, I underscore the principal findings of the study—among them the continuing powerful appeal of nationalism in the face of globalization, positive U.S.–China relations as the key to regional peace, the domestic character of many security issues, and the necessity of investing in human development—and address the implications for strengthening common security. The Asian way of inter-state dialogue is one way to promote security; but other ways are needed, such as confidence-building measures (CBMs), multilateral and bilateral cooperation to promote safe energy alternatives and protect natural resources and environments, human development assistance programs, social justice projects, humanitarian peacekeeping, and nuclear weapon–free zones. Neither strategies based on deterrence and military power, nor economic globalization controlled by a few powerful players, are capable of promoting security where people need it most.

## IDENTIFYING "ASIA"

How one comprehends "Asia," "Asia Pacific," or "East Asia" has a bearing on the larger questions of security that frame this study; namely, whether or not a unifying concept of regional security exists and what role outside powers like the United States should play in it. For some specialists, usually those who reside outside Asia, the region is too diverse—geographically, culturally, or politically, to be taken seriously. After all, the term "Asia" is itself a Western import; "Asia Pacific" must include all of the Americas that border the Pacific Ocean, from

Canada to Chile, yet may not include South Asia west of Burma; and "East Asia" has enormous differences when contrasting the Northeast with the Southeast sub-regions. Within Asia as well as outside it, no consensus exists on which countries belong in any one of the groupings, let alone on more important matters like security.

Asian officials and scholars are the first to point, sometimes with pride and sometimes defensively, to the historical and cultural differences among countries in the region. In some cases, such as Japan's feelings of racial superiority toward other Asians and China's occasional sense of cultural superiority, the differentness is palpable. All countries in Asia (including, arguably, Japan) have distinctive ethnic, religious, and language groups whose identity often is the basis of political disputes. But Asian as well as many Western observers vigorously dispute the notion made famous by Samuel Huntington, that a "clash of civilizations" (Islamic, neo-Confucian, Japanese, Western) is taking shape in Asia.[4] National distinctions are one thing, the idea of "civilizations" is quite another—particularly since the most serious rivalries in East Asia are occurring between countries of the same "civilization."

There is also the matter of great economic and political diversity across the region. Consider only East Asia: Japan, as an economic superpower and so-called elite democracy (because of long-time dominance by the Liberal Democratic Party), is in a class by itself. So is China, which, apart from Hong Kong, remains an authoritarian political system and a rapidly developing Third World country—socialist in form but fully involved in the global capitalist system, with a total trade that approached a half-trillion dollars in 2000, and host to $45 billion annually in foreign investments. Then there are the newly industrialized countries (NICs) or economies (NIEs)—South Korea, Singapore, Taiwan, and Hong Kong–China—in which one finds a high quality of life and (except for Singapore) competitive political systems within a clientele-based political culture; the other rapidly developing economies of Southeast Asia—Thailand, Malaysia, and Indonesia—plus the Philippines and Mongolia, each of which has embraced some democratic practices but is hobbled by one or another element of traditional elitism and authoritarianism;[5] and the most underdeveloped and authoritarian countries—North Korea, Burma, Cambodia, and Laos. Finally, Australia and New Zealand are two highly developed Western democracies.

Such a multitude of disparities—to which can be added geopolitical features such as divided states (China-Taiwan and the two Koreas), numerous disputes over small islands and borders, and assorted other problems of national integration—support those who argue that neither "Asia Pacific" nor "East Asia" has much meaning in terms of region. And if that is so, then notions such as Asian unity, Asian ways of resolving conflicts, and Asian approaches to development are more myth than reality. Indeed, for some analysts they are an excuse for refusing to face up to urgent issues, such as China's power, that demand concrete action based on national interest.[6]

But in fact, a case *can* be made for an Asian identity, so long as one first discards standards that are European in origin. Viewed through the lens of the European experience, Asia Pacific certainly lacks cohesiveness and extensiveness with respect to both security and economic/political integration—in East Asia, Northeast far more so than Southeast Asia. Still, from the standpoints of history, increasing interdependence, and self-perception, Asia Pacific, or at least East Asia, does have an increasingly separate identity. "Asianization" is a real phenomenon.[7]

## THE CASE FOR "ASIA"

Nationalism is the most powerful political force in the region, and the main ingredient of a shared Asian history. From the 1920s to the 1960s, nationalism, in the form of anticolonialism and anti-imperialism, drove popular revolutions and independence movements in several countries. As the Cold War intensified, national identity weakened as most governments felt compelled to choose sides and make concessions to U.S. or Soviet-Chinese aid, basing rights, or political positions. Nationalism was channeled into state building, sometimes (as in China, North Korea, and Indonesia) subsumed under an official ideology that justified authoritarian political power. The strong or "developmental" state, whether officially socialist or capitalist, emphasized a one-party-dominant political system and a high degree of central government intervention in economic planning and performance. In fact, the strong state (and weak society) model derived largely from the Cold War itself, as the United States (notably in Japan, South Korea, and Taiwan) and the Soviet Union (in China, North Korea, and North Vietnam) subsidized allied economies built around strong-armed leaders.[8]

With the end of the Cold War and of ideology's salience, nationalism around Asia has returned to the principle of *noninterference* that animated a number of state leaders in the 1950s, from China to Indonesia to India: calling for resistance to any major power that seeks to extend its influence in Asia through its foreign policies and the powerful international institutions over which it exerts great influence. But there is another dimension to nationalism as well that affects, even *in*fects, inter-Asian relations—historical memory. Japan's World War II–era aggressions, China's glory days of empire, Vietnamese expansionism and resistance to foreign rule, Indonesia's *konfrontasi* (policy of confrontation) with Malaysia under Sukarno—to recall these elements of the past is to expose suspicions that unite some parts of Asia against other parts.

A common interest in rapid economic development has also shaped an Asian identity. The developmental-state model evolved into an "Asia-Pacific capitalism" that stands apart from American and European capitalisms.[9] For most East Asian economies, the strong (and successful) state is one that shapes commercial policy by incorporating big business, banking, and professional bureaucratic interests in the policy making process. The state thus sets the conditions for systematic, integrated economic expansion at home and abroad. Japanese electronics and automobile production networks in Southeast Asia and Chinese family run businesses conglomerates are the outcomes of such strong-state policies, which aim at maximizing exports and accelerating economic growth.

External arrangements, such as participation in multilateral groups like APEC, are also a part of the growth-through-exports strategy. But they serve a political purpose as well: to help insulate Asian economies from excessive penetration by more powerful outsiders. That is precisely what happened after the collapse of several currencies in the 1997 financial crisis, when International Monetary Fund (IMF) bailouts occurred. Nevertheless, since the distinctiveness of state capitalism in Asia and the character of Asian regional cooperation constitute elements of an Asian identity, it seems highly unlikely that either one will change dramatically because of the crisis.

As is explored later on, the Asian emphasis on networking and consensus decision making, and on not mixing economic and security goals, is quite different from the European-American style (thus frustrating to some Western observers). The origins are worth pondering here, however. The Asian approach may well have cultural roots in a shared belief in cooperation through common effort. But even more so, it may be a reaction to the historical and more recent past—an insistence on independent development and treatment as equal partners; and a shared insecurity arising out of the end of superpower competition and its replacement with regional rivalry, especially between China and Japan.[10]

Third, Asian identity is a matter of self-perception. Whether or not the perception is accurate is beside the point. For all of their acknowledged differences, Asians also perceive themselves as having much in common. Some Asian notables, such as the longtime Singapore leader Lee Kwan Yew, equate identity with the notion of Asian values, as much to counteract the perceived corrupting effects of Western values (including the celebration of cultural diversity itself) as to promote what are said to be uniquely Asian ways of being and relating. Other Asian, as well as Western, commentators reject the notion that a modern Asian identity requires casting aside everything "Western." In fact, for some, hard-and-fast distinctions between sets of values are fruitless inasmuch as the origins of traditions such as personal freedom, tolerance, and the rule of law are by no means settled. These observers find the Asian difference today in the fusion of modern Western ideas, including multiculturalism, democratic practices, and human rights, with traditional Asian concerns, such as family, education, the paternalistic state, and social harmony.[11]

At bottom, the argument over *which* Asia may really be over *whose* Asia. It is a question of whether Asia should be treated as object or subject. Those who slight the notion of an Asian regional identity tend to belong to the Realist school, which is impatient with Asian claims to uniqueness and believes that in actuality Asian governments are (or should be) just as concerned as Western governments with issues of national power. The Realists regard Asia as a (security-) dependent region—dependent, that is, on the role of the United States as the "swing power."

What counts most in the Realists' security equation is not Asian nationalism, the importance of the noninterference principle is often quickly dismissed, but the strategic role of the United States and its "*anti*regional" policies.[12] The alternative view (which, for lack of a better term, will be called the Asian school) underscores the region-wide quest for independence in policy making. This school does not reject the Realists' balance of power thinking, but it does reject some of its implications, such as the desirability of alignment with or alignment against any one major power, and reliance mainly on military power for security rather than on other forms of power. Defenders of the Asian school remind us that political divisions created by the Cold War account for weak regional identity in Asia, and not only (as critics often say) cultural and historical differences. The preferred path to security therefore properly emphasizes cooperative activities on the basis of common interests (economic especially) rather than an overt balance-of-power strategy.[13]

The influence of Asian nationalism can be seen in this latter argument, whose thrust is not to repeat past patterns of alliance with this or that camp. Asia should control its own destiny to the extent possible. Realists scoff at this and observe that a U.S. strategic presence in the region is desired by most Asian governments. Asianists do not dispute this point either; but they note that Asian leaders are virtually unanimous in believing that the end of the Cold War is an opportunity at last to end the region's dependence on or suffering under great-power predominance. Such thinking certainly extends to the economic domain: American (as well as European) self-interest in pushing globalization while seeking to limit Asian states' efforts to protect against it is just the sort of pressure that challenges Asia's emerging sense of identity.

As we will see, neither of these schools pays much attention to the "other Asia," where ordinary people live. In this other Asia, security has an entirely different meaning from the one governments debate. Problems such as urban growth, environmental decline, food security, and rural poverty increasingly dominate the policy agendas of Asia Pacific and thus help define the region's commonality. Now, these *human* security issues are on the agenda too as some government leaders, after much prodding by nongovernmental organizations (NGOs), come to recognize how dependent social and economic stability is on both the people's and the environment's well-being.

## CHANGING RELATIONSHIPS
## IN A DIVERSE REGION: AN OVERVIEW

One way to appreciate the extensiveness of the changes in Asia Pacific security is to categorize them at the different levels—state, regional, and global—at which they have taken place over roughly the last twenty years. This multilevel approach may be of assistance in coming to grips with the different kinds of post–Cold War security problems that East Asia faces now, and may face in decades hence.

## Relations between States

There has been a remarkable number of diplomatic breakthroughs since the start of the 1990s, in which previously hostile countries either normalized or established relations: Russia and the People's Republic of China (PRC) with the Republic of Korea (ROK, South Korea, in 1990 and 1992 respectively); China with Indonesia, Singapore, Mongolia, and Laos (1990), and with Vietnam (1991); the United States and Vietnam (1995); and the Democratic People's Republic of Korea (DPRK, North Korea) with nearly all the ASEAN and European Union (EU) countries in 2000–2001. In addition, various bilateral agreements were negotiated to reduce tensions or forces, and/or to encourage deeper cooperation. North and South Korea signed accords in 1991 to remove nuclear weapons from the peninsula, defuse military tensions through confidence-building measures, and promote cultural and people-to-people exchanges. The accords had little effect, but in June 2000, in very different international circumstances, the spirit of those accords was revived when the two Korean leaders held an unprecedented summit meeting in Pyongyang.

Other tension-reducing agreements in the 1990s include the Russia-China agreement on border force reductions and nuclear weapon detargeting; the establishment by China and Taiwan of quasi-official committees to discuss common ("nonpolitical") issues such as hijacking and family visits; a Sino-Indian agreement to reduce border tensions; and agreements with Russia, Kazakhstan, Tajikistan, and Kyrgyzstan between the early 1990s and 2000 that provide for CBMs in military deployments and cooperation on border security. Economic opportunity and strategic calculation, sometimes in combination, account for these developments. In the Chinese case, for instance, the "opening to the outside world" during the 1980s gave priority to trade and foreign investment as the driving forces behind modernization. The PRC is now among the world's top ten trading countries and a favored location for foreign investment. Hong Kong aside, China's leading economic partners are all former enemy states: Taiwan, South Korea, Russia, and most prominently the United States and Japan. Or take the multilateral agreements just noted in Central Asia, which have been prompted not just by common concerns about ethnic minority unrest, but also in China's case by the need for access to the gas and oil fields of Kazakstan.

The economic and technological forces that comprise "globalization" have had diverse consequences around Asia, a subject explored in greater depth later in this chapter. They have undoubtedly contributed to the evolution of more pluralist and accountable political systems in Russia, South Korea, Thailand, Hong Kong, Taiwan, and Mongolia. The impact of globalization on countries with problems of national integration has been less clear. The crumbling of Indonesia's economy in the Asian financial crisis did more than simply pave the way for the end of one-man rule in 1998 (President Suharto); it served to open the door to East Timor's independence in 1999 and to separatist movements and communal violence in other outlying islands of the republic, such as in Aceh on Sumatra, among the Dayaks on Kalimantan, and in Irian Jaya on the western end of New Guinea. Hong Kong's integration with China since 1997 has been reasonably smooth, largely because Beijing has avoided interfering with Hong Kong's economy. But for PRC-Taiwan relations, globalization has produced economic closeness and increased political distance.

Globalization has meant enormous new wealth for Asian elites. The new prosperity has enhanced the potential for diplomatic tension as well as political and social instability. The scale of corruption, organized crime (in particular, its role in the smuggling of people and drugs), and labor migration and exploitation (especially of women and children) seems to be greater than ever before throughout Asia and worldwide. Relations between Thailand and Burma have become strained as a result of the drug trade, which targets Thai youth, corrupts politics in the poor northeast region, and makes Thailand a major transit point for the international drug trade.[14] Burma's heroin, combined with prostitution in Thailand, also makes for a regional AIDS epidemic that extends from eastern India across to southern China.[15]

Domestic political stability, I will stress throughout, profoundly affects foreign-policy thinking and behavior. Progress in democratization in South Korea, Thailand, and the Philippines has been conducive to foreign-policy initiatives such as the inter-Korean summit and the promotion of human rights and social justice within multilateral groups such as ASEAN. On the other hand, where the military looms large in politics (as in Burma, North Korea, and Indonesia), or where political authority is monopolized by a single party (as in China, North Korea, Burma, Cambodia, Laos, Malaysia, Vietnam, and Singapore), repression is likely to be the common reaction to groups demanding autonomy or respect for human rights. Political leaders in these countries are typically insecure and nationalistic, and thus they are as opposed to promoting a democratic or environmental agenda at home as abroad. The Burmese junta is a notorious example, with its efforts to manipulate the several ethnic groups that it has been at war with at various times, its horrendous human-rights record (especially in suppressing the political opposition), and (as noted above) its acceptance, if not outright involvement in, drug trafficking.[16]

The Indonesian military has a long history of violently suppressing separatist movements. Its withdrawal from East Timor in 2000 occurred only after it had armed paramilitary groups that forced people to flee East Timor, preventing a vote in favor of East Timor's independence. In the end, it took an Australian-led United Nations peacekeeping mission to restore order. Machine politics in Singapore and Malaysia, Mongolia's experimentation with democratic and market reforms, and China's repression of human rights activists, Tibetan monks, protesters on behalf of ethnic minorities, and religious groups all experience fallout across borders.

Environmentally, Asia's omnipresent push for economic development has taken an especially large toll, which will be explored further in chapter 2. The underside of the Asian "miracle" is that GNP increases, trade surpluses, and large-scale construction projects have meant not only more consumerism and more jobs, but also large-scale migration to cities, choking urban pollution, lowering water tables, and denuded forests, among other calamities.[17] Each of these problems affects politics at the global level; but they also affect state-to-state relations. For example, an issue in Sino–South Korean relations is China's refusal to allow North Koreans who manage to cross into China as they flee famine and despotism to be repatriated to South Korea instead of forced back into the North. Desertification in China's northern provinces carries "yellow sand" across the Koreas and over Japan. Since 1997 the haze from Indonesia's annual palm oil plantation fires, deliberately set by the companies to clear land, causes serious air pollution in Singapore and Malaysia. The ill treatment of migrant workers who perform "3-D" work (dirty, dangerous, and difficult) raises issues of discrimination internally, while externally it causes problems when (as happened in the late 1990s) those workers are forced to return to their home countries.

## Regional Developments

Regional changes have been a mixed bag of positive and potentially troublesome developments. In terms of regional cooperation, ASEAN accomplished the objective of universality beginning in 1995 when it admitted Vietnam, and later Laos, Cambodia, and Burma. Militarily, the Cold War's end meant the demise of the "Soviet threat" and a declining U.S. presence, from about 135,000 ground and naval forces in the western Pacific in 1990 to around 100,000 since 1996. Until the financial crisis of 1997–1998 set in, arms imports and official military spending had accelerated, as discussed below. But a number of international and bilateral agreements have helped to restrain arms buildups and deployments in East Asia and make progress in confidence building. They include the South Pacific (1986) and Southeast Asia (1995) nuclear weapon free zones, which ban the acquisition and use of nuclear weapons; China's and North Korea's decision to join the Nuclear Non-Proliferation Treaty (NPT) regime, whose life was indefinitely extended in 1995; the aforementioned North-South Korea denuclearization accord; reductions in the strategic nuclear weapons arsenals of the United States and Russia; international agreement to end nuclear-weapons testing under the 1996 Comprehensive Test Ban Treaty (CTBT); and a freeze on North Korea's putative nuclear-weapons program under the U.S.–DPRK "Agreed Framework" of October 1994, which created an international consortium—the Korean Peninsula Energy Development Organization (KEDO), whose principal members are the United States, South Korea, and Japan—to replace North Korea's nuclear power plants and provide for its oil needs.

Nevertheless, Northeast Asia continues to have the world's largest concentration of conventional weapons and weapons of mass destruction (WMD). Besides U.S. forces, which are based mainly in South Korea (around 37,000) and Japan (47,000), Chinese troops number 2.5 to 2.8 million, Japanese 237,000,

Russian 690,000, South Korean 633,000, and North Korean over 1.1 million. All of these armed forces also have substantial combat aircraft and naval (including submarine) strength, though of widely varying capability.[18] Nuclear arsenals remain incomprehensibly high and dangerously asymmetrical.[19] In 2000, the United States and Russia together still had over 30,000 deployed nuclear warheads, most of them on around 2,200 strategic (i.e., intercontinental) missiles and bombers. Russia's Pacific-based air and sea nuclear forces are smaller than in Soviet days, but relied on for deterrence perhaps more now than before;[20] and the U.S. submarine-based nuclear force is, in and of itself, probably sufficient to destroy every military target in Asia.

China, with about forty strategic delivery systems and over 400 deployed nuclear warheads, is a major nuclear and missile power.[21] It also has deployed 200–300 medium-range missiles opposite Taiwan. North Korea, despite its promising diplomatic engagements with the United States and South Korea, which in 2000 resulted in a DPRK-U.S. agreement to suspend missile tests, remains a mystery with respect to the extent of its nuclear weapons and missile programs. But it is fairly well-established that Pyongyang has received assistance on ballistic missile development from the PRC and Egypt. North Korea, South Korea, Taiwan, and even Vietnam all have deployed ballistic missiles with ranges of at least 100 kilometers; North Korea and China have long been accused by the United States of selling missile components and technology to Pakistan, Iran, and other Middle East countries; and Japan is certainly capable of developing long-range missiles as well as nuclear weapons on short notice.

Finally, this gloomy picture of WMD capabilities must note weaknesses in international arms-control agreements. North Korea, India, and Pakistan are the only three (of a total of forty-four) nuclear weapon–capable countries that have failed to at least sign the CTBT, thus preventing it from officially coming into force.[22] The NPT regime still does not include India and Pakistan; but even more significantly, lack of full safeguards on nuclear power facilities and adequate export controls have led to charges that some countries (China and North Korea) have transferred nuclear weapon materials. While the United States has usually been the source of those charges, its own record is blemished by failing, with Russia, to meet the original treaty's basic requirement of working toward nuclear disarmament.

Despite widespread adherence to the Chemical Weapons Convention (CWC) of 1997 that banned chemical weapons production, transfers, stockpiling, and deployment, research on and trade in such weapons or components apparently continues.[23] According to U.S. intelligence, North Korea, which is not a signatory of the treaty, and China and Russia (or at least Chinese and Russian export firms), which have signed and ratified the treaty, have supplied agents, equipment, and technology to Iran and other countries for use in manufacturing chemical weapons. Furthermore, North Korea may have active chemical and biological weapons programs.[24] These governments deny the charges, as they do charges of missile transfers; but the suspicions remain that they *are* engaged in these activities, adding to the complications of stabilizing relations between them and the United States, South Korea, and Japan.

The regional economic side presents a much more positive picture, but with troubling aspects nevertheless. At the macro level, the APEC economies account for more than one-half of global GNP. East Asia's share of world trade has doubled since 1970 to around one-fifth. Trade within East Asia and within the APEC group continues to rise as a proportion of countries' total trade. Tariffs and other barriers to trade have generally declined. APEC has sought to move in step with completion of the Uruguay Round and the evolution of the GATT (General Agreements on Tariffs and Trade) system into the World Trade Organization (WTO); and within the ASEAN-10, an AFTA (ASEAN Free Trade Area) has been progressively lowering tariffs, ultimately reaching zero by 2005. National economies have become more transnational, focusing on complementary factor endowments that can promote trade and attract investment. Whether pushed by business interests or by government policy, the phenomenon of "growth triangles" has spread. Examples include Greater China (China's Guangdong and Fujian provinces, Hong Kong, and Taiwan), the Yellow Sea Zone (north China and the Korean peninsula), and Sijori (Singapore, Johore in Malaysia, and Batam island in Indonesia). Japanese capital, especially since the mid-1980s when the yen was revalued, has led the way in the establishment of production networks around Southeast Asia. These have further integrated Japan's economy with the region.

Human and technology resources have been greatly affected by the trade push.[25] South Korea, Taiwan, and more recently China, have joined Japan as major sources of technological innovation and high-tech exports. Some countries, such as India and Singapore, have become booming centers for new computer firms and data processing. The acquisition of technology is a top priority in the trade policies of Asian (as, seemingly, of all other) countries. Education is the key: In a reversal of the traditional "brain drain," tens of thousands of students from Asia, led by PRC, Taiwan, and Japanese students, have received technology and business training in the United States and returned home to work or start new "dot com" companies. Indian and Vietnamese entrepreneurs residing in the United States have also begun returning home. At the same time, high-tech companies from some of these same countries have established "outposts" in Silicon Valley and the other advanced economies of the United States.

All of these developments have exacted costs, however. Richer and poorer Asian economies alike have been forced to open their trade and investment doors wider and much more quickly than they would have liked under the pressure of globalization. This has caused considerable resentment, such as bubbled to the surface in South Korea, where anti-IMF sentiment ran high for awhile after bailout loans were conditioned on allowing foreign firms to buy out or joint-venture with Korean companies and banks; in Malaysia, whose leader proclaimed that foreigners had conspired to create a currency crisis; and in Indonesia, where the IMF's intervention looked to many like a colonial imposition. Japan's use of its dominant investment position to promote its trade interests has caused friction. Most of its trade partners run persistent trade deficits with Japan, in part due to imports by Japanese transnational corporations (TNCs) of Japanese technology. TNCs in general have been accused by NGOs in their host countries and elsewhere of exploitative practices with regard to health and safety standards, employment of child labor, low wages, and extraction of natural resources (such as in the mining and timber industries) with little or no regard for the environmental consequences. Acquiring technology can lead to ugly international disputes—see chapter 4 on the U.S.–PRC conflict over high-tech trade that has military applications—especially because those who control it (the Americans and the Japanese) are increasingly reluctant to share it, whereas those who don't (the Chinese and the Koreans, for instance) resent their technological dependence.

The impact of rapid economic growth on individuals and communities in East Asia also gives reason to pause. The details are presented in the next chapter; here, we can briefly note some trends. It is possible to point to some bright spots as, for example, the World Bank does: the declining rate (percent) and number of people living in absolute poverty (defined as income of under $1 a day), declining infant mortality levels, rising life expectancy, reduced adult illiteracy, and increased secondary enrollment.[26] These trends, which are based on *average* figures for the region, compare favorably with those of other developing areas. Much of the improvement can be traced to poverty-reduction efforts in just two countries, China and Vietnam, both of which have undertaken socialist market reforms.

On the other hand, the road to be traveled to reach something approaching social justice is long indeed. Even before the financial crisis, Bruce Koppel wrote:

> Five hundred eighty-five million Asians do not have access to health care, and the average level of education ranges from two years for South Asian women to eight years for Filipino men. Each year, nearly 7 million Asian children die before their 5th birthday, and close to 300,000 women die in childbirth, with an additional 9 million incurring injuries, infections, and disabilities during pregnancy. Child malnutrition is more prevalent in South Asia than in sub-Saharan Africa.[27]

According to the Asian Development Bank (ADB), about 15 percent of East Asia's population and 40 percent of South Asia's were living in absolute poverty in 1996. Adding in those people forced into poverty by the financial crisis, a total of around 900 million people in Asia now are impoverished.[28] The World Bank's director acknowledged that the crisis had "wip[ed] out in a matter of months gains that had taken a generation to build."[29]

Across Asia, about one-quarter of the region's adults is still illiterate. Fewer than half of all girls are enrolled in secondary schools. Outside of sub-Saharan Africa, Asia-Pacific countries have the highest number of people with AIDS or the H.I.V. virus that causes it—over six million.[30] Populations are rapidly aging *because of* improvements in health care and declining fertility. For South Korea, Japan, and China, this development "will not only put pressure on national social security systems but, in addition, will have profound implications for long-term economic growth."[31] Asia's rapid urbanization adds to the aging problem: Population density, unemployment, and pressure on social services take a huge slice of budgets, diminishing the prosperity that great cities may seem to enjoy if one looks only at the skyscrapers.

Though economic growth of some kind is an essential condition of poverty alleviation, in East Asia it has been shown that growth by itself cannot *equitably* deliver the goods. As the aftermath of the financial crisis showed, while *economies* recovered, millions of *people* did not: According to the World Bank, it was, "a collapse that pushed millions back to the brink of poverty and decimated the savings of a whole generation of new middle-class citizens."[32] Later, the Bank's leader was more specific—41 million people were pushed into poverty.[33] Not surprisingly, "economic recovery" did not trickle down. A report on Indonesia, for example, while saying that "many claims [of an economic disaster] are exaggerated," found that "poverty rates have risen—by at least 25 percent." As a result, state budgeting for education declined, as did public health services, and the cost of food rose.[34] Naturally, these setbacks harmed the poorest families the most, which some might consider an economic disaster in a country where the poverty rate had been reduced to around 15 percent by the time of the financial crisis.

## Global Issues

Because of global interdependence, transnational and intra-state issues in Asia are on the agenda of international organizations. These include human rights, labor problems, the activities of transnational corporations and banks, peace-keeping, protection of the environmental commons, the maritime regime (seabed resources, territorial waters, and navigation rights), disarmament, and development assistance. Responsiveness to global issues also includes evidence of greater international "burden-sharing" by governments on global issues.

Political stability in East Asia is threatened by serious problems of governance. The passing of the era of radical rebellion ("communist insurgency," in the Cold War vernacular of Washington) has revealed other, equally intractable internal problems. In most one-party dominant systems, as well as in some other countries where politics have become more competitive (such as Malaysia and Indonesia since 1998), political successions are uncertain, the military's capacity to intervene in politics may be blunted but cannot be ruled out, and suppression of political critics and cultural minorities may lead to wider violence. Even in Taiwan, South Korea, and the Philippines, where democratic practices have taken root, national politics continue to be heavily influenced by corruption, personal rivalries, unstable parties, and even (as happened in Manila in 2001) the possibility of a coup d'état.

Nevertheless, looking back over the past twenty years leads to some degree of cautious optimism. Conditions for basic political liberties have greatly improved in several countries, among them Russia, South Korea, Taiwan, Thailand, and Indonesia. Most governments in East Asia, including China, have signed the basic United Nations human rights covenants—for example, those on "Civil and Political Rights" and "Economic, Social, and Cultural Rights" (which were drawn up in 1966), as well as conventions on torture, genocide, and discrimination against minorities and women. Systematic violations of the UN convenants continue, however. Naturally many Asian leaders resent being lectured to about such abuses of civil rights, but some of them acknowledge the need to confront abuses precisely as a means to sustain economic progress and ensure governmental legitimacy.[35]

Regarding *political rights*, many basic freedoms (such as press, personal movement, and speech) are still routinely denied around Asia. Respect for civil liberties and the rule of law is noticeably absent in China, North Korea, Vietnam, or Burma, all of which have at least signed the UN covenant, as well as in Indonesia, which has not signed it. Corruption and nepotism remain fixtures of the political scene, all the more so due to the extraordinary new wealth that market reforms have created. China, Nepal, Indonesia, Vietnam, and Russia, for example, have all had to grapple with serious official and business corruption, and with private gangs and politically powerful tycoons. Their effects have been to undermine civil-society tendencies, destroy public faith in the rule of law, and distort economies. On the other hand, in China and Vietnam, market reforms have contributed to the erosion of one-party rule. The Communist Party secretary has become a mere figurehead in many towns and villages, with real authority in the hands of local entrepreneurs. Institutional checks on the powers of the state or localities are only now appearing in a few countries, as is voting for representative government.

Protection of many *economic and social* rights has clearly improved in many countries of East Asia. However, the right to form independent labor unions and to strike has yet to be widely accepted. Discrimination against women and female children, in the home, at the workplace, and in educational opportunity, is well known, and of course occurs most frequently in situations of poverty and low literacy. But not entirely: Tens and perhaps hundreds of thousands of foreign women have been brought into Japan by criminal groups for what amounts to sexual slavery.[36] And it is well known that Japanese businessmen travel regularly to Thailand for sexual pleasure at the expense of children.

Ethnic minority groups endure various forms of abuse in all countries—in richer countries such as Japan and South Korea, to which migrant workers are moving in ever-greater numbers; in countries such as Indonesia and Malaysia, where Chinese communities tend to be the major business owners; and in poor countries such as the Philippines and Burma, where ethnic groups have long been in rebellion.

Environmental conditions in much of East Asia are cause for deep concern if not alarm. A short list of the kinds of problems each country faces would include the following:

*Water quality and availability*: China faces a crisis of both dwindling water for human and industrial use, and watershed deterioration. Water quality is also a serious issue in several other countries, developed as well as poor.[37]

*Forest destruction*, whether caused by illegal logging operations as in Cambodia and Thailand,[38] by timber exporters as in tropical Southeast Asia, or by individuals as in China, is adding enormously to desertification and global warming.

*Greenhouse-gas emissions*, due mostly to rapid industrialization and forest fires, are increasing much faster than the world average.[39] China and India have become major contributors to the so-called greenhouse effect.

*Global climate change*, brought about by the greenhouse-gas problem, is already threatening to inundate the South Sea islands in the not-too-distant future.[40]

*Fish habitats* are also threatened, due for example to overfishing to satisfy Japanese and southern Chinese tastes.

*Ecological destruction* is widening, such as that of coral reefs in Southeast Asia due to use of cyanide to stun fish, and of mangroves in Vietnam by shrimp farming.

*Reliance for electricity on nuclear power* is posing safety problems in Japan, South Korea, Taiwan, and the PRC, as well as difficulties in safely burying nuclear waste.

*Wildlife species* (including migratory species) are disappearing at an "alarming" rate because of deforestation in China, Thailand, and other parts of Southeast Asia, as well as in India, Australia, and Sri Lanka.

*Acid rain* is increasing, notably in Northeast Asia, with consequent destruction of crops and forests.[41]

*Unrecycled garbage* is adding to urban pollution, as in Japan.

*Air pollution* is at an appalling level in all of East Asia's major cities.

Environmental problems such as these compound the difficulties of achieving anything like sustainable development. In some cases this is due to increased poverty, in other cases to unregulated economic growth and the fixation on promoting trade with little or no regard for the product's origins. Insufficient state capacity, or will, to regulate and monitor the environment often stymies improvement—by now most East Asian countries have environmental protection agencies, but they are understaffed, underfunded, and no match for other bureaucracies. And official (civilian and military) and business corruption feeds exploitation of environment and resources for personal gain.[42] The failure of the state to protect the environment makes NGOs and community activism crucial to environmental protection, as is argued in the concluding chapter. A survey of country reports submitted by governments to the Earth Summit in June 1992 revealed that deforestation and the destruction of biodiversity have "reached critical proportions in Asia and the Pacific."[43] Commercial interests, not shifting agriculture, are the chief culprit in the rapid destruction of Southeast Asia's tropical forests; and none of the affected countries has a policy of sustainable forest management that might slow the destruction.[44]

"Five of the world's seven most polluted cities are located in the developing nations of Asia: Beijing, Calcutta, Jakarta, New Delhi, and Shenyang."[45] These and other "megacities" account for "the world's highest levels" of air pollution.[46] Much of it is caused by reliance on coal for winter heating. Lack of modern pollution controls on smokestacks, especially in China, contributes to the rapid increase of sulfur dioxide that carries acid rain across Northeast Asia.[47] Overfishing and offshore pollution are or may become serious problems in the South Pacific, the Yellow Sea, and the East (Japan) Sea. According to Greenpeace, millions of tons of toxic wastes from the major industrial countries are being shipped to (actually, dumped in) the poorest Asian countries.[48]

Poverty, rapid growth, and environmental decline add up to an enormous bill that also has wider political significance. The World Bank has estimated, for instance, that "developing East Asian countries will need to invest between $1.2 trillion and $1.5 trillion, or 7 percent of regional GDP, in transportation, power, telecommunications, and water and sanitation facilities in the next decade." Included in that estimate is around $200 billion to cope with rapid urbanization.[49] Who should pay? To protect whom? While promoting private investment as the chief source of such funding, the Bank made gross disbursements to Asia Pacific countries of over $34 billion between 1994 and 1999. But 80 percent of that amount was designated for only three countries: China ($12.6 billion), Indonesia ($6.9 billion), and South Korea ($8.1 billion).[50] That left very little for the poorest countries and communities. And nearly $13 billion of the total disbursements returned to the Bank in interest and fees. The Bank has also had a poor record, which it has acknowledged, when it comes to environmental protection, notably dam construction. But more recently it has begun to focus on the need for clean water, critical in China and several other countries.

Promoting private sector solutions to regional and global problems is at the heart of World Bank and IMF practices. Notwithstanding that unregulated, large-scale flows of private capital to East Asia were an important reason for the currency crisis—about $160 billion flooded into five East Asian "emerging markets" in 1995 and 1996 alone[51]—the World Bank remains convinced of private capital's salutary effects. Official development assistance (ODA) is small compared with direct private and portfolio (stock and mutual fund) investments, and the Bank's mission seems to be to get private capital back to the high level it was at (around $100 billion) before the 1997 crisis.[52] There are several problems with this approach that I take up in later chapters.

ODA and contributions to United Nations peacekeeping operations (PKOs) are two other forms of global burden-sharing. Japan occupies the number-one position worldwide in ODA loans and grants, giving over $14 billion in 1995.[53] As a percentage of GDP (0.28 percent), that is not a particularly impressive figure since the UN long ago set a target for all developed countries of 0.7 percent. It is also well known that Japanese ODA, about 60 percent of which goes to other Asian countries, is mainly intended to promote trade interests (hence, the largest amount to Indonesia), not sustainable development in the poorest countries. Still, Japan's ODA is almost twice the U.S. contribution. Australia and South Korea are the only other East Asian sources of ODA.

Support of UN PKOs is strong among Asia Pacific countries. For Japan, such support is a principal way to "make a contribution," as Japanese government figures often put it, to international peace and security. Thus, Japan pays about 20 percent of the UN's regular budget, higher than its share of world GNP (around 17 percent) and thus a source of some irritation.[54] Its UN assessment for peacekeeping missions runs about $264 million, just under Russia's assessment. By contrast, China's regular budget assessment is 0.74 percent (about $17 million); India's, 0.31 percent ($1.2 million); and Indonesia's, 0.14 percent ($1 million). When it comes to soldiers, however, the figures are reversed: Pakistan, India, and Malaysia have contributed the most personnel by far, and to the most number of UN PKOs, whereas Japan has contributed to only four PKOs and China to eight, always with civilians or soldiers in noncombat roles.[55] Crudely put, some countries are putting bodies on the line for collective security, and others mainly money or observers.

## TRENDS

In summary, the challenges to national and regional security in Asia Pacific are formidable. History counts heavily in Asia, and nationalism is central to political conflict—not just in the case of unresolved territorial disputes over islands, borders, and reunification of divided countries, but also with respect to policy making and in the tendency of governments to remember their victimization at the hand of a neighbor. But observers of East Asia and Asia Pacific generally ought not neglect those elements that bind the region together, including nationalism. Resistance to colonization in any form, including the controlling influence of global corporations and banks, and noninterference by outside powers in a country's internal affairs, are powerful ideas. Along with a common conviction that exports mean growth and thus political stability, and a self-perception of a new Asia with a globally relevant set of cultural and historical values, these notions create an Asian identity that cannot be dismissed simply because it doesn't fit in an Anglo-American framework.

The security picture is framed not only by identity issues but also by state-to-state relations, and by domestic, regional, and transnational developments. At every level, we can find cause for optimism as well as for pessimism. International relations in East Asia have improved enormously since the end of the Cold War, and common economic interests are a major reason for that. Political systems have become more competitive and accountable; economies have opened up and in some cases recovered from the shock of 1997; popular movements for social change and environmental protection have begun to dot the political map. But the negative side is at least equally prominent. Rapid economic growth has made for a very uneven "Pacific Century." Environmental problems are especially severe virtually everywhere thanks to industrialization, urbanization, and government action that is insufficient or throttled by corruption. Rapid urbanization, increased greenhouse-gas emissions, and extraordinary levels of deforestation are not merely matters for scientists; they compound the social costs of economic growth, add new dimensions to the problem of maintaining political stability, and are sources of regional and global concern. In many parts of Asia, human security, and human rights of all kinds, have not benefited from economic advances. The concentration of arms in Northeast Asia shows that the Cold War is not really over. Politics are unstable and undemocratic in many countries due to pervasive corruption, identity conflicts, entrenched interests, and outright authoritarianism.

In short, if it is difficult to define an Asian identity, it is even more difficult to characterize in a few words what has been happening in Asia, or any of its subregions, over the last twenty years. Yet policy making depends on characterizations. We must therefore examine these elements of security and insecurity in greater depth in order to arrive at a more nuanced set of conclusions.

## NOTES

1. "East Asia" refers to Northeast and Southeast Asia, including the Russian Far East and Taiwan. "Asia" includes the Indian subcontinent, the South Pacific, and Oceania as well as East Asia. "Asia Pacific" refers to all of these areas as well as the Americas facing the Pacific.

2. ASEAN's members are Thailand, Indonesia, Singapore, Philippines, Malaysia, Brunei, Vietnam, Laos, Burma, and Cambodia.

3. APEC's membership is based on economic status; members are "economies" rather than states. East Asian membership is almost universal—it includes Russia, Taiwan (as "Chinese Taipei"), and Hong Kong, but does not yet include North Korea, Vietnam, Cambodia, and Laos. Three Latin American countries are members: Mexico, Chile, and Peru.

4. Samuel Huntington, "The Clash of Civilizations?" *Foreign Affairs*, vol. 72, no. 3 (Summer 1993): 22–49.

5. Malaysia's politics is an example. By 2000, Prime Minister Mahathir bin Mohamad had ruled for nineteen years, the longest in Asia. His firing in 1998 of Anwar Ibrahim, deputy prime minister and presumed heir, and the subsequent arrest and conviction of Anwar on highly questionable corruption and sodomy charges, put Malaysia's judicial system and human rights record in a negative light.

6. See, for example, Gerald Segal, "'Asianism' and Asian Security," *The National Interest*, no. 42 (Winter 1995–1996): 58–65.

7. Robert A. Scalapino, "The United States and Asia: Future Prospects," *Foreign Affairs*, vol. 70, no. 5 (Winter 1991–1992): 26.

8. Richard Stubbs, "Asia-Pacific Regionalization and the Global Economy," *Asian Survey*, vol. 35, no. 9 (September 1995): 787–88. Stubbs cites Joel S. Migdal's 1988 study, *Strong Societies and Weak States*, on this particular point.

9. Stubbs, "Asia-Pacific Regionalization," 785–97.

10. Suisheng Zhao, "Asia-Pacific Regional Multipolarity: From Alliance to Alignment in the Post–Cold War Era," *World Affairs*, vol. 159, no. 4 (Spring 1997): 183–96.

11. Fareed Zakaria, "Culture is Destiny: A Conversation with Lee Kwan Yew," *Foreign Affairs*, vol. 73, no. 2 (March–April 1994): 109–26; Kim Dae Jung, "Is Culture Destiny? The Myth of Asia's Anti-Democratic Values," *Foreign Affairs*, vol. 73, no. 6 (November–December 1994): 189–94; Kishore Mahbubani, "The Pacific Way," *Foreign Affairs*, vol. 74, no. 1 (January–February 1995): 100–112; Amartya Sen, "Human Rights and Asian Values," *The New Republic* (July 14–21, 1997): 33–36.

12. See, for example, Barry Buzan, "The Asia-Pacific: What Sort of Region in What Sort of World?" in *Asia-Pacific in the New World Order*, ed. Anthony McGrew and Christopher Brook (London: Routledge, 1998), 68–87. See also Buzan and Gerald Segal, "Rethinking East Asian Security," *Survival*, vol. 36, no. 2 (1994): 3–21; Donald C. Hellmann, "America, APEC, and the Road Not Taken: International Leadership in the Post–Cold War Interregnum in the Asia-Pacific," in *From APEC to Xanadu: Creating a Viable Community in the Post–Cold War Pacific*, ed. Donald C. Hellmann and Kenneth B. Pyle (Armonk, N.Y.: M.E. Sharpe, 1997), 70–97.

13. Peter Drysdale and Andrew Elek, "APEC: Community-Building in East Asia and the Pacific," in *From APEC to Xanadu*, ed. Hellman and Pyle, 37–69; Andrew Mack and Pauline Kerr, "The Evolving Security Discourse in the Asia-Pacific," *The Washington Quarterly*, vol. 18, no. 1 (Winter 1995): 123–40.

14. Rodney Tasker and Shawn W. Crispin, "Flash Point," *Far Eastern Economic Review*, June 1, 2000, 24–26.

15. Susan Okie, "AIDS Outbreaks Follow Asia's Heroin Traffic," *Washington Post*, March 6, 2000, A9.

16. Bertil Lintner's reporting has long tracked the junta's repressions. See, for example, "Tightening the Noose," *Far Eastern Economic Review*, November 16, 2000, 30–33.

17. See Alan Burnett, *The Western Pacific: The Challenge of Sustainable Growth* (Sydney: Allen and Unwin, 1993).

18. For a precise listing, see a chart in "Conventional Forces in Northeast Asia," *Arms Control Today*, vol. 24, no. 8 (November 1994): 34.

19. See the Carnegie Endowment for International Peace Non-proliferation Project home page (www.ceip.org); Joseph Cirincione, "Assessing the Ballistic Missile Threat," Testimony before the Subcommittee on International Security, Proliferation and Federal Services, Committee on Governmental Affairs, U.S. Senate, February 9, 2000, online at www.ciep.org/programs/npp/bmtestimony.htm; and the Natural Resources Defense Council website (www.nrdc.org/nuclear/nudb).

20. Russian military leaders, such as Colonel General Vladimir Yakovlev, commander-in-chief of the RF Strategic Missile Force, believe that reliance on nuclear weapons is all the more necessary in an era of low budgets, aging weapons, and increasing WMD and conventional war capabilities among potential enemies. Yakovlev said in an interview that "for Russia, at least for the next several decades, there will be no alternative to nuclear deterrence. To that end it is necessary to maintain an approximate nuclear force balance between Russia and the USA in quantitative composition and fighting capacity terms at a minimum admissible level." Sergey Grigoryev, "Russia's Military Political Trump

Card," *Nezavisimoye Voyennoye Obozreniye* (Moscow), December 17–23, 1999; NAPSNet (Northeast Asia Peace and Security Network, Nautilus Institute), December 21, 1999 (online news service at www.nautilus.org).

21. Carnegie Endowment for International Peace Non-proliferation Project, "Countries Possessing Ballistic Missiles" (table), online at www.ciep.org/programs/npp/bmchart.htm.

22. As of May 2001, 160 countries had signed the CTBT and 76 of them had ratified it. Under the treaty's terms, all 44 nuclear weapon–capable states must deposit instruments of ratification for the treaty to come into effect. Thus far, 41 of those countries have signed the document and 31 of them have ratified it; but among the known nuclear-weapon states, the United States, China, India, and Pakistan have yet to ratify. For an up-to-date list, see the website of the Carnegie Endowment for International Peace (www.ceip.org) at //pws.ctbto.org.

23. As of March 2001, 143 governments had ratified or acceded to the CWC. See the Henry Stimson Center website for a list: www.stimson.org.

24. U.S. Central Intelligence Agency (CIA), Nonproliferation Center, "Unclassified Report to Congress on the Acquisition of Technology Relating to Weapons of Mass Destruction and Advanced Conventional Munitions, 1 January through 30 June 1999," 5, 6, and 8.

25. Richard P. Suttmeier, "The Technological Emergence of the Pacific Rim: Threat or Opportunity to the U.S.?" unpublished paper, February 1992.

26. World Bank, *The World Bank Annual Report 1996*, section 4, "East Asia and Pacific," online at www.worldbank.org. (Hereafter, *World Bank 1996.*)

27. Bruce Koppel, "Fixing the Other Asia," *Foreign Affairs*, vol. 77, no. 1 (1996): 100. This conclusion was acknowledged by the head of the World Bank when he said that China, the Philippines, Thailand, and Malaysia had rates of inequality "close to the averages in sub-Saharan Africa and Latin America, the world's most notoriously unequal region." James Wolfensohn, "Asia and the World Economy," address at Harvard University, June 12, 2000, online at www.worldbank.org, 8.

28. ADB, *Asian Development Outlook 2000* (New York: Oxford University Press), 177 and table 3.8, 193.

29. Wolfensohn, "Asia and the World Economy," 1.

30. Elizabeth Olson, "AIDS Infections Rise Globally, but Sub-Saharan Cases Stabilize," *New York Times*, November 25, 2000, A5, based on a World Health Organization report.

31. *World Bank 1996*, 9.

32. World Bank, *The World Bank Annual Report 1999*, East Asia section, online at www.worldbank.org. (Hereafter, *World Bank 1999.*)

33. Wolfensohn, "Asia and the World Economy," 8: "Moreover, we now know that the recent crisis sent 13 million East Asians below the poverty line of 1 dollar per day and 28 million East Asians below the line of 2 dollars a day."

34. "Effects of the Indonesian Crisis," RAND Corporation "Labor and Population Program Research Brief," January 31, 2000, online at www.rand.org/publications/RB/RB5026.

35. See, for example, the particularly forthright statement of Malaysia's deputy prime minister, Anwar Ibrahim, at a conference in Singapore. He said: "There cannot be an obsession with economic indices to the extent that one ignores that there remain in our midst considerable pockets of abject poverty and destitution. The pain and misery of exploited labour, including women and children, are very real wherever they occur. Social inequalities, corruption, denial of basic liberties and downright oppression are still rampant." *Far Eastern Economic Review*, June 2, 1994, 20.

36. Velisarios Kattoulas, "Bright Lights, Brutal Life," *Far Eastern Economic Review,* August 3, 2000, 50–55. The author reports one estimate that the sex industry in Japan accounts for about the same percentage of the GNP (1 percent) as Japan's defense spending!

37. Access to drinkable water ranges from 72 percent of the population in China to 76 percent in Thailand, 82 percent in the Philippines, and 34 percent in Indonesia. See Elizabeth Economy, "The Environment and Development in the Asia-Pacific Region," in *Fires Across the Water: Transnational Problems in Asia,* ed. James Shinn (New York: Council on Foreign Relations, 1998), 47. Destruction of forests and runoff lakes has led to disastrous floods in China, such as occurred in the Yangtze River in 1998, which may have cost $30 billion in damage.

38. "Forests that once covered 70 percent of the country now range over about 35 percent," said the London-based environmental lobbying group Global Witness. Much of the loss occurred in the 1990s. Logging was officially banned in Cambodia in April 1995, and an export ban was put in place, but to little apparent effect. "If this deforestation does not stop," King Norodom Sihanouk said, "Cambodia will be, alas, a desert country in the 21st century." (Seth Mydans, "Illegal Logging Ravages Cambodian Forests," *New York Times,* December, 22, 1996, online ed.) In Thailand, forest cover declined from 53 percent to 28 percent between 1961 and 1988. Economy, "Environment and Development," 52.

39. "Asia now is the source for only 17 percent of the greenhouse gases like carbon dioxide that are suspected of causing global warming, but its carbon dioxide emissions are rising at four times the world average. Just in the last few months, by one calculation, Indonesia's forest fires have released as much greenhouse gas as all the cars and power plants throughout Europe will emit this entire year. . . . The Asian Development Bank calculates that by the year 2020, the emissions will increase two to five times, depending in part on whether curbs are instituted." Nicholas Kristof, "Poisoned Lands," *New York Times,* November 28, 1997, A1.

40. "Fresh-water reserves have been contaminated. Whether it is a storm surge or the sea rising, the waters get into the fresh water. Climate change is the type of global issue not of our making, so it raises questions of equity and ethics," a Samoan official said, adding that the island nations will once again ask that larger nations cut back on their use of fossil fuels that heat the atmosphere. Barbara Crossette, "A U.N. Special Session on Climatic Threats to Island Nations," *New York Times,* September 5, 1999, online ed.

41. Crossette, 1999.

42. On official corruption and the weaknesses of environmental protection agencies, see Economy, "Environment and Development," 54–56. For examples drawn from Hong Kong, Taiwan, South Korea, and China of insufficient regulation and enforcement, including penalties for violations that are too low, see the articles in *Far Eastern Economic Review,* October 29, 1992, 31–42.

43. Jonathan M. Lindsay, "Overlaps and Tradeoffs: Coordinating Policies for Sustainable Development in Asia and the Pacific," *The Journal of Developing Areas,* no. 28 (October 1993): 22.

44. Gareth Porter, "The Environmental Hazards of Asia Pacific Development: The Southeast Asian Rainforests," *Current History,* vol. 93, no. 587 (December 1994): 430–34.

45. Economy, "Environment and Development," 48.

46. Environment Canada, "Fact and Figures: The Impact of Urbanization on APEC Economies," online at www.ec.gc.ca/apecmeet/rtab5k_e.htm.

47. See also Michael Richardson, "The Spoils of Growth," *International Herald Tribune* (Paris), June 3, 1992.

48. *The Korea Herald* (Seoul), February 3, 1994.

49. *World Bank 1996*, 8.

50. *World Bank 1999*, table 2-5.

51. Martin Hart-Landsberg, "The Asian Crisis: Causes and Consequences," *Against the Current*, no. 73 (March–April 1998): 26–29; Nicholas D. Kristof and David E. Sanger, "How U.S. Wooed Asia to Let Cash Flow In," *New York Times*, February 16, 1999 and subsequent issues.

52. See Wolfensohn, "Asia and the World Economy," 2–3.

53. This paragraph relies mainly on Carnegie Commission, *Preventing Deadly Conflicts* (New York: Carnegie Commission, 1997), table 6.1, 143.

54. Barbara Crossette, "U.S. Begins Lonely Fight to Cut Back Its U.N. Costs," *New York Times*, March 12, 2000, online. Japan also made additional voluntary contributions of over $200 million each to the UN missions in Kosovo and East Timor.

55. The principal source is Carnegie Commission, *Preventing Deadly Conflicts*, table 6.1, 143 and appendix 3.

*Chapter Two*

# Sources of Security and Insecurity

## GLOBALISM AND NEOREALISM

While there is no disputing the increasing importance of economic factors in world politics, Robert Gilpin tells us, "the core of the debate about the nature of the new world economic order is . . . whether economic factors will be a source of international cooperation or international conflict."[1] Globalists, or neoliberals, accent the capacity of economic interdependence to create a common stake in political stability and regional peace. Inter-state tensions over territory and contending nationalisms are acknowledged in Globalist analysis; but the pull of economic self-interest is considered the key to overcoming political differences. U.S. leadership, "liberal" policies that reduce state intervention in economies (through deregulation and privatization), a breakdown of barriers to trade and investment, a major role for global corporations, and information technology and other kinds of "soft" power are also important elements of the Globalist strategy.

Classical Realism, on the other hand, emphasizes power politics and the pursuit of national interests. Thus Neorealists stress the competitive side of global economics. Rapid economic growth and interdependence are likely to produce *increased* political tensions between countries, and even national-security threats. "Economic competition will become the pursuit of foreign policy and national security by other means," according to Gilpin's summary of the Neorealist position.[2] But those "other means" might still be military if rising economic power translates into a stronger military, as some Realists see happening in China.

The Globalist view, whose strongest partisan at the turn of the century was President Bill Clinton, resonated among several East Asian leaders who were also optimistic about the security value of economic cooperation. Their optimism was tempered by two intersecting concerns, however, one based on state power and the other on nationalism. From Japan to Indonesia, state leaders worry about the "liberal" economic prescriptions of the "Washington consensus"—the model of laissez-faire capitalism represented by the coordinated power of the United States, the IMF, and the World Bank[3]—which intrude into the state's decision making. Asian leaders also worry about the intentions of powerful and ambitious neighbors with questionable pasts. Hence the importance for East Asians to associate in informal, multilateral groups that can at least dilute the economic pressure coming from Washington as well as the political pressure coming from Beijing.[4]

Looking at East Asia, Neorealists are not only likely to stress how globalization can harm a country's economic security, but also why globalization cannot ultimately overcome political differences between states. They tend to regard East Asia's history of disputes as intractable and regional security as unstable without the presence of a "balancing" power—an issue discussed further in chapter 7. For Neorealists, East Asia, especially Northeast Asia—Japan, North and South Korea, China, Hong Kong, Taiwan, Russia, and Mongolia—will have to rely on an outside great power (which can only mean the United States) and its bilateral alliances if it is to continue enjoying both military and economic security.

Actually, what has been happening for some time in most of East Asia is that *both* economic interdependence *and* assertions of national self-interest are on the rise, just as they are elsewhere in the world.[5] Moreover, as was stressed in chapter 1, domestic sources of instability are becoming more pronounced—an aspect of the East Asia security picture that tends to receive minimal attention from Globalists and Neorealists alike. Substantial multilateral economic and (to a lesser extent) political interaction is taking place, regionally and sub-regionally, simultaneously with rising nationalism, anxieties about the future conduct of rising powers, energy and environmental concerns, shared concerns among state leaders about the consequences of globalization for state power, and profound inequalities and resentments among various social groups.

This chapter explores three closely connected issues: economic growth and interdependence, domestic and international disputes, and military security in East Asia. Geographically, emphasis is on Northeast Asia, the focal point of debate over *how* those issues interconnect. Questions are raised about the key assumptions behind Globalism and Neorealism: in the first case, the notion that rapid economic growth and cooperation on trade and foreign investment promote political stability within and between states; in the second, that national security is imperiled in East Asia by economic competition, rising nationalism, and accompanying military buildups. The overall theme is straightforward: Economic growth may harm as well as enhance cooperation and internal and regional stability. Cooperative efforts are valuable, but by themselves cannot overcome longstanding and recent political disputes between the region's states—no more in East Asia than anywhere else—nor can they, by themselves, lay the groundwork for stronger regional political or security cooperation. At the same time, the emphasis in Neorealist analysis on military threats is greatly exaggerated and, if made the core of security planning, it will undermine prospects for international cooperation.

Thus, it is not a matter of slowing down economic development efforts and regional economic integration for fear of feeding competitive impulses and nationalism. On the contrary, there is every reason to continue and enlarge economic cooperation, as well as to create or strengthen institutions that promote it, subject to two conditions that have long-term relevance for internal and external *security*: First, economic growth and interdependence must benefit all participants, including peoples and not just governments and TNCs. Second, economic change should strengthen national and shared natural environments and resources. It is with these two conditions in mind that the chapter includes an assessment of human and environmental conditions and their possible impact on state and regional security.

## NORTHEAST ASIA'S UNIQUENESS

### Northeast Asia within East Asia

The international political economy of Northeast Asia, excluding North Korea, has several characteristics in common with the rest of East Asia. There is a shared commitment to export-led growth, "open regionalism" (i.e., regional cooperation that is outward-looking and not an exclusive trading bloc), and protection of core economic sectors. In the post–Cold War era, the countries of Northeast Asia seek "comprehensive national strength" or "comprehensive security" rather than relying mainly on military power to protect their interests. They uphold the virtues of regional multilateral dialogue, not only for the economic benefits it will bring, but also as a means of obtaining domestic and regional political order.

Northeast Asia is also part of the East Asian pattern of "increasingly distinct subregionalized and localized economic integration" held together by "a complex division of labor and commodity chains" established through trade and foreign direct investment (FDI).[6] Japan has been the driving force, though not the only one, linking the two sub-regions of East Asia. Intrafirm ties among its transnational trading firms (*keiretsu*) have integrated industrial production and trade, mainly in the ASEAN countries.[7] This trend of increasingly *intra*-regional trade and investment began in the mid-1980s, when high growth rates around East Asia and increased consumerism coincided with currency revaluations (under the 1985 Plaza Accord) that led to a huge outflow of Japanese capital to the region.[8] China's emergence accelerated the trend. Intra-regional exports in East Asia rose from about 40 percent of total exports in 1986 to nearly 50 percent in 1991. In the same period, intra-regional imports increased from 51 percent to around 56 percent.[9] Trade among APEC countries, as a percentage of total Asia Pacific trade, increased over the same period from about 56 to about 65 percent.[10]

Meanwhile, FDI in China, the four Asian NICs, and four of the ASEAN countries (Thailand, Philippines, Indonesia, and Malaysia) has come overwhelmingly from within the region: from the NICs themselves (e.g., Hong Kong and Taiwanese investments in China, and South Korean investments in Southeast Asia), and from Japan.[11]

Another integrating trend in East Asia is *sub*-regional, as seen in the emergence of trade and investment zones that are sometimes called natural economic territories (NETs). The Bohai Bay, for instance, is the focal point of major South Korean investments in North China (Liaoning, Shandong, and Jilin provinces) and booming Korean–Chinese trade.[12] Multination development projects, such as the Tumen River Area Development Program (TRADP), sponsored by the United Nations Development Program (UNDP), also aim to promote sub-regional economic cooperation. Situated at the juncture of Russia, China, and North Korea, TRADP also includes South Korea and Mongolia, with Japan as observer and most likely financier. But Japan has been strapped for cash, and the program has yet to get much beyond the planning stage.[13]

## Northeast Asia's Distinctiveness

The Northeast Asia trade and investment picture fits with the overall features of East Asia.[14] Despite the drag on sub-regional economic cooperation created by North Korea's minuscule role in international commerce, trade and FDI rose dramatically in the 1990s. Intra-regional trade as a percentage of total trade was in fact higher among the Northeast Asia countries (over 29 percent in 1995) than in ASEAN (around 21 percent). Japan, of course, is the principal trade partner of its neighbors; it accounted for 31 percent of Northeast Asia trade in 1995. But the PRC and Hong Kong together accounted for over 42 percent, and Taiwan for nearly 12 percent. All those countries or territories rely substantially on intra-regional trade; only Russia has limited trade dependence on Northeast Asia. FDI in Northeast Asia grew about five times between 1990 and 1995 to nearly $45 billion, or more than twice the figure for ASEAN. FDI in China accounted for over 80 percent of the total inflow, a commentary both on China's importance and the still-limited openness to foreign investment of South Korea and Japan.

While Northeast Asia is part of the regionalization phenomenon, it is strikingly different from the rest of East Asia in several key respects. Northeast Asia is by far the most militarized region, as we have noted. Despite being in a common cultural zone (Confucian), the Northeast Asian countries have very little experience of sub-regional multilateral cooperation. Their political and economic diversity sets them apart from Southeast Asia. Political disputes between Northeast Asian states are far more numerous and volatile than in Southeast Asia. Most of the major unresolved territorial questions having to do with sovereignty—such as between Japan and Russia (over the four so-called Northern Island groups in the Kuril Islands chain), Japan and South Korea (over Takeshima or Tokdo island in the Japan, or East, Sea), and China and Japan (over Diaoyutai or Senkaku, tiny islands in the East China Sea)—are in Northeast Asia. The only one that is not—the Spratlys (Nansha in Chinese) and the Paracels (Xisha) in the South China Sea—involves six claimants representing both sub-regions.

The fact that Northeast Asia has two industrial powerhouses and a third (China) on the way, while also containing many of the world's largest cities, accounts for its severe environmental problems. Though the sub-region shares some such problems with the rest of East Asia, such as deforestation and marine pollution, Northeast Asia's problems differ in magnitude and in the degree of difficulty in achieving cooperative action at the state level.[15]

## POLITICS AND ECONOMIC COOPERATION

### The International Political Economy of East Asia

The neoliberal argument that as economic cooperation and integration grow in East Asia, political problems between states will gradually be overcome, certainly has some merit: Economic development needs have indisputably provided new incentives for state leaders to leapfrog or shelve their political differences. In fact, it might be said that the *diversity* of economic development levels, particularly in Northeast Asia, has created complementarities that have helped promote both greater economic interaction and political rapport.[16] Improved relations between China and South Korea, China and Russia, Russia and South Korea, and China and Taiwan can be accounted for largely through their differences in capital availability, labor costs, and technological capabilities. Involvement for economic cooperation in regional groups such as ASEAN, APEC, and TRADP, and in global organizations such as the WTO,[17] clearly has had beneficial effects in building trust and crafting economic policies on the basis of mutual interests. Indeed, a threat to common economic interests may create opportunity for policy coordination, as happened among the major economies, including China, during the Asian financial crisis.[18] If North Korea should open up to regional trade, investment, and multilateral economic cooperation, there is every reason to think that its political relations with South Korea and the rest of East Asia will markedly improve. With good reason scholars suggest that economic cooperation may sometimes be considered a kind of CBM or step toward developing a "common political language."[19]

While political relationships may often benefit from increased economic contact, there are several points to consider. First, political steps, including a "clearing of the atmosphere" to create goodwill, usually precede the decisive improvement of economic relationships. Secondly, businessmen influence, but do not ordinarily *make,* foreign policy. Trade bureaucracies are responsible for foreign economic policy; except in Japan they do not normally shape the political character of external relations. The place of economic interest becomes a *strategic decision* and must be fitted into a larger-than-economic framework of national interest that includes not only external but also domestic political objectives. Third, common economic interests may help, hurt, or have little effect on political and security relations. In Northeast Asia there are numerous examples to show that economic cooperation and political disputes may take place simultaneously, so that closer economic ties may not significantly erode political differences. Consequently, increased bilateral and regional economic integration may contribute to political tensions between states and/or to greater regional *in*security.

Each of the above three points deserves additional comment. Concerning the first point, diplomacy has proven essential to a significant improvement in economic relations between countries. Russian–South Korean and Sino–South Korean commercial relations, for instance, did not receive a major boost until formal diplomatic relations were established in the early 1990s. The Russia-ROK entente came about as the result of parallel trends in their foreign policies: Mikhail Gorbachev's determination (initially expressed at Vladivostok in 1986), to reduce the arms race, normalize relations with Asian neighbors, and promote common security through economic and other modalities; and Roh Tae Woo's "Northern policy" of opening the door to South Korean relations with the socialist world. China and South Korea began to develop commercial relations before 1992 through trade liaisons; but the huge leap in South Korean–Chinese trade was only possible after Beijing made the political decision to ignore Pyongyang's protests and establish full diplomatic relations with Seoul. Consequently, at least through 2000, bankers and traders were relatively bullish on Northeast Asia as compared with Southeast Asia, inasmuch as tensions had diminished between the two Koreas and China-Taiwan, whereas political uncertainties had gripped several of the ASEAN states.[20]

On the second point, a common interest in economic growth does not typically spring from purely economic motives; it is part of a larger set of strategic objectives. This observation is easiest to see in China's expanding trade ties with Northeast Asia since the mid-1980s.[21] Fundamentally, the expansion occurred because of the Deng Xiaoping-led leadership's twofold commitment to rapid economic reform and a "peaceful, independent foreign policy." As Chinese leaders have long recognized, reduced political tensions with neighboring states are a prerequisite to economic development. This is the essential meaning of the expression frequently employed by PRC leaders that China "needs a long period of international quiescence." The substantial increase in China's border trade with Russia and trade with Japan (China's principal trade partner) flowed from political decisions in 1980 through 1982 concerning a change in China's basic direction—and in terms of the increases of recent years in Sino-Russian trade, from four summit meetings between 1992 and 1996 that led to their proclamation of a "strategic partnership."[22] Moreover, China views trade not merely as an instrument of economic growth, but also as a potential source of leverage in regional affairs. China for the first time can become the pivotal "bridge" in Northeast Asia's division of labor, working with rather than competing against Russia and Japan to create mutually beneficial economic relationships that may also promote more stable regional relationships.[23]

The third point brings us closest to the security problem in East Asia: Economic cooperation may ease political tension, but not enough to keep disputes from turning violent. The integration of the "Greater China" economic zone has ameliorated tensions between China and Hong Kong and between China and Taiwan. While business leaders in Hong Kong generally support close economic ties with the PRC and a dominant role for pro-Beijing representatives in the new Hong Kong government, Hong Kong's future autonomy is in doubt. How democratically the Hong Kong legislature functions, how the Beijing-appointed leadership handles issues of personal and institutional autonomy, and what security role the People's Liberation Army (PLA) garrison plays in the Hong Kong Special Administrative Region are among many unknowns. In Taiwan, too, business leaders have generally pushed hard to end the government's ban on direct economic and other contacts with China. They have succeeded in loosening the ban but politics rule: Taiwan's spectacular economic growth has promoted cultural and political pluralism, enhanced Taiwan's international standing, and led its presidents to toy with the explosive idea of separate sovereignty rather than accept Beijing's principle of "one China." In fact, this evolution was contrary to what Beijing leaders seem to have anticipated in the early 1980s; they thought the mainland's economic reforms would narrow the gap between the two societies and facilitate reunification.[24] Consequently, even though China and Taiwan are major trade and investment partners, military buildups continue on both sides of the Taiwan Strait. Few doubt Beijing's warnings of a military response to a declaration of independence by Taiwan.

East Asia's trade relations with Japan have consistently been unbalanced in Japan's favor. As one Korean analyst has observed, Japan's trade surpluses are symptomatic of a structural defect in regional trade: They compel the NICs and the ASEAN states to seek trade surpluses with the United States.[25] This is because of the regionalized pattern of production networks. Japanese and other TNCs in Southeast Asia and China import components and capital goods from Japan and the NICs, then export finished products mainly to the United States and the EU, not to the Japanese market.[26] Except for China, Japan has run huge trade surpluses with East Asian countries, and the United States has run huge trade deficits with Japan and China—around two-thirds of its total trade deficit in recent years. ASEAN, China, and the NICs have become caught in the middle of political warfare between Washington and Tokyo over "unfair competition" and managed trade.

Russian, Chinese, and South Korean trade with Japan provides still other examples of how economic ties have failed to overcome political differences. Suspicions of Russian intentions concerning the disputed Northern Islands remain intense among the Japanese elite and public. More than half a century after World War II, the two countries still have not signed a peace treaty. China's large trade volume with Japan, about $66 billion in 1999, has not dispelled historical Chinese hostility toward Japan or the sense of some Chinese strategists that Japan will fully re-arm and become a future threat.[27] South Korea–Japan trade and technology interdependence is very high but also one-sided in Japan's favor. At times as much as 90 percent of South Korea's trade deficit has been accounted for by Japanese imports. As a result, interdependence only reinforces long-standing Korean grievances over Japanese colonialism and occupation between 1910 and 1945.

The best that economic cooperation can accomplish with countries that have long-standing political differences is to create a basis of cooperation on which to build—one that might evolve into a deeper political understanding. The examples cited underscore the importance of trade politics (and internal affairs in general) in the debate over interdependence. Whether or not interdependence or its sequel, globalization, moves states in the direction of conflict or cooperation often depends on developments such as the state's response to social and economic strains, the influence of interest groups, the stability and accountability of political parties and other institutions, intra-leadership conflicts, and the state's mobilization of nationalism on behalf of international objectives.[28] Technological advances, especially in telecommunications, influence each of those conditions. Worldwide support of the students and workers at Tiananmen in 1989, the democratic resistance in Burma, and popular demonstrations against corrupt government in the Philippines all were enormously facilitated by the communications revolution.[29]

Moreover, as economies mature, internationalize, and seek lower production costs through foreign investment, a multitude of new problems arise at home and abroad. We see these problems in Korea and Southeast Asia today: labor's concerns about the export of jobs; government and business confrontations with workers over labor costs and unionization; and international concerns about the exploitation of workers and environment as consequences of foreign investment in manufacturing and resource (e.g., timber and ore) extraction. Economic globalization in general can have salutary consequences for international relationships in East Asia, as we have discussed. But it can also expose a country to dangers, such as the spread of drugs and AIDS, the power of organized crime, and the ease of arms smuggling. All these problems increase the militarization of borders and cities in the name of internal security.

## The Economics of Insecurity

If the post–Cold War era were marked by a new equality between states, the economic basis for international cooperation would probably be much stronger than it is in fact. But *hegemony*, not equality, is still the name of the game in East Asia's international politics (see chapter 7), undermining some of the optimism of the Globalist view. The terrorist attacks on New York City and the Pentagon on September 11, 2001 reinforced that conclusion: It led to President George W.

Bush's proclamation of a "war on terrorism" and a bombing campaign in Afghanistan to destroy terrorist bases and eliminate the Taliban regime.

But while terrorism revealed globalization in its most horrifying dimension, it did not alter the fact that in East Asia, concerns about external attack have greatly abated. Security-dependent partners of the United States, such as South Korea and Japan, accepted U.S. leadership of the antiterrorism campaign and offered Washington concrete assistance. In the long run, however, looking beyond the war in Afghanistan, neither U.S. allies nor ideological and economic competitors such as China (which also lent support to the war) are going to accept U.S. leadership on all issues or bow to American policy goals. On the economic side, for example, the United States's aggressive push to liberalize capital markets and open economies up for its TNCs has led to backlashes, such as Japan's and South Korea's upset over IMF policies during the financial crisis and China's upset over U.S. conditions that had to be met before Washington would approve Beijing's entry into WTO. Those kinds of nationalist responses are likely to continue, with or without concerns about terrorists.

Economic growth and integration may in fact contribute to regional insecurity. Even when they proceed smoothly, unencumbered by external conflict, they may unleash internal forces that will upset the apple cart. Within states, for instance, China's and Russia's unbalanced regional development has clearly exacerbated tensions between center and region. As regions and localities make their own economic development choices, their interests are likely to diverge from national policy. The conflict can become acute when scarce resources, such as water, are involved, as in China;[30] when the question arises of how to share tax and other revenues (as in Beijing's longstanding struggles with Shanghai and Guangdong Province); or when policy making authority is at stake (as in former Russian President Boris Yeltsin's tug of war with Primorskiy regional leaders). Chinese local leaders have engaged in protectionism to maintain a hold on certain commodities, creating independent "dukedoms." In the extreme, differences between local governments and Beijing are even capable of bringing the central government's legitimacy into question and eventually producing political fragmentation. Military intervention and civil war may result, as happened in Russia in the 1991 revolt against Yeltsin's authority. These dire consequences are all the more likely to occur if economic reforms fail and lead to the intensification of authoritarian rule.[31] Alternatively, they could occur if the benefits of reforms continue to be unfairly distributed, as is the case between coastal and inland Chinese provinces. Much depends on whether or not political institutions and legal options exist to moderate these imbalances.

Growing gaps between regions of countries need not portend a breakup; but they could affect these countries' international relations. Governments and NGOs may prefer doing business with regional rather than with central authorities. Strong ties have developed in China between local and foreign investors, such as between Fujian Province and Taiwan entrepreneurs, and between Shandong Province and South Korean firms. At some point, these relationships may intrude into the foreign policy arena, producing resistance to the central government's preferences—for example, to Beijing's use of force against Taiwan, or to Moscow's interest in cutting a deal with Tokyo that would concede Russian claims to the Northern Islands.

Economic development becomes a potential source of interstate conflict when it clearly advantages one side, occurs without sufficient regulation, or exacerbates a preexisting problem. This is especially problematic in Northeast Asia, because of the large gaps in development levels between states. There is reason to suspect, for example, that South Korea's dramatic economic and technological leap forward in the 1990s contributed to North Korea's sense of insecurity, its professed fear of "absorption" of the South, and perhaps its resort to a nuclear weapon option as a desperate equalizer. In the Japan-Russia case, frictions are likely to multiply as the result of the Russian Far East's dependence on Japanese capital and technology and the lack of a multilateral Northeast Asia framework that might facilitate Russia's marketing of its products.[32] Free trade and growth triangles can just as easily produce disputes as cooperation, depending on how evenly the benefits are distributed.[33]

Transnational environmental and energy problems, many of which stem from economic development patterns, are likely to impose a whole new set of long-term security challenges.[34] Transboundary acid rain from Chinese, Japanese, and Korean coal-fired industrial plants heads the list because of its pervasive effects on regional air quality, agriculture, and climate.[35] China's rapid economic growth will soon make it the world's largest source of carbon dioxide emissions. These and other greenhouse gases, such as sulfur dioxide, contribute significantly to regional air pollution and to the global warming problem. Northeast Asia's dependence on imported oil—including China, which became a net oil importer in 1993—makes all countries vulnerable to developments in the Middle East and elsewhere along oil routes. Competition for new energy sources links territorial disputes with energy security, as in the South China Sea. Rapidly increasing energy requirements expose countries and populations to major accidents from nuclear power plants, oil tanker spills, and ocean or land dumping of nuclear and other wastes.

As national economies prosper, new trade and investment rivalries may emerge. Now that the PRC and ASEAN economies (most recently including Vietnam's) are leaping ahead, their manufactured exports are challenging more expensive South Korean manufactured exports, compelling Korean business to internationalize more rapidly but also putting pressure on local Korean businesses and labor to hold down costs. In Southeast Asia, Japan and South Korea are in intense competition for market position in automobiles. Sometime in the future, it is likely that China and some of its southern neighbors, such as Thailand, Malaysia, and Vietnam, will be competing for (and disputing over) markets in commonly produced goods. Nor is it beyond challenge that as multilateral economic cooperation moves forward, nationalism will prevail over economic openness, privileging members of the bloc and limiting access to everyone else.[36]

## ENVIRONMENTAL AND HUMAN SECURITY

### Human Underdevelopment

Unbalanced and unregulated economic growth—sharp gaps in income between people and between regions, widespread corruption, large-scale rural migration to cities, forced resettlement of populations, and severe damage to water, forests, and other ecosystems, for example—may imperil national security and undermine regional relations. Gross figures on economic growth may go up, but they are likely to mask the real social, economic, and potentially the political costs of failure to heed the signs of social disaffection and environmental destruction. A central government's legitimacy, its ability to maintain social cohesion, and the space it allows (if any) for wider political participation are likely to decline, running the risk of mounting social protest and political violence, in some cases directed against ethnic minorities. Nor can governments prevent the pernicious effects of unbalanced growth by relying on trade, foreign investment, or the military.[37]

Social justice has not been well served, as the discussion in chapter 1 documented. When there are two billion poor people living on less than two dollars a day, as is the case in Asia as a whole,[38] the notion of "human development" takes on special significance. Table 2.1 shows the UNDP's "human development index" ranking for developing countries of East Asia before and after the financial crisis.[39] It points up yet again the great disparities within the region when it comes to meeting basic needs as measured by indicators such as literacy and mortality rates, drinkable water, quality of health care, purchasing power income, and gender equality. By another UNDP measure known as the "human poverty index," fewer than one-fifth of people living in Singapore, China, and Thailand experience basic human deprivations; but over one-fifth of people living in Indonesia, Vietnam, Myanmar, and Cambodia do—not to mention in India, Pakistan, and

**Table 2.1. UN Development Program Human Development Index: Ranking for Developing Countries of East Asia, 1995 and 1998ª**

|  | 1995 | 1998 |  | 1995 | 1998 |
|---|---|---|---|---|---|
| Singapore | 28 | 24 | China | 106 | 99 |
| Hong Kong, PRC | 24 | 26 | Vietnam | 122 | 108 |
| South Korea | 30 | 31 | Indonesia | 96 | 109 |
| Brunei | 35 | 32 | Mongolia | 101 | 117 |
| Malaysia | 60 | 61 | Myanmar | 131 | 125 |
| Thailand | 59 | 76 | Cambodia | 140 | 136 |
| North Korea | 75 | —ᵇ | Laos | 136 | 140 |
| Philippines | 98 | 77 |  |  |  |

ª Ranking based on *all* countries (174) ranked. Taiwan was not ranked.
ᵇ Not ranked.
*Sources:* For 1995, UNDP, *Human Development Report* 1998, table 1.3, 21; for 1998, UNDP, *Human Development Report* 2000, 158–59.

Bangladesh.[40] Widespread poverty in the outlying islands of Indonesia,[41] and the southern, mainly Muslim Philippines, has long underpinned political violence. North Korean "food refugees"—anywhere from 100,000 to 200,000 people seeking escape from five years of famine—have illegally found refuge in China.[42] In Thailand, Indonesia, and the Philippines, and (in South Asia) India, Pakistan, and Bangladesh, the abuse, sale, and virtual enslavement of millions of children stand in sharp contrast with overall figures for Asia Pacific (for example, with respect to malnutrition and infant mortality) that show improvement in the status of children.[43] The condition of women in most Asian countries is also deplorable.[44]

The effects of the financial crisis also include higher unemployment and underemployment, rising income inequality, and new uncertainties for migrant workers. IMF structural adjustment programs in South Korea, for instance, required corporate downsizing and a substantial cut in public service employment. Unemployment, which was 2 percent when the financial crisis hit, reached close to 8 percent in 1998. (In early 2001 it was just under 5 percent.) Some social groups, in South Korea and elsewhere in East Asia, suffered much more than others. Low-skilled workers, women workers, and older workers were fired first and rehired last.[45] Workers in rural areas were affected even more than urban workers. Hundreds of thousands of migrant workers in East Asia, typically those involved in construction and other hard-hit sectors, were forced to return home, as noted below. For all these labor groups, the absence of a reliable social safety net meant a sudden plunge into poverty.[46] Among the affected countries, only in South Korea and (more recently) in China are unemployment benefits available, health coverage is limited throughout the region, and retraining programs for displaced workers are virtually unknown.

But it is the longer-term effects of unbalanced, unfettered economic growth, and not merely the financial crisis, that have led to widening income gaps and unemployment everywhere in East Asia and undermined social stability. China is a good example: Even though the PRC has received high marks from the UNDP for progress in "human development," and from the ADB for dramatically lowering the rate of poverty,[47] and even though per capita real GNP rose substantially between 1988 and 1995, China is "one of the more unequal of Asian developing countries."[48] With very rapid growth of GNP and personal income has come increasing income inequality not only within rural and urban areas, but even more so nationally and regionally.[49] Unemployment figures, though inexact, may amount to nearly 10 percent of the urban population and about 30 percent of the rural population.[50] These disparities are rather dramatic in a society that had once prided itself on egalitarianism and a strong social safety net.

The social consequences of these inequities may be explosive. For one thing, China's western provinces, which are home to large ethnic minority populations, are significantly poorer than the coastal provinces. The geography of human development closely follows the unequal distribution of the benefits of growth.[51] Furthermore, China today has a so-called floating population of *at least* 100 million people (by official counts) who have drifted from rural areas into cities in search of jobs. This figure is likely to rise quickly once China's entry in the WTO is complete and the impact of agricultural imports is felt in the countryside. Though these migrant workers make important contributions to local economies, they are often badly treated and they amount to enormous pressures on city services. Rising income gaps and unemployment surely contribute to China's increasing crime and gangsterism, which plays a part in an emerging AIDS crisis as poor people in rural areas and drug users sell their blood or re-use needles.[52] Official corruption and the emergence of a privileged elite in China are reflections of income inequality. Political leaders and their children are deeply involved in the major business entities, go abroad for study and pleasure, and have unique opportunities to amass personal fortunes.

Legal and illegal immigration from poorer to richer societies have reached large proportions. In the 1980s there were about one million foreign workers in seven East Asian countries; but by 1997, the number had increased to around 6.5 million. Most such workers are from elsewhere in East Asia, and about one-quarter of them work illegally.[53] Some of those countries, such as China and Malaysia, are both sources and recipients of migrant workers.[54] Large numbers of migrant workers have moved in recent years from China to Russia, from Indonesia to Malaysia, from Burma and Cambodia to Thailand, from the Philippines and Vietnam to South Korea, from the Philippines, Thailand, and Malaysia to Taiwan, from North Korea to Russia, and from the Middle East to Japan. But for all their value in taking on jobs at the low end of the salary and status scales, these immigrants pose new challenges of human rights, cultural identity, and citizenship that nearly all governments in East Asia will have to contend with for many years to come.[55]

The devastating effects of the financial crisis on employment caused several countries to cut back on the number of foreign workers at the very time when jobs were in short supply back home. Malaysia's detention and repatriation of Indonesian workers strained their relations, as did Thailand's repatriation of several hundred thousand Burmese workers.[56] In most cases, these workers have no legal protection in case of difficulties. Though their cheap labor may be welcome, working conditions are often deplorable, the risks of AIDS through prostitution have greatly increased,[57] and the very presence of foreign workers in large numbers (as in the case of Chinese workers in Russia's Far East) may incur nationalist resentment.

## Environmental Destruction

Economic changes in East Asia are occurring at the expense of the environment. The regional picture is shocking. As just one example: "Throughout Asia, 2.7 million people die from diseases related to air pollution every year."[58] China's situation is especially revealing. Economic reforms and the rise of consumerism have given a huge boost to industrial and home construction, and to energy demands. Inevitably in a country where environmental protection lags far behind production goals, the severity of toxic waste discharge, deforestation, soil erosion, ozone-destroying emissions, and acid rain is extreme.[59] Forest destruction and overgrazing in north China, for example, have turned about one million square miles, or 27 percent of the country's total area, into desert. Fertile land is literally being blown away at a rapid pace.[60] Deforestation finally led to the Chinese government to ban logging—in twelve provinces in 1998 and, eighteen in 2000— only to have logging operations shift to Burma's tropical forests, thereby simply exporting the destructive practice.[61]

Problems such as these are not merely ecological; they are political as well, as they have the potential to become sources of internal instability. For example, the ambitious, $30-billion effort to harness the Yangzi River's power at Three Gorges Dam has already led to popular protests. More than one million people will be displaced by the required flooding of the dam area, water supplies may be poisoned by effluents, and the dam itself might collapse under the weight of siltation.[62] A different kind of environmental problem is posed by China's unusually high (70 percent) reliance on coal for energy. China is already one of the world's leading producers of electricity. But should global warming come to pass, it would significantly affect China's agriculture. The impact on farming populations, local economies, and food supplies might be great enough to create food shortages.[63] Rural migrations to the cities would grow even larger.

Severe damage is also occurring to the Asia Pacific commons: waterways, air, and fisheries. Aggressive economic growth in East Asia has decimated forests, polluted air and water, increased toxic waste disposal, and strained local capacities to store wastes. These practices sometimes spill over borders and thus become sources of political disputes, such as China's "yellow sand" air pollution that annually invades the Korean peninsula, oil dumping in the Yellow and East (or Japan) Sea, and overfishing all along the Western Pacific. Competing claims to seabed resources complicate the picture as the Russian-Japanese and Japanese-Korean disputes over access to fisheries attest.[64] The Russian navy's nuclear waste dumping in the Sea of Japan created a furor in Japan when it came to light in 1994. Taiwan's announcement in January 1997 that it would ship up to 200,000 tons of low-level nuclear waste to North Korea for storage caused protests by residents and environmental groups in Taiwan, as well as by South Korea, China, and other governments.[65] Taiwan dropped its plans but a deal later was made with the PRC to bury low-level nuclear waste there, probably in one of the western provinces mainly inhabited by ethnic minorities.[66] In February 1997, when Indonesia announced it would build a number of nuclear power plants, the first of which would be sited in a volcanic region, Australians complained, pointing to the catastrophic regional effects of a meltdown.

Thus, a more plausible scenario than open warfare for the unraveling of East Asian security is widespread popular protest and exodus brought on by severe environmental decline, with China as the chief candidate. Problems such as China faces are also faced by other rapidly developing countries, but to lesser degrees. The combined effects of drought, rivers running dry, greatly reduced farmland and farm output, poisoned water supplies, desertification, and rising sea levels in coastal cities are unimaginable, yet all these things are happening now.[67] South Korea and Taiwan also face serious environmental problems that are direct consequences of rapid economic development, among them heavy air pollution in major cities, inadequate capacities for handling radioactive waste from nuclear power plants (they provide about 35 percent of South Korea's electricity and 30 percent of Taiwan's), and toxic spillages in waterways. The differences between their situations and China's are not just a matter of scale, but also of politics: South Korea and Taiwan are democratizing, allowing for political and legal remedies as well as for media attention. Business and political corruption, authoritarianism, and environmental degradation in Taiwan and South Korea have galvanized citizen protests and political reforms. Citizen action in Taiwan (involving nuclear power) and South Korea (water pollution and nuclear power), for example, has stopped some projects that threatened the environment.[68]

"Asia" increasingly means megacities, not farm villages. Urban population is about to exceed rural population. There are now seven megacities with 8 million or more residents, and fifty-six cities in East Asia with populations of 1 million or more.[69] The strain such explosive growth puts on city governments is enormous, in terms of waste disposal, unemployment, clean water availability, air pollution, and health care—nor are these just local problems. The large amount of capital needed simply to meet minimal health and welfare standards, as well as the potential for social unrest if they are not met, make East Asian urbanization a matter of regional and even global concern.

The H.I.V.-AIDS crisis centered in East Asia is another example. Attention is increasingly being drawn to the rising number of intravenous drug users in China, and to the neglect of public officials, mostly for political reasons, to deal with H.I.V. infection and the rapidly increasing numbers of people who develop AIDS. Cases of AIDS are increasing by about 30 percent a year in China. It is likely that a significant proportion of such cases can be found in the border region with Burma, where drug trafficking is a major industry.[70] Thus, China and its neighbors, along with the drug consumer countries, have a common interest in stemming an interrelated, international problem of public health and crime that threatens to spiral out of control.[71]

## Environmental and Energy Cooperation

The environmental and human dimensions of national and regional security are not typically addressed in Western or Asian discussions.[72] That they will require lengthy multilateral dialogue and cooperation at the state and supranational organization levels seems certain, and not only because the issues bear directly on the long-term economic and social well-being and potential political stability of several countries and sub-regions. The fact that the economically advanced countries, starting with the United States and Japan, are far greater exploiters of the environment than the Asian NICs raises the ante of political dialogue.[73] With democratization and spreading educational opportunity and information technologies, moreover, citizen groups (of the kind that have already emerged in Taiwan, Hong Kong, Thailand, and South Korea) are going to be increasingly vocal about not putting off remedies to some post-industrial era. As has happened in Western Europe and North America, and indeed to some extent influenced by their examples, civil society in East Asia will gradually widen. With that, demands are bound to grow stronger for allocating money to human and natural sources of national security.[74] East Asian governments that deny NGOs a voice may one day face a new kind of insurgency, nonideological but passionate over human and environmental rights.

That being said, it is also the case that environmental cooperation at all levels—bilateral and multilateral, regional and international—is intensifying around East Asia.[75] Several countries in Northeast Asia (China, Japan, South Korea, and Russia) have signed bilateral environmental agreements with each other that cover, for example, ocean dumping, acid rain, and fisheries' management. Under the Green Aid Plan, Japan has made environmental ODA and environmental technology transfers key components of its foreign policy, mainly in relations with China. At the multilateral level, examples are the Northwest Pacific Action Plan (NOWPAP—Japan, Russia, China, ROK) under the UN Environment Program; TRADP for the Tumen River area; and KEDO for energy assistance to North Korea. A network has been established for environmental training and education under the United Nations Conference on Environment and Development.[76] Several international agreements are pertinent to protecting Asia Pacific's marine environment.[77] Multilateral ventures take various forms. NOWPAP seeks by a regional convention to protect and manage the coastal and marine environments in the Japan (East) Sea and Yellow Sea areas. Multination scientific groups have formed in East Asia to discuss transboundary air pollution and acid rain. ASEAN has had a Southeast Asian Programme on Ocean Policy, Law and Management since the early 1980s. TRADP developed a "Strategic Action Plan" in 1997 to identify transboundary environmental problems and enlist international assistance to resolve them. APEC has focused on capacity building to protect urban, ocean, and agricultural environments.

NGOs have also been actively cooperating across borders. The North-East Asia and North Pacific Environmental Forum (NEANPEF), for instance, brings together representatives of NGOs, governments (including the PRC and DPRK), business, and academia from several Asia Pacific countries for periodic strategy sessions and joint research.[78] Its strategy is to head off security tensions that may arise from large-scale transboundary environmental problems, such as flooding, forest fires, river contamination, and threats to biodiversity. The Atmospheric Action Network of East Asia embraces NGOs from Japan, South Korea, Taiwan, Hong Kong, Mongolia, China, and Russia.[79] As another example, the Nautilus Institute for Security and Sustainable Development in Berkeley, California, and the Center for Global Communications in Tokyo collaborated in a three-year project to produce policy recommendations concerning energy and environmental security.[80]

At the global level, most governments have signed the major international environmental conventions, including Agenda 21 on sustainable development (which came out of the 1992 Earth Summit in Rio de Janeiro), the UN Convention on the Law of the Sea (UNCLOS, which includes protections for marine pollution), the Convention on International Trade in Endangered Species, the Montreal Protocol to phase out chlorofluorocarbons (CFCs), the Convention on Biological Diversity, and the 1997 Kyoto Protocol on greenhouse gas emissions. The UN's Economic and Social Commission for Asia and the Pacific (ESCAP) has sponsored conferences on the regional environment and helped to establish regional networks devoted to environmental policy research, desertification, and environmental journalism.[81] China and Indonesia have been major recipients of World Bank loans for rural and urban environmental projects.

Some huge hurdles remain to be overcome before environmental cooperation can claim significant achievements.[82] One is the question that is ever-present in North-South debates on development: Who should pay for environmental cleanup and damages? Third World East Asian countries such as China and Malaysia have insisted that before they consider putting environmental protection on a par with economic development, the West must assume major financial responsibility for cleanup and technology transfers. Second, lack of multilateral coordination and the diverse capacities of states that are party to environmental commitments can undermine cooperation, especially when historic animosities need to be overcome as well. For example, unless the Tumen River project can overcome funding and other obstacles, there will be dire consequences for regional fisheries and water quality. Third is the failure of regional economic fora, notably APEC, to incorporate environmental goals in trade and investment planning. As will be noted again in the next chapter, accepting a "sustainable development" agenda is one thing, and actually improving the environment through regulation or incentives is another.[83]

## TERRITORY: GROUNDS FOR CONFLICT?

Nowhere is the contradiction clearer between economic cooperation and political conflict than in East Asia's numerous territorial disputes.[84] It is apparent to all that the disputes over the Paracels and Spratlys, not to mention other island groups in East and Northeast Asia, concern potential undersea gas and oil deposits and not simply sovereignty.[85] Economic interdependence may moderate these disputes, but it will not make the claims disappear. Rapid economic growth in East Asia has intensified the search for energy and other resources. Most resource analysts project sharp increases in Asia's fossil fuel and nuclear-energy needs during coming decades. Reliance on external sources of energy is bound to be accompanied by security concerns—about maintaining unimpeded access to the resources, controlling access at the source if possible, and the potential military implications of a rival state's energy picture.[86]

Because of China's interests, the case of the South China Sea (SCS) dispute illustrates the potential for large-scale conflict, but also the opportunity for creative conflict resolution. Armed clashes occurred between China and Vietnam in 1974 and 1988. In February 1995, the Chinese navy occupied Mischief Reef, claimed by the Philippines.[87] In addition, there have been a few smaller incidents involving PRC naval shows of force directed at Vietnam's islets, though they have subsided since Vietnam's entry into ASEAN in 1995.[88] China's energy requirements are relevant here. A net crude oil importer since 1993, China by one estimate will run out of proven reserves in twenty years if it maintains a modest 8 percent annual economic growth rate and does not find new oil reserves at home.[89] What impact might that have on the PRC's diplomatic and military posture with respect to the SCS islands? To some observers, the impact is already apparent in the Chinese navy's modernization program, Beijing's refusal to submit the sovereignty issue to regional or international arbitration, and China's periodic run-ins with patrol boats of the Philippines, a friendly ASEAN state.[90]

These developments notwithstanding, the implications drawn from them can easily be exaggerated. Behind China's claims lie several possibly competing impulses. One, very much influenced by the far more important Taiwan question, is to demonstrate an unswerving commitment to a matter of sovereignty. Another, no doubt pushed by China's navy, which wants a blue water capability, is to show that China is capable of defending state interests that lie beyond its borders. A third PRC impulse may be to promote its 1992 proposal for joint development of ocean resources. And a fourth, which is of more recent vintage, is to show China's commitment to the peaceful settlement of disputes with ASEAN as a whole, and not exclusively on a bilateral basis.

Thus far, in this clash of interests, internationalism has won out: China's use of force has abated, whereas its willingness to discuss its claims within the multilateral framework of ASEAN has strengthened.[91] Strategic opportunism may be behind China's changed approach. It can attempt to weaken the American argument that bilateral security alliances are the centerpiece of East Asian security; and a more accommodating PRC stance lowers the risk that ASEAN will unite against a "Chinese threat" or (for example, on the PRC-Taiwan dispute) take a position opposite China's.[92] In any event, China's policy meshes with ASEAN's own "balance of politics," which includes engaging China through private diplomacy rather than public criticism and promoting common economic development interests as the basis of peaceful region.[93] What is at work here (to be explored further in the next chapter) is one aspect of the consultative, common security model of security, buttressed by elements of Globalist thinking about the beneficial political effects of economic cooperation.

# ARMS AND INSECURITY

## Arms Spending and Imports

Arms spending and buildups offer another insight to the state of security in Asia, as well as to the negative international consequences of economic development.

Official military spending throughout Asia has been on the upswing for the last two decades; in the 1990s, it jumped 20 percent in Northeast Asia and 25 percent in Southeast Asia, generally outpacing military spending in other regions.[94] The sharpest increases occurred in the prosperous days of the 1980s and early 1990s, when several East Asian countries, led (in percentage terms) by Singapore, Japan, South Korea, and Taiwan, went on buying sprees.[95] (See Table 2.2 for 1992–1996.) As one result, "Asia's share of world expenditure on arms transfers rose from 15.5 percent in 1982 to 34 percent in 1991,"[96] at a time

**Table 2.2. East Asia Military Expenditures, 1992, 1996, 1999 (in $U.S. billion[a])**

|  | 1992 | 1996 | 1999 |
|---|---|---|---|
| **NE Asia** | | | |
| Japan | 48.80 | 51.00 | 51.10 |
| PRC[b] | 13.80 | 13.70 | 18.40 |
| N Korea[c] | 2.10 | N/A | N/A |
| S Korea | 13.10 | 15.40 | 15.00 |
| Mongolia | .28 | .17 | .17 |
| Taiwan | 10.00 | 10.10 | 9.30 |
| **SE Asia** | | | |
| Brunei | .34 | .32[b] | N/A |
| Indonesia | 2.30 | 2.70 | 2.30[b] |
| Malaysia | 2.00 | 2.30 | 2.20 |
| Burma | 3.00 | 3.60 | 2.90[b] |
| Philippines | .85 | 1.10 | 1.00[b] |
| Singapore | 2.80 | 4.00 | 4.90[c] |
| Cambodia | N/A | .11 | .09[b] |
| Vietnam | .46 | N/A | N/A |
| Thailand | 2.90 | 3.50 | 2.60 |
| **Oceania** | | | |
| Australia | 7.70 | 7.60 | 8.30[b] |
| Fiji | .03 | .03 | .03 |
| New Zealand | .77 | .65 | .71 |

[a] Figures calculated at 1995 prices and exchange rates.
[b] SIPRI estimate.
[c] SIPRI uncertain figure.
*Source:* SIPRI database, online at www.projects.sipri.org/result_milex. php?send

when the global trend was in the opposite direction.[97] Mainly, the spending was for purchases of air and naval weapons and equipment with long-range capabilities.[98]

A common view among specialists in the early 1990s was that in a region with many rivalries and few mechanisms for conflict management and dispute resolution, arms acquisitions tended to stoke the fires of uncertainty about others' intentions and contributed to further demand for weapons.[99] The reasons for the buildup varied from country to country: military modernization for its own sake, intraservice rivalry, uncertainty about the ambitions of China, increased requirements for patrolling the seas (due, for example, to territorial disputes, ASEAN's creation of 200-mile Exclusive Economic Zones (EEZs) following signing of the UNCLOS, and piracy), the allure of high-tech weapons, the enticements of official profiteering from arms sales, and a wide range of internal security concerns. But a constant factor was that sophisticated weapons became affordable (and always available) as long as economic growth rates were high.[100]

Imports of major conventional weapons by *all* Asian countries declined, however, between the 1987–1990 period (when they were worth about $47 billion) and 1991–1994 (around $30 billion).[101] Besides India, the leading Asian arms-importing countries in the first half of the 1990s were Japan and the newly industrializing economies, including China.[102] For the second half of the 1990s (see table 2.3), the leading arms recipients in Asia, ranked on a global basis, were Taiwan (1), South Korea (4), India (6), Japan (7), and China (9).[103]

Due to the financial crisis, weapons acquisitions from outside East Asia declined substantially in 1998 and 1999,[104] strongly suggesting that they were driven by the availability of cash more than by external security threats. The number of armed forces personnel declined in nearly all armies in ASEAN as well. Overall military spending tended to level off. In Northeast Asia, military spending increased significantly only in China (see table 2.2 for 1999); but weapons imports generally rose, in some cases (South Korea and China) sharply.[105]

The principal reasons for these trends have been the persistence of animosities between countries and internal security concerns.[106] The first reason is clear enough: Not only in the two divided countries of Northeast Asia but even within ASEAN—meaning among Singapore, Malaysia, and Indonesia—suspicions and mistrust have continued to inhibit cooperation on security matters, perhaps more so than the so-called China threat. The second and more usual reason is that newer sources of security concern had jumped to the top of most countries' agendas: drug trafficking, piracy, protection of the EEZ, environmental decline, communal violence, and (because of the financial crisis) a dramatic increase of illegal migration and refugee problems amidst economic calamity. All these matters have led to "a redirection of security attention from external to domestic environments."[107]

Table 2.3.   Arms Transfers to Asia in the Late 1990s: The Ten
Leading Importing Countries[a]

| World Rank for Period | Recipient | 1995–1999 Total Value |
|---|---|---|
| 1 | Taiwan | $13,936 |
| 4 | South Korea | $ 6,011 |
| 6 | India | $ 4,637 |
| 7 | Japan | $ 4,343 |
| 9 | China | $ 3,994 |
| 12 | Pakistan | $ 2,873 |
| 14 | Malaysia | $ 2,574 |
| 16 | Thailand | $ 2,394 |
| 17 | Singapore | $ 1,740 |
| 22 | Indonesia | $ 1,331 |

[a] In $US million at 1990 prices. Only "major conventional weapons"
imports are counted in this table.
Source: SIPRI Yearbook 2000, Appendix 7A.1, 368–71, online ed.

## Weapons Exports and Production

The main exporter of conventional weapons in East Asia is China, which ranked sixth in the world among all suppliers of major conventional arms as the 1990s ended. In the early 1990s, China had cumulative sales of just under $6 billion.[108] As the discussion in chapter 4 will point out, however, China's arms sales, including sales of missiles, declined steadily in the remainder of the decade. Actual PRC arms deliveries came to about $2.2 billion for the 1995–1999 period, including a mere $79 million in 1999.[109] Beijing's motivations for sales have often been ascribed to money-making and market share opportunities; but as the geographical locus of its arms sales shifted in the 1990s from the Middle East to Asia (notably to Burma and Pakistan), the more usual political objectives to acquire influence and sustain friendly states seemed to become more important.[110]

Indigenous arms production in East Asia is an important feature of the arms story. With rapid growth and sophisticated civilian or military-industrial technological bases, several countries besides China (mainly North and South Korea, Singapore, and Indonesia) have been able to invest increasing funds in weapons research, develop military technologies, and build their own arms plants. (In part, the reasons may also relate to the drive for economic development: to make a profit; to exchange arms for resources, such as oil; and to develop or acquire high technologies for use in nonmilitary industries.) Exports of homemade arms can then be used to purchase military technologies and, most critically, acquire high-tech weapons. Examples are Beijing's purchases in the 1990s of advanced Russian jet fighters (the Su-27) and antimissile-capable ships, and North Korea's sales of missile components to the Middle East. Besides China, North Korea, Taiwan, and South Korea have the capability to develop nuclear and chemical weapons along with the missiles to deliver them.

From the standpoint of "comprehensive security"—that is, nonmilitary forms of security—information and high technology must also be figured in the regional security picture. Acquiring, using, controlling, and protecting these sources of economic and potentially military power have become matters of utmost sensitivity. Adherence to international agreements governing proprietary information is bound to be an ongoing problem in Asia, for economic and political reasons and not merely because of cultural differences. For a number of years, South Korean, Chinese, and other industrial product exporters' dependence on Japanese technology has been a major irritant in relations.[111] Starting in the mid-1990s, U.S. aerospace, nuclear-power, and supercomputer exports to China came under scrutiny in Washington over the question of diversion of sensitive dual-use technologies to PRC military research institutes and weapons factories, and to new nuclear weapon states such as Pakistan. (See chapter 5 for further discussion.) The basic issues here are simply put: Acquiring high technology has become a principal goal of most countries' trade policies; countries will spare no effort, including illegal means, to acquire high technology; the line between military and commercial high-technology is very thin and hard to recognize; and controlling technology trade to guard against theft or diversion is extremely difficult. Japan discovered as much when its semiconductors and other components were found to be incorporated in the very North Korean *Taepodong 1* missile that was flight-tested over Japan in 1998.[112]

In sum, armaments are increasing in number, sophistication, and range across Asia; military budgets continue to go up; force modernizations have generally stalled in Southeast Asia (though probably not for much longer) but not in Northeast Asia; and military establishments, even in ASEAN, continue to do their own planning independently of one another, reflecting continued rivalry.[113] These factors inhibit opportunities for building a regionwide arms control regime or agreement to reduce armed forces and budgets. They also mean that the real defense burden in every country—the cost of savings from military spending that might have been invested in other forms of security—will continue to fall where it always does, on the shoulders of working people.

But the arms buildups do not amount to an arms race. East Asia is far from becoming another Middle East; concerns that force modernizations might raise tensions and contribute, in combination with internal political changes, to open conflict have not been borne out. In a Realist world, after all, acquiring more and better weapons is perfectly rational.[114] Besides, the figures on arms acquisitions and military spending have never been as foreboding as some analysts claimed.[115] Thus far, conventional weapons acquisitions have outpaced efforts to restrain them; but that conclusion holds true everywhere else. Nevertheless, significant progress in arms control has been made, mainly with respect to WMD and shorter range missile systems; and Asian governments continue to develop their own distinctive approach to security, such as ASEAN's quiet diplomacy with China to keep the SCS islands disputes at least on the back burner. With the onset of the financial crisis and the refocusing on internal security problems, there is less talk of an arms race and more talk about meeting "human security" needs, as chapter 3 relates.

## Feeding the Arms Race

Sometimes lost in the analysis of arms in East Asia is the role of supplier countries such as the United States, Europe, and Russia. Their arms-making industries see fast growing East Asian economies as money making opportunities, all the more so since the end of the Cold War significantly reduced military spending in most parts of the world. Keeping East Asia armed with expensive, top of the line conventional weapons is big business—and for the Russian economy, much more urgently so than for the others. Desperately needing export markets, and pressed by a politically powerful military-industrial complex to preserve its scientific and technical assets, the Russian government needs to do everything possible to push arms sales.

Over roughly the last twenty years, an arms sales pattern has emerged that generally looks as follows: The United States has sold arms mainly to its allies and security treaty partners (Japan, Taiwan, Thailand, South Korea, and the Philippines); British, French, German, and other European arms have gone mostly to the ASEAN states and South Korea; Russian sales have been almost exclusively to China, India, and North Korea; and Chinese arms have gone to Burma and Thailand. The United States is far and away the leader here, selling mostly to countries that can afford the best weapons and thus typically taking over 60 percent of market share in East Asia.[116] Worldwide, between 1995 and 1999, the United States ranked first in major conventional weapons sales with deliveries valued at over $53 billion. In the same period, Russia was a distant second with $14.6 billion in deliveries; China, as mentioned, ranked seventh at around $2.2 billion. (France, Britain, Germany, and Netherlands ranked third through sixth.) U.S. domination of the arms export market may be seen in the fact that its total exceeded by $10 billion the combined total exports of the next *nine* countries.[117] Asian governments often observe that in seeking security through advanced weapons and technologies, they are merely following the example set by the major powers during and since the end of the Cold War.

What has changed is the locus of arms production—not so much in terms of Chinese and Korean arms exports, but even more in the greatly expanded number of agreements on co-production and local production of arms under license, such as between the United States and Japan and South Korea. These trends show the persistence of arms sellers to increase exports, if not of finished weapons then of military technology.[118] In doing so, however, the sellers are adding to regional fears of particular states (namely, China and Japan) in contradiction to the sellers' professed desires to help stabilize the region.

Any suggestion that East Asian countries exercise restraint in arms acquisitions is not going to be well received, and not just because of mutual suspicions. There is also the matter of a double standard: The United States and other arms-exporting countries have been transferring weapons for decades, reaping great profits along the way. Asians may also feel insulted by the implication that they are less responsible than their Western counterparts in the use of high-tech weapons. Arms control in Asia may also be hard to achieve because of the perceived interests it protects: Just as weapons manufacturing in Asia is taking off, Western suppliers want to rein it in and seemingly protect their turf. The world arms market, after all, reflects Western corporate as well as national concentrations of power, with U.S. firms providing over one-third of worldwide arms sales.[119]

## CONCLUSION

As one scholar has concluded, "On balance, increasing interdependence in Northeast Asia has fostered a more stable and peaceful regional security environment." But the restraining effects of interdependence do not ensure conflict prevention.[120] Nor is globalization a panacea for many of the underlying causes of inter- and intra-state conflict, as the depressing statistics on human development and the environment in East Asia make clear. The deeply felt effects of the global economy can and do have a multitude of consequences for regional security; but precisely how those effects will play out depend on many internal factors, including the competence and adaptability of state leaders.[121] To those qualities might be added another: the ability of leaders to recognize how crucial the promotion of human and environmental security is to real national security.[122]

But despite the opportunity state leaders have to turn attention and resources to such real security needs, the trends in military spending and arms transfers around East Asia show little in the way of new thinking. Countries continue to tread the path of military modernization in search of security, following the example set by the United States and other major powers. The debate over responsibility for perpetuation of the arms-for-security paradigm is reminiscent of the North-South debates over human rights and the environment. What all these debates have in common is competing notions of development. As such, neither neo-Realism, with its emphasis on national interests and the balance of power, nor Globalism, which relies so heavily on economic forces to defuse conflicts, offers a resolution.

One possible way out of the arms-for-security trap is recourse to regional or global mechanisms for dealing with underlying issues of insecurity. Such mechanisms might devise limits on the production and sales of weapons, for example, establish an Asian peacekeeping force, or create incentives for governance that accord with common standards of social and economic justice. Clearly, however, East Asian governments are not ready for that level of cooperation. But a regional consultative model has been put in place. Its impact on security is the subject of the next chapter.

# NOTES

1. Robert G. Gilpin, "The Debate About the New World Economic Order," in *Japan's Emerging Global Role*, ed. Danny Unger and Paul Blackburn (Boulder, Colo.: Lynne Rienner, 1993), 23.

2. Gilpin, "The Debate," 25.

3. See Wiliam Greider, *One World, Ready or Not: The Manic Logic of Global Capitalism* (New York: Simon & Schuster, 1997), 264, 277.

4. Note Gilpin's observation that as the United States and Europe seek to assert their economic predominance, "the East Asian economies will be continually pressured to harmonize the 'East Asian' model of economic development with the predominant neoclassical economic model of the West" as stated in "APEC in a New International Order," in *From APEC to Xanadu*, ed. Hellmann and Pyle, 35. As for concern about devising a "balance of politics" to deal with China, see Allen S. Whiting, "ASEAN Eyes China: The Security Dimension," *Asian Survey*, vol. 37, no. 4 (April 1997): 299–322.

5. Joseph S. Nye Jr., "What New World Order?" *Foreign Affairs*, vol. 71, no. 2 (Spring 1992): 85.

6. Xiangming Chen, "China's Growing Integration with the Asia-Pacific Economy," in *What Is in a Rim? Critical Perspectives on the Pacific Region Idea*, ed. Arif Dirlik (Boulder, Colo.: Westview, 1993), 111.

7. Mitchell Bernard and John Ravenhill, "Beyond Product Cycles and Flying Geese: Regionalization, Hierarchy, and the Industrialization of East Asia," *World Politics*, vol. 47, no. 2 (January 1995): 171–209; Yasuhiro Maehara, "The Role of Foreign Direct Investment in the Economies of East Asia," *Joint U.S.–Korea Academic Studies*, vol. V (1995): table 3, 79.

8. "In the four-year period 1986–89 [Japanese] FDI grew at an average annual rate in excess of 50 percent. By the end of this period Japan was the world's single largest source of FDI, with an annual outflow amounting to $48 billion (up from $6.5 billion in 1985). . . . In fact, Japan's investment in manufacturing in other Asian countries in the years 1986–89 exceeded the *cumulative* total for the whole of the 1951–85 period." Bernard and Ravenhill, "Beyond Product Cycles," 181.

9. Maehara, "The Role of Foreign Direct Investment," 87.

10. Peter Drysdale and Ross Garnaut, "The Pacific: An Application of a General Theory of Economic Integration," in *Pacific Dynamism and the International Economic System*, ed. C. Fred Bergsten and Marcus Noland (Washington, D.C: Institute for International Economics, 1993), 183–85, including table 1, 183–84. On intra-APEC trade, see also Susumu Awanohara and Nayan Chanda, "Uncommon Bonds," *Far Eastern Economic Review* (November 18, 1993): 17.

11. Maehara, "The Role of Foreign Direct Investment," 78–79.

12. South Korea–China trade came to over $15 billion in 1995, about five times what it was in 1990. See Jung Mo Kang, "The Economic Necessity of the Northeast Asia Economic Sphere," *Global Economic Review*, vol. 27, no. 1 (Spring 1998): table 3, 68. It was $25 billion in 1999. Further discussion of the ROK–PRC economic relationship is in chapter 6.

13. On TRADP, see Andrew Marton et al., "Northeast Asian Economic Cooperation and the Tumen River Area Development Project," *Pacific Affairs*, vol. 68, no. 1 (Spring 1995): 9–33, and Icksoo Kim, "Tumen River Area Development Program and the Prospects for Northeast Asian Economic Cooperation," *Asian Perspective*, vol. 19, no. 2 (Fall–Winter 1995): 75–102.

14. I rely here on figures provided by Jung Mo Kang, "The Economic Necessity of the Northeast Asia Economic Sphere," *Global Economic Review*, vol. 27, no. 1 (Spring 1998), 65–72.

15. For a very comprehensive treatment, see Miranda A. Schreurs and Dennis Pirages, eds., *Ecological Security in Northeast Asia* (Seoul: Yonsei University Press, 1998).

16. Both the economic complementarities and the deficiencies are well outlined by Jung Mo Kang, "Economic Necessity," 67.

17. For example, both Taiwan and PRC specialists anticipate that the entry of both in WTO will help to bypass political differences and focus on meshing their trade and investment policies with WTO's rules. See Julian Baum, "Chen's Dilemma," *Far Eastern Economic Review* (May 25, 2000): 22–24.

18. Mike M. Mochizuki, "Security and Economic Interdependence in Northeast Asia," Asia/Pacific Research Center, Stanford University, May 1998, 19; online at aparc.stanford.edu. At that time, China defended the "East Asian development model" and refused to devalue its currency, which would have worsened chances of recovery for the Southeast Asian economies. As one PRC observer said: "China is no longer a big economic power considering only its own interests, but rather, has become a global economic, trade and financial country shouldering far more responsibilities than ever before." Dai Xiaohua, "'East Asian Model': A Few Problems, But It Works," *Beijing Review*, no. 12 (March 22–29, 1998): 9.

19. Edward A. Olsen, "The Tumen Project CBM: An American Strategic Critique," *Asian Perspective*, vol. 19, no. 2 (Fall–Winter 1995): 53–74. Guo Binqi writes: "In the process of common development, the personnel and cultural exchanges that accompany economic cooperation will push forward each country's people toward further mutual understanding and mutual trust. Thus, 'common development' economically will gradually lead to a 'common language' politically. This will be helpful in resolving the Japan-Russia territorial question, problems on the Korean peninsula, and other contradictions. It will also be helpful in improving political and diplomatic relations between countries and in the peace and stability of the Northeast Asia region." Guo, "Development of the Tumen River Area and Economic Cooperation in the Northeast Asia Region," *Xiboliya yanjiu* (Siberian Studies), no. 1 (1995): 11.

20. Tom Holland, "Asia's New Fissure," *Far Eastern Economic Review* (June 29, 2000): 14–16.

21. See Gaye Christoffersen, "Economic Reforms in Northeast China: Domestic Determinants," *Asian Survey*, vol. 28, no. 12 (December 1988): 1245–63.

22. In 1999 Russia was China's ninth-ranked trade partner with total bilateral trade of $5.7 billion. About 80 percent of the trade consisted of Russian exports to China. But the total was less than 2 percent of China's total trade. *Renmin ribao* ( People's Daily, Beijing), February 13, 2000, English online ed.

23. Christoffersen, "Economic Reforms," 1255–57.

24. A number of editorials in the official *Renmin ribao* made this projection; see, for example, issues of July 12 and December 5, 1987. Needless to say, such ideas are no longer to be found in *Renmin ribao*.

25. Kak-Soo Shin, "Japan's Regional Role in Asia: A Korean Perspective," *Korea and World Affairs*, vol. 17, no. 2 (Summer 1993): 281–82. Shin cites (p. 290) a cumulative Korean trade deficit with Japan of about $66 billion as of 1992, but that figure is much higher today. See chapter 6.

26. Bernard and Ravenhill, "Beyond Product Cycles," 203.

27. For Chinese views of Japan, see Bonnie S. Glaser, "China's Security Perceptions: Interests and Ambitions," *Asian Survey*, vol. 33, no. 3 (March 1993): 252–71.

28. See Samuel S. Kim, ed., *East Asia and Globalization* (Lanham, Md.: Rowman & Littlefield, 2000).

29. In the Tiananmen case, it was the fax machine; in Burma, the Internet; and in the Philippines, text messaging on mobile phones that reportedly (*New York Times*, January 20, 2001, online) were used to bring people out to a mass protest that brought down President Joseph Estrada.

30. Elizabeth Economy, *Reforms and Resources: The Implications for State Capacity in the PRC* (Cambridge, Mass.: American Academy of Arts and Sciences, 1997).

31. Gerald Segal, *China Changes Shape*, Adelphi Paper No. 287 (London: IISS, 1994), and "Tying China Into the International System," *Survival*, vol. 37, no. 2 (Summer 1995): 60–73.

32. Tsuneo Akaha, "Japan-Russia Economic Relations and Their Implications for Asia-Pacific Security," in *Power and Prosperity Economics and Security Linkages in Asia Pacific*, ed. Susan L. Shirk and Christopher P. Twomey (New Brunswick, N.J.: Transaction Publishers, 1996), 205.

33. See Amitav Acharya, "Transnational Production and Security: Southeast Asia's 'Growth Triangles,'" *Contemporary Southeast Asia*, vol. 17, no. 2 (Spring 1995), 173–85.

34. For a good, brief overview, see the final report of a three-year American–Japanese collaboration: Nautilus Institute and Center for Global Communications, "Energy, Environment and Security in Northeast Asia: Defining a U.S.–Japan Partnership for Regional Comprehensive Security," December 1999, online at www.nautilus.org/papers/energyu/finalreport.html.

35. Esook Yoon and Hong Pyo Lee, "Environmental Cooperation in Northeast Asia: Issues and Prospects," in *Ecological Security,* ed. Miranda A. Schreurs and Dennis Pirages (Seoul: Yonsei University Press), 69–71.

36. The notable example was the Malaysian proposal, made in 1990 by Prime Minister Mahathir bin Mohamad, to create a yen-based bloc of Asian states that would have excluded the United States. Japan's unwillingness to support the proposal, for fear of alienating Washington, led to the alternative of incorporating the "EAEG" in APEC as the East Asian Economic Caucus (EAEC).

37. For some provocative essays on this issue as it relates to Southeast Asian experiences, see W. Scott Thompson and Kenneth M. Jensen, eds., *Rapid Economic Growth, Conflict, and Peace in Southeast Asia* (Washington, D.C.: United States Institute of Peace, 1997).

38. *Asian Development Outlook 2000*, 177.

39. UNDP, *Human Development Report 1998* (New Delhi: Oxford University Press, 1998), table 1.3, 21.

40. *Human Development Report 1998*, table 1.7, 26.

41. East Timor is the best-known case; but since its independence, the Indonesian government has faced several other rebellions that stemmed from or were pushed along by social injustice. See, for example, John McBeth and Margot Cohen, "Tinderbox," *Far Eastern Economic Review* (January 9, 1997): 14–15.

42. Elisabeth Rosenthal, "Famine in North Korea Creates Steady Human Flow into China," *New York Times*, June 10, 2000, online ed.

43. See the wrenching assessment by Robin Wright, "The Littlest Victims of Global 'Progress,'" *Los Angeles Times* "World Report" supplement, January 15, 1994, 1. The report is largely based on findings by UNICEF (the United Nations Children's Fund) and

other international organizations. On child slavery in South Asia, see *Japan Times* (Tokyo), September 20, 1995, 5.

44. See John-Thor Dahlburg, "Closing the Gap for Women," *Los Angeles Times,* "World Report" supplement, April 16, 1994, 1, 11. Overall in the Third World, about two-thirds of the illiterate adult population is female, according to UNESCO, mainly due to intentional gender discrimination in early education.

45. See International Labor Organization, *The Social Impact of the Asian Financial Crisis* (Bangkok: ILO Regional Office for Asia and the Pacific, April, 1998), 27; online at www.ilo.org/public/english/bureau/intpol/bangkok/index.htm.

46. International Labor Organization, *The Social Impact,* 25.

47. UNDP, *The China Human Development Report* (New York: Oxford University Press, 1999); *Asia Development Outlook 2000.* The latter source (p. 179) points out that, based on China's national poverty line, 9 percent of the population was living in poverty in 1998, compared with 28 percent when the economic reform era began in 1978.

48. *The China Human Development Report,* 54.

49. *Asia Development Outlook 2000* (p. 62) provides unofficial estimates of 208 million rural poor (23 percent of the rural population) and 12–15 million urban poor (5–6 percent). For regional and national figures, see pp. 54–57. On rural and urban income gaps, one Chinese source reports that the highest one-fifth of urban households (in 1994) accounted for about 44 percent of all income, while in rural areas, the top one-fifth of households accounted for nearly 49 percent of all income. Li Qiang et al., "China's Comparative Gap Between Rich and Poor," *Xinhua wenzhai* (New China Digest, Beijing), no. 2 (1996), trans. *Inside China Mainland,* vol. 18, no. 6 (June 1996): 70–74.

50. *Asia Development Outlook 2000,* 62–63, reporting World Bank and other estimates, which are considerably higher than official Chinese figures.

51. See *The China Human Development Report,* 61–62.

52. Elisabeth Rosenthal, "In Rural China, a Steep Price of Poverty: Dying of AIDS," *New York Times,* October 28, 2000, online ed.

53. ILO, *Social Impact,* 27 and table 2.16, 28.

54. Paul J. Smith, "East Asia's Economic Transformation and Labor Migration," in *Fire Across the Water: Transnational Problems in Asia,* ed. James Shinn (New York: Council on Foreign Relations, 1998), 74–75.

55. For an excellent overview and analysis, see Mike Douglass, "Unbundling National Identity: Global Migration and the Advent of Multicultural Societies in East Asia," *Asian Perspective,* vol. 23, no. 3 (1999): 79–127.

56. Sheldon W. Simon, "Arms Control, the Economic Crisis, and Southeast Asian Security" (paper prepared for the International Studies Association annual meeting, Washington, D.C., February 16–20, 1999), 8–9.

57. *Korea Times* (Seoul), October 29, 1997.

58. *Asia Development Outlook 2000,* 178.

59. Vaclav Smil, *China's Environmental Crisis: An Inquiry into the Limits of National Development* (Armonk, N.Y.: M.E. Sharpe, 1993).

60. Cao Jiaxiang, "China's Desertification Problem," *World Press Review* (August 2000): 44–45, taken from an article in the Shanghai newspaper, *Wenhui bao,* April 18, 2000.

61. See John A. Pomfret, "China's Globalizing Economy Ravages Border Forests," *Washington Post,* March 26, 2001, online ed.

62. On the protests, see Economy, *Reforms and Resources,* 53. Economy's report notes a number of other citizen protests occasioned by Beijing's policies on water and

land. Among the many critiques of the Three Gorges project, see Jonathan Spence, "A Flood of Troubles," *New York Times Magazine* (January 5, 1997): 34–39.

63. See Patrick E. Tyler, "China's Inevitable Dilemma: Coal Equals Growth," *New York Times*, November 29, 1995, 1.

64. On the legal complications that accompany such environmental and resource issues, see Choon-ho Park, "Current Legal and Political Disputes in the Yellow Sea," in *The Regime of the Yellow Sea: Issues and Policy Options in the Changing Environment,* ed. Park et al. (Seoul: Yonsei University Institute of East and West Studies, 1990), 39–48.

65. South Korea brought its protest to the UN General Assembly in June 1997, during a special session to follow up the 1992 "Earth Summit" on sustainable development held in Rio de Janeiro. The shipment was suspended, but the deal between Taiwan and North Korea remained alive as of mid-2000.

66. Erik Eckholm, "China and Taiwan Pursue Secret Nuclear Waste Deal," *New York Times*, March 14, 2000, A6.

67. See, for example, the *New York Times*, July 23, 2000, report on the drying up of the Songhua River in Heilongjiang province, a major agricultural region that normally would be quite full as a result of springtime rains. And see Cao, "China's Desertification Problem," which reports that 80 percent of northern China, or 27 percent of its total territory, is desert as the result of forest destruction and overgrazing.

68. In the South Korean case, for example, see the discussion of environmental politics and citizen protest by Norman R. Eder, *Poisoned Prosperity: Development, Modernization, and the Environment in South Korea* (New York: M.E. Sharpe, 1996).

69. Tasman Institute, "Environmental Priorities in Asia and Latin America," Report to the Monash Group, November 7, 1997 (www.arts.monash.edu.au/ausapec/epala8.htm).

70. "The spread of AIDS is accelerating rapidly and we face the prospect of remaining inert against the threat," states an extraordinarily blunt report by a committee of eminent Chinese experts that was sent to China's leaders earlier this year. It adds: "Owing to government indifference, AIDS prevention and control is gravely ineffective." (Elisabeth Rosenthal, "Scientists Warn of Inaction as AIDS Spreads in China," *New York Times*, August 2, 2000, online.) Chinese media reports say there are about one million people with H.I.V. in China, and the number is expected to climb rapidly (*Washington Post*, January 15, 2001). As is true of other social and environmental issues, political considerations undermine research and regulations: "The central government doesn't seem to realize how serious this is," said Qiu Renzong, a bioethicist at the Chinese Academy of Social Sciences, with clear exasperation. "We have not yet had an effective risk reduction strategy, because some departments are very conservative. They think chastity is more important than condom use. They say that the only way to prevent H.I.V. transmission is to rely on China's traditional values!"

71. On the drug trade in Asia, with emphasis on opium growing and heroin trafficking, see Stephen E. Flynn, "Asian Drugs, Crime, and Control: Rethinking the War," in *Fire Across the Water*, ed. Shinn, 18–44.

72. Two exceptions are Walden Bello, *People and Power in the Pacific: The Struggle for the Post-Cold War Order* (London: Pluto Press, 1992), and Desmond Ball, "The Most Promising CSBMs in the Asia/Pacific Region" (paper prepared for the conference on "The Asia-Pacific Region: Links Between Economic and Security Relations," Institute on Global Conflict and Cooperation, University of California, San Diego, May 13–15, 1993).

73. For example, China, with almost five times the U.S. population, has carbon emissions that are a bit more than one-half those of the United States. Per capita, China's

emissions are more than seven times lower. Jeffrey Logan et al., *Climate Action in the United States and China* (Princeton, N.J.: Woodrow Wilson Environmental Change and Security Project, May 1999), table 1, 3.

74. The rising tide of environmental NGOs is covered by Alvin Y. So and Yok-Shiu Lee, eds., *Asia's Environmental Movements* (Armonk, N.Y.: M. E. Sharpe, 1999); Elizabeth Economy, "The Environment and Development in the Asia-Pacific Region," in *Fire Across the Water,* ed. Shinn, 57–59 and Miranda A. Schreurs, "The Future of Environmental Cooperation in Northeast Asia," in *Ecological Security,* ed. Schreurs and Pirages, 212–13.

75. Among many sources, see Yoon and Lee, "Environmental Cooperation," 75–78; and Schreurs, "The Future of Environmental Cooperation in Northeast Asia," 209–18.

76. The UNCED program is the Network for Environmental Training at Tertiary Level in Asia-Pacific (NETTLAP). See John E. Hay, Atsutoshi Oshima, and Gillian D. Lewis, "Capacity Building for Sustainable Development in Asia," *Asian Perspective,* vol. 23, no. 3 (1999): 7–32.

77. Among them are the UN Convention on the Law of the Sea, the London Convention of 1975 on ocean dumping of waste, and the International Convention for the Prevention of Pollution from Ships (the MARPOL Treaty of 1978).

78. See, for example, the Yueyang Declaration issued from the Forum's meeting in China in December 1998. (Text in Nautilus Institute special report, January 15, 1999; ES-ENA@nautilus.org.) The declaration urged strengthening cooperation between NGOs and others, enhancing the management of biodiversity in the region, and developing an ecosystems approach to wetlands and forest protection.

79. Schreurs, "The Future of Environmental Cooperation," 212.

80. Their final report—Nautilus Institute and Center for Global Communications, "Energy, Environment and Security in Northeast Asia: Defining a U.S.–Japan Partnership for Regional Comprehensive Security," December 1999—is online at www.nautilus.org/papers/energy/finalreport.html.

81. Schreurs, "The Future of Environmental Cooperation," 214–15.

82. Sources for this paragraph include Elizabeth Van Wie Davis, "Global Conflicts in Marine Pollution: The Asian Pacific," *Journal of East Asian Studies,* vol. 10, no. 1 (Winter–Spring 1996), 192–222; Jason Hunter, "The Tumen River Area Development Program, Transboundary Water Pollution, and Environmental Security in Northeast Asia," talk at the Woodrow Wilson Center, Environmental Change and Security Project, January 7, 1998, via Nautilus Institute (APRENet@nautilus.org).

83. The Nautilus Institute has been a frequent critic of APEC's half-hearted commitment to the environment. See, for instance, Jason Hunter, "APEC: Promise or Peril in the Asia-Pacific?" Nautilus Institute paper, online at www.nautilus.org/vforum.html; and Lyuba Zarsky, "APEC, Globalization, and the 'Sustainable Development' Agenda," *Asian Perspective,* vol. 22, no. 2 (1998): 133–68.

84. For a full list, which goes beyond the disputes concerning sovereignty over various island groups, see Ball, "The Most Promising CSBMs," table 2, 28.

85. Michael Leifer, "Chinese Economic Reform and Security Policy: The South China Sea Connection," *Survival,* vol. 37, no. 2 (Summer 1995), 44–59, and Andrew Mack and Desmond Ball, "The Military Build-up in Asia-Pacific," *The Pacific Review,* vol. 5, no. 3 (1992): 206–7.

86. See, for instance, Kent E. Calder, *Pacific Defense: Arms, Energy, and America's Future in Asia* (New York: William Morrow, 1996), and Calder, "Asia's Empty Tank," *Foreign Affairs,* vol. 75, no. 2 (March–April 1996): 55–69.

87. See Gerald Segal, "East Asia and the 'Constrainment' of China," *International Security*, vol. 20, no. 4 (Spring 1996): 107–135.

88. Simon, "Arms Control," 27.

89. Mamdouh G. Salameh, "China, Oil and the Risk of Regional Conflict," *Survival*, vol. 37, no. 4 (Winter 1995–96): 133–46.

90. See, for example, Segal, "East Asia and the 'Constrainment' of China," 118–23.

91. See Allen S. Whiting, "ASEAN Eyes China: The Security Dimension" *Asian Survey*, vol. 37, no. 4 (April 1997), 299–322, and Rosemary Foot, "China in the ASEAN Regional Forum: Organizational Processes and Domestic Modes of Thought," *Asian Survey*, vol. 38, no. 5 (May 1998): 425–40.

92. On Taiwan, ASEAN's public position has been in agreement with Beijing's, namely, that Taiwan is a domestic Chinese problem, that a peaceful settlement by the two parties is preferable, and that Taiwan's policies are partly responsible for the tensions. One ASEAN specialist has also acknowledged a self-interested motive: ASEAN "does not want to set a precedent that would enable others to intervene in their domestic affairs in the future." Jusuf Wanandi, "ASEAN's China Strategy: Towards Deeper Engagement," *Survival*, vol. 38, no. 3 (Autumn 1996), 125.

93. Whiting, "ASEAN Eyes China," 300–301.

94. See table, "World and Regional Military Expenditure Estimates, 1990–99," SIPRI database online at www.projects.sipri.se/milex/mex_wnr_table.html.

95. *SIPRI Yearbook 1992*, appendix 7A, 254–68 and table 8B.3, 311–14; International Institute for Strategic Studies, *The Military Balance 1992/93* (London: IISS, 1993), 220.

96. Desmond Ball, "Arms and Affluence: Military Acquisitions in the Asia-Pacific Region," *International Security*, vol. 18, no. 3 (Winter 1993/94): 79.

97. From 1984 to 1989, major conventional arms imports in Asia (excluding Japan and Oceania) went from $8.3 billion to about $16 billion, whereas worldwide they declined in the same period from $34.3 billion to $22.2 billion. *SIPRI Yearbook 1992*, appendix table 8B.1, 308.

98. Ball, "The Most Promising CSBMs," 31–42, gives detailed tables on these military acquisitions.

99. Mack and Ball, "The Military Build-up in Asia-Pacific," 206–7.

100. The most comprehensive picture is provided by Malcolm Chalmers, *Confidence-Building in South-East Asia* (Boulder, Colo.: Westview Press, for the University of Bradford, 1996), 61–199. See also Michael T. Klare, "The Next Great Arms Race," *Foreign Affairs*, vol. 72, no. 3 (Summer 1993): 136–52, and Kusuma Snitwongse, "Economic Development and Military Modernization in Southeast Asia," in *Power and Prosperity*, ed. Shirk and Twomey, 19–34.

101. SIPRI, *SIPRI Yearbook 1995: Armaments, Disarmament and International Security* (London: Oxford University Press, 1995), appendix table 14A, 510.

102. SIPRI, *SIPRI Yearbook 1995*, table 14.2, 494. Taiwan, China, Thailand, South Korea, and Indonesia were among the top twenty recipients worldwide from 1990 to 1994, according to this table.

103. Based on actual *deliveries* of major conventional weapons. Asian states (including Malaysia, Pakistan, Thailand, Singapore, and Indonesia) occupied nine of the top twenty positions among all arms-importing states from 1995 to 1999, much as they had between 1990 and 1994. Taiwan's purchases were valued at $13.9 billion for the period covered. See *SIPRI Yearbook 2000*, table 7A.1, 368, at the SIPRI database, online at www.projects.sipri.se/armstrade.

104. For instance, in 1997 Northeast Asian countries imported $7.1 billion worth of major conventional weapons, and Southeast Asian countries imported $2.1 billion worth. In 1999 the comparable figures were $5.8 billion and $1.6 billion for the two regions. See *SIPRI Yearbook 2000*, appendix 7B, 374, online at www.projects/sipri.se/arm-strade/facts_and_figures.html.

105. *SIPRI Yearbook 2000*, 368–71.

106. On Southeast Asia, see Simon, "Arms Control," 3–5.

107. Simon, "Arms Control," 5.

108. *SIPRI Yearbook 1995*, table 14.1, 493.

109. SIPRI arms transfers database, in *SIPRI Yearbook 2000*, table 7A.2, 372, online ed. It should be noted that in 1999, Chinese arms sales agreements worldwide surged to around $1.8 billion. Steven Lee Myers, "Led by U.S., Arms Sales Surge Globally," *New York Times*, August 21, 2000, online ed.

110. See Evan S. Medeiros and Bates Gill, *Chinese Arms Exports: Policy, Players, and Process* (Carlisle, Pa.: U.S. Army, Strategic Studies Institute, August 2000), 9–11. On the general problem of incentives for arms exports, see Steven E. Miller, "Arms and East Asia: Supplier Motivations and Arms Transfer Control," *The Korean Journal of International Studies*, vol. 24, no. 4 (Winter 1993): 405–30.

111. Bernard and Ravenhill, "Beyond Product Cycles," 201.

112. Nicholas D. Kristof, "North Korean Missile Parts Said to Be from Japan," *New York Times*, July 9, 1999, online ed. The components were probably acquired by North Korea from third countries (China denies being the source), with Ukraine identified as a probable source of expertise in missile development. See *Korea Times*, February 10, 1999, based on research by the Monterey Institute of International Studies Center for Nonproliferation Studies.

113. Simon, "Arms Control," 36.

114. For example, military spending among the (then) ASEAN Six was generally below the level (4.5 percent of GDP) that the International Monetary fund said should be the maximum. These "countries today are compensating for the underdevelopment of their external defence capabilities and are building up to a level that, in other regions, would be considered normal," writes Leszek Buszynski, "ASEAN Security Dilemmas," *Survival*, vol. 34, no. 4 (Winter 1992–93): 100, 106. See also Ball, "Arms and Affluence," 79–95.

115. For example, defense expenditures in East Asia as a percentage of intra-East Asian trade volume declined significantly in each of the past two decades. (Hadi Soesastro, ed., *Indonesian Perspectives on APEC and Regional Cooperation in Asia Pacific* [Jakarta: Centre for Strategic and International Studies, 1994], table 3, 375.) As a share of GDP, they were stable or declining in seven East Asian countries (Indonesia, Japan, South Korea, Malaysia, Singapore, Taiwan, and Thailand) between 1981 and 1990. Ian Anthony et al., "Arms Production and Arms Trade," in *SIPRI Yearbook 1993: World Armaments and Disarmament*, SIPRI (London: Oxford University Press, 1993), 454–55.

116. For example, U.S. conventional arms sales in East Asia accounted for 62 percent of all countries' sales between 1988 and 1992. *SIPRI Yearbook 1993*, table 10.10, 444.

117. Based on data in the *SIPRI Yearbook 2000*, table 7A.2, 372, online ed.

118. Anthony et al., "Arms Production and Arms Trade," 455; Frances Fukuyama and Kongdan Oh, *The U.S.–Japan Security Relationship after the Cold War* (Santa Monica, Calif.: RAND National Defense Research Institute, 1993), 61 (discussing the U.S.–Japan co-production agreement on the FSX fighter plane).

119. Based on Congressional Research Service data. U.S. sales in 1999 were about $11.8 billion out of a worldwide total of $30.3 billion. The U.S. total was more than that of all European companies combined. Steven Lee Meyers, "Led by U.S., Arms Sales Surge Globally," *New York Times*, August 21, 2000, online ed. In 1991, by contrast, forty-seven U.S. arms firms accounted for about 61 percent of total arms sales by the 100 largest companies. Next were forty West European firms, with 33 percent of total arms sales. *SIPRI 1993*, table 10.3, 428.

120. Mochizuki, "Security and Economic Interdependence," 30.

121. See the excellent introduction by Samuel S. Kim to a collection of national studies, "East Asia and Globalization: Challenges and Responses," in *East Asia and Globalization*, ed. Kim, 1–30.

122. I stress that theme in contemporary world politics in *Global Politics in the Human Interest*, 4th ed. (Boulder, Colo.: Lynne Rienner, 1999).

## Chapter Three

# The Asian Way

## APPROACHES TO SECURITY

How have the Asia Pacific states responded to their diverse security problems? How have they been able to overcome competitive impulses and negative histories to cooperate in ways that dampen tensions? Does the "Asian way" or "ASEAN way" work? Two points may be useful background to answering these questions.

First, we should note the strikingly different paths to enhancing security taken in Europe and Asia. Europe, prompted by the Mikhail Gorbachev–George Bush nuclear initiatives, moved steadily after the fall of the Berlin Wall in 1989 to overcome Cold War divisions, reduce military spending and arms imports, and expand economic and security integration. The EU—acting through the Conference on (later, Organization for) Security and Cooperation in Europe (CSCE, then OSCE)—and the North Atlantic Treaty Organization (NATO) constitute a security community. It conducts UN-authorized peacekeeping operations, as in Bosnia, Kosovo, and Macedonia, in an effort to deal with contending nationalisms; as of the end of 1999 the EU had a 60,000-troop rapid reaction force for conflict resolution and other missions. Europe is also at the cutting edge when it comes to collectively addressing, if not resolving, the destabilizing consequences of transnational issues such as the exploitation of migrant labor, deprivations of human rights, and transnational environmental problems.

The tendency in Asia Pacific, on the other hand, is that governments rely mainly on their own resources and on the congealing effects of economic interdependence for security rather than, as in Europe, on security structures with a common mission, high degree of integration, and binding commitments. Post–World War II history provides one of the reasons for this difference—the separate, and opposite, ways in which regional organizing evolved in Western Europe and East Asia.[1] Simply put, in Europe, the march toward a European

Community took place in the context of systematic political decision making by a variety of coalitions, the formation of NATO in 1948, and the full-fledged integration of Germany in European affairs. In East Asia, on the other hand, cooperative, institutionalized political decision making has been fitful; no military alliance has provided the glue for a sense of community; and Japan has only been reintegrated economically in the region. In East Asia, common economic interests must therefore substitute for a history of political cooperation that is lacking.

The second preliminary observation is that Asian governments have tended to sidestep the arms buildup issue. Officials usually argue that increases in military spending and arms acquisitions are not out of the ordinary, and that it is prudent to enhance military capabilities should the worst case occur. Left unsaid, but understood, is that "the worst case" certainly includes conflict with neighbors with whom one is now at peace.[2] Even more, it includes the potential for conflict with China.[3] Asian governments prefer, however, to accent the positive possibilities deriving from regional prosperity and not draw attention to worst cases.

## The Path to the Asian Way

As was argued in the early discussion of an Asia Pacific identity, three sources stand out as being responsible for Asia's distinctive approach to security issues. The first is nationalism—the common conviction that Asians must develop their own means of achieving security. Colonial rule, agreements and treaties orchestrated by the major powers during the Cold War, and big-power interventions had taken control of Asia's destiny out of Asian hands. With the achievement of impressive levels of economic growth in most of East Asia, national leaders now have the self-confidence to organize for security in their own way. Thus, it is a matter of pride that ASEAN on its own established the ASEAN Regional Forum (ARF) in 1994 to promote security dialogue.[4]

A second source of the Asian approach is the Cold War history of bilateralism in security relations. The United States took the lead in this regard, with strong support from Japan. Bilateral security arrangements that the United States concluded with East Asian allies (Japan, South Korea, Taiwan, Philippines, and Thailand) were alternatives to reliance on multilateral organizations.[5] Politically, however, these arrangements had the effects of dividing Asia against itself and ensuring U.S. control of all security initiatives.[6] Economically, they tied U.S. allies to imports of U.S. arms. Militarily, bilateralism was founded on a rigid conceptual attraction to the balance of power, which argued that alliances against a common enemy, meaning the "Sino-Soviet bloc," provided the best insurance against aggression. That argument, which gained momentum with the Korean War, not only promoted the long-term maintenance and forward deployment of U.S. military forces and bases in East Asia; it also blocked discussion of naval and other kinds of arms control measures that multilateral regimes might enact.[7]

In the post–Cold War period, the objective conditions for bilateralism and forward deployment of U.S. forces have changed. There no longer is a single (Soviet) threat for the United States and its allies to deter. Nor is China the expansionist power that the U.S. alliance system was meant to contain. Revolutionary nationalism and communist internationalism both actually died even earlier, with the end of the war in Vietnam in 1975. Today, Asia has many rivalries, but no common enemy. Most ASEAN leaders regard China as the greatest potential threat to regional order; but there is no common desire to be party to a military organization to contain it. Koreans north and south regard Japan (and Japanese) with much greater suspicion than they do China, while some security specialists in Japan and China still consider Russia the greatest threat to their countries. The India-China relationship warmed early in the 1990s, then took a large step back over India's nuclear weapon tests and budding naval competition in the Indian Ocean. The Thai government is frequently at odds with Burma and Cambodia over refugees and drugs; Thailand and Cambodia have an historic concern about Vietnamese aspirations; and Laotians are concerned about Thailand's intentions. Singapore-Malaysia tensions flare periodically, still suffering the pangs of their separation in 1965. The paradox is that Asian nationalisms now must compete in the decision making of Asian governments with thriving, increasingly multinational and sub-regional commercial relationships and with tactical diplomatic alliances, some of which cross over traditional Cold War lines.

The third source of the Asian approach is economic: Rapid growth in much of the region necessitated multilateral cooperation, not merely to facilitate further growth, but also to avoid political frictions that would threaten it. Increased economic interdependence, a Brunei official has written,

> could result in vulnerability, especially because of reliance on foreign investments and markets. [Asia Pacific leaders] accepted the fact that, as nations drew together, free access to markets, unimpeded sea lanes and access to resources were indispensable for further economic progress. They also became aware that those factors could be potential sources of conflict.[8]

For that very reason, closer economic ties in Asia Pacific have aimed at bridging political differences and creating new sets of intersecting interests. As just one example, when the annual report for 1999 on foreign investment in the ASEAN countries was submitted and showed substantial declines everywhere except in Singapore, the foreign ministers agreed with the request of one member (probably Singapore) not to make the report public.[9] Their action showed just how politically sensitive economic vulnerability is, and why banding together is considered crucial to the association's success.

The Asian way may be distinguished with respect both to style and substance: first, by emphasis on informal arrangements rather than institution-building to solve intergovernmental problems and gain cooperation; second, by preference for economic rather than military measures to produce security (in the belief that where security cooperation may not be directly attainable, economic development through interdependence is); third, by reliance on reassurances through dialogue rather than rule making in regimes or agreements to resolve or mitigate disputes.[10] Chart 3.1 shows the Asian way in the context of other security models, while chart 3.2 depicts the model's essential features.

ASEAN is often cited by its supporters for promoting regional security by developing

> a trend . . . toward the institutionalization of regular, intensive and continuous interaction and intercommunication among its member states. This has sustained the "getting-acquainted process," familiarization and consensus, and indeed, confidence-building among the member states. Such a trend, moreover, will help to iron out differences and even neutralize conflicts, actual as well as potential, among the ASEAN member states.[11]

The writer further observed that ASEAN's unique approach had helped reduce each state's military burden, thus enhancing its economic development opportunities and economic cooperation—all of which insulated the region from external interference.[12]

The Asian way reflects present day realities in the region in several regards: It is consistent with nationalism and contemporary political thinking in Asia, where there is a widespread concern about control of regional affairs, or a regional organization, by a single power; the lack of a consensus in support of global norms or regional rule making; respect for regional diversity and concern about overly Western formulations; an almost universal interest in comprehensive security focused on outward-oriented economic development; and a preference in actionable disputes for flexible options rather than reliance (as, for example, in NATO) on legal conditions or automaticity. The Asian way also seeks to convey a culturally specific approach to conflict—the emphasis on consensus, personal relationships, and indirect, nonconfrontational styles. Inclusivity, flexibility, avoidance of pressure tactics (such as sanctions), and the pursuit of limited, practical, and modest goals are the preferred ways of conducting public affairs.[13]

Western critics have had great difficulty accepting the effectiveness of groups that rely so much on informality and action by consensus, that are slow to come to agreement, and (especially in APEC's case) that deliberately delink security from economic issues.[14] As one long-time observer of Asian security affairs has written, the "utilitarian" and "cognitive" dimensions of security building need more attention in East Asia—that is, arrangements for dialogue and policy assessment of issues affecting cooperation. It should not be assumed, he said, that functional ra-

**Chart 3.1.     Alternative Security Models to the Asian Way**

*Confidence and security building measures* (CBMs, CSBMs): on the model of the Organization for Security and Cooperation in Europe—agreements that emphasize transparency in preventing arms buildups and miscalculations.

*Collective security:* on the NATO security treaty model for responding to external threats to the peace.

*Multiple functionalism:* groups with different purposes and memberships, but together comprising a "regional security web."

*Two-track regionalization:* the Japanese two-tiered approach of sub-regional cooperation to settle disputes and regionwide political dialogue to promote strategic reassurance.

*Conflict prevention:* the ASEAN security model, relying on common economic interests and dialogue to serve as forms of preventive diplomacy.

*Single-issue regime:* a multilateral regime devoted to negotiating the resolution of one problem, such as arms reductions or accidents at sea.

*Track II:* activities of international NGOs on issues such as transboundary pollution, human rights, and arms control.

*Track III:* civil society popular movements for internal security (i.e., democracy and human rights).

**Chart 3.2.     Characteristics of Asian Approaches to Security**

• Passive rather than active collaboration; reliance on coordination and communication.

• Comprehensive definition of security.

• Consultative, not hegemonic or coalition building.

• Consensual, not contractual.

• Loose rather than tight organization and mission.

• Open (inclusive) rather than closed (exclusive) membership.

• Conciliatory rather than coercive purposes.

tionality will suffice to create common ground.[15] In fact, many Asian analysts believe that the numerous points of difference and contention among Asia Pacific countries must be confronted, lest politics overwhelm common economic interests.[16] The combined effects of the financial crisis, violence in East Timor, and China's assertiveness have raised questions about the capacity and effectiveness of APEC and ASEAN to respond to regional problems. But how to do so while preserving the integrity of the Asian way, its raison d'être, is the overriding challenge.

## MULTILATERALISM ASIAN STYLE

**Weak Multilateralism**

Despite the size of the Asia Pacific security agenda, regional leaders have very carefully limited the scope and purposes of their security-building efforts. A major reason is the recognition that a consensus is usually lacking to reach binding agreements on specific problems such as arms control and territorial disputes. Multilateralism means different things to different governments. For example, whether or not a multilateral venture should have a leader, and which state that might be; how universal membership in a multilateral group ought to be; what "security" purposes a multilateral organization ought to have (to deter aggression? to promote dialogue? to keep the peace?). Furthermore, whether or not multilateral activities should be encompassed by a formal organization; and what new conflicts and tensions multilateralism itself might occasion, such as between sub-regions, between proto- and nonleaders, between developed and developing economies, and between members and nonmembers—these are among the practical considerations that make formal multilateral security cooperation unattractive at present to most of the region's leaders.

There is also a strong belief in Asia, as there is outside it, that a European approach to security is incompatible with Asian realities: East Asian authorities cite quite different histories, geographies, cultural mixes, and experiences at cooperation; their region's lack of a shared strategic philosophy equivalent to Europe as a "common home"; and the fundamentally different kinds of security problems the two regions must confront.[17] Geographically, for instance, Europe's security conflicts have been over land and Asia's over maritime issues. Politically, whereas post–Cold War Europe has mainly dealt with confidence building and conflict prevention (stabilizing boundaries, peacekeeping, and arms control), East Asia has been preoccupied with domestic instabilities, territorial disputes, and the establishment of norms of good behavior in inter-state relations. These differences account for ASEAN's embrace of a multitrack forum, the ARF, for dealing with security problems rather than adoption of an Asian variation of CSCE, which was emphatically rejected in the early discussions about a regional response to security problems.[18]

To a far greater degree than in the EU countries, domestic politics in East Asia greatly constrain effective multilateral cooperation. Forging political compromises, healing social rifts, and determining how and where public funds will be spent all detract from attention and resources for conducting foreign affairs. For example, Japan's ability to assume more regional security responsibilities (such as the United States would like), or for that matter make *any* significant departure from a reactive foreign policy, depends on mollifying both right and left in the Diet as well as on changing the legendary bureaucratic domination of the policy making process. PRC leaders probably differ over how to assert Chinese nationalism on matters such as Taiwan while sustaining a booming economy that is so reliant on foreign investment. Russian diplomacy with Japan, and prospects for finally resolving the Northern Islands dispute, depend substantially on domestic factors: in Moscow, a strong presidency and stable political conditions; in Tokyo, the government's perception of the public's tolerance for a negotiated settlement that does not lead to recovery of all four islands. Indonesia's ability to continue as the core state in ASEAN is inseparable from the stability and integrity of its political system, the recovery of its economy, and a peaceful resolution of secessionist bids. ASEAN governments in general are plagued by political and social disorders of one sort or another.

In such circumstances, there is no easy way to achieve consensus on "domestic" issues that affect national and regional security. Though Thailand and the Philippines have sought to soften the nonintervention principle so that refugees and human rights can be matters of common discussion, Indonesia and other members have resisted. And in South Korea, whether or not Kim Dae Jung can promote a "soft landing" for unification with North Korea depends on the outcome of domestic affairs: How effectively he can deal with right-wing criticism ("red-baiting," it is being called), for instance, and how he can sustain economic aid to North Korea while his own economy has serious problems.

These considerations frame what is possible and desirable around Asia when it comes to working together. They have led governments to opt for what might be called "weak multilateralism" in both economic and political cooperation. What follows is an overview of these cooperative efforts.

## Economics: APEC and Other Regional Groups

On the economic side, APEC is of course the most important group at the official (Track I) level. (Other intergovernmental economic organizations are the Asian Development Bank, founded in 1966, and Asia-Europe Meeting (ASEM), which started in 1996.) But private, nongovernmental activities (so-called Track II) are crucial too, since they helped create the path to APEC and often shape its agenda and initiate projects beyond APEC's capacity.[19] Among the prominent groups is the Pacific Economic Cooperation Council (PECC), which is a forum for deliberating trade policy. It was PECC's discussions on regional economic cooperation, beginning in 1980, that eventuated in the formation of APEC. PECC sought to preempt a global movement toward regional trading blocs by creating a Pacific voice for an open trading system.[20] It brings together business, academic, and (in unofficial capacities) government representatives from around the Pacific Rim (including Latin America) and from other multilateral organizations.

The Pacific Basin Economic Council (PBEC) is an organization of national committees of business leaders founded in 1967 on the initiative of a Japan-Australia business committee.[21] The Northeast Asia Economic Forum (NAEF), an NGO created before the Cold War ended, sponsors conferences to promote economic cooperation. Like the other groups, it attracts big business and government officials in hopes of spurring serious cooperative development projects regardless of overt political barriers. In the case of NAEF, it has done that: The Tumen River project (TRADP) emerged directly out of the Forum's bridge-building efforts, specifically with North Korea in mind.[22] Lastly, in recognition of the EU's significant place in East Asia's economy, there is the Council for Asia-Europe Cooperation, which helped launch ASEM.

APEC's significance lies in the simple fact that its membership represents about one-half of world trade and world income. It has been described as "a novel experiment in regionalism with global objectives." On one hand, APEC needs to identify shared interests within a region of highly diverse economies. On the other, because of the importance of the U.S. and European markets, and concern in East Asia about being shut out of the NAFTA zone and the EU, APEC also needs to operate according to the new global order, which has meant "strengthening a rules-based, nondiscriminatory, multilateral economic system."[23] The notion of APEC as a "forum of economies" accurately reflects what it is and is not: a consultative body that seeks to harmonize trade and investment policies rather than make binding decisions.

In political terms, APEC is a pluralistic entity—there are no leaders, no formal structure, no binding decisions, and no weighted voting. There *is* an openness to wide national participation, to working by consensus and building trust, and to respect for the principle of sovereignty no less than that of interdependence. From the standpoint of its least powerful members (i.e., those in ASEAN), which are the real core of APEC and which are anxious to avoid being dominated by U.S. economic decisions, we might say that APEC is a *strategy for engaging* the United States in consultative problem solving.

Over the years APEC has avoided institutionalizing; but as discussions and missions have become more complex, it has had to accept some degree of administrative growth. Thus, while not creating a central decision making bureaucracy, APEC has established a permanent secretariat in Singapore, policy-based groups, and several working groups (e.g., on fisheries, human resources development, and telecommunications). Recommendations to the ministerial and senior officials level also come from an Eminent Persons Group of intellectuals, comprised mostly of economists.

NGOs, on the other hand, have literally had to force their way in APEC's door, which they did in 1996 at an APEC ministerial meeting in Manila. Their activism has focused on the environmental and labor consequences of open trade—for instance, the destruction of mangrove forests as a result of shrimp farming, or the clearcutting of forests to maximize export of raw logs, or the low wages and poor health and safety conditions of workers in processing and assembly industries. Their argument has been that APEC's aim to harmonize product standards and tariffs amounts to a "race to the bottom" in terms of environmental and labor standards. NGOs have helped to inject the notion of sustainable development in the capacity-building activities of APEC's working groups; but they remain outside of the APEC policy process. As a group, APEC has yet to accept either that environmental goals should be an intrinsic part of commercial policy making or that the popular constituencies that NGOs represent have valid interests in the outcome of APEC's deliberations.[24]

## Security: ASEAN, ARF, and Other Groups

On the security side, the Five Power Defence Arrangements of 1971 (FPDA) is a largely consultative framework involving Britain, Australia, New Zealand, Malaysia, and Singapore. Its central purpose has been to provide visible defense support of Malaysia and Singapore through basing and joint maneuvers. But FPDA does not provide a formal security guarantee and is not a treaty alliance.[25] Nor does it reflect Southeast Asia's search for regional legitimacy, which goes to the heart of ASEAN. Since its founding in 1967 by five of the ten current members (Thailand, Indonesia, Philippines, Singapore, and Malaysia), ASEAN's emphasis has had two overriding purposes: to build trust among the states of the region, initially through economic and cultural interchange, and to insulate the region from great power interference.[26] Events in the mid-1960s provided the backdrop to ASEAN's formation—several high profile disputes within the region, most seriously Indonesia's "crush Malaysia" campaign and the war in Vietnam.

ASEAN's chief concerns were to put those disputes to rest and to break the historical pattern of entrapment in "major power rivalry and intervention"—to extract Southeast Asia from its long history of colonial rule, external pressure, and bilateral alignments.[27] At Kuala Lumpur in November 1971, the ASEAN-5 announced that they sought to "secure the recognition of, and respect for, South East Asia as a Zone of Peace, Freedom and Neutrality [ZOPFAN], free from any form or manner of interference by outside Powers."[28] ZOPFAN expressed the hope that the major powers would accept the principles of noninterference, peaceful coexistence, and pacific dispute resolution in their foreign policy conduct. Other countries would then take ASEAN seriously and thus increase ASEAN's leverage in dealing with the major powers.[29] Toward that end, ASEAN in 1972 opened its doors to "dialogue partners," principally the big powers, by creating a Post-Ministerial Conference (ASEAN-PMC) to discuss regional cooperation.[30]

The other aspect of ASEAN's search for a new security model lay in the overriding concern with national development, and therefore with domestic sources of insecurity. "Noninterference" also applied here, in the form of respect for each other's sovereignty and equality. That much became clear in February 1976, when the five heads of state signed a Declaration of ASEAN Concord and a Treaty of Amity and Cooperation (TAC) in Southeast Asia. The Declaration was designed to push forward the ZOPFAN idea and "exert all efforts to create a strong ASEAN community" through economic, political, and social cooperation. Poverty, subversion, and social inequities were identified as threats to stability. In the TAC, the same principles that underlay ZOPFAN were restated, but in the context of promoting self-restraint in intra-ASEAN relations. The TAC even created a mechanism, the High Council, to serve much like the UN secretary general in facilitating the resolution of disputes among the ASEAN-5.[31] Protocols to the TAC in 1987 and 1998 allowed other states to subscribe to its principles.

Only with the end of the Cold War, however, was ASEAN able to make a credible and effective effort to secure its goals. That is because until then, its appeals were undermined by communist insurgencies, North Vietnam's victory over the United States, and the fact that all the ASEAN states except Indonesia had major power military bases on their soil.[32] Economically, inspired by APEC, ASEAN created a free trade area (AFTA) in 1993 that aims to reduce or eliminate trade barriers among its members. Though somewhat behind schedule, about 90 percent of trade within AFTA is currently subject to between 0 and 5 percent tariffs.[33] Intra-ASEAN trade (a total of about $86 billion in 1997) has grown to nearly one-quarter of its total trade.[34] In the political arena, two large uncertainties in East Asia—the U.S. commitment and the SCS dispute[35]—helped galvanize sentiment by 1991 in favor of an explicit agreement in the ASEAN-PMC to discuss security issues for the first time. Those discussions launched the process that established the ARF in 1994, with Australian foreign ministry officials taking the lead and Japan providing strong support. ARF brings together the same twenty-two countries that are in the PMC, plus North Korea. The United States is a member, but it was an early and vigorous opponent of the ARF concept, which at bottom was regarded as undermining the dominant position of the United States in East Asian security based on bilateral treaty commitments.[36]

The dilemma faced by the ASEAN countries has been that, individually and collectively, they lack bargaining power. Throughout the Cold War the ASEAN states were consistently at the mercy of the big powers, without the resources and the intrinsic importance that were needed to leverage commitments from them.[37] Thus, when ASEAN came together around the notions of neutrality and nonintervention, the question arose: How could the ASEAN states make the major powers respect those principles without having to align with them or accept some form of security guarantee from them? There was no ready answer: "Instead, ASEAN states continue to rely upon their traditional security ties with outside powers, whether or not such relations [e.g., Thailand's treaty ties to the United States] undercut the efforts of its ASEAN partners to support and gradually sever their reliance on external deterrence commitments."[38]

But in the ARF, ASEAN was able partially to resolve its dilemma with a model midway between security self-reliance and dependence. As a "forum," ARF promotes discussion of comprehensive-security issues.[39] Its focus now and for the foreseeable future is on confidence-building measures and preventive diplomacy. Not being a collective security organization, since it lacks a military arm and a decision making apparatus, ARF cannot *deter* conflict by use or threat of force, nor dispatch peacekeepers to monitor or enforce a settlement. It can only look to develop conflict-resolution resources at a later time,[40] which to some observers means that ARF is in the business of "conflict avoidance."[41] But that is a harsh judgment, given ARF's recent origins and diverse membership. What it can do, in response to or anticipation of threats to the peace, is exploit its capacity to bring together ASEAN and other regional leaders for dialogue on terms of equality. Asian officials have variously described this capacity as "the development of friendship rather than the identification of enemies," and building "security with others rather than against them."

Such inclusive multilateralism is quite at odds with its predecessor, the "exclusive bilateralism" of U.S. security policy during the Cold War.[42] Thus, for example, whereas American bilateralism focused on containing China during the Cold War (and now again, the Chinese charge), ASEAN's approach has been to avoid confronting China, no matter the concerns about its future intentions. Instead, ASEAN seeks to bring China into its tent and seek its commitment to principles and practices of common interest. It has accomplished that objective: China is involved in several different tracks of the ASEAN process, including most recently (in 1999) the "ASEAN+3" summit meetings, which are designated as an annual event to bring together the heads of state of China, South Korea, Japan, and ASEAN.

Engagement is not the only element of ASEAN's China strategy—delicately offsetting Chinese power is another. Though not widely acknowledged within ASEAN, the decisions to admit Vietnam and Burma were probably motivated in part, on *all* sides, by the hope that ASEAN's bargaining position with China would be strengthened, and China's weakened. Vietnam would no longer have to stand alone in its dispute with China over the SCS islands; and Burma, China's principal arms customer in East Asia and an increasingly pivotal player in the Sino-Indian strategic competition in South Asia, would be less exposed to Chinese influence.[43] The admission of Vietnam, it should be noted, was not considered provocative by Beijing, since by the time it occurred (1995) PRC-Vietnam relations had normalized; thus it could be accomplished in the name of inclusiveness. But larger membership can be advantageous in dialoguing with China, reinforcing the various ASEAN declarations that urge self-restraint when disputes occur.

Furthermore, bilateralism has its place in the ASEAN way. For one thing, the five U.S. security alliances in East Asia are very much counted on in ASEAN's security thinking. ASEAN's interest in ARF stems from a belief that a strong U.S. military presence in East Asia is an essential ingredient of regional stability. The clearest evidence of this is the stopover and resupply arrangements that a number of ASEAN governments have conducted with the U.S. Navy, and ASEAN's reliance on U.S. weapons sales. ASEAN scholars have frequently pointed out that a continuing U.S. role in maintaining the Asian balance of power was among the crucial factors in the decision to create ARF in the first place.[44] The near-universal belief in ASEAN is that a U.S. regional presence promotes security through strategic reassurance, particularly against China via the U.S.–Japan Security Treaty but also, in some thinking, against the possibility of a military resurgent Japan.[45]

At the same time, however, ASEAN leaders recognize that the U.S. presence cannot be counted on forever or in every dispute. U.S. forces and bases in Asia were cut back after the Vietnam War. The two major U.S. bases in the Philippines had to be abandoned in the early 1990s, precipitating a shift in Pentagon strategy from "bases" to "places" for U.S. training programs and naval access (see chapter 7). The U.S. Congress has periodically pared military budgets and shown little taste for strengthening security commitments in East Asia other than to Taiwan. And U.S. national security strategy has centered in recent years on the Middle East, central Europe, and "global threats" such as drug trafficking. Based on these trends, multilateralism was "seen as a necessary 'insurance policy' by [ASEAN] policymakers," who believed "the U.S. security umbrella can no longer be taken for granted."[46]

Bilateralism also backstops ASEAN's multilateralism in another basic sense: When it comes to resolving disputes among the members, the recourse has been to bilateral negotiations and commissions—"the dispute provisions in the 1976 Bali Treaty of Amity and Cooperation, ASEAN's touchstone, have never been invoked."[47] Thus, ASEAN operates at two distinct levels: its declarations of principles promote norms of conduct, but actual disputes are managed through state-to-state diplomacy. As pointed out above, this is the difference between conflict resolution, which has not yet been entertained within ASEAN/ARF, and conflict avoidance or prevention.

ASEAN-PMC and ARF are "Track I" (intergovernmental) activities. Track I is reinforced and informed by nongovernmental activities in Track II and Track III.[48] Track II consists of academic and semi-official fora devoted to policy discussions and research. Just as, on the side of economic cooperation, APEC sponsors study centers in each member economy, on the security side ASEAN-Institute for Strategic and International Studies (ASEAN-ISIS) embraces institutes of strategic and international studies in several countries. In recent years quite a number of policy institutes and think tanks have emerged around Asia Pacific; all seek to feed into the regional policy dialogue. The Council for Security Cooperation in the Asia Pacific (CSCAP) was established in 1993 by ten ASEAN-ISIS institutions to facilitate regional security dialogue in ARF. It brings together military and civilian officials and academics for informal policy discussions; participants attend in their private capacities.[49] Similarly, Northeast Asia Cooperation Dialogue was inaugurated in 1994 by the Institute on Global Conflict and Cooperation at the University of California, San Diego, for private study of a wide range of security problems by scholars, government, and military officials from Northeast Asia and the United States. As discussed below, workshops on the South China Sea dispute have become important Track II contributions to confidence building in that disputed region.

Track III activities consist of other NGOs that represent grassroots interests. Unlike Track II organizations, these NGOs have particular constituencies and political causes, such as environmental protection, arms control, and human rights. They may be national or transnational in organizational scope, and civil society or popular movement in purpose. Some participate in Track II activities, while others choose to influence Track II and Track I activities from the outside.

Examples of Track III organizations that have transnational programs are the Nautilus Institute, which as mentioned is active in alternative energy, environment, and nuclear weapons issues around East Asia; Asia Watch and Human Rights Watch; Amnesty International; and Japan's Sasakawa Peace Foundation, which mainly funds policy research and intellectual exchange.[50] On the national side, South Korean and Taiwan environmentalists, Japanese antinuclear and women's groups, Thai and Filipino civil society groups, and Chinese farmers' associations are examples of Track III activities.

## Form Over Structure

Three structural characteristics of Asian-way regional groups stand out. One is a "soft," least-common-denominator approach to security. Unlike Europe, where political affinities and mutual defense needs are the glue of security cooperation, Asian states find common ground in their commitment to rapid, outward-oriented economic development. In ASEAN—and borrowing from Japan—security is defined comprehensively, with emphasis on nonmilitary (especially economic) rather than military capabilities. The guiding concept is that each society's development and internal stability will contribute to the state's and the region's security, including the ability to resist external pressure or attack.[51] A cooperative approach to interdependence will, in this view, undergird security and, through consistent dialogue, provide a common language in managing intra-regional disputes.

A second characteristic, consistent with "weak multilateralism," is Asia's avoidance of strong organizations and institution building. Again in contrast with the European experience, cooperation in East Asia has been marked by decentralized leadership, informal structures and processes, and a preference for consultation over clear mandates.[52] ASEAN reflects functionalism without integration.[53]

The third characteristic of Asia's regional groups is their unbalanced memberships. Though inclusiveness is a shared norm of ASEAN and APEC, neither organization has fully attained it.[54] One reason may be the Cold War legacy of major power domination.[55] Another reason often mentioned by Asian officials is that regional groups should not become "mini UNs." A third is the simple fact that APEC, by bringing together economies rather than governments, has more flexibility than ASEAN. It allows APEC to give Taiwan and Hong Kong separate status alongside the PRC. And since Taiwan cannot officially take part in the ASEAN or ARF process, any attempt at a multilateral Asian response to the Taiwan Strait problem is automatically stymied.

Inclusiveness also has drawbacks. Bringing Vietnam, Burma, Laos, and Cambodia into ASEAN further complicates an already difficult process of consensus building. Moreover, ASEAN's origins and evolution make it far more suitable for dealing with conflicts in Southeast than in other parts of Asia. The emphasis on multilateral dialogue, CBMs, and codes of conduct has yet to be fully accepted in Northeast or South Asia, where the possibilities of armed conflict remain strong. Perhaps most importantly, ASEAN and ARF are not the same thing. Though they operate on the same underlying principles of consensus and trust building, they have different memberships and security purposes. The question of "ASEAN-ization" of ARF is divisive: Should ASEAN be the natural leader of ARF, as it assumed it would be, or must it share leadership (and therefore security agenda and action orientation) with Australia, China, Canada, the United States, and other nonmembers?[56] The China factor looms large here, inasmuch as the ASEAN members of ARF must tread a difficult path between placating China and responding to the Western membership, which prefers that ARF move quickly ahead and take on conflict resolution functions.[57]

Regarding security, ASEAN as a group has increasingly come to embrace domestic stability as an important matter along with economic growth. That means "corruption, collusion, and nepotism" (KKN, as the Indonesians say); human-security issues such as labor, poverty, and environmental protection; finance; and democratization. ARF's security menu is more traditional—territorial disputes, internal wars, external penetration. Preventative diplomacy, its ministers agreed in July 2001, will receive increased attention, but only in disputes *between* states. The actual commitment to dealing with either of these security agendas is weakened by several factors. The obvious one is that ASEAN's members have different levels of interest in and support of both ASEAN and ARF. Thailand and the Philippines are perhaps the leading activists in both groups, whereas Indonesia and the Indochinese states (Laos, Cambodia, Vietnam) are among the most conservative.

The extent of enthusiasm for ASEAN and ARF often correlates with a country's domestic politics—the more stable and democratic a country, the stronger is its support for ASEAN and ARF. The role of NGOs enters the picture here: In those ASEAN countries where the strong state tradition still flourishes, NGOs are viewed as sources of inter-state friction that weaken ASEAN solidarity. In the late 1990s, for instance, Indonesian students' protests of human rights in Rangoon, Singapore, press criticism of Mahathir's governance, and calls by Indonesian environmental groups for Singapore, Malaysia, and Brunei to sue Indonesia before the International Court of Justice for allowing forest fires to burn unchecked all drew the wrath of their governments.

Finally, there are important differences between ASEAN and APEC. As one prominent Indonesian scholar has written, "ASEAN has been cautious about APEC from the beginning." The concern stems from "vast disparities in income, technology, and skill level among the APEC economies [that] could lead to asymmetrical dependence, heightened tension, and North-South polarization within APEC."[58] In a word, ASEAN worries that APEC will be pushed too quickly by the United States and Japan in the direction of institutionalizing itself, thus forcing less developed economies to accept rules and timetables that make them vulnerable. "Processes are more important than structures," ASEAN advocates insist.[59] Left unstated is a related political issue: The more APEC institutionalizes, the less effective ASEAN's efforts might be at bridging disputes among its members. Should APEC become a more tightly integrated, action-oriented group, lest the gaps between richer and poorer, less democratic and more democratic members become potentially divisive.

## Views of the Major Powers

The task of actually building a workable mechanism for multilateral security in Asia Pacific is formidable for reasons that go beyond the conflict-ridden histories of intra-Asian relationships. The three major states whose cooperation is essential to multilateral endeavors—the United States, Japan, and China—are of very different persuasions about it. The persistent U.S. preference for bilateralism is not limited to regional security matters. Other examples may be found in Washington's separate, often muscular handling of trade disputes with Japan, South Korea, China, and Taiwan; its insistence on a single standard of human rights, which it has applied (or not applied) depending on the character of relations with particular governments; its economic diplomacy in Asia on behalf of U.S.-based multinational corporations; and its inconsistent policies on nuclear proliferation (compare, for example, Washington's hard line with China and Iran, and its softer lines with North Korea and Japan).

Despite the end of the Cold War, little has changed since Secretary of State James Baker's seminal article that defined U.S.–Asia policy in terms of spokes in a wheel, with bilateral security treaties with the United States being the main spoke and multilateral arrangements and a regional military presence being secondary spokes.[60] Clinton's approach was somewhat more amenable than Baker's to regional multilateral dialogue, via APEC on economic matters and ASEAN-PMC and ARF on security matters. But these groups were never regarded as substitutes for U.S. treaties, forward deployments of forces, and unilateral action when necessary—most clearly in 1996, when two U.S. carrier battle groups moved close to Taiwan in response to PRC missile tests. As Joseph Nye, Clinton's assistant secretary of defense for international security affairs and a point man on Asia policy, said when the Defense Department announced a floor of 100,000 troops in East Asia: "While we are indeed stressing the increased importance of multilateral institutions, it's not at the cost of our primary attention to reinforcing the traditional security alliances we have in the region." [61]

China's support of multilateral initiatives is largely confined to economic matters, where its own development can be assisted. Thus, APEC's consultative approach and action on a voluntary basis have Beijing's full support, as does the expansion of ASEAN's ties with Northeast Asia under "ASEAN+3."[62] Chinese analysts argue that it is premature to organize more ambitious partnerships given the disparate interests and economic levels of the participants. Beijing policy makers are evidently fearful lest China become just another "goose" in Japan's formation—a resource that feeds Japanese industries without gaining technological compensation. Hence, to cite a specific example, in Northeast Asia China has called for a building block approach that includes lesser forms of cooperation, such as a Yellow Sea economic zone and increased bilateral trade.[63]

When it comes to regional security, Beijing endorses ASEAN's founding principles, but not all its modalities. Noninterference, equality, mutual benefit, and peaceful coexistence have been staples of PRC foreign policy since the 1950s, when Chinese diplomacy sought Third World support for its anti-imperialist rhetoric. But even as China becomes increasingly comfortable with multilateral fora such as ARF for dialogue, exchanges of view, and other elements of cooperative security,[64] its own tradition of bilateralism (which doubtless has strong support in the military) makes Beijing draw the line at CBMs and preventive diplomacy that might intrude into its "internal affairs," such as Taiwan. China likewise has resisted more deeply institutionalizing the ASEAN way. Here, China has some of the same misgivings as the ASEAN states themselves, such as that a NATO-like organization would become an instrument of compulsion and intervention, as happened in the Kosovo conflict.[65] Thus, when it comes to Taiwan, Tibet, and the Spratly Islands, no Chinese government is going to yield its sovereign prerogative and the right to act unilaterally. Since the ASEAN states, too, worry about foreign interference in their domestic affairs—for example, Indonesia, ever since the UN-sponsored, Australian-led peacekeeping mission to ensure East Timor's independence—there is a mutuality of interests with Beijing. Officially, ASEAN supports Beijing's view that Taiwan is a Chinese matter; and, like China, most ASEAN governments probably suspect that a formal multilateral security body would become a vehicle for imposing U.S. standards, such as on human rights.

The PRC's position on multilateral security frameworks is evolving, however, as the ARF "Workshops" on the SCS show (see below). In tandem with its deepening involvement in regional and global economic arrangements (the WTO, ADB, World Bank, and IMF), Chinese leaders have become increasingly accepting of arms control regimes and regional CBMs. This trend, discussed in chapter 4, appears to be the consequence of an emerging internationalism in Chinese security thinking that shows how PRC national interests can be advanced through multilateral involvement.

Japan's interest in Pacific-wide economic cooperation goes back to the 1960s, whereas its entry in discussions of cooperative security date from the late 1980s. In the former case, Japan's large trade, investment, and ODA commitments in East Asia, and its reliance on the region for natural resources, dictate its support of regional economic cooperation. With Australia, it took a leadership role in creating APEC and bringing a reluctant United States into it.[66] The interest in security dialogue was prompted by the end of the Cold War and the need to rethink the role of the U.S.–Japan Security Treaty, concern about a U.S. withdrawal from Asia, and a desire (expressed in the Miyazawa Doctrine of the new prime minister, Miyazawa Kiichi, in 1992) to form a "global partnership" with Washington on behalf of international security. In 1991 Japan's foreign minister, Nakayama Taro, had proposed using ASEAN-PMC to promote "a sense of mutual reassurance." The Miyazawa Doctrine proclaimed that Japan would adopt a "two-track approach" to Asia Pacific security. On the first track, Japan would contribute to the settlement of regional disputes. The fighting in Cambodia prompted Miyazawa to push the Peacekeeping Operations bill through the Diet so that Japan, for the first time in post-war history, could dispatch noncombat personnel in support of UN missions. On the second track, Japan would promote regional political dialogue (in what later became the ARF).[67]

The notion that promoting dialogue and transparency in defense policies can build trust among regional adversaries, without requiring the formation of a military alliance or Asian equivalent of CSCE, is widely held among Japanese policy makers. Though hardly amounting to a revolutionary change in foreign policy, the idea at its inception did reflect a new Japanese interest in Asian regionalism— "re-Asianization," in a word[68]—and a desire to expand outward from the traditional low posture in international affairs. But Japan would have to do so in a way that would calm fears of Japanese remilitarization and redefine the U.S.–Japan relationship so as to create a place for multilateral initiatives. In large part re-Asianization was linked to Japan's economic stake in East Asia: using the "trinity" of trade, aid, and investment to promote Japan's resource and manufacturing needs in East Asia. But that has not been a straightforward task for a Japan, which has always had an identity problem with its fellow Asians. It has always been burdened not only by its previous efforts to impose a "new order" in Asia, but also by its self-interested uses of ODA and FDI to promote its trading firms its relatively protected home market, and the tendency of Japanese in official positions to make offhand remarks that justify past colonial practices and even suggest racial superiority to other Asians. Whatever the explanation of where this identity problem originated—in the political culture, in Japan's insularity, or in the U.S. occupation period—it has been antithetical to multilateral cooperation.

As a consequence, regional groups—mainly APEC and ASEAN, but also the ADB, to which Japan, along with the United States, is the largest lender[69]— serve a useful purpose for a Japan that does not want to lead but wants to be liked.[70] They "provide a convenient framework for Japan to take a leadership role in regional affairs without causing undue concern on the part of other Asian countries."[71] And, of course, APEC and ASEAN (that is, ASEAN-PMC and ARF) help promote a sense of Asian community that is hospitable to Japanese capital and products. In keeping with the Miyazawa Doctrine, moreover, APEC in particular is a way for Japan to ease into a co-leadership role with the United States. Co-leadership has never occurred, of course, because Japan's economy slowed dramatically by the late 1990s and the political system failed to reform. Nevertheless, those Japanese commentators who believed that Asian regional arrangements, especially on the economic side, would help integrate China in the new post–Cold War Asia order and keep the Americans engaged were correct. Both those trends serve Japan's interest in preventing China-Japan rivalry from overheating.

The growing European involvement in Asia Pacific cooperation should also be noted.[72] ASEM provides a regular forum for senior-level economic policy discussions. In terms of security issues, Britain's withdrawal from Hong Kong in

1997 eliminated the last European troops from East Asia. But the EU is a member of ASEAN-PMC and ARF, European arms accounted for about one-third of ASEAN arms imports during the buildup period, Britain is a key player in the FPDA, and French and other European soldiers have been involved in peacekeeping in Cambodia and East Timor. Now that the EU has created a rapid reaction force, it is interested in deeper security dialogue with Asian countries, perhaps through ASEM.[73] Europeans see such dialogue as a necessary extension of economic interdependence, due to the fallout from Asian labor migration, the drug trade, and the global effects of the financial crisis.

American, Chinese, and Japanese policies on Asian multilateralism are influenced by a common heritage of bilateralism and a cautiousness about participation. An example of this caution, and what it means for regional security cooperation, emerged at the November 1993 APEC summit meeting in Seattle. The U.S. delegate, Winston Lord, proposed striving for an Asia Pacific community with "a shared sense of destiny, a shared vision and a shared family sense." He contrasted this modest hope with "a big integrated community with a 'capital C.'" China went further: It reportedly objected to translating "community" as "organization" in the final communiqué. APEC, said China's President Jiang Zemin, "should be an open, flexible, fairly loose forum for economic cooperation."[74] Prime Minister Hosokawa Morihiro of Japan flatly ruled out formation of a NATO-like security grouping, proposing instead to rely on "political and security dialogue among countries in the region to further increase a sense of reassurance."[75] Malaysia's Prime Minister Mahathir refused to attend out of fear the Americans were out to take over the organization and, perhaps, try to resurrect the Southeast Asia Treaty Organization (SEATO) that was founded in 1954 and disbanded in 1977.

## IS ASIA VULNERABLE?

Pessimism underlies most Western analyses of the Asia Pacific region's future security. One writer suggests that it stems from the fact that Asia, unlike Europe, did not undergo a system change with the end of the Cold War.[76] That is, it lacks the coherence necessary to do what the Europeans have done with respect to security cooperation: organize for collective defense. As a result, East Asian states are arming without arms control and allowing a "power vacuum" to form that can only be filled in one of two ways: either by an emerging great power such as China, or by a reliable great power like the United States.

In chapter 2 I disputed the pessimistic assumptions about an arms race in East Asia. Asia's presumed divisiveness is also exaggerated. The suggestion in this chapter is that the "Asian" or "ASEAN" consultative model, though not an antidote to every kind of regional dispute, and least of all to human security issues, fulfills important functions that compensate for its vulnerability.

## Reevaluating Asia's Cohesiveness

Asia Pacific's cultural, racial, religious, and other differences are often mentioned as obstacles to closer cooperation. This generalization may do a disservice to people's capacity to adapt to diversity. Such a capacity has long been apparent in Japan, South Korea, Malaysia, Singapore, and most of the rest of East Asia, where important elements of Western religion, culture, technology, and political thought have readily been absorbed.[77] It also fails to recognize that, at least in inter-state relations, common economic interests can have tension-reducing, bridge-building political effects, just as they have in Europe—for example, in the environmental arena, as previously discussed. In fact, ASEAN might take some pride in its ability to avoid war with one another. In terms of internal conflict, ethnic and religious tensions are plentiful and they have led to significant violence—for example, against Chinese in Indonesia (as recently as the spring of 1998) and Vietnam, by Chinese against Tibetans, in several outlying islands of Indonesia, and by Muslim groups in the Philippines and even Malaysia (in 2000). Such tensions may yet explode into large-scale civil wars that cross frontiers: Turkic and Muslim populations along China's borders with Kazakhstan and Turkistan are future candidates. But these are not present dangers, nor do they compare in violence and destructiveness with Russia's war in Chechnya or the NATO conflict with Yugoslavia over Kosovo. At the least, we may say that internal conflicts are no greater a security concern in East Asia than in Central Europe and Central Asia.

It remains to be seen whether or not Europe will actually be as economically and politically stable as is often claimed. Comparisons with Asia Pacific sometimes fail to consider the widespread disillusionment with change that has infected (for example) Germany over unification and foreign workers, France and Italy over political scandal, the European Union over unemployment, and the former Soviet bloc over democracy and privatization. In fact, the economic, environmental, and political gaps between western and eastern Europe remain formidable; several former Soviet republics have slid back into communist-style absolutism. If anything, Europe's troubles have sensitized Asians to approaching similar problems in different ways—as for example in South Korea's rejection of the German model of unification through absorption, and China's determination not to follow the Soviet/Russian example by putting political reform on the same fast track as economic reform.

Nationalism in Asia Pacific countries must again be emphasized as a source of cohesion as well as of mutual suspicion. For example, China's president, Jiang Zemin, has sought to make common ground with ASEAN on the basis of a "new international order" with Asian values, such as peaceful coexistence and opposition to U.S. "gunboat diplomacy" and "economic colonialism."[78] When the United States tried to influence ASEAN not to accept Burma's membership, on the grounds of its human rights record, the effort boomeranged—not only because of ASEAN's commitment to inclusiveness, but also because it offended a common nationalism centered on the noninterference principle.[79] ASEAN, said the Indonesian foreign minister, "has one cardinal rule, and that is not to interfere in the internal affairs of other countries." The West must realize that "this is our organization, not theirs."[80]

In December 1995 ASEAN announced the treaty that made Southeast Asia a nuclear weapon free zone (NWFZ).[81] Within the zone, which embraces the entire region, nuclear weapons testing, development, production, acquisition, transport, use, or deployment are prohibited, as is nuclear waste dumping. The treaty, which follows similar instruments that declared Latin America and Africa NWFZs, fulfills the promise of ZOPFAN to create such a zone. It gives ASEAN a certain moral force on the nuclear issue at a time when nuclear weapons testing has apparently ended but the acquisition and possession of nuclear weapons have not.

Nationalism is also behind concerns in East Asia about financial globalization's threat to erode economic sovereignty. The power of IMF structural adjustment loans and the inroads of foreign corporations have been sources of concern in economies as diverse as Malaysia, Japan, Indonesia, and South Korea. Malaysia's Prime Minister Mahathir has been the most outspoken on this subject. When, in 1990, he called for creation of an all-Asian "East Asian Economic Group" to be headed by Japan, China and some other regional governments supported the idea, and Japan showed interest. But the United States, fearing a victory for the Japanese model of "managed trade," came out strongly against the proposal, and Japan backed off.[82] The EAEG thus became "EAEC," a "caucus" within APEC, instead. Then, during the financial crisis, Japan proposed the establishment of an Asian Monetary Fund (AMF), with substantial Japanese financial backing. Again the United States objected, since the idea clearly would weaken the power of the "Washington consensus." Tokyo was forced to take AMF off the table, even though the idea had plenty of support around East Asia.[83] That did not keep Japan from coming up with a new plan for aiding troubled East Asian economies.[84] And a version of AMF, designed to make available foreign exchange reserves on a swap basis in the event of another financial crisis, did get launched in 2000 at ASEAN's initiative.[85] These responses to economic globalization are as much political as economic, for they have in common a quest for greater Asian self-reliance and fear of Western economic hegemony.[86]

## THE ASIAN WAY: STRENGTHS AND LIMITATIONS

From our discussion, a great gulf is apparent between most Asian and most Western notions about defining and effectively dealing with security in the Asia Pacific. Nearly all of the region's governments are anxious to promote economic cooperation and rely on consultative methods to manage political conflicts. Very few are willing to make defense commitments, embrace organized forms of strategic cooperation, or join arms control regimes wholeheartedly. Yet government and academic experts across East Asia are troubled by the emergence of unsatisfied, potentially irredentist regional powers and the lack of a clear U.S. security policy for Asia Pacific. Sensing trouble ahead, they are searching for a "third way" between U.S.-dominated bilateralism, which is passé, and EU-style multilateralism, which is far into the future.

Whether or not Southeast Asians have found a third way is a matter of some contention. Labeling and evaluating the "way" is difficult. One supporter calls it a "quasi-security community," but that may be stretching the point.[87] Another writer calls ASEAN an example of a modern-day "entente cordiale," whose chief purposes are to moderate disputes among themselves and find ways to fend off the great powers that surround them.[88] Still a third view, from the inside of the ASEAN process, believes it practices preventive diplomacy "through the promotion of cooperative security and by means of informal diplomacy."[89] Some analysts (especially those from the ASEAN states) tend to credit ASEAN with great success at building sub-regional unity and a preventive approach to security. Critics (usually Western) insist that ASEAN's informality has made it largely an exercise in symbolism and fuzzy declarations that has accomplished little in preventing or settling disputes or promoting arms control.

Western and Asian approaches share at least one fundamental bedrock ingredient: mistrust. In the Western case, however, mistrust is embedded in Realism's view of the world as comprised of self-interested, aggrandizing states; whereas in the East, mistrust is a product of history and clashes of cultures ("nations") that, with patience and emphasis on economic self-interest and dialogue, can be overcome. Hence, the West seeks to lock adversaries into detailed agreements, which become substitutes for mere promises of good behavior. Asians, while also leery of promises, tend to rely on informal contact over a long time, during which the "habit of dialogue" is cultivated. Hard bargaining over specific security concerns may eventually occur; but it should be preceded by growing trust, which is most likely to occur in areas such as trade. Moreover, the multitude of other bilateral and multilateral arrangements, such as on the environment, can be seen as undergirding ASEAN's "soft" security-building approach by extending the web of regional cooperative activities.

Predictably, critics attack ASEAN's limited *military* usefulness. ARF, they maintain, not only is unfit as a model for other parts of East Asia, but also as a response to post–Cold War security problems in Southeast Asia such as arms buildups and China's claims in the Spratlys.[90] Examining ASEAN's involvement in Vietnam's invasion of Cambodia in 1978 and in the eventual settlement of the war, which was the organization's most important venture into security issues, provides contrasting answers to questions of its utility in conflict management.[91] The ASEAN states became involved to protect the security of some of them and in order to reaffirm their common commitment to principles of nonintervention and noninterference. They effectively employed a mix of diplomatic moves that contributed to Vietnam's eventual withdrawal under the 1991 UN-sponsored settlement. As an outside actor, however, ASEAN's effectiveness was ultimately linked to that of other parties—major governments, international organizations, and individuals—and to changing local and global circumstances. Certain conditions of conflict, such as the exhaustion of the combatants, and favorable international circumstances must prevail for an organization committed to dialogue to work well. By itself, ASEAN could not prevent, contain, or terminate Vietnam's intervention.

ASEAN's inability to respond to the crisis in East Timor showed the limits of its capacity even more than did Cambodia. "Inaction and inertia were reinforced by the weakness of pre-existing mechanisms for policy coordination and joint action," two critics have argued.[92] Both before and after East Timor overwhelmingly voted in favor of independence from Indonesia in August 1999, ASEAN looked on as pro-integration militias, with Indonesian army support, carried out killings and the forced flight of innocent civilians. "Noninterference" became a dodge for some member states that preferred not to offend Indonesia. (The initially mild U.S. reaction, informed by many years of military cooperation with the Indonesian army and concern for Jakarta's economic recovery, doubtless reinforced ASEAN's passivity.) In the end, Australia led the UN peacekeeping force that took over for the Indonesian army in East Timor, while several ASEAN states remained on the sidelines and ARF did nothing. Only Thailand and the Philippines contributed troops, and there was considerable bickering within ASEAN that reflected old quarrels.[93] Protection of human rights under preventive diplomacy thus suffered a major blow.

## OPTIONS FOR THE ASIAN WAY

### Another Look at Confidence Building

The Asian/ASEAN approach is no assurance of effectiveness or comprehensiveness in dealing with the multitude of security matters on the regional agenda. As Alagappa observes, a regional group such as ASEAN seems to function best in combination with organizations (such as the UN) at other levels. The UN peacekeeping mission in East Timor supports that observation, in more ways than one: Neither ASEAN nor ARF has a military force of its own or a shared security doctrine that would enable either one to dispatch a peacekeeping mission. Precisely for that reason, cynics argue that the ASEAN model is a formula for futility at best and, at worst, for evasion—avoiding difficult situations altogether, choosing rhetoric and face-saving gestures over strong (i.e., military) countermeasures that it lacks, and responding to "actions at less than a level that would trigger an international response or that would disrupt interdependent ties."[94]

These criticisms do point to a major flaw in ARF, but they may not be fair, and the flaw itself need not be fatal to ARF's future. After all, ARF has only been in existence since 1994; it is a forum, not an alliance; it can only act on the basis of consensus among an extraordinary array of parties; and certain issues of vital interest to one or more members are simply unapproachable by ARF (though admittedly, East Timor was not one of them, the Indonesian government urged ASEAN to get involved). Thus, ARF makes no pretense of being a conflict resolution mechanism, as we have been saying. Beyond that, there is much to be said for dialogue in and of itself. Exchanges of view in informal settings can be a crucial first step to conflict prevention or resolution, particularly when the conflict is between suspicious parties, between parties that do not regularly meet, or on vexing issues that seem to have no way out.

Moreover, ARF can point to some modest achievements.[95] It has created a multitrack, mutually reinforcing process that brings a variety of governmental and nongovernmental players together, thus promoting the "habit of dialogue." The "habit" has extended to military officials, whose meetings under the ARF umbrella constitute a first in regional interactions. It has helped turn China's attitude around from skeptic to involved partner in the ASEAN/ARF process. And in a region that had been almost totally lacking in multilateral security organizations, ARF pioneered a new approach.

## Revisiting the South China Sea Dispute

As the SCS disputes show, ARF has been something more than a "talking shop." The Workshops on Managing Potential Conflicts in the South China Sea, which began under Indonesian initiative in 1990, have achieved concrete results.[96] Their informality—as a Track II activity, participation occurs in a private capacity—allows Taiwan officials to attend along with PRC delegates. As a result of the second workshop, all the parties to the dispute issued a formal ASEAN Declaration on the South China Sea in July 1992 that committed them to resolve matters peacefully, not to use force, and to exercise restraint. Subsequent workshops became more substantive, and technical matters such as marine environment and navigational safety in the disputed waters were worked out. China's participation deepened, yielding agreements with Vietnam and the Philippines on codes of conduct. China gave ground on several positions, such as by agreeing to multilateral negotiation with ASEAN of conflicting claims, acknowledging freedom of navigation through the SCS waters it claims, and recognizing the UN Convention on the Law of the Sea (UNCLOS) as the basis for resolving claims. As the workshops process became more complex, it was opened to outside specialists and organizations, including NGOs; and the process thus tended to overlap with other ASEAN and ARF activities concerned with the SCS. At an ASEAN ministerial meeting in July 2000 in Bangkok, China agreed to join work on developing a code of conduct with ASEAN as a whole.

These developments show that, on the positive side, ARF has at least accomplished two things in the SCS dispute. First, its process has reduced tensions, helped restrain the use of force, and possibly cleared a path to a new, comprehensive understanding among the parties. Second, ARF has engaged China in dialogue. Given that China has a fulsome history of using force in conflicts with its neighbors, keeping China at the table and willing to discuss ways to avert a military solution is no small achievement. Third, the dialogue process may encourage confidence building at the bilateral level. The China-Vietnam accord of December 25, 2000, to resolve the long-standing boundary disputes in the Gulf of Tonkin may be an example. The accord, which follows on a border agreement between the two countries in 1999, as well as prospects of expanding trade, covers territorial waters and exclusive economic zones, but not the Spratlys or the Paracels.[97] In time, those remaining problems may be resolved.

Nevertheless, a process-oriented approach to regional security is bound to have drawbacks. Workshops are not negotiations, and bargaining on disputed sovereignty has not occurred. ASEAN and its offshoot groupings cannot adjudicate problems such as mutual suspicions and disagreements about tactics, it can only "dialogue" about them when the parties are willing. The SCS Workshops are a good example of the limitations these create.[98] The different domestic capacities of the participants, in terms of expertise as well as commitment to see the process through, have posed a substantial obstacle to a settlement. Furthermore, though confidence building has been promoted, it has yet to lead to agreements on military CBMs that would implement the pledges of the 1992 Declaration. For example, military contacts between commanders responsible for the SCS area, and/or mutual force reductions in disputed areas, have yet to be accepted. The best China has done so far is to publish military white papers as a means of accommodating ASEAN's desire for greater transparency. But these documents, though a welcome departure from past secrecy, shed little light on PRC intentions with respect to security policy or weapons deployments.

Agreement on implementing the Law of the Sea convention so as to deal with overlapping EEZs has yet to occur. Nor has the Chinese proposal for joint development been seriously explored. All that has happened so far is a pledge by the parties, in keeping with the UNCLOS, "to submit to adjudication if negotiations between the parties concerned do not bring a solution within a reasonable time or if the disputes persist to the degree that they endanger peace and stability in the South China Sea region."[99]

These are important shortcomings; but given the number of parties and the long-standing suspicions that divide them, it hardly seems fair to judge that the ASEAN way has failed in the SCS. "Western" security models have also proven weak at overcoming similarly complex problems. No process guarantees the implementation of agreements; and the absence of an interactive, trust-building component in a political settlement effort may ultimately cause any agreement to unravel. Ultimately, the greatest obstacle to a settlement is "the obsession with sovereignty" and the politically driven reluctance of parties to back away from the status quo and toward cooperation.[100]

## The Human Security Dimension

The Asian financial crisis shook ASEAN at its roots. A great deal of soul searching occurred afterwards, deepened by violence in Indonesia, the world's fourth-largest country in population and a potential candidate for widespread fragmentation. Two kinds of criticisms emerged from within ASEAN: one that argued the need for a new political maturity, the other that insisted the organization must address people victimized by rapid, unregulated economic growth.

On the first count, a distinguished Indonesian scholar, Jusuf Wanandi, has led the way. His argument is straightforward—to survive, ASEAN must come of age and "be turned into a Southeast Asian Community." Finding inspiration rather than difference in the EU's evolution, Wanandi stated:

> ASEAN's integration should be rules-based and supported by better institutionalized regional cooperation. . . . To become a community, ASEAN needs more norms and institutions. It will not be as elaborate as those of the EU, but it surely must involve more than a state-to-state based institution.

To cope with the specific challenges of globalization that East Asia failed to meet in 1997, Wanandi said, ASEAN will have to breach the walls of sovereignty. That is, people's identity will need to become regional as well as national; and NGOs and, as in Europe, civil society groups will have to be brought fully into the process of creating a sense of community.

What Wanandi was proposing represented new thinking in at least two fundamental respects. First, he was calling for a major change in the way ASEAN (and, one might add, APEC too) functions, so that NGOs of various kinds are regarded as having important roles in community building rather than being viewed as threats to the state. Second, he was questioning a narrow understanding of ASEAN's noninterference principle, saying that the financial crisis had shown how the principle had done the region a disservice. "[T]he strategy of development in the crisis countries needs to be changed," he argued; "domestic instabilities should also be a concern of other members, because they could have regional spillovers."[101]

Wanandi's observations have been echoed elsewhere in East Asia. Thai officials have been emphatic in calling upon regional governments to address the negative human consequences of globalization. As the foreign minister said, economic success "rested on fragile foundations":

> We gave inadequate attention to the preservation of our environment. We embraced free markets and globalization with open arms but with minimal supervision and discipline. In our rush to catch up, we became fixated on growth rates and on the façade of progress and prosperity. And in the end we became victims of our own success. In my opinion, the origin of the current financial and economic crisis is deeply rooted in our sociopolitical structures. It is indeed a systemic problem. For we have equated order, stability, and continuity with growth. And we assumed that the prosperity achieved as a consequence of that system was to be sustained. In the end, it has proven to be an illusion and a fragile bubble of growth.[102]

The minister went on to remind listeners that human resources are "our most precious asset," and that all governments must face up to the challenge of providing for "human security, the desire for equality and social justice."

Nevertheless, though human security is now on ASEAN's agenda, the call for justice is rather tepid and can only be backed by such resources as the individual members provide.[103] The same can be said of major common environmental hazards such as the intense pollution (officially, "haze") from Indonesia's annual summertime palm oil plantation fires.[104] Serious human rights violations that systematically occur in half the ASEAN countries cannot be papered over either, especially as ASEAN membership is supposed to lead to improved conditions in Burma,[105] Cambodia, and other authoritarian countries. So long as important internal problems such as these receive only lip service, ASEAN's reputation will suffer and, as in East Timor, the credibility of its commitment to conflict prevention will be questioned.

## NOTES

1. I am indebted for this observation to Joseph M. Grieco, "Political-Military Dynamics and the Nesting of Regimes: An Analysis of APEC, the WTO, and Prospects for Cooperation in the Asia-Pacific," in *Asia-Pacific Crossroads: Regime Creation and the Future of APEC*, ed. Vinod K. Aggarwal and Charles E. Morrison (New York: St. Martin's Press, 1998), 246–51.

2. See Andrew Mack and Pauline Kerr, "The Evolving Security Discourse in the Asia-Pacific," *The Washington Quarterly*, vol. 18, no. 1 (Winter 1995), 131, 135.

3. The ASEAN view is to engage China "to tame the tiger" (as a Thai defense scholar put it), not alienate it by publicly characterizing its intentions as aggressive. A senior Malaysian official said it would be "crazy and self-destructive" to form a bloc against China; much better would be to "achieve progress" with it. See *Defense News*, October 24–30, 1994, 10.

4. See the article by a foreign ministry official of Brunei, Pengiran Osman Bin Pengiran Haji Patra, "The Future Course of the ASEAN Regional Forum: Openness and the Regional Approach to Disarmament," *Disarmament*, vol. 18, no. 2 (1995): 145–57.

5. Sheldon W. Simon, "Regional Security Structures in Asia: The Question of Relevance," in *East Asian Security in the Post–Cold War Era*, ed. Simon (Armonk, N.Y.: M.E. Sharpe, 1993), 14. During the Cold War, bilateralism was also pursued by China and the USSR against "U.S. imperialism," but (except in the case of North Korea) without the overarching structure of mutual defense treaties and basing arrangements.

6. As Tsuneo Akaha has written, U.S.-sponsored bilateralism "obviated development of any regionwide forum for political dialogue. Virtually every international scheme that was attempted in the region during those [Cold War] years . . . either presumed adversarial relations among the Asian countries or [as with the Southeast Asia Treaty Organization] was designed to promote cooperation among some Asian countries to the exclusion of others." Akaha, "Japan's Security Policy in the Posthegemonic World: Opportunities and Challenges," in *Japan in the Posthegemonic World*, ed. Akaha and Frank Langdon (Boulder, Colo.: Lynne Rienner, 1993), 97.

7. Andrew Mack, "Naval Arms Control and Confidence Building for Northeast Asian Waters," *The Korean Journal of Defense Analysis*, vol. 4, no. 2 (Winter 1993): 135–37.

8. Pengiran Osman Bin Pengiran Haji Patra, "Future Course," 147.

9. Wayne Arnold, "Asian Group Declines to Release Study on Foreign Investment," *New York Times*, August 24, 2000, online. Reportedly, FDI in ASEAN fell 22 percent in 1999 after having fallen 21 percent in 1998.

10. See Patrick M. Morgan, "Comparing European and East Asian Regional Security Systems" (paper prepared for the annual meeting of the International Studies Association, Acapulco, Mexico, March 1993), 14–15, and Miles Kahler, *Institution-Building in the Pacific*, Research Report 93-03 (San Diego, Calif.: Graduate School of International Relations and Pacific Studies, 1993) for stimulating discussion.

11. J. Soedjati Djiwandono, "The Role of ASEAN in the Asia-Pacific Region," in *Regional Cooperation in the Pacific Era*, ed. Dalchoong Kim and N. Sopiee (Seoul: Yonsei University, 1991), 391.

12. Djiwandono, "The Role of ASEAN," in *Regional Cooperation*, ed. Kim and Sopiee, 397–98.

13. See Desmond Ball, "The Most Promising CSBMs in the Asia/Pacific Region" (paper prepared for the conference on "The Asia-Pacific Region: Links Between Economic and Security Relations," Institute on Global Conflict and Cooperation, University of California, San Diego, May 13–15, 1993), 52–59.

14. For one such critique, see Donald C. Hellmann, "America, APEC, and the Road Not Taken: International Leadership in the Post–Cold War Interregnum in the Asia-Pacific," in *From APEC to Xanadu: Creating a Viable Community in the Post–Cold War Pacific*, ed. Donald C. Hellmann and Kenneth B. Pyle, (Armonk, N.Y.: M.E. Sharpe, 1997), 70–97.

15. Desmond Ball, "The Benefits of APEC for Security Cooperation in the Asia-Pacific Region," in *Power and Prosperity: Economics and Security Linkages in Asia-Pacific*, ed. Susan L. Shirk and Christopher P. Twomey (New Brunswick, N.J.: Transaction Publishers, 1996), 36–37.

16. Ali Alatas, "Basic Principles, Objectives and Modalities of APEC," in *Indonesian Perspectives on APEC and Regional Cooperation in Asia Pacific*, ed. Hadi Soestro (Jakarta: Centre for Strategic and International Studies, 1994), 25.

17. See, for example, Alexei V. Zagorsky, "Confidence-Building Measures: An Alternative for Asian-Pacific Security?" *The Pacific Review*, vol. 4, no. 4 (1991): 345–57; and Kwa Chong Guan, "Reflections on Prospects of Asia-Pacific Multilateralism," in *Multilateral Activities in South East Asia: Pacific Symposium*, ed. Michael W. Everett and Mary A. Sommerville (Washington, D.C.: National Defense University Press, 1995), 166–70.

18. See Michael Antolik, "The ASEAN Regional Forum: The Spirit of Constructive Engagement," *Contemporary Southeast Asia*, vol. 16, no. 2 (September 1994): 118–19.

19. See Lawrence T. Woods, *Asia Pacific Diplomacy: Nongovernmental Organizations and International Relations* (Vancouver: University of British Columbia Press, 1993).

20. Andrew Elek, "The Challenge of Asian-Pacific Economic Cooperation," *The Pacific Review*, vol. 4, no. 4 (1991): 324–25.

21. Chungsoo Kim, *Regional Economic Cooperation Bodies in the Asia-Pacific: Working Mechanism and Linkages*, Working Paper No. 90-01 (August 1990), Korea Institute for International Economic Policy, Seoul; and Lawrence T. Woods, "Non-governmental Organizations and Pacific Cooperation: Back to the Future," *Pacific Review*, vol. 4, no. 4 (1991): 312–21, provide useful histories and summaries of these organizations' activities.

22. See Mark J. Valencia, "The Northeast Asia Economic Forum: Achievements and Future Prospects," in *Politics and Economics in Northeast Asia: Nationalism and Regionalism in Contention*, ed. Tsuneo Akaha (New York: St. Martin's Press, 1999), 315–28.

23. Peter Drysdale and Andrew Elek, "APEC: Community-Building in East Asia and the Pacific," in *From APEC to Xanadu*, ed. Hellmann and Pyle, 39.

24. For a review of these issues, see Lyuba Zarsky and Jason Hunter, "Environmental Cooperation at APEC: The First Five Years," *The Journal of Environment & Development*, vol. 6, no. 3 (September 1997): 222–51.

25. Malcolm Chalmers, *Confidence-Building in South-East Asia* (Boulder, Colo.: Westview Press, for the University of Bradford, 1996), 28–29.

26. A good source for the background and evolution of ASEAN is Daljit Singh, "ASEAN and the Security of Southeast Asia," in *ASEAN in the New Asia: Issues and Trends*, ed. Chia Siow Yue and Marcello Pacini (Singapore: Institute of Southeast Asian Studies, 1997), 122–35.

27. Kwa, "Reflections," in *Multilateral Activites*, ed. Everett and Sommerville, 168–69.

28. This and other official ASEAN documents are available in full on the ASEAN web site, www.asean.or.id.

29. Chalmers, *Confidence-Building*, 22–24.

30. The "dialogue partners" are Australia, Canada, New Zealand, South Korea, the European Union, Japan, the United States, China, India, Russia, Mongolia, the UNDP, and UNESCO. Pakistan currently has the status of sectoral dialogue partner. Its efforts to join ARF have so far failed because of India's opposition.

31. Note article 10 of the TAC: "Each High Contracting Party shall not in any manner of form participate in any activity which shall constitute a threat to the political and economic stability, sovereignty, or territorial integrity of another High Contracting Party."

32. Singh, "ASEAN and the Security of Southeast Asia," in *ASEAN in the New Asian*, ed. Chia and Pacini, 123–25.

33. The AFTA implementing agreement of January 1, 1993, may largely have been a response to the formation of other regional trading blocs, against which the (then) ASEAN-6 needed protection. In 1994 AFTA's principal targets were to reduce tariff rates among the members to 0–5 percent within fifteen years, and to encourage foreign direct investment (FDI). (See Park Chin Keun, "The ASEAN Free Trade Area: Concepts, Problems and Prospects," in *AFTA After NAFTA*, Joint Korea-U.S. Academic Symposium, vol. 4 [1994], 127–42.) Subsequently, the members decided to accelerate the timetable and reduce tariffs to zero by 2003. But the addition of new members, and post-financial crisis concerns to protect some industries, forced a compromise so that now the target is elimination of all import duties among the ASEAN-6 by 2010 and among the other four least-developed countries (Burma, Vietnam, Laos, Cambodia) by 2015.

34. Trade statistics from the official ASEAN web site; see note 28.

35. Larry M. Wortzel, *The ASEAN Regional Forum: Asian Security without an American Umbrella* (Carlisle Barracks, Pa.: U.S. Army War College, 1996), 20–23.

36. Mack and Kerr, "The Evolving Security Discourse," 124–26; Wortzel, *The ASEAN Regional Forum*, 16.

37. An excellent review of the Cold War with specific reference to the issue of bargaining power is by William T. Tow, *Encountering the Dominant Player: U.S. Extended Deterrence Strategy in the Asia-Pacific* (New York: Columbia University Press, 1991), esp. 272–301.

38. Tow, *Encountering the Dominant Player*, 315.

39. At its second annual meeting in 1995, the ARF recognized that "the concept of security includes not only military aspects but also political, economic, social and other issues." Chairman's statement, quoted in Daljit Singh, "Evolution of the Security Dialogue

Process in the Asia-Pacific Region," in *Southeast Asian Perspectives on Security*, ed. Derek da Cunha (Singapore: Institute of Southeast Asian Studies, 2000): 39–40.

40. See the official statement, "The ASEAN Regional Forum: A Concept Paper," at the ASEAN website.

41. David B. H. Denoon and Evelyn Colbert, "Challenges for the Association of Southeast Asian Nations (ASEAN)," *Pacific Affairs*, vol. 71, no. 4 (Winter 1998–99): 506.

42. The quotations are from a Malaysian and an Australian foreign minister. See Amitav Acharya, "Making Multilateralism Work: ARF and Security in the Asia-Pacific," in *Multilateral Activities*, ed. Everett and Sommerville, 180.

43. This point is also made by J. Mohan Malik, "Burma's Role in Regional Security— Pawn or Pivot?" in *Burma: Prospects for a Democratic Future*, ed. Robert I. Rotberg (Washington, D.C.: Brookings Institution Press, 1998), 122.

44. See Singh, "Security Dialogue." Rizal Sukma, "ASEAN and the ASEAN Regional Forum: Should the 'Driver' Be Replaced?" unpublished paper, Center for Strategic and International Studies, Jakarta (July 1999); author interviews in Singapore and Jakarta, August 1999.

45. Singh, "ASEAN and the Security of Southeast Asia," in *Multilateral Activities*, ed. Everett and Sommerville, 128–31.

46. Acharya, "Making Multilateralism Work," in *Multilateral Activities*, ed. Everett and Sommerville, 182.

47. Denoon and Colbert, "Challenges," 506.

48. For overviews, see Chalmers, *Confidence-Building*, 152–59, and Jusuf Wanandi, "The Role of Intellectual Exchange," in *The Asian Crisis and Human Security: An Intellectual Dialogue on Building Asia's Tomorrow*, ed. (Tokyo: Japan Center for International Exchange, 1999), 104–14.

49. On CSCAP see Paul M. Evans, "The Council for Security Cooperation in Asia Pacific: Context and Prospects" (paper prepared for the Conference on Economic and Security Cooperation in the Asia Pacific, Canberra, Australia, July 27–29, 1993).

50. On Sasakawa and other Japanese NGO activities, see Takashi Shirasu and Lau Sim-Yee, "Nongovernmental Initiatives in Japan for Regional Cooperation," in *Politics and Economics*, ed. Akaha, 329–45.

51. Simon, "Regional Security Structures," in *East Asian Security*, ed. Simon, 21; Mack and Kerr, "Evolving Security Discourse," 123–40.

52. These are among the characteristics of Asia's "strategic culture," as Desmond Ball calls it. It also includes "longer time horizons and policy perspectives" than in the West, different approaches to war, and informality in structures and processes of decision making. ("The Most Promising CSBMs," 6–7.) See also Kahler, *Institution-Building in the Pacific*.

53. Renato Cruz De Castro, "The Association of Southeast Asian Nations as an *Entente Cordiale*," *Asian Perspective*, vol. 24, no. 2 (2000), 59–85.

54. PBEC's membership, for instance, is heavily weighted in favor of the advanced Pacific Rim economies. In APEC, Hong Kong and Taiwan are members; but they do not belong to the ASEAN-PMC. North Korea is not included in either APEC or the ASEAN-PMC. The ARF does not include India, Hong Kong, or Taiwan. North Korea was not invited to join until 2000, following the North-South Korean summit.

55. Ball, "The Most Promising CSBMs," 7–9.

56. I am indebted to Sukma, "ASEAN and the ASEAN Regional Forum"; see also Acharya, "Making Multilateralism Work," in *Multilateral Activities*, ed. Everett and Sommerville, 186.

57. Singh, "Evolution of the Security Dialogue Process," 48.

58. Soesastro, "APEC," 177.

59. Soesastro, "APEC," 179.

60. James A. Baker III, "America in Asia," *Foreign Affairs*, vol. 70, no. 5 (Winter 1991–92): 1–18.

61. *Washington Post*, February 28, 1995.

62. See, for example, Zhang Yunling, "China and APEC: Interests, Opportunities, and Challenges," in *From APEC to Xanadu*, ed. Hellmann and Pyle, 195–202.

63. Pu Chenghao, "The Future of Strategy and Cooperation in the Regional Economic Development of Northeast Asia," *Shehui kexue jikan* (The Social Sciences), no. 6 (1993): 67–71.

64. See, for example, A. Ying, "New Security Mechanism Needed for Asian-Pacific Region," *Beijing Review*, no. 33 (August 18–24, 1997): 6–7. More recently, PRC leaders have referred to the dialogue and consultation process with ASEAN as a "new security concept" that contrasts with the Americans' approach based on "hegemonism." See Carlyle A. Thayer, "China's 'New Security Concept' and ASEAN," *Pacific Forum*, online at www.csis.org/pacfor/cc/003Qchina_asean.html.

65. See, for example, Guo Zhenyuan, "Prospects for Security Cooperation in the Asia-Pacific Region," *Beijing Review*, no. 28 (July 11–17, 1994): 20–22.

66. Yoichi Funabashi, *Asia-Pacific Fusion: Japan's Role in APEC* (Washington, D.C.: Institute for International Economics, 1995), 55–66.

67. See Yoshihide Soeya, "Japan's Multilateral Diplomacy in the Asia-Pacific and Its Implications for the Korean Peninsula," *Asian Perspective*, vol. 19, no. 2 (Fall–Winter 1995): 223–41.

68. See Kenneth B. Pyle, "Japan and the Future of Collective Security," in *Japan's Emerging Global Role*, ed. Danny Unger and Paul Blackburn (Boulder, Colo.: Lynne Rienner, 1993), 107–8.

69. The ADB, which has fifty-seven member-countries, loaned $9.4 billion in 1997 at the height of the financial crisis and $5.9 billion in 1998. Japan took the lead in financing loans to the poorest Asian countries. *Asian Wall Street Journal*, May 1, 1999, online ed.

70. On these characteristics, see Masaru Tamamoto, "The Japan that Wants to be Liked: Society and International Participation," in *Japan's Emerging Global Role*, ed. Unger and Blackburn, 37–54.

71. Akio Watanabe and Tsutomu Kikuchi, "Japan's Perspective on APEC: Community or Association?" in *From APEC to Xanadu*, ed. Hellmann and Pyle, 141. The authors were referring only to APEC, but their view seems equally applicable to ASEAN and ARF.

72. This paragraph relies mainly on Charles E. Morrison, Akira Kojima, and Hanns W. Maull, *Community-Building with Pacific Asia: A Report to the Trilateral Commission* (New York: Trilateral Commission, 1997), chapter 7.

73. Shada Islam, "Cross Purposes," *Far Eastern Economic Review* (July 20, 2000): 24.

74. *International Trade Reporter* (Bureau of National Affairs), November 24, 1993, 1978–79.

75. *Far Eastern Economic Review* (December 2, 1993): 14.

76. See Morgan, "Comparing European and East Asian Regional Security Systems," 7–8.

77. Frank B. Gibney, "Creating a Pacific Community: A Time to Bolster Economic Institutions," *Foreign Affairs*, vol. 72, no. 5 (November–December 1993): 20–25.

78. Associated Press, Bangkok, report of September 4, 1999; NAPSNet, same date.

79. Michael Vatikiotis, "Friends and Fears," *Far Eastern Economic Review* (May 8, 1997): 14–15.

80. Seth Mydans, "Burma Gains Observer Status in Asean," *New York Times*, July 22, 1996, online ed.

81. Text of the treaty may be found at the ASEAN web site.

82. Joseph M. Grieco, "Political-Military Dynamics," in *Asia-Pacific Crossroads: Regime Creation and the Future of APEC*, ed. Vinod K. Aggarwal and Charles E. Morrison (New York: St. Martin's Press, 1998), 245–46.

83. South Korea's Prime Minister Kim Jong-pil said of it (and of the parallel concept of an East Asian economic community): "It is necessary for us to have a mindset that problems that take place in Asia should be resolved by the hands of Asians." *Korea Herald* (Seoul), September 3, 1999; NAPSNet, same date. Kim was addressing a Japanese audience.

84. The plan is named after then-Finance Minister Miyazawa Kiichi. As of mid-1999, Japan had pledged $79 billion in loans and aid to Southeast Asia, including $30 billion under the Miyazawa Plan. A "New Miyazawa Plan" subsequently pledged an additional $30 billion.

85. The project is called the Chiang Mai Initiative after the Thai city in which it was discussed. See "The Joint Ministerial Statement of the ASEAN + 3 Finance Ministers Meeting, 6 May 2000, Chiang Mai, Thailand," at the ASEAN website; and for commentary, see G. Pierre Goad, "Asian Monetary Fund Reborn," *Far Eastern Economic Review* (May 18, 2000): 54.

86. For example, ASEAN's finance ministers echoed the criticisms of Malaysia and a number of academic experts when they (very politely) called for greater transparency in IMF and World Bank loans, in credit ratings of Asian economies, and in short-term capital flows—all of which exacerbated the financial crisis in 1997. See "Joint Ministerial Statement of the Third ASEAN Finance Ministers Meeting, 20 March 1999, Hanoi, Vietnam," at the ASEAN website.

87. Noordin Sopiee, "ASEAN and Regional Security," in *Regional Security in the Third World*, ed. Mohammed Ayoob, 229.

88. De Castro, "The Association of Southeast Asian Nations."

89. Hasjim Djalal and Ian Townsend-Gault, "Managing Potential Conflicts in the South China Sea," in *Herding Cats: Multiparty Mediation in a Complex World*, ed. Chester Crocker et al. (Washington, D.C.: U.S. Institute of Peace, 1999), 109.

90. "Debating Asian Security: Michael Leifer Responds to Geoffrey Wiseman," *Pacific Review*, vol. 5, no. 2 (1992): 167–69; Buszynski, "ASEAN Security Dilemmas," 91–95.

91. I rely here mainly on Muthiah Alagappa, "Regionalism and the Quest for Security: ASEAN and the Cambodian Conflict," *Journal of International Affairs*, vol. 46, no. 2 (Winter 1993): 439–67.

92. Wade Huntley and Peter Hayes, "East Timor and Asian Security," NAPSNet Special Report, February 23, 2000, online via Nautilus.org.

93. Michael Vatikiotis and Ben Dolven, "Missing in Action," *Far Eastern Economic Review* (September 30, 1999): 14.

94. Buszynski, "ASEAN Security Dilemmas," 106.

95. Singh, "Security Dialogue," mentions several of these points as well.

96. See Djalal and Townsend-Gault, "Managing Potential Conflicts," in *Herding Cats*, ed. Crocker et al., 109–33; and Wanandi, "ASEAN's China Strategy," 117–28.

97. *New York Times*, December 26, 2000, A12.

98. Djalal and Townsend-Gault, "Managing Potential Conflicts," 120–23.

99. Djalal and Townsend-Gault, "Managing Potential Conflicts," 127.

100. Djalal and Townsend-Gault, "Managing Potential Conflicts," 129.

101. Jusuf Wanandi, "ASEAN's Challenges for Its Future," *Global Beat*, online at www.nyu.edu/globalbeat/asia/Wanandi012399.html.

102. Speech of Surin Pitsuwan, in *The Asian Crisis and Human Security*, 22.

103. See the "Joint Communique of the Thirty-Third ASEAN Ministerial Meeting, Bangkok, Thailand, 24–25 July 2000," ASEAN website.

104. The plantation fires occurred mainly in Riau province, Sumatra (southwest of Singapore) and in Indonesian Borneo (Kalimantan). Forest-clearing fires during two previous summers had cost an estimated $4 billion in lost tourist dollars, hindrances to shipping, and public health. (See *International Herald Tribune*, August 7–8, 1999.) The August 1999 fires provoked very public expressions of concern in Singapore, Malaysia, and Brunei; and ASEAN called for more study and surveillance. But all these were inadequate and futile efforts that, to some critics in ASEAN itself, showed the need for penalties instead of more dialogue. See the Reuters report in *Observer* (Jakarta), August 8, 1999.

105. Frustration in some of the ASEAN countries, notably Thailand, over Burma's resistance to political change did finally lead to the opening of a dialogue between the generals and Aung San Suu Kyi, the opposition leader, as 2001 began. A Malaysian serving as special UN representative facilitated the opening. See Beril Lintner, "A Ray of Hope," *Far Eastern Economic Review* (January 25, 2001): 22–23.

## Chapter Four

# China Rising: Threat or Opportunity?

### WHAT DOES CHINA WANT?

The extraordinary successes of China's post-1978 economic reforms have been a source of pride and self-confidence within the country. But China's rise has received mixed reviews elsewhere. PRC leaders see the reforms as a pathway to creating a strong and prosperous country, achieving long-denied international recognition, completing national integration, and securing China against external interference. An economically and politically stable China will make positive contributions to world peace, China's leaders insist. Outside China, the country's striking economic and social advances are applauded everywhere. But what a "strong and prosperous" China means for the security of its neighbors, starting with Taiwan, is a matter of widely varying opinion. Just as within China the prevailing belief is that the country's history of underdevelopment and fragmentation argue for looking inward, outside China some observers believe an economically rising and dissatisfied power inevitably will bully other countries. In focusing this chapter on the People's Liberation Army (PLA), China's armed forces, the intent is to give some context to the debate over what China's rise means for East Asian security.

By all accounts, Deng Xiaoping's leadership of China's drive to join the ranks of the NICs was prompted by two basic considerations: that China's security, international status, and the survival of a socialist one-party system depended on an open door policy to gain access to capital and technology; and that the danger of a major war had receded, enabling China to take advantage of ten to fifteen years of relative peace in which to pursue a growth strategy.[1] These conclusions, as well as subsequent external events—most especially, the collapse of the Soviet Union, the Gulf War, Taiwan's rising international stature, and NATO's Kosovo operation—have had direct consequences for the PLA.

This chapter has two main sections. The first provides an overview of China's military modernization and its implications for the PRC's external behavior.

91

Trends such as the PLA's increasing influence in top-level policy making, rising military spending, improvements in weapons production and acquisitions, and changes in strategic doctrine have led some observers to conclude that China seeks hegemony in Asia and must be contained. The conclusion here is that China's external behavior, and the PLA's influence, will continue to be subject to significant constraints, beginning with the kinds of internal social and environmental problems noted in chapter 2. In the second section, discussion turns to U.S.–China relations—the political and structural roots of growing tension, the seemingly intractable Taiwan problem, and prospects for creating a common security agenda despite inevitable areas of disagreement.

## THE MILITARY AS AN INFLUENCE GROUP

China's military-industrial complex, which includes the PLA and all enterprises concerned with armaments, has always been a major player in the affairs of party and state. Its influence has traditionally been reflected in significant military representation in the Chinese Communist Party Central Committee and higher party organs; in occasional direct intervention in political affairs, starting with the Cultural Revolution in the 1960s and most dramatically in the 1989 student-worker demonstrations at Tiananmen; and in the ability to command scarce resources (educational, scientific, and technological) to support strategic weapons programs even in times of political chaos.[2] Despite cutbacks in the military budget and personnel in the 1980s, the military ultimately benefited from China's economic takeoff and the PLA's loyalty at Tiananmen.

For one thing, the PLA's mission widened: Not only would it be responsible for defending China's offshore "strategic frontiers" (see below); it would also have to devote more effort to internal security, dealing with subversion, ethnic nationalism, and other threats to socialism and the state.[3] The PLA's political clout also grew. In 1992, at the time of the 14th National Party Congress, PLA leaders became a strong presence on the Central Military Commission (CMC), the key organ of party authority over the military (presided over from 1981 to 1989 by Deng Xiaoping and thereafter by President and party General Secretary Jiang Zemin). The military's budget in the 1990s and beyond rose annually by over 12 percent. Deng gave the green light for import-export corporations under the PLA and the State Council to become more autonomous of state control, which included exporting arms and keeping the profits.[4]

The PLA's enhanced stature and mission at a time of China's rapid economic growth have led to its becoming closely identified with a vigorous post–Cold War Chinese nationalism. All Chinese leaders are firmly committed to "comprehensive national strength" and the pursuit of China's longstanding national objectives—recovery of Taiwan to complete unification, border security, modernization, and great power status. The PLA, as guardian of national security and the Chinese party-state, has unique roles to play in China's pursuit of those objectives. The PLA can argue, from the standpoint of national pride as much as from bureaucratic self-interest, that China's time has arrived to stand up. Its senior commanders made that argument numerous times in the 1990s. They pressed Deng and Jiang Zemin to take tougher stances against U.S. "interference" in Chinese affairs, usually with support from the communist party's "leftists."[5]

Yet self-interest may be a more important factor in the PLA's policy advocacy than is commonly thought. As Allen Whiting has maintained in his examination of assertive Chinese nationalism, it tends to be "more a function of factional politics than of substantive issues."[6] In the cases of PLA naval deployments in the South China Sea in 1988 and 1995, and the Chinese missile exercises near Taiwan in 1995 and 1996, the PLA clearly pushed for a strong Chinese stance on behalf of sovereign interests. Though the two cases presented very different issues of sovereignty, they had two things in common as far as the PLA was concerned: first, they offered the PLA *opportunities to show its indispensability, notwithstanding the end of the Cold War, for protecting Chinese national interests*; and second, they provided PLA leaders, especially in the air force and navy, with arguments for more rapidly acquiring modern weapons to deal with pressing national security responsibilities.[7] This conclusion is not meant to diminish the saliency of PLA nationalism in the PRC's external behavior, nor to dismiss the possibility that it may turn from assertive to aggressive. The key point, though, is that assertive nationalism has domestic political sources and is not merely indicative of an outwardly directed hostility.

As Michael Swaine's study shows, senior PLA leaders, active and retired, have been increasingly active in representing the professional soldier's viewpoint on defense policy.[8] That influence will probably continue to grow, since two of the military's strongest advocates—Generals Zhang Wannian and Chi Haotian, the defense minister—are vice chairmen of the CMC.[9] Still, the PLA does not have a blank check in weapons procurement, external security affairs, or party decision making. As in the past, China's budget priorities and strategy are set by the top party leaders in accordance with political objectives. The PLA must compete for resources with other interest groups, some of which, like the state-run industrial enterprises, are already a huge drain on the central budget. Thus, while on one hand the PLA has been able to count on increasing state financial support, its funding—and perhaps its autonomy—has been set back by Jiang Zemin's order in 1998 that PLA-run businesses be shut down, due mainly to extensive corruption and its impact on morale.[10] In addition, the PLA's resources are being absorbed by other missions and activities besides external security, as I discuss later.

Perhaps the most important internal constraint on the PLA's role in national security is the nature of army-party relations in China. The PLA leadership prides itself on professionalism and is wary of becoming the tool of a particular political faction. Though various commanders and units have been dragged into the middle of political battles, senior PLA commanders have typically not been willing participants. The protests of several of them against using the army to suppress the Tiananmen demonstrators in 1989 showed as much. Nor does it appear that PLA leaders are about to challenge the long-standing rules of the game in party-army relations and become more interventionist. Political loyalty to the supreme leader is essential to regime survival; without it, as Mikhail Gorbachev discovered, the system itself may come apart.[11]

Greater PLA participation in decision making is still largely a matter of consultation, collaboration, and representation, not institutional lobbying or efforts to dominate the security policy making process.[12] Most observers of the Chinese military are of the view that barring some threat of political chaos and a consequent vacuum of authority, PLA leaders would prefer to sit on the sidelines in a dispute among China's elite. That choice would probably be preferred by Jiang Zemin as well. Though he has periodically shown considerable deference to the military, such as by elevating a number of younger commanders to general and making visits to local units, Jiang has no military background and is widely believed not to command strong loyalty from any of the PLA's senior leaders.

## THE MILITARY BUDGET

China's official military budget rose to $14.6 billion in 2000, or about 13 percent (8.29 percent, according to Beijing) of total state spending.[13] The official budget thus nearly doubled since 1995 and more than tripled since the mid-1980s. As is widely known, the official budget greatly understates actual military spending, since it does not include spending for military research and development (R&D), weapons acquisitions, military construction, and the one-million man People's Armed Police (PAP), among other items. If all spending for military purposes were included, a reasonable estimate is that the PRC military budget was actually about $36–42 billion in 2000.[14] That figure puts Chinese military spending fourth in the world, just behind Japan.

Both Chinese and Western sources raise important qualifications about the two sets of figures, however. PRC sources often point out that (official) military spending is low in comparison with other countries, such as Japan and India not to mention the United States, both in gross terms and on a per-soldier basis. Beijing also notes that over half of the (official) budget is eaten up by soldiers' salaries, operations and maintenance, and inflation.[15] Many Western sources concur, adding that as a percentage of GDP and central government spending, the PLA's budget held steady or even went down between the mid-1980s and the late 1990s.[16] Though those percentages increased in 2000, so did the costs of keeping a large military intact. It will be hard for PLA commanders quickly to create the modern army they want. Added to that consideration is a deeper one: The lesson PRC leaders drew from the Soviet Union's downfall was that it was due to excessive military spending.[17]

Nevertheless, the argument is often made that the PLA has significant extra-budgetary income, notably in four areas: extra central government funds, profits from the conversion of military enterprises to civilian production, arms sales, and (until Jiang Zemin's 1998 order) PLA-run or invested businesses. These sources, while substantial, do not seem to add much to the PLA's military capability. For one thing, some significant portion of the central leadership's off-budget allocations to the PLA go to what are basically nonmilitary purposes, such as support of military conversion (although "reverse conversion" may enable the PLA to acquire foreign military or dual-use technologies) and to retraining demobilized soldiers. Secondly, profits from the sales of converted military-industrial enterprises and PLA-run businesses likewise, according to Chinese sources, stayed within the enterprises or the units.

Only in the case of arms sales, it would appear, are profits used by the PLA for military purposes, probably for R&D as one means of keeping defense industries afloat. But, as noted earlier, arms sales dropped dramatically in the 1990s—China delivered only $79 million worth of arms in 1999[18]—due to changes in the international situation, poor quality and reliability of Chinese arms, compliance with missile nonproliferation agreements, and U.S. opposition to PRC missile sales.[19] China's share of arms sales in its two main markets, Asia and the Middle East, has declined to very small percentages,[20] as have Chinese sales of surface-to-surface, surface-to-air, and antishipping missiles.[21] Moreover, since 1998 China has had in place arms export regulations that for the first time provide a legal and administrative framework to cover military exports and penalize violations. If faithfully implemented, the new rules may further restrain China's sales of major weapons systems.[22]

Given China's size and technical backwardness relative to the major military powers, even PRC military spending in the range of $100 billion a year, which would be roughly twice the size of Japan's current military budget, would not be out of line for a country seeking to catch up.[23] For China, however, the problem is that real spending of such amounts is extremely unlikely in the foreseeable future. It would require a major, and politically dangerous, reorientation of economic planning. It would arouse anxieties throughout Asia, particularly in Japan, quite possibly setting off an arms race that might result in a nuclear-armed Japan independent of the United States. A sudden burst of Chinese military spending might also jeopardize efforts to satisfy the ordinary soldier's and the defense scientist's needs for better wages and working conditions.

## CHINA'S MILITARY PRODUCTION

Acquiring technology and simultaneously promoting military and economic modernization are central state objectives. While PRC leaders hope defense technology innovation can be accomplished by indigenous commercialization, they must also rely on import-export industrial corporations that in some substantial part service the military's needs. In 1999, these corporations—representing the nuclear, shipbuilding, ordnance, aerospace, and aviation industries—were reorganized into ten "enterprise groups" (*jituan gongsi*) and made responsible to the State Council.[24] Besides exporting arms, the corporations market many kinds of products besides weapons, export or import directly or through third countries, and make use of Chinese branch companies operating abroad.[25] Within China, the corporations are also leaders in military-industrial conversion, a project that Deng Xiaoping pushed beginning in the mid-1980s. Aerospace, officially considered the "center" of high tech development, and nuclear power, which by 2020 might account for five percent of China's total energy production, are leading sectors in conversion, along with electronics.

China is a major weapons producer, with a full array of conventional weapons and the ability to deliver nuclear weapons across the Pacific. The evidence suggests, however, that China's own production of weapons and improvements in military technology continue to be beset by management and organizational problems. The military-industrial complex seems still to be inefficient and uncoordinated—plagued, as it has been since the 1980s, by a great deal of unutilized or underutilized capacity, uncooperativeness between research units, and bureaucratic redundancy.[26] (These problems may lend some truth to Chinese government's claims that it doesn't always know what its arms firms are doing, and to the claims of some of the firms that they cannot account for the behavior of their subsidiaries.) Frequent reorganizations such as the one described above of China's bureaucratic system for integrating weapons production, military exports, and arms control reflect these management problems. But though some positive results have occurred, the system as a whole is still dogged by some distinctive weaknesses: problems of indigenizing imported technology, a brain drain of younger scientists, wasteful use of human resources, an "irrational" R&D process, and outdated facilities for producing advanced weapons.[27]

Nor is China is a position to shift new resources into military R&D. Two characteristics of such spending stand out. First, the amounts, so far as they can be known at all (and information is exceedingly sparse on this issue, especially as the Chinese do not report it as a separate category of military spending), are rather small in relation to total official military spending.[28] Second, at around $1 billion a year (in 1994), spending on military R&D is extremely small compared with that of all other countries with high military expenditures excluding Japan and Russia.[29]

There is always the danger of underestimating China's military R&D and production, however. After all, China has produced a wide range of sophisticated weapons and military-related technology. The ability of its defense scientists to do what is asked of them, from nuclear submarines to satellites, should not be doubted.[30] Furthermore, Western analysts often tend to underestimate China's capabilities because its manufacturing processes do not follow those of the United States. A final cautionary point is that China's great strides in nonmilitary scientific research may yet redound to the benefit of the military sector; "Chinese technology programmers now understand defense requirements as thoroughly derivative of developments in the commercial sphere."[31] It seems sensible to conclude, along with two Western specialists, that so long as the PLA remains committed to its current internal and peripheral security agenda, China's military-industrial complex will be able to keep pace with the its weapons requirements.[32]

## WEAPONS ACQUISITIONS

Despite other pressing budgetary obligations, China is willing to spend large sums for weapons and high technology. In Russia, China has found an important new channel for modern arms acquisitions (such as the jets and diesel submarines mentioned before), technology transfer, and technical help. Access to Russian technology and scientists may now be considered a substitute for exports to achieve defense modernization.[33] But the other side of the coin is more impressive: the number of *closed or highly restricted* sources of weapons and technology; the poor Chinese record when it comes to *absorbing foreign military technology* and moving into serial production of foreign-designed weapons; and the *declining attractiveness* for Chinese scientists and engineers of working in the military sector.[34] Indeed, apart from Russia and Israel, China has no consistent external sources of top-of-the-line weapons. Notwithstanding their friendship and cooperation treaty of July 2001, Sino-Russian relations will always be subject to the instability of Russian politics, the susceptibility of Russia's cooperation to Western pressures, and historical animosities between the two countries' leaders.[35] Washington has tried to block various Israeli weapons deals with China.[36] Overall, "while there appears to be a willingness [by China] to spend on some items, this tendency is not as yet indicative of a massive effort to upgrade the Chinese military through shopping sprees abroad."[37]

The quality of Chinese weapons continues to be unreliable, notwithstanding impressive accomplishments in aerospace. A high proportion of PRC combat aircraft, for instance, perhaps 90 percent, are of "pre-1966 design."[38] That proportion will change somewhat with the acquisitions from Russia, but not enough to put China's air force on a par with the United States and Russia. At sea, Chinese frigates and destroyers similarly are said to be in desperate need of modernizing to bring their armaments and construction up to world standards.[39] As a regional force, the PLA Navy (PLAN) may seem formidable against any one local foe. But it should be remembered that its victories in the South China Sea were against very weak Vietnamese forces, that the ASEAN military forces are equipping themselves with modern weapons too, and that the Chinese navy still has serious weaknesses should it choose to operate far from home ports.[40] The U.S. Navy's reported estimate is that China "will lack [naval] logistic support and adequate air defense and [antisubmarine warfare] capabilities for the foreseeable future."[41] Even with Chinese purchases of two Russian missile-capable destroyers and the S-300 antiaircraft missile system in late 1996, that assessment remains unchanged.[42] Rumors that China will acquire an aircraft carrier have been around for several years, yet remain just that: rumors. Even if China did find the money to acquire one, it is difficult to see how that would convert China into a true naval power. China lacks many of the ingredients of naval prowess, though we may expect that it will continue devoting resources to submarine and antisubmarine warfare development, surface-to-surface ballistic missiles, and air refueling capability to lengthen the range of attack aircraft.

## DOCTRINE AND MISSION

Military doctrine sits uncomfortably somewhere between national intentions and objectives, which are ultimately matters of political judgment, and military capabilities. Doctrine provides clues to actual behavior, but is by no means the only or even the most important indicator of it. Nor may weapons—including their research, procurement, and manufacturing—be in synchrony with doctrine. In fact, the Chinese case shows doctrine sometimes in search of weapons to support it, and sometimes being pushed by weapon technology.[43]

Chinese doctrine and strategic intent are also not necessarily closely connected. It is one thing for the military services to show interest in use of nuclear weapons in combat, preemptive attack, and strategic retaliation, and quite another thing to be actively planning for these actions. Especially since the Gulf War, PLA doctrine has been more affected by the *potentialities* of high tech weapons than by any new strategic design. In the case of the PLAN, for instance, there seems to be an understanding that capabilities, as well as political considerations, limit what can be done in the name of "active offshore defense"—and that even acquiring an aircraft carrier would not by itself resolve the logistical difficulties of going to a more aggressive posture.

Thus, while military doctrine indicates the direction a military establishment thinks it needs to go to *prepare* for action and the probable scenarios in which action will take place, it cannot by itself be taken as a signal of offensive intent. Nor does offensive intent reveal itself in current Chinese military doctrine. For example, Chinese strategists have written a good deal about deterring and fighting a limited nuclear war, and the PLA's strategic nuclear warheads and missiles are being modernized and expanded. But doctrine is well ahead of capabilities in this area, so much so that (as we see in China's hostile reaction to the Americans' theater missile defense [TMD] idea) Beijing fears its deterrent will be undermined even before it fully develops it.

Where doctrine, capabilities, and strategy mesh most clearly is with respect to nearby conflicts. The leadership's goal is to put muscle behind those Chinese territorial objectives (reunifying with Taiwan, maintaining authority over Hong Kong and Tibet, and securing borders) that are directly related to its historic mission of national reunification and integration. Hence the PRC has invested mainly in rapid reaction forces, short-range ballistic missiles, and air and naval weapons for offshore defensive and offensive missions[44]—the kind of capability most useful for dealing with nearby contingencies such as another Taiwan Strait crisis.

The PLA's doctrine also does not reveal all of its mission. China's growing domestic dislocations may compel the PLA to assume more internal responsibilities. Rising crime (enough to prompt a nationwide anticrime campaign and a sharp increase in executions in 1996), farmers' sometimes violent protests against public officials, strikes by workers laid off from state-owned enterprises, potential environmental protests in Neimenggu (Inner Mongolia) and the Three Gorges Dam area, and the huge influx of unemployed peasants into major cities are already putting pressure on local police and public security forces. Ethnic nationalist unrest in the far western provinces, especially among Muslim populations, is becoming a particularly difficult problem for Beijing. Numerous casualties among security forces and citizens have been reported in the various protests, the largest of which have required intervention by the army and the PAP, which is under PLA authority.[45] In 1994, public order was regarded by Chinese authorities as a serious problem in 17 of 29 provinces; by 2001, cities all over China were being ordered to create anti-riot units, an indication that the PAP was insufficient.[46] The PLA has acted as an "occupation force" in villages surrounding the town of Pingyuan, Yunnan, where local authorities have been conducting a war on drugs. (Army units were preceded by over 2,000 troops of the PAP in 1992.) The combination of ethnic minorities, heroin, and big money is making life tenuous for some centrally appointed politicians.[47]

Though the scope of disorder in China should not be exaggerated, it certainly commands the attention of the top leaders. The references to "hostile foreign forces" that will stir up public opinion in order to subvert socialist rule seem to occur whenever demonstrations take place, whether in 1989 or in 2001, when adherents of the Falungong religious sect protested against official repression. One cannot rule out the resumption of demands for political change, including legal reform, by an aroused citizenry, raising the specter of Tiananmen. In the name of restoring public order, army units may again be called upon to do what they generally detest: crack down on demonstrators. The latest national defense law seems to anticipate an expanded PLA role in containing domestic political protests.[48] Hong Kong, where civil liberties have come under increasing assault since the PRC's assumption of authority, could be a test case. The law governing the PLA's Hong Kong garrison leaves plenty of room for the military to carry out intelligence, security, and business activities despite assurances that the PLA will not have authority over the Hong Kong political administration.[49] Nor is it out of the question that, as happened during the Cultural Revolution, army units will be fighting one another, with one group representing the military and the other the criminals. Military officers in coastal and border provinces who are supposed to be safeguarding the public are believed to be among those engaged in smuggling guns, drugs, and other goods.

## THE PLA AND CHINA'S EXTERNAL BEHAVIOR

It might be said that even though China is not able to produce or acquire weapons sufficient to challenge the United States, it has the conventional and unconventional capability to intimidate nearby countries. This is no doubt true, as Beijing proved at Mischief Reef in the Spratlys in 1995 and in the Taiwan Strait. But neither case offers firm evidence either of aggressive Chinese designs in Asia, or of military domination of foreign policy. These were not instances of national security crises. Rather, the central party leadership's objective was to demonstrate, through a show of force, its firm commitment to defend China's interest in ultimately recovering Taiwan—and to stopping Taiwan's drift toward a declaration of independence. At the same time, Beijing was careful to avoid a direct confrontation, out of an appreciation of the high price, in economic and strategic terms, that it would have to pay if it chose to use aggressive force.

The two cases also alert us to be careful not to fall into the Cold War era analytical trap of treating China as a monolith, a unitary decision maker. Assertive nationalism surely is a commonality among PRC decision makers; but there very probably are differences among the top leaders, even within the PLA, over how quickly and at how much risk China should seek to complete its nationalist agenda. Nor is a narrow nationalism the only foreign policy motivator. The security and economic benefits of diplomatic engagement with Asia-Pacific neighbors—normalizing relations with India and Vietnam; establishing economically and strategically important ties with the Central Asian states in a six country grouping now called the Shanghai Cooperation Organization; deepening contacts with ASEAN and ARF—are important to the Chinese military as well as to party leaders. PLA analysts see those kinds of relationships as alternatives to the American bilateral alliance system in building regional security without hegemonic dictation.[50] Adherence to international norms, such as through participation in international arms control arrangements, has also gained high-level support (see discussion below).

In fact, the constituency in China that favors the peaceful settlement of disputes and low-risk security policies may be broader still as the result of the economic reforms. Local entrepreneurs and province governors in the coastal areas have a great deal at stake when tensions rise over Taiwan or the SCS. Though little is known about their foreign policy views, it is likely that they put regional economic development interests above the immediate satisfaction of China's territorial ambitions. And it is conceivable that in today's China, local leaders in coastal provinces have clout with higher authorities.

The capabilities of the PLA have not been tested in combat since 1979, when China suffered serious losses at the hands of Vietnam. The years of entrepreneurial activity, with lost training time, may have taken a further toll on preparedness. In any case, while there is no reason to underestimate the PLA in a limited engagement, the PLA's ability to project power is open to question. The most careful study of PRC capabilities with respect to Taiwan concludes that

China has no military options—neither ballistic missile threats nor a blockade or invasion—that stands any chance of success, independently of U.S. involvement. As the commander-in-chief of the U.S. Pacific Command said in 1997: "In our estimate, it will be about one and one-half decades before China could field a military with a modernized, force projection capability."[51]

## China Threat?

Analysts who see China as a present or future threat to its neighbors often, and mistakenly, assume a direct connection between capabilities and intentions, and between hardware numbers and real war capabilities. In a word, there may or may not be one. A growing military budget, and improvements in weapons produced or acquired, may be explained in several ways besides a menacing intention: as a consequence of bureaucratic competition and influence; as a "natural" outgrowth of increased national prosperity; as a response to perceived external threat or rivalry; and as a normal step in modernizing weapons and equipment. Furthermore, analysts need to be cautious about attributing malevolence and successful military operations to a country's military buildup without at least considering the same about other countries. A common standard needs to apply to all, lest the analysis rest on Cold War ideological suppositions about the behavior of communist as opposed to capitalist, or socialist as opposed to democratic, countries.[52] It would be interesting to know, for example, why the same analysts who believe China is a threat to the international order, (with its weak defense-industrial base, poor quality weapons, and low military spending relative to its size), see no threat in the United States and Japan. Granted, both countries are democracies, but their military assets dwarf China's, and they have long histories of intervention in Asia.

Thus far, at least, although China's military doctrine, assertive nationalism, behavior in nearby waters, and efforts to modernize the PLA are consistent with interpretations of an assertive China, the evidence favors a cautious view of PRC strategic intentions. Over the last decade, the PLA has become more autonomous and self-confident; but it has not acted in unrestrained and aggressive ways. China's dependence on the world economy, its need of friendly relations with bordering countries, and numerous serious weaknesses in the PLA and the military-industrial complex are among the constraints on external adventurism. When, in April 2001, a U.S. electronic surveillance aircraft collided with a Chinese jet fighter off the China coast and was forced to make an emergency landing on Hainan island, this very issue of nationalist sensitivities versus developmental priorities came to the fore. The latter won out. "Everything in the end is determined by economic development," said an official commentary.[53] China's need to keep growing, and mounting domestic political and social problems that accompany growth, are likely increasingly to absorb the attention and resources of political and military leaders alike. It thus makes no sense to treat China as a rogue state or rising hegemon, lest it become one.

## THE INSTABILITY OF U.S.–CHINA RELATIONS

China's economic reforms and the end of the Cold War might have opened the door to an era of good feeling and deepening contacts between the United States and China. Instead, those events removed some obstacles, only to see them replaced by others. U.S.–China relations over the last decade have blown hot and cold, seemingly unable to come to rest on a set of mutually acceptable principles that would, in effect, update the 1972 Shanghai Communiqué that concluded President Richard M. Nixon's path-breaking trip to China. As a result, China's economic rise appears just as threatening to some American leaders as did Mao Zedong's revolution.

At the heart of the tensions lie a host of fundamental differences rooted in ideology and history. These are well known. Here, I want to accent two other factors: contention between the two schools of thought introduced in chapter 2—Globalism (neoliberalism) and Neorealism—and structural asymmetries between the United States and China. Globalism on the U.S. side influences China policy by relying on trade, investment, and economic sanctions as levers for transforming the PRC party-state system. It was ascendant in American policy making from the early 1980s until the Tiananmen crackdown. It resurfaced again, as "economic diplomacy," in the period bracketed by the summit meetings of October 1997 and June 1998 between President Clinton and PRC President Jiang Zemin. Realism, expressed in concern over China as a threat to U.S. power-political interests, was the dominant force between the 1989 Tiananmen debacle and China's missile tests near Taiwan in 1996.[54] Realism became firmly entrenched in 1999, and by the time Clinton left office in January 2001, a relationship that had once been characterized as a "strategic partnership" rested on shaky pillars.[55] Under President George W. Bush, China was officially considered a "strategic competitor," a designation that lasted until October 2001, when he reached out for Chinese cooperation in the antiterrorism campaign.

Beijing policy makers have also struggled to find an appropriate balance between the two schools—essentially, between geopolitics and economic interdependence—particularly when it comes to policy toward the United States. Their basic guideline still seems to rely on Deng Xiaoping's sixteen-character instruction of the early 1990s, which called for "enhancing cooperation" with Washington and "avoiding confrontation."[56] PRC leaders see the United States as being central to China's achievement of rapid and sustained economic growth. However, they also see U.S. "hegemonism" and "power politics" at work, obstructing China's attainment of other paramount national interests: reunification with Taiwan, independence of action at home, and international acceptance as a great power. Aware that long-term U.S. policy is to promote China's rise precisely in order to democratize and thus tame it—an objective, incidentally, that must remind PRC leaders of the U.S. strategy of promoting "peaceful evolution" in the late 1950s and early 1960s—Beijing chafes at America's status as the sole superpower even as it curries favor with U.S. commercial interests. Thus, in the same years that U.S. Realism has been ascendant, Chinese Realists have been especially vocal in their criticism of the United States for abusing its superpower status and seeking to contain China.[57] The July 2001 treaty with Russia may be understood as the Realists' defensive response to American hegemonic power, specifically concerning ballistic missile defense.

Our examination of U.S.–China relations begins with the policy making and structural factors that seem to account for the constant tensions between Washington and Beijing. There follows a case study of one policy arena—U.S. transfers of advanced technology to China—whose politics embrace the most intractable and controversial issues in the overall relationship: China's military capabilities and intentions, the U.S. policy of engaging versus containing China, and the Taiwan question.

## The Realist-Globalist Debate

U.S. policy toward China today is a combustible mixture of Cold War geopolitics and post–Cold War geoeconomics. Realists and Globalists share a commitment to perpetuating global primacy, universalizing American values, and transforming China politically while containing its power strategically. That the two schools have become so deeply at odds over China policy testifies to the prominence of opposing domestic political forces that are engaged on each side. In the U.S. case, members of Congress, heads of transnational corporations (TNCs) that do business with China, the press, and NGOs such as labor, religious, and civil rights groups, all hold strong views about China. Especially since the 1989 crackdown at Tiananmen, China has become a major "intermestic" issue in U.S. politics, engaging a wide variety of interest groups and many Congress members who usually pay no attention to foreign policy issues.[58] The negative view of China is informed by Cold War ideology—a deep mistrust of China's communist leaders—and not merely by empathy for the victims of authoritarianism. The positive view expects economic and technological forces ultimately to cause the party-state to wither away and be replaced by civil society.[59] The U.S. policy making community seems to be divided along similar lines on how best to interpret and manage a rising China (see below).

For over twenty years, Chinese Globalists, starting with Deng Xiaoping himself, have been making two essential points: first, that China needs a "peaceful international environment" in which to push forward economic development; second, that a peaceful, prosperous, and politically stable China is as much in the world's best interest as it is in China's best interest. In the course of the economic reforms and now economic globalization, a strong Globalist constituency has emerged in the international economic and arms control bureaucracies under the State Council. Their agenda includes promoting positive relations with the West, positioning China to be a powerful economic competitor, actively engaging the PRC in East Asian multilateral fora, and making a modest contribution to UN collective security efforts such as international peacekeeping missions. The Ministry of Foreign Affairs would seem to be the most consistent follower of Deng's formula for cooperative relations with the United States, as well as the key supporter of multilateral diplomacy.[60] One reason the 2001 spy plane incident did not escalate to become a crisis in China–U.S. relations may be that the ministry's (and the U.S. State Department's) diplomats took charge rather than the military.

To the extent internationalism serves specific Chinese interests, it has the backing of central party-state leaders. Deciding to support the U.S. antiterrorism campaign is an example: Though the war resulted in a resumption of U.S. ties with Pakistan, China's key ally in South Asia, it lent legitimacy to China's pursuit of its own ethnic "terrorists," and for a time pushed controversial issues in relations with the United States into the background. But those same leaders embrace the Realism and assertive nationalism often associated with the PLA when it comes to matters of state sovereignty. There, the top priority is reunification with Taiwan, and the chief obstacle is the United States. U.S. pressure tactics and "interference" in matters of state sovereignty, from support for religious and political dissidents to military aid to Taiwan, provide rallying points for Chinese nationalism.[61] They also help China make the case in Asia for its "new security concept" based on mutual trust and multilateral cooperation.

Both elements in the PRC elite believe that China's domestic political stability and economic strength are the keys to its international influence; that increased involvement in international trade and investment is essential to China's continued rapid growth; and that military modernization is a vital part of national self-strengthening. They share a belief that China's moment in history has finally arrived.[62] When it comes to protecting the PRC's core interests, Chinese Realists and Globalists differ only (though importantly) on the price of international exposure—in a word, how much China should sacrifice in policy making autonomy in order to acquire the means of self-strengthening. While all members of the elite seem to agree, for example, that adjusting to economic globalization is a necessity for China, even though it will involve painful sacrifices, they probably have differences that reflect a competing desire to protect the national economy.[63]

Chinese and U.S. Realists perceive each other within the standard parameters of state sovereignty and national security. Their primary field of play is the *bilateral relationship*, where strong philosophical and policy differences often outweigh perceptions of mutual benefit. In official circles, the American Realist view of China is most strongly represented in the Pentagon, the CIA, and parts of the State Department. In the Pentagon, even though China was depicted as being a "constructive partner" during the Clinton years, it was also described as a future "global peer competitor" or regional military challenger of the United States by 2015.[64] In the last days of the Clinton administration, the chairman of the Joint Chiefs of Staff, Henry H. Shelton, said: "I am firmly convinced that we need to focus all elements of U.S. power and diplomacy on ensuring that China does not become the twenty-first-century version of the Soviet bear."[65] The combination of a capitalist-style economy and a communist dictatorship could prove unsustainable, and threaten regional stability, Shelton said—a point also made by CIA analysts.[66] Nevertheless, the Pentagon supported engagement of China, and its contacts with PLA counterparts, mainly for confidence building, were extensive during most of the Clinton years. Under George W. Bush, *all* forms of contact with China were reassessed soon after his term began. Following the spy plane incident, hardliners around the president, led by his vice president, secretary of defense, and chief national security adviser, reportedly took over China policy making.[67]

U.S. Realists seem to premise engagement on U.S. leadership to shape the world in ways hospitable to democratization, open markets, and its own rules of order. Strategically, engagement was never meant to suggest any significant departures from primary reliance on Cold War deterrence doctrine and the forward deployment of U.S. power in the Pacific.[68] So far as China policy is concerned, Realism means continuing to arm Taiwan—indeed, some of the largest military sales to Taiwan occurred under Clinton and one of Bush's earliest major decisions was to offer Taiwan a large new menu of weapons—strengthening defense ties with Japan, and pushing ahead on TMD in Asia.

U.S. Globalists and Realists agree on the primacy of national over global interests and the inextricable relationship between economic and political interests on one side and security interests on the other. In Asia, both groups assume that the United States must be the preeminent power and that the network of bilateral U.S. security treaties in Asia and forward military deployments remains the best way to protect security interests.[69] Furthermore, Globalists and Realists accept the need to "engage" China for the sake of China's and the region's stability—which sometimes includes using sanctions when China's behavior does not measure up to U.S. expectations. But American Globalists argue that regional and global interdependence create important common security interests that, except where they touch on vital matters of sovereignty, ought to transcend political differences with China. They also maintain that the post–Cold War national security agenda must give high priority to nonmilitary issues, such as environmental protection, economic growth, and population planning.

U.S. Globalists take Chinese leaders seriously when they say their country needs a long period of peace in order to sustain rapid economic growth. Negotiations and summitry are therefore ordinarily better tools than confrontation and punishment to keep China on that path, and to resolve policy differences. While certain Chinese domestic and international conduct should be criticized and even militarily confronted, Globalists say China's conduct should not be subject to linkage, which can only ratchet up tensions, feed PRC nationalism, and damage the overall relationship without producing desired results. To judge from remarks by Clinton, a weak China is of greater concern to Globalists than a strong one.[70] While therefore accepting the importance of bilateral defense treaties to deter China, Globalists prefer transnational and multilateral channels such as TNCs, United Nations agencies, arms control agreements, and trade-promoting fora such as the WTO and APEC to advance U.S. foreign policy objectives. And foremost among those objectives is to transform the Chinese political system itself.[71]

The U.S. Globalist view centers on the proposition that engaging China is also unavoidable, since it plays a global role in environmental, economic, and security issues.[72] Mirroring Deng's instruction, they believe that shared interests should be the focal point of policy; confrontation should be deemphasized. As one State Department official under Clinton said:

> We must not demonize China. Some Americans tend to think that because China is not a democratic friend, it is necessarily an enemy, and must therefore be opposed. That is a false choice, and one we would not be long in regretting if we made it. To treat China as an enemy is to ensure that it will behave as one. Some advocate a policy of containment toward China. Such a policy would forfeit the historic opportunity to enlist China's participation in meeting common challenges and would disrupt relations with our allies, none of whom see the wisdom of such a policy.[73]

Although Globalists acknowledge China's capacity for troublemaking in East Asia, they consider a direct conflict with the United States unlikely in view of Beijing's reliance on Western capital, markets, and technology.[74] As evidence, they point to ways in which the strategic dialogue with China has borne considerable fruit, such as PRC commitments on arms control and its cooperation to reduce tensions on the Korean peninsula. Where Realists see self-interested Chinese behavior on global issues—protectionist trade practices, rejection of commitments to reduce greenhouse gases, and restrictions placed on Western news outlets and Internet activity—Globalists point to positive steps China has taken in these areas. For instance, China is credited with responsible global citizenship in refusing to devalue the renminbi during the Asian financial crisis.[75] In 2001 it ratified the UN Covenant on Economic, Social, and Cultural Rights, and thus had ratified five of the six major human rights instruments. (China has signed but not ratified the Covenant on Civil and Political Rights.) And its record on arms control, while spotty in the U.S. view, is typically regarded favorably by Globalists, who tend to give China the benefit of the doubt in grey areas such as missile transfers.

Notwithstanding some questionable aspects of that record—as with the U.S. record, it should be added[76]—the fact remains that the PRC has taken steps on international security that not very long ago seemed inconceivable. On arms control, for example, between the early 1990s and 2001 Beijing signed and ratified the NPT's indefinite extension, signed the CTBT, ratified the CWC (it had acceded to the Biological and Toxin Weapons Convention in 1984), indicated its support for a Fissile Material Cut-Off Treaty, issued three white papers on national defense in the interest of greater transparency,[77] reached nuclear detargeting arrangements with Russia and the United States, and agreed to abide by the restrictions on missile exports of the Missile Technology Control Regime (MTCR).[78] Beijing also instituted regulations on dual-use chemical exports and on nuclear exports, assertedly incorporating the two control lists of the Nuclear Suppliers Group even though it has not yet joined it.[79] China participated in six UN peacekeeping operations and supported various sub-regional and international environmental agreements.

In assessing Chinese Globalism, two conclusions suggest themselves. One is that an arms control community has evidently emerged in China, one that has convinced its political leaders that the country's global interests are better served by helping to shape the rules of international negotiations than by continuing to be a rejectionist. That community is gradually becoming more focused and institutionalized, such that arms control policies are now matters of debate, internally and internationally.[80] Second, China's new willingness to participate in multilateral international security arrangements is contrary to Realist assumptions about state behavior and runs counter to its traditional power-maximizing ideology.[81] It apparently has done so in part to avoid the stigma of standing outside widely supported regimes, and in part to be better positioned to take advantage of international "goods," such as technology and loans, to which a good citizen is normally entitled.

## The Structural Dilemma

Feeding the Realist-Globalist debate, and further complicating it, is a set of structural asymmetries in U.S.–China relations. One asymmetry is that China is a rising power while the United States seeks to preserve its place as first-among-equals in post–Cold War international politics. The Chinese can only explain with reference to hegemony why the United States is dissatisfied with the kind of China it supposedly always wanted—a China that has peacefully marketized its economy and allowed it to be subject to global forces. Acting in its global-system role as the only superpower, the United States is constantly seeking to transform China, forcing China to bend to rules of behavior made in America. In arms control, for example, Washington was able to obtain PRC promises not to export cruise missiles and nuclear power technology to Iran; and it got China's agreement to abide by conditions of the MTCR even though China was not consulted when those limits were determined.

Though Chinese analysts find engagement a welcome alternative to containment, many warn that engagement is hardly neutral. It arises out of necessity, not American generosity; and its notion of "constructive" international behavior promises constant friction whenever China's performance fails to measure up to U.S. standards.[82] The U.S. tendency to set preconditions ignores Chinese interests and suggests less partnership than hierarchy in the relationship. Thus, "engagement without considering legitimate Chinese concerns and interests could be, and has been, interpreted by the Chinese as a comprehensive containment strategy aiming to belittle, destabilize, and hold back China."[83]

A second structural problem lies within the two countries' political economies. The United States is a global economy, driven more than ever by economic and technological forces that have powerful and diverse domestic constituencies. As the case study that follows of high tech exports indicates, such commercial interests command a president's attention, a fact that has had obvious positive consequences for China's development. But it also has a negative aspect: U.S. economic interests demand rules on market open-ness and transparency that China, as a developing country, cannot readily accept or quickly implement.[84] China's priority is rather to acquire foreign technologies through joint ventures and other means.[85] Thus, Chinese enter-prises, including multinational firms and those belonging to the military-industrial complex, do not necessarily share the objectives of American and other countries' TNCs, or the neoliberal agenda in the WTO for harmonizing trade rules.

These structural factors tend to have polarizing effects that exacerbate the tug of war between Realists and Globalists. While hegemony motivates U.S. policy to pressure China on a host of issues, economic and technological forces seek to pull China into the U.S.-dominated international system as a means of open-ing up its political economy. The first encourages clashes of nationalisms. The second, by relying on instruments of global interdependence, widens opportu-nities for accommodation but also intensifies competitive interests. As one Chi-nese Realist has remarked, "more extensive engagement [with the United States] is likely to create more frictions."[86]

The structural factor also has strategic implications for the so-called balance of power in Asia. From the perspective of U.S. Realists, a rising, undemocratic China is a threat to the balance. But to the Chinese, maintaining the "balance" is code for keeping the status quo, which is American predominance. Chinese Realists evidently aim to redress such a balance. Investing in antisatellite and cy-ber warfare and improving the range and accuracy of intercontinental ballistic missiles may prove the "China threat" to some Americans, but from a Chinese standpoint such actions are necessary to offset huge U.S. strategic and East Asia theater advantages.[87]

## THE PERILS OF COMMERCIALIZING U.S.–CHINA RELATIONS

Because of their military implications, the transfer of U.S. advanced technology to China is one policy arena in which the clash between Realists and Globalists in the two countries, and between U.S. commercial interests and PRC military interests, has been played out. The political issues raised by these transfers, which involve equipment and information as well as technology, reveal why U.S.–China relations have been so difficult to manage.

"Engagement" has resulted in five areas of controversy in recent years. These areas, listed below, have raised questions in the United States about China's mil-itary capabilities and intentions, U.S. security, and the advisability of using technology and scientific exchanges to engage China.

- Acquisition (in the United States or elsewhere abroad) by Chinese firms, whether or not affiliated with the PLA, of advanced technology and equip-ment with military applications.

- PRC acquisitions of dual-use technology or technical information from U.S. corporations doing business in China.
- PRC re-exports to third countries of U.S.-provided components or materials applicable to producing weapons of mass destruction.
- PRC espionage in U.S. nuclear laboratories.
- Contributions to the Clinton re-election campaign by PRC military sources so as to influence decisions on high tech exports to China.

In this section, I make reference to most of these issues but deal mainly with the first one, advanced technology exports in the supercomputer, aerospace, and nuclear energy sectors to China. Common to these exports is that they involve huge, highly competitive markets in China, and therefore large potential profits for U.S. firms; the technologies have national security implications on both sides of the Pacific; and they bring into play crosscutting domestic political forces. Until the late 1990s, advanced technology exports to China had strong bipartisan support in Washington because they served both strategic and commercial interests. That ceased being the case after the Cold War.

## The Background before Clinton

What seems to have been forgotten in the heat of U.S.–China tensions as the 1990s ended is that the relationship was always based on mutual self-interest. The Cold War provided one such overriding interest: the Soviet threat. It was sufficient to motivate a modest strategic partnership and to put Taiwan on the back burner.[88] Once the USSR collapsed, however, the partnership lost its center. Globalism in the form of commercial gain has yet to be able to compensate for the loss of compelling Realist interests in putting U.S.–China relations back on an even keel.

Under Nixon, as we now know from the recently released Kissinger papers on conversations in 1971 with PRC leaders, anti-Sovietism included substantial intelligence sharing—satellite data on Soviet troop deployments—that Kissinger said was necessary to deal with a Soviet nuclear threat to China.[89] Before Gerald Ford left office, he approved the sale to China of two advanced computers with military applications. Under Jimmy Carter, following establishment of diplomatic relations with China in 1979, military sales (but not weapons) to the PRC were accelerated.[90] U.S. electronic listening posts in China were established to intensify monitoring of Soviet troop movements. Leading American nuclear arms scientists and security officials visited Chinese weapons laboratories and test sites, starting an ongoing exchange program that would also bring Chinese nuclear physicists to the United States.[91] And the two countries coordinated arms shipments to Afghanistan. When PRC leaders worried about a Soviet attack on China while the PRC was invading Vietnam (which Deng told Carter about two weeks before it began), daily U.S. briefings provided them with intelligence on Soviet intentions.[92]

Were it not for these and subsequent tangible forms of strategic cooperation, U.S. arms sales to Taiwan might have undermined the new relationship with

Beijing. At the time of normalization, Deng Xiaoping was apparently deeply concerned about the possibility of continued U.S. arms sales to Taiwan after termination of the U.S.–Republic of China Mutual Defense Treaty. To Deng, the sales would remove any incentive for Taiwan leaders to negotiate reconciliation with the mainland—and there were many PRC overtures for peace talks with Taiwan in the early 1970s.[93] Washington refused to reassure Deng in writing; and in 1979 Deng's worst suspicions materialized when the U.S. Congress passed the Taiwan Relations Act (TRA). It obligates the United States to assist Taiwan with "defensive" arms, resist threats to its security, and regard non-peaceful efforts to determine Taiwan's future as "a threat to the peace and security of the Western Pacific area." During the 1980s, U.S. arms sales to Taiwan amounted to over $600 million a year, a clear violation of U.S. assurances to China contained in the August 1982 so-called third communiqué.[94] To counter the TRA, in 1981 and 1982 Chinese leaders (Ye Jianying and Deng Xiaoping) proposed terms of peaceful unification with Taiwan based on the "one country, two systems" formula. Taiwan's response to PRC overtures was not encouraging as it undertook a policy of "Taiwanization" and democratization under President Chiang Ching-kuo.

Perhaps to ease China's pain and dampen its protests of U.S. arms sales to Taiwan, the Reagan administration expanded relations with Beijing in a number of ways. President Reagan paid an official visit to China in April 1984; President Li Xiannian repaid the visit in July 1985. U.S. criticism of China's human rights record continued, but more softly than before. Beijing's policies on Tibet, intellectuals, and human rights were now evaluated in the larger context of its greatly improved economic and social conditions.[95] At the strategic level, Beijing's concern about the Soviet threat abated. But some U.S. analysts worried about a possible reforging of PRC–USSR security ties as well as about supporting China as a counterweight to the Soviets.[96] They successfully made the case that strategic ties to China needed to be upgraded to "prevent a widening of the military gap between the PRC and the U.S.S.R," and to reward China's cooperativeness on Afghanistan. As a result, China was granted a new export status nearly comparable with that of U.S. NATO partners, enabling Beijing to modernize specific weapons programs, such as fighter aircraft and artillery. U.S. commercial interests were also influential in the decision to promote Chinese purchases of U.S. technology and U.S. investments in China. The resulting easing of export licensing requirements for high tech sales to China enabled China to purchase a variety of once-banned items, including dual-use equipment (such as computer equipment usable in nuclear programs,[97] and Sikorsky helicopters). In all, between 1982 and 1988, U.S. military sales deliveries to China amounted to about $237 million.[98]

More direct military exchanges with China also took shape, highlighted by Defense Secretary Caspar Weinberger's September 1983 visit and the first U.S. naval port call in late 1986. And in 1985 the two countries signed the Nuclear Cooperation Agreement, which the administration hailed as a milestone in promoting nonproliferation, but which was also supposed to help boost U.S. exports of U.S. nuclear energy "materials, facilities and components."[99] Implementation of the agreement did not begin until 1998 due to opposition in Congress.

One other component of U.S.–PRC cooperation in the Reagan years was commercial satellite launches, a subject that would come back to haunt the Clinton administration. The U.S. commercial satellite industry received a major boost from Reagan's determination to keep China militarily and commercially tied to the United States. Despite the known risks of technology diversions to PRC state corporations with ties to the PLA, the Reagan administration in December 1988 signed agreements with China on safeguards and liability that cleared the way for later presidents to approve the launching of U.S. communications satellites by the relatively low-cost Chinese *Long March* rockets.[100]

Due to the Tiananmen crackdown, the George Bush administration and U.S. allies in the Coordinating Committee on Multilateral Export Controls (COCOM) suspended further liberalization of export controls concerning China. Proliferation concerns also prompted Bush to step in to prevent a sale of satellite components in 1991. But some U.S. sales to China of dual-use high tech equipment continued, as well as previously noted waivers for satellite launches. High-level visits by U.S. officials resumed, at first secretly and then openly. In 1992, military exports to China already in the pipeline, valued at about $36 million, were granted clearance by Bush—the same year in which he angered Beijing by allowing Taiwan to purchase 150 F-16s, a deal worth nearly $6 billion, and by resuming visits to Taiwan by senior U.S. officials.

With the end of the Cold War, commerce became the glue keeping U.S.–China relations in a tenuous balance. The shift from strategic factors to "intermestic" ones exposed the relationship to new domestic political strains in both countries—all the more so as China's rapid rise brought nationalism to the fore. Two trends now became primary: The importance of China in U.S. global strategy sharply declined, for Moscow no longer needed to be contained nor could be counted on to keep China preoccupied; and reunifying with Taiwan became a more urgent matter in China, especially to PLA leaders. China moved from strategic partner to problem-state: a human rights violator, unfair trade partner, and potential threat to the balance of power in East Asia. The PRC's combination of an open door economy "without political restraint" now gave U.S. Realists pause; China became "the great power in the [East Asia] region about which U.S. strategists should worry most over the long term."[101] Likewise, for some Chinese analysts, the United States had also transformed. It now seemed less like a partner than a great power once more out to "contain" China and solidify its two-China policy. Assessing the great transformation in U.S.–China relations, one Chinese commentator concluded that among the problems that the end of the Cold War had brought back to the surface, "the greatest . . . is ideological differences."[102]

## Clinton's Policies

In the Clinton administration, high-level attention was given to ensuring that science and technology decisions meshed with foreign policy objectives, including commercial goals. Though one U.S. priority was to "curb the proliferation of strategic technologies," promoting trade competitiveness was also an objective—as it turned out, a somewhat higher one than nonproliferation.[103] COCOM's disbandment in 1994 symbolized the new reality.

The reasons for Clinton's support of high tech exports to China are clear enough. First, they are important elements in the U.S. trade balance, which by 1998 was around $60 billion in deficit with China. Second, the market in China is huge. For instance, nuclear power plants in China have an estimated market value for foreign investors of $60 billion. Commercial aircraft sales to China are expected to be around $110 billion over the next decade or so—one-tenth of the world market.[104] China's energy plans over the next fifty years call for a massive, and extremely expensive, increase in nuclear power plants to supply electricity.[105] And China is expected to command a sizable share of launchings in the estimated $171 billion U.S. commercial satellite business.[106] Finally, politicking on China policy is a high priority for U.S. multinationals, which have a major stake in China (accounting for roughly 5 percent of FDI there). They have pushed hard and often for expanding trade with China, granting exceptions for advanced technology sales, and avoiding sanctions.[107] And to accent their interests, high tech corporations were major contributors to the Clinton election campaigns.[108]

Consequently, there seemed to be a presumption in the Clinton administration in favor of dual-use exports to China. As one senior State Department official said:

> Well, we have restrictions on dual-use technology, and of course they attempt to provide the balance between keeping us competitive commercially and preventing . . . risks to our national security in transfers of technology. We look at whether or not China could acquire the article in question from another source before making a decision. If it could acquire it from another source, we would generally make it available. We try not to disadvantage our American business in that respect.[109]

The clearest sign of a permissive attitude toward technology sales to China came during 1996. Overruling Secretary of State Warren Christopher, Clinton shifted licensing responsibility for communications satellites from the State Department to the Department of Commerce. The decision evidently was influenced by pressure on the president from U.S. executives of satellite manufacturers—specifically, Hughes Electronics Corporation, a major player in the competition for placing satellites aboard Chinese rockets, and Loral Space and Communications, which is in the telephone satellite business—to shorten the approval time of satellite exports. Concerns in the Pentagon and the State Department about the potential for China to gain access to encryption technology with application to antisatellite warfare were overruled.[110]

Between January 1990 and April 1998, $312.8 million in commercial export licenses were approved for sales to China of the most sensitive items on the munitions list—mainly ($237 million), satellites and satellite equipment that required a presidential waiver.[111] In all, from 1993 to 1998, about $3 billion worth of U.S. dual-use technology was approved for sale to China, making China by far the largest beneficiary of U.S. licensing decontrols.[112] The trend toward giving China the benefit of the doubt on high tech sales lasted until 1998, when Congressional pressure as a result of the Loral-Hughes case forced a reevaluation. Control over licensing was returned to the State Department in March 1999.[113]

## China's Policies

A principal task of the enterprise group corporations in China's military-industrial complex is to acquire militarily useful advanced technology,[114] all the more so since the Gulf War, when U.S. "smart" weapons demonstrated their power. The PLA's specific interest of late is in electronics for information warfare (for example, for antisatellite, microwave, and laser weapons); it has even invited foreign firms to invest in China's defense electronics sector.[115] Selling weapons and related technologies for a profit was, as previously noted, one route for the PLA to augment its weapons R&D funding. With Jiang Zemin's July 1998 order to close down PLA commercial activities, the military's incentive for acquiring technology has probably increased.[116] As for the group corporations, some of them were among the Chinese companies in the United States that violated customs laws and sales contracts in pursuit of military-related equipment and technologies.[117] (The violations are apart from the controversy over Chinese government-backed contributions to the 1996 U.S. presidential campaign, which included allegations of donations to the Democratic Party by officials with ties to the PLA.[118]) But as always, there must be a willing seller as well as a willing buyer—and from time to time, it appears, the U.S. seller has cared less about national security considerations than about profits and market opportunities. Such appears to have been the case with Hughes and Loral in their dealings with two Chinese state corporations, China Great Wall Industry Corporation and China Aerospace, both of which are in the missile as well as the satellite launch business.

The Chinese leadership typically distances itself from the acts of PRC corporations, arguing that they operate autonomously. When the corporations get into trouble abroad, Beijing typically maintains that their acts are undertaken without central authorization, presumably by greedy corporation heads with the connivance of lower-level officials or businesses. Such excuses lack credibility when companies transfer dual-use equipment to third countries, as the United States charged two PRC corporations with doing when they apparently sold WMD components to Pakistan and Iran in the 1980s and 1990s. But when state and PLA-affiliated companies acquire militarily useful technology and information, at home or abroad, they may well be acting independently. Beijing's stance is that it deserves to be trusted, not treated as an enemy state, and that sales of high tech equipment are a sign of such trust. Thus, it attaches a political weight to such sales, which no doubt the U.S. corporate community carries with it back to Washington when it lobbies on behalf of high tech sales.

## The Control Issue

Several cases came to light of loose controls over high tech exports and scientific exchanges. But only in a few was it clearly established that the PLA acquired technology or militarily useful information. One is the Hughes-Loral case, which apparently involved two instances (in 1995 and 1996) of unauthorized transfers of information to Chinese scientists working on the *Long March* rocket, which had experienced several failed launches.[119] McDonnell Douglas Aircraft evidently was lax in allowing machine tools from a $1.6 billion commercial jet sale in 1994 to China to be diverted to a Nanchang military plant, where cruise missiles were believed to be produced. The belated discovery of the diversion two years later suggests a reluctance on the part of the Commerce Department to ensure Chinese and U.S. corporate adherence to the terms of the sale.[120] In a third case, at the same time that Washington had suspended $10 million of Export-Import Bank financing for U.S. businesses in China, it approved visas for six Chinese nuclear engineers to enter the United States and participate in an advanced power reactor project—clearly because of U.S. competition with France, Germany, and other countries for China's nuclear plant business.[121] Several sales of telecommunications equipment to China have had the potential to enhance the PLA's communications and targeting capabilities if the equipment were transferred to it.[122] The United States also exported a large number of high-performance computers to China, including forty-seven so-called supercomputers, following Clinton's 1995 easing of export controls. In at least one case, an unauthorized diversion occurred. While PLA access to U.S. supercomputers was not established, U.S. nuclear experts cited their potential application to China's nuclear testing.[123]

China's strategic weapons program may have been helped by espionage over a twenty-year period at U.S. nuclear weapons laboratories, an effort that apparently gained momentum in the Reagan years of strategic partnership. The full extent of the damage done by virtue of espionage remains unclear. (The CIA, the Energy Department, and other U.S. agencies agreed that warhead design secrets and technology were stolen, but disagreed as to whether or not those secrets accounted for China's advances in nuclear weapon design. See further discussion below.) In three cases publicized by U.S. agencies, espionage between 1983 and 1995 supposedly facilitated China's miniaturization of strategic warheads (the W-88) for submarines and long-range missiles, its development of a neutron bomb (the W-70), and its development of a warhead for the long-range mobile DF-31 missile.[124]

The tilt toward promoting economic diplomacy with China detracted from another favored Clinton objective, however: nuclear nonproliferation. Several times during his presidency, Clinton had to contend with internal debate over whether or not PRC corporations had exported missiles, technology, or equipment to Pakistan that would assist its nuclear weapons program. Sanctions were imposed on the corporations, but were lifted each time in exchange for China's promise to abide by the terms of the MTCR. The last such understanding was announced in late 2000, with Beijing agreeing to license its aerospace companies that are engaged in the export of missile-related items and not to assist any country to develop ballistic missiles for a nuclear weapons program. Perhaps China will keep the companies on a tight leash; but the real winners are business interests—the PRC and U.S. companies that, as a result of the new understanding, will again be able to put American telecommunications into orbit on Chinese rockets.[125]

## IMPLICATIONS FOR U.S.–CHINA RELATIONS

Neither neoliberalism nor Neorealism contains appropriate solutions to the problems that beset U.S.–China relations. Neoliberalism, relying on the instruments of "globalization," seeks to enmesh China in a web of external nonmilitary relationships that ultimately will ease it out of authoritarianism. But neoliberalism has no answer for the social, political, and economic dislocations that globalization causes or intensifies—and therefore no answer for China's resort to repression of striking workers, angry farmers, environmental and ethnic activists, and political reformers seeking to create new parties. Nor is neoliberalism able to deal sensitively with Chinese nationalism or carefully enough with transfers of militarily sensitive technology to or from China. Neorealism, on the other hand, leads us back to the Cold War era of confrontations with China. It makes highly questionable assumptions of a China threat, greatly exaggerating PRC capabilities and intentions while neglecting sources of Chinese weakness. Rising Chinese nationalism, which can be interpreted as a matter of national pride and international assertiveness, is instead viewed as undergirding truculence and aggressive behavior.

The contest between these two policy thrusts frustrates and angers not only the Chinese leadership, but also its professional America watchers.[126] As they see it, China has in many ways peacefully evolved into the kind of country that Washington hoped for, only to face a new round of criticism because its political evolution has failed to keep pace with market reforms. Thus, from a Chinese point of view, it is not only that the Americans do not appreciate Beijing's mounting difficulties in containing social forces that market socialism has unleashed. Even more fundamentally, the Americans can never be satisfied—they want a stable, capitalistic, *and pluralistic* China that respects everyone's "rights" all at once, and based on standards made in America. Such a perceived agenda has negative consequences on several levels. It provides the glue of nationalist resentment among all Chinese, whether Realist or Globalist. It makes the job of China's America watchers, who must explain the politics behind U.S. pressure tactics, even harder. And it adds to the insecurities of the Chinese leadership, which already faces daunting social challenges that it chooses to meet with repression.[127]

Even commerce, which is the one clearly common interest between China and the United States, is problematic, as the story of strategic trade reveals. The problem of *what* to trade with China represents the parting of the ways between those who believe trade can help create civil society in China, despite inevitable disagreements, and those who suspect that China will manipulate trade with the United States to hone a comparative advantage and become a challenger, economically and strategically, for Asia-Pacific leadership.

## Reforming Strategic Trade Policy

It stands to reason that U.S. policy toward China will be muddled by a diversity of influences and interests that seek to guide it. Clearly, however, the Globalists have won most of the important battles—those in the trade and international security arenas—by arguing that sanctions and linkage politics ought only be pursued on a selective basis, that U.S.–China economic interdependency matters greatly for the U.S. economy (consumers and jobs as well as corporate sales),[128] and that changing China's behavior can best be accomplished by long-term economic engagement. The Clinton-Jiang 1997 summit, combining commercial and arms control agreements, demonstrated the paramount nature of economics in the relationship. It removed roadblocks to nuclear energy, aircraft, and probably supercomputer deals. Jiang in fact signed several billion dollars' worth of agreements before leaving the United States. In return he reassured Washington of China's intention not to transfer nuclear weapon materials to Iran, and agreed that China would join one (the Zangger Committee) of the two (along with the Nuclear Suppliers Group) international regimes for controlling nuclear exports.[129] But the internal bickering in Washington over Chinese behavior and intentions has not abated.

In attempting to sort out whether or not the U.S. engagement policy has been self-defeating, we must first of all consider several imposing practical problems when it comes to identifying high tech commodities that might lend themselves to military use. Distinguishing military from civilian uses of technologies is difficult, and likely to remain so as advanced sensing and information processing technology available from civilian goods becomes an increasingly important source for China of military components. It is also hard to be certain of the actual identity of the PRC buyer, or to monitor the final destination of the exported item. China can buy from third parties, as it may have with supercomputers, or through various front companies that can mask diversions, making export controls fairly useless.[130] Lastly, in the broadest sense the goal of nonproliferation will continue to be weakened by globalization of high technology, and neither

Chinese officials, anxious to acquire whatever technology they can however they can, nor U.S. officials and corporate heads, anxious to maintain market advantage, are reliable channels for preventing diversions of technology.

On the other hand, there is the danger of blowing issues of unauthorized access to technology and technical information out of proportion. So far as business contacts are concerned, the actual number of cases of diversion is small; there is no evidence of a systematic, centrally directed Chinese effort to use government or private companies to acquire advanced technology for the PLA;[131] and the evidence is not conclusive that China's military capabilities have been measurably enhanced by the diversions.[132] Nor has it been well established that U.S. safeguards against diversion have been frequently, much less systematically, bypassed.[133] In fact, Clinton administration officials contended that overall, it had a strong record of discovering and reversing illegal diversions to the PLA, punishing U.S. corporations that failed to guard against diversions, and working with Chinese authorities to prevent shipments of materials to potential nuclear-weapon states.[134] There are also long-term *gains* to be considered, to the U.S. economy and businesses, from technology transfers to China, as well as *advantages* to U.S. national security of access by foreign scientists to U.S. nuclear-weapons laboratories.[135]

As for the espionage cases, other kinds of qualifications are in order. Foremost among them is that the danger to the security of the United States and its allies is easily exaggerated, considering the enormous U.S. edge over China in strategic weapons numbers, accuracy, and reliability of delivery. China's fundamental aim in strategic weapons modernization clearly seems to be to achieve a credible second-strike capability by improving the survivability of its strategic forces.[136] While it may be that China gained from espionage, no evidence has been produced to show a change in PRC nuclear doctrine, deployment, or capability as the result of supposedly stolen secrets.[137] As many weapons experts have pointed out, it is a huge step from nuclear weapon codes to production and deployment—and no evidence has been brought forward to show that China acquired and put the codes to such use.[138] As Beijing quite plausibly insists, whatever improvements China has made—in missile warhead miniaturization, maintenance of its nuclear stockpile, and other areas of military modernization—have mainly been the result of the ingenuity of its own scientists and access to sources other than spies.[139] Hence, correcting lax security practices in U.S. weapons laboratories there would seem to be a more cost-effective approach than limiting scientific exchanges with China or cracking down on a presumed widespread Chinese spy network.[140]

## POLICIES FOR ENGAGING CHINA

It is not possible to change the structural circumstances of U.S.–China relations, or to find a common enemy that might serve as the glue of a new strategic partnership. But different U.S. policies can help reduce the structural gap and restore a more positive, accommodating relationship. To do so, U.S.–China policy needs to take account of the enormous and ongoing transformation in Chinese national security thinking and (especially) practice that has occurred since Mao's passing. Departing from engagement with China would leave the field open to Neorealists on both sides, creating the danger of a return to vilifying Cold War era rhetoric, miscalculations, tit-for-tat retaliations, and possibly open conflict. For all its deficiencies, the Globalist approach to U.S.–PRC security issues is correct: reciprocity and cooperation in the many areas of common interest. Moreover, the case against China is weakened by American double standards when it comes to arms control, arms transfers, and human rights. Lecturing other countries on "responsible" behavior and measuring their performance in terms of one's own standards cannot bridge the gap in one's own policies between rhetoric and reality. It also encourages nationalist resentment. Leadership by example is often more convincing.[141]

Rather than constantly berate China, U.S. policy makers would be wise to address the "perceptual gap" in U.S.–PRC relations. Clearly, both governments fall short of having a firm understanding of the other's political and social systems, values, notions of "reform," "rights," and other key ideas, and strategic cultures (including responses to threat perceptions and willingness to use or deploy force). The two sides can agree to lower the rhetoric of disagreement. They should acknowledge that neither is a threat to the other. And they should recognize that while certain areas of difference are simply going to remain so—most prominently, human rights—both sides reserve the right to protest conditions in the other's country and to draw international attention to them.

Some recent studies underscore the potential for miscalculation and misperception in U.S.–China relations, especially in the absence of CBMs and frequent high-level dialogue.[142] Such findings reinforce the case for augmenting high-level dialogue, particularly between military leaders.[143] Military-to-military contacts have been buffeted by strains in bilateral relations—such as the Tiananmen crackdown, the Taiwan Strait crisis of 1996, the intervention in Kosovo, and the spy plane incident—as well as by resistance in the U.S. Congress. Yet there is no substitute for such direct exchanges of views, which include opportunities for each side to assess the other's military capabilities.[144] The same logic applies to expanding military contacts in multilateral settings. China began bilateral security dialogues with Japan and various kinds of military-to-military contact with South Korea in the 1990s; and of course China has extensive military exchanges with Russia and North Korea. What is missing is periodic, institutionalized security dialogue at the multilateral level, such as a U.S.–PRC–Japan security dialogue and a Northeast Asia dialogue forum that would include the two Koreas and Russia. The strong attachment of the United States and China to bilateralism on security issues is a byproduct of their structural imbalance, and a serious obstacle to transcending Cold War politics.

A major U.S. objective should be to do nothing that would give Chinese nationalists ammunition for demanding a crash program to upgrade military capabilities, as distinct from ordinary weapons modernization, and for backtracking on commitments to arms control. U.S. policy should aim at supporting Chinese Globalists through steps that reduce military capabilities and promote multilateral approaches to security. One example is in arms control, where American ideas to create a missile defense and space force have put it at odds with proposals by China and other countries to stop the militarization of space.[145] Clearly, however, reaching an understanding concerning Taiwan will be the litmus test of common security prospects.

## Untangling the Taiwan Knot

Ever stronger economic bonds between the PRC and Taiwan have made business interests the chief safeguard of their peaceful political relations. Taiwan–PRC trade in 2000 surpassed $30 billion, and Taiwan investment in the mainland for the first time amounted to about one-half of Taiwan's total FDI. Much of the business stems from Taiwan's information technology industry, which has been attracted to the mainland because of cheap labor.[146] In all, "more than 200,000 business people from Taiwan live and work in the PRC, employing about 3 million workers."[147] Yet, aside from the demilitarized zone that divides Korea, the Taiwan Strait is the most dangerous place in East Asia—not only because of competitive mutual force deployments,[148] but perhaps moreso because of opposing political and military commitments. The U.S. president must operate within a legally mandated commitment to Taiwan's defense; and the United States is the principal supplier of weapons and military technology to Taiwan. China, meanwhile, has acquired and deployed weapons that are clearly intended to augment its capacity to deter another U.S. naval interposition in the Taiwan Strait area—and thus add to Taiwan's nervousness. As for Taiwan, its principal goal is to sustain the drive for international acceptance and neutralize Beijing's pressure to accept the "one-China" principle.

As one U.S. official has said with specific reference to Taiwan, U.S.–PRC tensions are lowest when their overall relations are good.[149] In 1995 and 1996, for example, when U.S.–China relations were severely strained, the cross-Strait dialogue was suspended. Taiwan's presidential election was the occasion for PRC missile tests and a U.S. display of naval power. When the dialogue resumed in October 1998, U.S.–China relations had warmed in the glow of the Clinton-Jiang summits. Then came TMD, arbitrary detentions by Chinese authorities, the spy plane incident, new U.S. weapon sales to Taiwan—and a serious downturn in relations.

The lesson here is that U.S. policy should emphasize areas of common interest in China precisely in order to keep PRC–Taiwan dialogue alive and exchanges flourishing. Military maneuvers at a time of diplomatic hostility are a recipe for miscalculation, even when they appear to work. Though they may be politically satisfying to pro-Taiwan members of Congress, they undermine the engagement policy and may lead to disastrous miscalculations. Thus, although it might be argued on the U.S. side that Beijing was deterred in 1996 and reduced to saber rattling, in Chinese eyes the crisis was a victory for a coercive strategy designed to forestall a drift toward Taiwan independence.[150] At the same time, however, the U.S. deployments set a bad precedent, and may have given pro-independence forces in Taiwan, including President Lee, unintended confidence.[151] Some PRC analysts are inclined to think that it did much more—it was part of a calculated plan to play the "Taiwan card" as part of its overall strategy to contain China.[152] The PLA's subsequent missile buildup opposite Taiwan may be interpreted as a response to that perceived strategy.

The dangerous new element in the mixture is the U.S. TMD system and the possibility that Taiwan will join it. TMD has provoked a great deal of protest from Beijing, which views it as directed against China, because of its implications for Japan's militarization (since Japan has agreed to join the system)[153] and for arms control (the 1972 Anti-Ballistic Missile Treaty) as well as for Taiwan's future. A fully functioning TMD would essentially neutralize China's ballistic missile capability opposite Taiwan and thus undermine Beijing's capacity to intimidate Taiwan should Taiwan seek independence. The system might add to Taiwan's defense, but at the probable cost of a severe rupture of U.S.–China relations, since in Beijing's view a TMD that included Taiwan would "mean creation of U.S.–Taiwan joint defense and the formation of [a] military alliance."[154] From that angle, TMD would reduce rather than improve Taiwan's overall security.[155]

While protecting Taiwan from PRC attack is a legitimate U.S. interest, there is no indication that the Chinese missile buildup across the Taiwan Strait has attack in mind. Michael O'Hanlon has convincingly shown the serious limitations on *any* PRC option for militarily resolving the Taiwan problem, whether by coercion (a blockade or missile attack) or outright invasion.[156] China's intentions, moreover, seem to be only partly related to capabilities. While it has been acquiring naval power and deploying missiles in ways that signal a warning to Taiwan, its other air and naval deployments do not indicate a readiness to make war. Uncertainty concerning the U.S. response to another Taiwan crisis may be an important constraint on Chinese decision making; but that may not be the most important constraint. U.S. involvement, O'Hanlon argues, is not even necessary in most conflict scenarios in light of Taiwan's capabilities and Chinese military deficiencies.

Should the United States deploy TMD and extend its protection to include Taiwan, Chinese leaders would feel compelled to respond. One countermeasure might be to get back in the business of exporting longer-range missile technology, thus reversing China's agreement to abide by terms of and consider formally joining the MTCR.[157] A second step would be to intensify space warfare capabilities designed to disrupt U.S. command and control systems in East Asia.[158] A third option is to accelerate development of long-range missiles—in number, accuracy, or configuration (i.e., with multiple warheads)—that might be used to deter a U.S. defense of Taiwan in a crisis. In fact, some senior U.S.

intelligence analysts are convinced that overcoming TMD may be a factor in China's drive to acquire strategic weapons information from the United States, through espionage and otherwise.[159] The regional consequences are potentially alarming, since—again according to members of the U.S. intelligence community and many other specialists—an increase of China's nuclear missile forces would probably lead India and Pakistan to do the same, thus touching off another round of the nuclear arms race.[160]

Though the PLA has been modernizing its missile forces for some time, the strategic balance in East Asia has not been altered. But a continuing competitive weapons buildup on Taiwan and the mainland is bound at some point to become dangerously destabilizing. Indeed, it is possible that another crisis over Taiwan might tip the balance in the ongoing debate among PLA strategists from minimum deterrence to a more ambitious level.[161] Taiwan is reportedly building—and has supposedly already successfully tested—its own missile defense system, called "Sky Bow II," that will supplement the *Patriot* defense of Taipei.[162] Moreover, the United States has already provided Taiwan with quite an array of air and sea defensive systems.[163] One authoritative study summarized U.S. military assistance to Taiwan as follows:

> From 1991 to 1998, arms transfer agreements (primarily U.S.) signed by Taiwan totaled $17.3 billion, while arms deliveries (primarily U.S.) received by Taiwan totaled $20 billion—the second highest (after arms received by Saudi Arabia). . . . In addition to hardware, beginning after tensions in the Taiwan Strait in 1996, the Clinton Administration is said to have quietly expanded the sensitive military relationship with Taiwan to levels unprecedented since 1979 . . . to "software," including discussions over strategy, military thinking, logistics, command and control, and plans in the event of an invasion.[164]

Any improvement of Taiwan's defenses must be weighed against the regional tensions it will probably produce. More is not always better, especially as Taiwan's military procurements tend to be motivated by "traditional bureaucratic rivalries [among the services] or even personal considerations, rather than on rigorous analysis of overall warfighting needs based on an integrated threat-centered defense strategy." There is the additional problem of "the failure of the ROC military to fully assimilate and maintain its more advanced weapons."[165] As a RAND Corporation study of a possible war scenario over Taiwan concluded, even in the (unlikely) event of an all-out PRC invasion of the island, Taiwan's defense needs are much more modest than either the Taiwan military or the Pentagon usually thinks—mainly, improved air defenses, training, and information sharing rather than new weapons systems.[166] Unfortunately, the Bush administration did not agree, though its weapons offering to Taiwan in the spring of 2001 did not include the most advanced weapons the United States had available.[167]

The Taiwan question cannot be unbundled from the overall problems in U.S.–China relations; nor can it be disentangled from domestic politics in all three countries. Every U.S. president, no matter how strongly committed to "engaging" China, will have to deal with a Congress divided on how to treat China, with an unpredictable Taiwan government that has strong support in Congress, and with internal bureaucratic debate. During 1999, for instance, Clinton had to distance his administration from Taiwan President Lee Teng-hui's public campaign to have Taiwan–PRC issues considered "special state-to-state relations." While warning China to act with restraint on Taiwan, Clinton nevertheless privately reassured Jiang that Washington's "one-China" policy remained unchanged and reiterated the "three no's": no U.S. support for Taiwan independence; no support for two Chinas or one China, one Taiwan; and no support for Taiwan's entry into international organizations that require sovereignty for membership. Taiwan leaders chafed at Clinton's statement; but when Chen Shui-bian succeeded Lee in the presidency, he accepted the U.S. insistence on restraint.[168] Not so with Taiwan's Congressional supporters, who pushed for approval of closer U.S.–Taiwan military cooperation.[169]

On the Chinese side there are different kinds of domestic political considerations. As noted, the PLA for a number of years has been an advocate of toughness in dealing with the United States, and its voice is prominent in the pivotal Central Military Commission. Moreover, no Chinese leader can afford to appear supine on issues of national sovereignty, least of all Taiwan. Though "public opinion" does not have the same political meaning in China that it has in Western democracies, nationalist sensitivities are easily aroused in a rising China. The demonstrations against the U.S. bombing of China's Belgrade embassy were unusual, but as responses to American "bullying" and "hegemony" in world affairs, they were consistent with themes that appear regularly in the official press, over the Internet, in commentaries by PLA leaders, and in books by nationalistic young intellectuals.[170] Among the latter group is a "new left" (*xin zuo pai*) that is angry about the United States's persistent efforts to control and contain China. Though not an organized group, these people speak for a constituency that yearns for the times under Mao when China stood up to "U.S. imperialism."[171] Anti-Americanism among young Chinese, as reflected in opinion polls and popular books, is widespread, fed by negative portrayals of China in the U.S. media as well as by policy conflicts and trends, such as economic globalization, that are perceived as equivalent to Americanization.[172] China's leaders cannot ignore these voices, and may feel compelled to play to them.

A logical way to resolve the conflict would be an exchange of China's assurance not to use force for Taiwan's promise not to seek independence. That approach is not likely to work, however, since Beijing has always, as a matter of principle, reserved the right to decide the method of unification with Taiwan. Chas. Freeman has proposed another approach that has much to recommend it: "one China, but now now." The United States would continue to adhere to the one-China principle, but pressure Taiwan not to declare independence.

U.S. policy can no longer hope to deter war exclusively by keeping Beijing at bay. The United States must also discourage decisions and actions by Taipei that could leave Beijing with little choice but to react militarily. . . . Hence the United States should state unequivocally that it will not support or endorse any unilateral change in Taiwan's status by either Beijing or Taipei.[173]

Clinton's China trip in June 1998, during which he upset Taiwan authorities by publicly embracing the "three no's," was consistent with "one China, but not now."

One problem with "but not now," *as announced policy,* is that it keeps the American hand in the Taiwan question for a long time to come. Beijing cannot accept such a position, which contradicts public statements that it will not tolerate separation from Taiwan "indefinitely." An alternative U.S. policy that simply preserves the status quo and allows events to run their course—*one China and peaceful PRC–Taiwan relations*—serves not just the interests of all three parties, but equally those of the people who live on both sides of the Taiwan Strait. Tensions between China and Taiwan will rise and fall even then; but the status quo has too many benefits for either side to prefer a military confrontation. As time goes on, as exchanges deepen across the Strait, and as Taiwan does not openly challenge the one-China principle, it is reasonable to expect that China's leaders will become more open-minded about Taiwan's quest for higher international standing (e.g., travel by its leaders and membership as a territory of China in all regional and international bodies).

Second, all sides should agree as a matter of common interest to promote tension reduction in the Taiwan Strait area. Arms control and confidence-building measures, and avoidance of provocative moves by either side that threaten to alter the status quo, are essential. A reduction in PLA missile strength facing Taiwan is important, as is the verifiable redeployment of other weapons, such as submarines, that appear to be directed at Taiwan. Taiwan's willingness fully to open up direct trade, transportation, and other linkages to the mainland would be helpful.[174] Taiwan leaders have proposed various CBMs and cooperative projects that would promote common security.[175] On the U.S. side, tension-reducing steps should include a reduction of high tech arms sales to Taiwan and a decision against involving Taiwan in TMD. The longer Taiwan and the PRC are able to avoid serious tensions, and the broader their economic, tourist, and other interactions become, the greater the likelihood of a peaceful resolution—and of PRC–U.S. cooperation on common security issues.

## A Strong China or a Weak One?

The critical underpinning of the arguments advanced here is a changed perception of Chinese and U.S. security needs. China's nationalistic assertiveness is a given; its expansionism is not. For those analysts inclined to emphasize the dangers of China's rise, it is important to take into account not only the constraints

on the military mentioned earlier. Additionally, the social and economic complications of economic growth need to be considered, since many of them have implications for the country's stability. These include the mountain of debt accu-
mulated by state-owned enterprises and the banking system; problems arising
from economic decentralization, such as uncollected tax revenue; huge numbers
of migrant workers, unemployed, and underemployed; serious environmental
problems mentioned earlier, such as deforestation and air pollution; water
scarcity;[176] ethnic unrest; corruption, smuggling, drug trafficking, and other previously unknown criminal behavior, some of it involving high-level officials;[177]
and the inevitable clamor for political change.[178] With China's entry in WTO, the
Globalist vision for China will be sorely tested, since China is likely to experience still greater instabilities, at least in the short term. The Beijing leadership's
responses to unrest will not be to the liking of the U.S. government and many
domestic American interest groups.[179]

In the search for a new basis of partnership with China, the United States
would do well to focus on practical forms of cooperation that address the domestic sources of Chinese insecurity. Clinton was right to remind Americans of
the dangers that a weak China could pose; Chinese intellectuals need no re-
minding.[180] Equally important, however, is that neither a strong nor a weak
China is a matter of American choice. A strong China is inevitable; it cannot be
prevented. The core issue is likely to be that a strong China will be preoccupied
with internal problems that will offset external ambitions—except when paramount issues of sovereignty arise. Regional stability is thus best served not by
presuming that a strong China will be aggressive, nor by seeking to weaken
China through balance-of-power tactics, but rather by helping provide China
with the means of securing its people's livelihoods and protecting its resource
base—in a word, helping to refocus its security agenda in ways that also promote regional security. Such a *common security* agenda should be part of a
larger post–Cold War U.S. reappraisal of national and regional security frameworks, as I propose in chapter 7.

As noted, the prerequisites to common security are positive U.S.–China relations, foremost on the Taiwan issue, and a serious investment in multilateral approaches to security building. China has consistently rejected multilateral security
arrangements as being both premature and having the potential to be directed
against it. For China to rely on multilateral fora, such as in the South China Sea
disputes, it must be convinced that they will give PRC interests a fair hearing and
not be used by the United States to "gang up" on China. The U.S. Commander in
Chief, Pacific, Admiral Dennis Blair, put the matter this way:

The competing South China Sea claims provide nations with the opportunity to experience the benefits of collective dispute resolution. Success in this case will increase confidence that we can move from ancient balance-of-power thinking to approaches of security pluralism suited to the challenges of the twenty-first century.[181]

## NOTES

Portions of the chapter have appeared elsewhere: in Melvin Gurtov and Byong-Moo Hwang, *China's Security: The New Roles of the Military* (Boulder, Colo.: Lynne Rienner, 1999), especially ch. 7; "China's Military Modernization: Implications for Security Policy," in *The Future of China and Northeast Asia*, ed. Tae-Hwan Kwak and Melvin Gurtov (Seoul: Institute for Far Eastern Studies, Kyungnam University Press, 1997), 127–46.

1. Huan Xiang, "A Year of Turmoil, Transformation, and Disquiet," *Renmin ribao* (Beijing), January 2, 1988, 6.

2. See John W. Lewis and Xue Litai, *China's Strategic Seapower: The Politics of Force Modernization in the Nuclear Age* (Stanford, Calif.: Stanford University Press, 1994).

3. See *Xinshiqi Mao Zedong junshi sixiang di fazhan* (Development of Mao Zedong's Military Thought in the New Period) (Beijing: PLA Press, 1991), 113–14.

4. On the organization of these corporations, see John Frankenstein and Bates Gill, "Current and Future Challenges Facing Chinese Defence Industry," *China Quarterly*, no. 146 (June 1996): 401–403.

5. For specific instances of PLA protests, see Allen S. Whiting, "Chinese Nationalism and Foreign Policy After Deng," *China Quarterly*, no. 142 (Summer 1995): 295–316.

6. Whiting, "Chinese Nationalism and Foreign Policy After Deng," 315. Whiting appropriately distinguishes "assertive" from the more intense "aggressive" nationalism. Both kinds of nationalism identify a foreign enemy, but aggressive nationalism seeks to mobilize for action against it.

7. Concerning PRC motives in the South China Sea, see John W. Garver, "China's Push Through the South China Sea: The Interaction of Bureaucratic and National Interests," *The China Quarterly*, no. 132 (December 1992): 999–1028. On the Taiwan Strait exercises, see Gurtov and Hwang, *China's Security*, ch. 8.

8. Michael D. Swaine, *The Role of the Chinese Military in National Security Policymaking* (Santa Monica, Calif.: RAND Corp., 1996), 13.

9. They were named to the CMC in 1995. See Swaine, *The Role of the Chinese Military*, 15–16.

10. The businesses, usually estimated at around 20,000, were run by headquarters and military units at all levels of authority. They ranged from bars and hotels to rental of military property such as ships and planes. See Gurtov and Hwang, *China's Security*, and Thomas J. Bickford, "The Business Operations of the Chinese People's Liberation Army," *Problems of Post-Communism*, vol. 46, no. 6 (November–December 1999): 28–36. Jiang's demand for divestiture reportedly led to serious differences with PLA leaders over accusations of unlawful military activities, compensation for enterprises the PLA gives up, enterprises the conglomerates may keep, and possible investigations of the conduct of senior officers. See Susan V. Lawrence and Bruce Gilley, "Bitter Harvest," *Far Eastern Economic Review* (April 29, 1999): 22–27. Apparently, Jiang's order has not been fully carried out. See Mark Magnier, "Chinese Military Still Embedded in the Economy," *Los Angeles Times*, January 9, 2000.

11. On the importance of this lesson for PRC leaders, see Andrew Scobell, "Playing to Win: Chinese Army Building in the Era of Jiang Zemin," *Asian Perspective*, vol. 25, no. 1 (2001): 73–105.

12. Swaine, *Role of the Chinese Military*, 13, 34–35, 74.

13. John Pomfret, "China Plans Higher Defense Spending," *Washington Post*, March 6, 2000. The Chinese source is PRC State Council, News Bureau, *2000 nian Zhongguo*

*de guofang baipishu* (White Paper on China's National Defense in 2000), *Renmin ribao* (People's Daily, Beijing), November 6, 2000, online at www.peopledaily.com.cn.

14. Pomfret, "China plans." For balanced assessments of the military spending issue, see David Shambaugh, "China's Military: Real or Paper Tiger?" *Washington Quarterly*, vol. 19, no.2 (Spring 1996): 21, and Michael D. Swaine, "Chinese Military Modernization: Motives, Objectives, and Requirements," in *China's Economic Future: Challenges to U.S. Policy*, U.S. Congress, Joint Economic Committee, 104th Cong., 2d Sess., August 1996 (Washington, D.C.: U.S. Government Printing Office, 1996), 333.

15. China's three defense "white papers" issued since 1995 typically make these points. See, for example, the 1998 paper, "China's National Defense," in *Beijing Review*, no. 32 (August 10–16, 1998): 20; and *2000 nian Zhongguo de guofang baipishu*, part 3, 3, which states that 67 percent of the 2000 military budget was devoted to salaries and operations and maintenance and only 33 percent to equipment/weapons. Between 1987 and 1993, for example, China's *real* (inflation-adjusted) official military spending rose only 6.4 percent, far less than that of most Asian governments. U.S. General Accounting Office, *National Security: Impact of China's Military Modernization in the Pacific Region*, Report to Congressional Committees GAO/NSIAD-95-84, 1995, 26.

16. For example, Chinese figures ("China's National Defense," tables 3 and 4, 22) show that *official* military spending as a proportion of GDP declined steadily between 1978 and 1997, when it was 1.09 percent—lower than several other countries except Japan (0.99 percent). In 2000, China reported that the figure was 1.31 percent, again lower than the other major military powers. (*2000 nian Zhongguo de guofang baipishu*, part 3, p 4.) For generally supporting views of the PRC position, see Swaine, "Chinese Military Modernization," 333–34, and Shambaugh, "China's Military," 23.

17. Scobell, "Playing to Win."

18. *SIPRI Yearbook 2000*, table 7A.2, 372, online ed.

19. "Total Chinese arms exports declined 75 percent from 1990–98. China's share of the world arms market also declined significantly, especially in exports to developing countries." Medeiros and Gill, *Chinese Arms Exports*, viii–ix, 5–8.

20. Evan S. Medeiros and Bates Gill, *Chinese Arms Exports*, 8–12, and Richard F. Grimmett, *Conventional Arms Transfers to Developing Nations, 1987–1994*, Congressional Research Service Report No. 95-862F, August 4, 1995, table 1E, 34; online version (via www.fas.org).

21. Between 1987 and 1990, for example, China delivered 900 of these missiles; but between 1991 and 1994, it only delivered 270. Grimmet, *Conventional Arms Transfers*, table 3, 49.

22. Medeiros and Gill, *Chinese Arms Exports*, 26–27.

23. For a similar argument, see Bates Gill and Taeho Kim, *China's Arms Acquisitions from Abroad: A Quest for 'Superb and Secret Weapons,'* SIPRI Research Report No.11 (Oxford, U.K.: Oxford University Press, 1995), 98–99.

24. James Mulvenon, *Chinese Military Commerce and U.S. National Security*, RAND Paper DAR-1626-CAPP (June 1997), 26; Arthur S. Ding, "Is China a Threat? A Defense Industry Analysis," *Issues & Studies*, vol. 36, no. 1 (January–February 2000): 63–65; Medeiros and Gill, *Chinese Arms Exports*, 41–51 and, for a chart that depicts the place of military industries in the PRC organizational hierarchy, appendix 3, 93.

25. Mulvenon, *Chinese Military Commerce*, 13, reports that there are at least twenty to thirty PLA-affiliated companies in the United States, for instance.

26. For appraisals in the 1980s and early 1990s, see Richard A. Bitzinger, *Chinese Arms Production and Sales to the Third World*. RAND Note N-3334-USDP. (Santa Monica, Calif.: RAND Corporation, 1991), 26–28; Frankenstein and Gill, "Current and Future Challenges," 407–16; Bates Gill and Lonnie Henley, *China and the Revolution in Military Affairs* (Carlisle Barracks, Pa.: U.S. Army War College, 1996), 32–33; Gill and Kim, *China's Arms Acquisitions*; and Wendy Frieman, "China's Defense Industries," *The Pacific Review*, vol. 6, no. 1 (1993): 51–62.

27. A good overview is provided by Ding, "Is China a Threat?" 49–75.

28. Gill and Kim, *China's Arms Acquisitions*, 100–101.

29. Eric Arnett, "Military Technology," in *SIPRI Yearbook 1995*, 376.

30. See John Lewis and Xue Litai, *China Builds the Bomb* (Stanford, Calif.: Stanford University Press, 1988), and Lewis and Xue, *China's Strategic Seapower*.

31. The quotation is from Evan A. Feigenbaum, "Who's Behind China's High Technology 'Revolution,'" *International Security*, vol. 24, no. 1 (Summer 1999): 106; and see Wendy Frieman, "China's Defence Industries," 60–62.

32. Frankenstein and Gill, "Current and Future Challenges," 426.

33. Nazir Kamal, "China's Arms Export Policy and Responses to Multilateral Restraints," *Contemporary Southeast Asia*, vol. 14, no. 2 (September 1992): 133–35.

34. Gill and Kim, *China's Arms Acquisitions*, 35–43, 102.

35. Evidently, the extent of Russia-China closeness is a subject of dispute in Russian decision making circles. One foreign ministry specialist decried "some hotheads [who] already call for a Moscow-Beijing 'axis,'" as well as those Russians who worry about China's "demographic expansion" in the Far East. Russian policy, he wrote, should be guided by mutual economic interests and a balanced relationship with other countries, especially Japan. Evgeniy Bajanov, director of the Institute of Contemporary International Studies, Diplomatic Academy, RF Foreign Ministry, "Strong Rear As a Basis for Successful Offensive," *Obshchaya Gazeta*, no. 3 (January 9–15, 1997); and the same author's "Giants' Flexible Diplomacy," *Moskovskiye Novosti*, no. 5 (December 22–29, 1996), both excerpted in NAPSNet, January 14, 1997.

36. Israel for over a decade sold China technology (with a strong presumption that some of it originated in the United States) for jet fighters, tanks, and air-to-air missiles. See Jeff Gerth, "5 Charged in Plot to Export Arms," *New York Times*, November 16, 1989, 1; Michael R. Gordon, "Israel Sells Arms to China, U.S. Says," *New York Times*, October 13, 1993, 1; and Rowan Scarborough, "Chinese Arsenal Born in America," *Washington Post*, April 23, 2001.

37. Gill and Kim, *China's Arms Acquisitions*, 100.

38. Bates Gill, "Arms Acquisitions in East Asia," in Stockholm International Peace Research Institute, *SIPRI Yearbook 1994: World Armaments and Disarmament* (London: Oxford University Press, 1994), 556.

39. Gill and Kim, *China's Arms Acquisitions*, 103–104.

40. See Michael G. Gallagher, "China's Illusory Threat to the South China Sea," *International Security*, vol. 19, no. 1 (Summer 1994): 169–94.

41. Eric Rosenberg, "China's Weapons Buying Spree is on the Upswing," *Defense Week*, May 24, 1993, 2, via Center for Defense Information, online at www.cdi.org.

42. One informed Russian view is that these and other weapons sold to China are clearly intended for use in the Taiwan Strait and not, as some Russians are said to have argued, against Russia itself. (A. Surikov, "China Buys a War," *Pravda-5*, September 17, 1996, 3.) U.S. officials expressed no concern that these transactions went beyond nor-

mal modernization to pose a threat of a Russo-Chinese alliance. See, e.g., "Pentagon Spokesman's Regular Briefing," January 16, 1997; NAPSNet, same date.

43. Frankenstein and Gill, "Current and Future Challenges," 408.

44. In this latter group are *Sovremmeny*-class guided-missile destroyers. China purchased two such destroyers, and the first of them appeared in the Taiwan Strait in February 2000. Reportedly, the ships will be armed with *Sunburn* antiship missiles that are nuclear-capable but would probably have conventional warheads. See Craig S. Smith, "New Chinese Guided-Missile Ship Heightens Tension," *New York Times*, February 9, 2000, 1.

45. For some early examples, see Greg Austin, "The Strategic Implications of China's Public Order Crisis," *Survival*, vol. 37, no. 2 (Summer 1995): 7–23. In Xinjiang Province, for example, Moslems staged a "rebellion" in 1990: see Daniel Southerland, "China Confirms 22 Dead in Clash in Western Area," *Washington Post*, April 23, 1990. Uighurs have been fighting Chinese authorities in Xinjiang province since 1996, with thousands arrested: see Patrick E. Tyler, "Ethnic Strain in China's Far West Flares with Bombs and Rioting," *New York Times*, February 28, 1997, 1. John Pomfret of the *Washington Post* has written several articles on the urban and rural protests and the strong official reaction in most cases, including use of the army. See, for example, "Miners' Riot a Symbol of China's New Discontent," April 5, 2000 (in the mining town of Yangjiazhangzi; the largest known outbreak of violence over jobs and corruption); "Chinese Workers are Showing Disenchantment," April 23, 2000 (reporting the large increase in annual labor disputes since the early 1990s—to around 120,000 in 1999); "Separatists Defy Chinese Crackdown," January 26, 2000 (on the three-year-old campaign of Uighurs in Xinjiang who are seeking independence, evidently with external support, in what once was East Turkistan); and "Chinese Farmers Riot Over Taxes," August 31, 2000 (on farmer riots involving perhaps 20,000 in various townships of Jiangxi province, southern China). Farmer protests in Jiangxi resulted in a second major intervention by police and PAP forces a year later; see Erik Eckholm, "Chinese Raid Defiant Village, Killing 2, Amid Rural Unrest," *New York Times*, April 20, 2001, online ed.

46. Erik Eckholm, "Chinese Officials Order Cities to Bolster Riot Police Forces," *New York Times*, January 30, 2001, online ed.

47. Patrick E. Tyler, "China Battles a Spreading Scourge of Illicit Drugs," *New York Times*, November 15, 1995, 1.

48. A news article cited General Chi Haotian, the defense minister and CMC vice-chairman, as saying that "the law covers not only plans for repulsing foreign armed invasions, but also for instituting crackdowns on attempts to split the motherland, and on any rebellions or armed riots aiming to overthrow the socialist system." *China Daily*, May 13, 1996; NAPSNet, May 16, 1996.

49. Willy Wo-Lap Lam, "China's 'Great Wall of Steel' Could Enclose Hong Kong," *Japan Times* (Tokyo), November 22, 1996.

50. For a concise discussion, see Ronald N. Montaperto and Hans Binnendijk, "PLA Views on Asia Pacific Security in the 21$^{st}$ Century," *Strategic Forum*, no. 114 (June 1997): 1–4.

51. "Statement of Admiral Joseph W. Prueher, U.S. Navy, Before the House National Security Committee, Posture Hearing," March 6, 1997, 13 (mimeo.).

52. A prominent example of such an analytical bent is Richard Bernstein and Ross H. Munro, *The Coming Conflict with China*.

53. The article, by "Commentator," always an authoritative byline, said: "Strength determines everything. If the economy doesn't keep growing, if comprehensive national power doesn't keep strengthening, national security will lack a material foundation and basic guarantor. We will then have no way to struggle for our place among the world's

peoples. We should deeply recognize that we are still in the preliminary stage of socialism, there are still certain gaps in our economic strength, and the foundation of our national defense construction still is rather weak. Everything in the end is determined by economic development, everything depends on having a stable environment for development." *Renmin ribao*, April 7, 2001, online ed.

54. The continued prominence of the Cold War paradigm in U.S. policy was well described by two American China scholars: "Since the spring of 1989 China has gone from being perceived as reformist, poor, and weak to being seen as totalitarian, prosperous, and strong. . . . [Today] some Americans . . . regard China has a political pariah, an economic competitor and a potential strategic rival—the ingredients that go into making enemies." Scott Kennedy and Michael O'Hanlon, "Time to Shift Gears on China Policy," *Journal of East Asian Affairs* (Winter–Spring 1996); online via Nautilus Institute, www.nautilus.org.

55. See Jane Perlez, "Hopes for Improved Ties with China Fade," *New York Times*, February 12, 1999, A6. Following that article, U.S.–China relations deteriorated dramatically when Chinese Premier Zhu Rongji's official visit (in April) failed to wrest American agreement to China's entry into the World Trade Organization, and (in May) when NATO bombers killed three Chinese in a mistaken bombing raid over Belgrade that hit the PRC embassy. Though some of the diplomatic damage was repaired subsequently—the two countries reached agreement on WTO, and Washington compensated the bombing victims—it was not enough to overcome lingering suspicions and disagreements on other issues.

56. The other two parts of the instruction are "to increase mutual trust" and "to reduce trouble." See Quansheng Zhao, *Interpreting Chinese Foreign Policy: The Micro-Macro Linkage Approach* (Hong Kong: Oxford University Press, 1996), 221.

57. For example, see Steven Mufson, "China Puts Forth Persistent, Caustic Anti-U.S. Themes," *Washington Post*, August 13 1996.

58. See Kenneth Lieberthal, "Domestic Forces and Sino-U.S. Relations," in *Living With China: U.S./China Relations in the Twenty-First Century*, ed. Ezra F. Vogel (New York: W.W. Norton, 1997), 258–63. Among the internal Chinese issues that engage the attention of U.S. interest groups are religious freedom, treatment of workers, prisoner labor, trade, intellectual property rights, and political dissent.

59. Illustrative of the debate over China's intentions are two articles: Richard Bernstein and Ross H. Munro, "The Coming Conflict with America," and Robert S. Ross, "Beijing as a Conservative Power," both in *Foreign Affairs*, vol. 76, no. 2 (March–April 1997): 18–32 and 33–44, respectively.

60. Lieberthal, "Domestic Forces" in *Living with China*, ed. Vogel, 270, provides a few specific examples. See also Gurtov and Hwang, *China's Security*, 8, 58–59, and Jianwei Wang, "Managing Conflict: Chinese Perspectives on Multilateral Diplomacy and Collective Security," in *In the Eyes of the Dragon: China Views the World*, ed. Yong Deng and Fei-Ling Wang (Lanham, Md.: Rowman & Littlefield, 1999), 73–96.

61. Concerning the surfacing of nationalism in Chinese views of the United States from 1999 on, see Xiaoxiong Yi, "Dynamics of China's South Korea Policy: Assertive Nationalism, Beijing's Changing Strategic Evaluation of the United States, and the North Korea Factor," *Asian Perspective*, vol. 24, no. 1 (2000): 71–102.

62. On these and other elements of Chinese security thinking, I draw from Gurtov and Hwang, *China's Security*, chs. 1–2.

63. For an interesting discussion of China's "global nationalism," see Thomas G. Moore, "China and Globalization," *Asian Perspective*, vol. 23, no. 4 (1999): 65–95.

64. William S. Cohen, *Report of the Quadrennial Defense Review 1997* (May 1997), www.dtic.mil/defenselink.

65. Speech to the National Press Club, December 14, 2000, in *New York Times*, December 15, 2000, A22.

66. George J. Tenet (Director of Central Intelligence), "The Worldwide Threat in 2000: Global Realities of Our National Security," statement before the Senate Select Committee on Intelligence, February 2, 2000; online at www.nyu.edu/globalbeat/usdefense/Tenet020200.html.

67. See Steven Mufson, "Clash with China Strengthens Hard-Liners," *Washington Post*, April 23, 2001, online ed.

68. Walter B. Slocombe, Undersecretary of Defense for Policy, "U.S. Security Interests in the Pacific," statement before a hearing of the House Committee on International Relations, Subcommittee on Asia and the Pacific, May 11, 1998, via Internet.

69. On the U.S. side, examples of the melding of Globalism with Realism may be seen in Joseph S. Nye Jr., "East Asian Security: The Case for Deep Engagement," *Foreign Affairs*, vol. 74, no. 4 (July–August 1995): 90–102; and U.S. Department of Defense, Office of International Security Affairs, *The United States Security Strategy for the East Asia-Pacific Region* (November 1998), 30–31.

70. As in Clinton's speech before the U.S. Institute of Peace, Washington, D.C., April 7, 1999, in which he said: "As we focus on the potential challenge that a strong China could present to the United States in the future, let us not forget the risk of a weak China, beset by internal conflicts, social dislocation and criminal activity, becoming a vast zone of instability in Asia." Text provided by NAPSNet, April 8, 1999.

71. The clearest statement of that objective was Clinton's speech at Johns Hopkins University on March 8, 2000, in which he argued that bringing China into the World Trade Organization would promote the export to China not only of products, but also of individual freedom and political reform. Full text in *New York Times*, March 9, 2000, online ed.

72. As Clinton told Jiang in December 1995, "The greatest threat to our security that you [in China] present is that all of your people will want to get rich in exactly the same way we got rich. And unless we try to triple the automobile mileage and to reduce greenhouse gas emissions, if you all get rich in that way we won't be breathing very well." So Clinton expressed the hope of environmental and economic cooperation to develop China in nonthreatening ways. Thomas L. Friedman, "Gardening with Beijing," *New York Times*, April 17, 1996, A23.

73. Statement of Jeffrey Bader, Deputy Assistant Secretary of State for East Asia and Pacific Affairs, U.S. Congress, House Committee on International Relations, Subcommittee on Asia and the Pacific, *Hearing: Sino-American Relations and U.S. Policy Options*, 105th Cong., 1st Sess., April 23, 1997 (Washington, D.C.: U.S. GPO, 1997), 4.

74. Joseph S. Nye Jr., "Conflicts After the Cold War: Realism, Liberalism, and U.S. Interests," in *The Future of American Foreign Policy*, 3d ed., ed. Eugene R. Wittkopf and Christopher M. Jones (New York: St. Martin's/Worth, 1999), 68–82.

75. Murray Weidenbaum and Harvey Sicherman, "The Chinese Economy: A New Scenario," *Wire* (Foreign Policy Research Institute), vol. 7, no. 1 (January 1999), online via fpri@aol.com.

76. For example, the failure of the U.S. Senate to ratify the CTBT; the consistent U.S. rejection of a no-first-use policy with respect to nuclear weapons, which China has long supported; the maintenance of very large strategic nuclear forces long after the Cold War

ended; and inconsistent application of nuclear nonproliferation policies, the notable case being Israel.

77. The first paper, "China: Arms Control and Disarmament," was issued in 1995. The second, which provides a full listing of China's accessions to international arms control agreements, is Information Office of the State Council, "China's National Defense," in *Beijing Review*, no. 32 (August 10–16, 1998): 12–34. The third paper was issued in October 2000 by the same Information Office. The Chinese text, "White Paper: China's National Defense in 2000," was published online by *Renmin ribao*, November 6, 2000.

78. For the full record, see Monterey Institute of International Studies, Center for Nonproliferation Studies, "Chinese Participation and Positions Regarding Various Arms Control and Nonproliferation Agreements, Organizations, and Regimes," April 1999, online at cns.miis.edu/cns/projects/eanp/fact/cregime.htm.

79. Sha Zukang, Director General of the Department of Arms Control and Disarmament, Ministry of Foreign Affairs, "Some Thoughts on Non-Proliferation," speech to the 7th Annual Carnegie International Non-Proliferation Conference, Washington, D.C., January 11–12, 1999, mimeo.

80. See the conference reports of the Monterey Institute for International Studies, *Individuals, Institutions and Policies in the Chinese Nonproliferation and Arms Control Community*, Monterey, Calif. November 6–9, 1997, and *U.S.–China Conference on Arms Control, Disarmament and Nonproliferation*, Beijing, September 23–25, 1998. A chart depicting the organization of China's arms control community can be found online at the Monterey Institute's Center for Nonproliferation Studies website: www.cns.miis.edu/cns/projects/eanp/pubs/chinaorg.htm.

81. Alastair Iain Johnston, "But Is It Socialization? International Institutional Effects on Chinese Arms Control Policy," MIT Security Studies Program Seminar, May 13, 1998.

82. Wang Jisi, "U.S. Policy Toward China: Containment or Engagement?" *American Studies in China*, vol. 2 (1995): 24–39. Wang heads the Institute of American Studies in the Chinese Academy of Social Sciences, Beijing.

83. Deng and Wang, "Introduction: Toward an Understanding of China's Worldview," in *In the Eyes of the Dragon*, ed. Deng and Wang, 10.

84. As a Chinese host of U.S. visitors said, "China is most concerned with its own internal development and the United States is most concerned with trying to maintain international order. Therefore, our agendas are different." David M. Lampton, "A Growing China in a Shrinking World: Beijing and the Global Order," in *Living with China*, ed. Vogel, 121.

85. See Richard P. Suttmeier, "Does 'Globalization' Matter? Technology and the Changing Context of U.S.–China Relations," *In Depth*, vol. 4, no. 3 (Fall 1994): 65–83.

86. Wang Jisi, "U.S. Policy Toward China," 31.

87. In ICBMs, for instance, China is believed to have only "about 20" land-based missiles (CSS-4 class that can reach the United States), whereas the United States has thousands of missiles that can hit Chinese targets. The ICBM China successfully tested in August 1999, believed to have a 5,000-mile range (the mobile DF-31), "will be targeted primarily against Russia and Asia." National Intelligence Council, "Foreign Missile Developments and the Ballistic Missile Threat to the United States Through 2015," 8, online at www.cia.gov/cia/publications/nie/nie99msl.html#rtoc12.

88. Robert G. Sutter, *The China Quandary: Domestic Determinants of U.S. China Policy, 1972–1982* (Boulder, Colo.: Westview, 1983), 20–21. Anti-Sovietism was not the only common policy; others were strategic stability on the Korean peninsula and ensuring that Taiwan did not pursue independence or nuclear arms.

89. Michael Dobbs, "Kissinger Offered China Satellite Data in 1973, Papers Show," *Washington Post*, January 10, 1999.

90. Linda Mathews, "400 Permits to Ship High Technology to China Approved," *Los Angeles Times*, September 11, 1980. The deal was announced in Beijing by William J. Perry, then undersecretary of defense. It included electronics gear, equipment for a helicopter plant in Harbin, radar and instrumentation systems, and computers. Perry was also reported to have said that China was willing to supply the United States with critical metals for aircraft manufacturing. See also Sutter, *China Quandary*, 113–14.

91. William J. Broad, "Spies vs. Sweat: The Debate Over China's Nuclear Advance," *New York Times*, September 7, 1999, A14. As Broad reports, these exchanges, which were later the subject of much criticism by U.S. congressmen who believed it enabled the Chinese to steal U.S. nuclear secrets, actually greatly increased U.S. knowledge of China's nuclear weapons programs.

92. George Lardner Jr. and R. Jeffrey Smith, "Intelligence Ties Endure Despite U.S.-China Strain," *Washington Post*, June 25, 1989.

93. The full story of the U.S.–PRC talks that led to normalization is told by Patrick Tyler, "The (Ab)normalization of U.S.–Chinese Relations," *Foreign Affairs*, vol. 78, no. 5 (September–October 1999): 93–122. On PRC peace overtures and other conciliatory moves, see Sutter, *China Quandary*, 41–43.

94. In the third communiqué, the U.S. promised that arms sales to Taiwan "will not exceed, either in qualitative or in quantitative terms, the level of those supplied in recent years" since 1972, and that "it intends gradually to reduce its sale of arms to Taiwan, leading, over a period of time, to a final resolution." Beijing would later charge that the United States never abided by that agreement, most flagrantly with Bush's approval of the sale in 1992 of 150 F-16s. PRC State Council, Taiwan Affairs Office and Information Office, *The Taiwan Question and Reunification of China*, August 1993, 9.

95. See Harry Harding Jr., "Breaking the Impasse Over Human Rights," in *Living With China*, ed. Vogel, 168–69.

96. Harry Harding, *A Fragile Relationship: The United States and China since 1972* (Washington, D.C.: Brookings Institution, 1992).

97. Letter of Frank C. Conahan, Director, U.S. Government Accounting Office, to Congressman Al Swift, in which it is reported that "the Department of Commerce approved 1,080 licenses to export dual-use, nuclear-related items to the PRC during the period July 1, 1981 to June 30, 1982" valued at $103 million. Computers and computer equipment accounted for around 80 percent of the total value.

98. Harding, *A Fragile Relationship*, table 371.

99. U.S. Department of State, "U.S.-China Nuclear Cooperation Agreement," *Current Policy*, no. 1729, n.d.

100. U.S. Senate, Select Committee on Intelligence, *Report on Impacts to U.S. National Security of Advanced Satellite Technology Exports to the People's Republic of China (PRC), and Report on the PRC's Efforts to Influence U.S. Policy*, 106th Cong., 1st Sess., May 1999, 3–4, online at www.apbonline.com/911/1999/05/06/report.htm. After Tiananmen, these launches required a presidential waiver. George Bush signed three waivers for nine satellite launchings, and Clinton signed eight waivers for eleven launchings. Brent Scowcroft and Arnold Kanter, "What Technology Went Where," *Washington Times*, June 5, 1998

101. Richard K. Betts, "Wealth, Power, and Instability: East Asia and the United States After the Cold War," *International Security*, vol. 18, no. 3 (Winter 1993–94): 75. In criticism of liberal theorists, Betts further argued: "Gambling that democracy will underwrite peace is a

reasonable risk, but compounding the wager by gambling that wealth will produce democracy some time in the future is compromising balance of power norms too much" (75).

102. Jin Canrong (Institute of American Studies, Chinese Academy of Social Sciences), "Sino-US Relations: An Overview," *Beijing Review*, no. 43 (October 21–27, 1996): 10.

103. See the discussion of the 1994 "Title V report" of the U.S. State Department's Office of Global Affairs in Suttmeier, "Does 'Globalization' Matter?" 69–70.

104. Boeing Company estimate in *New York Times*, April 24, 1997, C3.

105. Richard P. Suttmeier and Peter C. Evans, "China Goes Nuclear," *The China Business Review*, September–October 1996, 16–21; Nigel Holloway, "No Sale Just Yet," *Far Eastern Economic Review* (June 19, 1997): 14.

106. A Merrill Lynch estimate for the U.S. industry's sales by 2007; see Shawn W. Crispin, "Technical Problem," *Far Eastern Economic Review* (February 25, 1999): 31.

107. Julia Chang Bloch, "Commercial Diplomacy," in *Living With China*, ed. Vogel 204. There is, however, concern among industrialists, namely, that China might eventually erase the U.S.'s competitive edge as they acquire advanced electronics and other technologies.

108. For instance, Hughes Electronics and Loral Space and Communications together contributed $2.5 million to the Democrats between 1991 and early 1998. The money, and other forms of support of Clinton's causes, seemed to represent good investments in light of Clinton's previously noted waivers for commercial satellite exports to China. Loral's chief executive accompanied Secretary of Commerce Ron Brown to China, there won a telephone satellite deal, and successfully petitioned the president to shift licensing authority over satellites to the Commerce Department. More generally, the U.S.–China Business Council took the lead in lobbying on behalf of TNCs. For an account of the business community's pressure tactics, see David E. Sanger, "How Push by China and U.S. Business Won Over Clinton," *New York Times*, April 15, 1999, 1.

109. Testimony of Jeffrey Bader, *Hearing: Sino-American Relations and U.S. Policy Options*, 12–13.

110. Jeff Gerth and David E. Sanger, "How Chinese Won Rights to Launch Satellites for U.S.," *New York Times*, May 17, 1998, 1; Jeff Gerth and John M. Broder, "The White House Dismissed Warnings on China Satellite Deal," *New York Times*, June 1, 1998, A13. Even in the Defense Department and the CIA, opposition to dual-use sales to China has come from the rank-and-file, not necessarily from the leadership. Both William J. Perry, the Secretary of Defense, and John M. Deutch, the Director of Central Intelligence, regarded efforts to restrict dual-use sales as "a hopeless task," in Perry's words. *New York Times*, October 19, 1998, A14.

111. Harold J. Johnson, U.S. Government Accounting Office (National Security and International Affairs Division), *China: U.S. and European Union Arms Sales since the 1989 Embargoes*, testimony before the U.S. Congress, Joint Economic Committee, GAOA/T-NSIAD-98-171, April 28, 1998, 6–7.

112. *New York Times*, October 19, 1998, A14.

113. As a sop to the industry, the State Department promised to review satellite licenses within thirty working days. But it remained up to the Pentagon to render a final judgment of the national security implications of such sales. See *New York Times*, January 22, 1999, A11. In February 1999, the Clinton administration canceled a Hughes satellite sale worth $450 million. Once again, the Commerce Department approved the sale, but the State and Defense Departments objected. The satellite was intended for a regional

telephone network; but the departments cited the fact that the buyer, a PRC company based in Singapore, included PLA investors, thus possibly giving the PLA access to technology that could improve ICBM accuracy and enabling it to control use of the satellite once in orbit. *New York Times*, February 23, 1999, 1. As noted later, Clinton cleared the way for Chinese launches of U.S. communications satellites just before he left office.

114. As implied in the 2000 defense white paper, *2000 nian Zhongguo de guofang baipishu*, part 3, 4.

115. On the PLA's targeting of information systems, see the testimony of James R. Lilley, former U.S. ambassador to China, in U.S. Congress, Senate, Select Committee on Intelligence, *Hearing on People's Republic of China*, 105th Cong., 1st Sess., September 18, 1997 (Washington, D.C.: U.S. GPO, 1998), 18–19. Regarding PLA solicitations of foreign firms, see James Harding, "China Courts Arms Suppliers," *Financial Times* (London), July 14, 1997.

116. Matt Forney, "China Draws Line in the Sand on PLA," *The Asian Wall Street Journal*, December 15, 1998; *New York Times*, March 21, 1999.

117. Mulvenon, *Chinese Military Commerce*, 28–29.

118. One set of political contributions is said to have been made by China Aerospace and China International Trust and Investment Corporation (CITIC), corporations that stood to benefit from removal of licensing requirements from satellite deals with Hughes Electronics Corporation and Loral Space and Communications. See: Jeff Gerth, "Democrat Fund-Raiser Said to Detail China Tie," *New York Times*, May 15, 1998, A1; and Jeff Gerth and David E. Sanger, "How China Won Rights to Launch Satellites for U.S.," *New York Times*, May 17, 1998, online ed. A second contribution to the Clinton re-election campaign, amounting to $300,000, apparently came from the Intelligence Bureau of the PLA General Staff Department via a Chinese American businessman, according to the U.S. Justice Department. *Los Angeles Times*, April 4 1999; *Far Eastern Economic Review* (April 15, 1999): 12–13.

119. Jeff Gerth, "U.S. Business Role in Policy on China is Under Question," *New York Times*, April 13, 1998, 1; *New York Times*, May 7, 1999, A19. Scientists of the two companies had been asked by the Chinese to assess the causes of two rocket booster failures in which Hughes and Loral satellites were to be launched.

120. It remains unclear whether McDonnell Douglas or its Chinese partner, CATIC, was responsible for the obfuscation about the jets' equipment that allowed the export license to be issued. Jeff Gerth and David E. Sanger, "Aircraft Deal with Chinese is Questioned," *New York Times*, October 30, 1996, 1.

121. Bloch, "Commercial Diplomacy," 203–4.

122. Mulvenon, *Chinese Military Commerce*, 30. In one instance, the end user was COSTIND.

123. A supercomputer was diverted in 1997 to a military research facility in Hunan rather than shipped as agreed to a science institute in Beijing. The system was sold to a Hong Kong company that resold it, thus avoiding the licensing requirement. When U.S. authorities discovered the diversion, they investigated and sought to retrieve it; but the Chinese refused to allow the supercomputer to be inspected. Jeff Gerth, "U.S. Complains to China About Supercomputer," *New York Times*, July 2, 1997, online. On the supercomputer sales, see Jeff Gerth, "China Buying U.S. Computers, Raising Arms Fears," *New York Times*, June 10, 1997, 1, and Barbara Opall, "China Possesses Hundreds of U.S. Supercomputers," *Defense News*, June 16–22, 1997, 1.

124. *New York Times*, May 14, 1999, 1. Published reports at the time lent credence to U.S. government allegations that an employee of Chinese descent at the Los Alamos National Laboratory, Wen Ho Lee, transmitted highly sensitive nuclear weapon design data via computer to China. (Walter Pincus, "U.S. Cracking Down on Chinese Designs on Nuclear Data," *Washington Post*, February 17, 1999; James Risen and Jeff Gerth, "China Stole Nuclear Secrets for Bombs, U.S. Aides Say," *New York Times*, March 6, 1999, 1.) Though unauthorized downloading of computer files did occur, it never led to proof that information was passed on to PRC sources. To the contrary, Lee, who was jailed on espionage charges, was released; the judge castigated the U.S. government for misleading him on the evidence and apologized to the accused. On the case and the faulty journalism that contributed to the spying charges, see Robert Scheer, "No Defense: How the *New York Times* Convicted Wen Ho Lee," *The Nation*, October 23, 2000, 11–20.

125. See Jane Perlez, "China to Halt Sales of the Technology to Launch A-Arms," *New York Times*, November 22, 2000, 1.

126. See, for example, *New York Times*, February 28, 1999.

127. What China sees as threats to internal security and to its ability to persist in economic and political reforms, the United States sees as state repression and failure to live up to commitments on improving human rights. See the annual report of the U.S. State Department, "China Country Report on Human Rights Practices for 1998," February 26, 1999, online at www.state.gov.

128. The U.S. corporate community and Heritage Foundation estimate that between 190,000 and 200,000 American jobs are linked directly to China trade. U.S. Congress, *Hearing: Sino-American Relations and U.S. Policy Options*, 26.

129. A month before the summit, Premier Li Peng signed off on new nuclear trade export control regulations that the United States had also insisted upon.

130. See Barbara Opall, "China Possesses Hundreds of U.S. Supercomputers," *Defense News*, June 16–22, 1997; and Feigenbaum, "Who's Behind," 11.

131. Mulvenon, *Chinese Military Commerce*, 27.

132. The U.S. Senate Select Committee on Intelligence merely stated that "the technology transferred to the PRC during these two launch failure investigations [that were aided by U.S. companies] may improve the PRC's space launch and ballistic missile programs." See *Report on Impacts to U.S. National Security of Advanced Satellite Technology Exports to the People's Republic of China (PRC), and Report on the PRC's Efforts to Influence U.S. Policy*, 106th Cong., 1st Sess., May 1999, 15; online at www.apbonline.com/911/1999/05/06/report.html.

133. Scowcroft and Kanter, "What Technology Went Where"; Risen and Gerth, "China Stole Nuclear Secrets," *New York Times*.

134. Briefing at the Carnegie Endowment for International Peace by Gary Samore, Special Assistant to the President and Senior Director for Nonproliferation and Export Controls at the National Security Council, March 17, 1999, online at www.ceip.org; testimony of Stanley O. Roth, Assistant Secretary of State for East Asian and Pacific Affairs, before the Senate Foreign Relations Committee, May 14, 1998 (transcript), 7 (referring to a reported Chinese shipment to Iran in 1998 of chemicals that could supposedly be used to convert uranium).

135. The advantages include increased understanding of how to improve the safety of nuclear weapon stockpiles, enhance command and control of nuclear weapons, and prevent theft, smuggling, and other avenues of nuclear weapon proliferation. Among the few places where such advantages were mentioned are Bill Richardson (U.S. Sec-

retary of Energy), "Don't Quarantine Our Scientists," *New York Times*, May 7, 1999, A25, and the unclassified introduction to the April 1999 report by the panel headed by Admiral David Jeremiah, which reviewed an interagency panel's "Damage Assessment" of alleged Chinese espionage at U.S. nuclear laboratories (CIA press release, online at www.odci.gov/cia/public_affairs/press_release/0421kf.html).

136. See "The Intelligence Community Damage Assessment on the Implications of China's Acquisition of US Nuclear Weapons Information on the Development of Future Chinese Weapons," April 21, 1999, press release online at the CIA web site.

137. This includes the work of the U.S. House of Representatives Select Committee on U.S. National Security and Military/Commercial Concerns with the People's Republic of China, the so-called Cox Committee chaired by Christopher Cox, Republican of California. That committee's work was politically driven; it set out to prove that espionage explained China's successful miniaturization of its nuclear weapons. For a survey of the doubtful aspects of the report, see Walter Pincus, "China Spy Gains Overvalued, Two Former Lab Directors Say," *Washington Post*, May 30, 1999.

138. The Damage Assessment panel cited above was unable to determine "whether any [nuclear] weapon design documentation or blueprints were acquired" by China. It also stated: "To date, the aggressive Chinese collection effort has not resulted in any apparent modernization of their deployed strategic force or any new nuclear weapons deployment."

139. The above-cited "Damage Assessment" concluded that China's nuclear weapons program was "probably accelerated" by espionage. But the report also said: "We believe it is more likely that the Chinese used US design information to inform their own program than to replicate US weapon designs." A top-secret report prepared for the president in November 1998 by U.S. counterintelligence officials concluded that "Beijing's exploitation of U.S. national laboratories has substantially aided its nuclear weapons program," mainly in the area of nuclear stockpile "stewardship." Jeff Gerth and James Risen, "1998 Report Told of Lab Breaches and China Threat," *New York Times*, May 2, 1999, online ed. If stewardship was the principal Chinese gain, however, perhaps that should count as a contribution to strategic stability, since the better China can maintain its existing weapons, the less reason it has to produce more of them or find ways (as the United States has found) to test them without formally violating the CTBT. Finally, there is the question of double standards. Accusations of Chinese misbehavior could just as easily be applied to the United States. Take spying, for instance: the apparent discovery of spying by China was itself the result of espionage—by U.S. agents in China and from intercepted Chinese communications. Associated Press report, Washington, D.C., April 23, 1999.

140. See Avery Goldstein, "How to Deal With Beijing," NAPSNet Special Report, March 29, 1999, online.

141. For an excellent discussion of how the United States can lead by "acting like the responsible great power that it wants China to become," see Samuel S. Kim, "China As a Great Power," *Current History*, vol. 96, no. 611 (September 1997): 246–51. *Per contra*, see Douglas H. Paal, "China and the East Asian Security Environment: Complementarity and Competition," in *Living With China*, ed. Vogel, ch. 2. Paal favors engaging China, but on the all-too-familiar basis of balance-of-power management designed to move China toward "constructive" and not "counter-productive" behavior.

142. Susan M. Puska, *New Century, Old Thinking: The Dangers of the Perceptual Gap in U.S.–China Relations* (Carlisle Barracks, Penn.: Strategic Studies Institute, U.S. Army

War College, 1998); Michael Pillsbury, *Dangerous Chinese Misperceptions: The Implications for DoD*, report (Washington, D.C.: Office of Net Assessment, 1998).

143. For a good review of U.S.–China military exchanges, see Kenneth W. Allen and Eric A. McVadon, *China's Foreign Military Relations*, Report no. 32 (Washington, D.C.: Henry L. Stimson Center, October 1999), 71–77.

144. There was improvement in this area as a result of the Clinton–Jiang summit in 1997. Regular high-level strategic dialogues began in December 1997, and the Military Maritime Consultation Agreement of January 1998 to prevent misunderstanding during air and sea maneuvers. (See Department of Defense, *The United States Security Strategy*, 34.) Military exchanges were restored in January 2000 with the visit to Washington of Lt. Gen. Xiong Guangkai, Director of Intelligence and Deputy Chief of the PLA general staff, to hold the third round of Defense Consultative Talks. These steps no doubt contributed to the resumption in June 2000 of long-suspended arms control talks. An effort to resurrect the joint China–U.S. commission on defense conversion would be another positive step. The commission was established in 1994 but was killed by the U.S. Congress. Concerns about China's diversion of U.S. technologies to military uses would seem to be considerably outweighed by the common interest in promoting China's civilian applications of military-industrial facilities and technologies.

145. In February 2000, the PRC, with Russian support, officially proposed to ban the use of space for military purposes, including testing and deploying weapons. The proposal was clearly intended to preempt U.S. plans to deploy a theater or national missile defense system and thus breach the U.S.-USSR 1972 Anti-Ballistic Missile Treaty.

146. David Brown, "Dialogue in Neutral: Private Sector in Gear," *Comparative Connections*, www.csis.org/pacfor/cc/004Qchina_taiwan.html.

147. Raymond F. Burghardt, Director of the American Institute in Taiwan, "The U.S. Role in Asia-Pacific Security," speech to the Asia-Pacific Security Forum Conference "The Dynamics of Asia-Pacific Security: A Fin-de-Siecle Assessment," December 17, 1999; NAPSNet special report, December 21, 1999.

148. As one careful study of weapons acquisitions by Taiwan and the PRC has concluded, they "not only are engaged in a competitive arms process, but [their] competition is heavily weighted toward the types of weapons that have the potential to destabilize the existing military balance" between them. Michael D. Wallace, Brian L. Job, Jean Clermont and André Laliberté, "Rethinking Arms Races: Asymmetry and Volatility in the Taiwan Strait Case," *Asian Perspective*, vol. 25, no. 1 (2001), 187.

149. Stanley O. Roth, Senate testimony of May 14, 1998, 8.

150. As Suisheng Zhao has written, PRC strategy sought to "send a loud message to Taipei and Washington: If Taiwan independence emerges and if foreign countries interfere in what Beijing considers China's internal affairs, then Beijing would settle it by military means." Zhao, "Taiwan: From Peaceful Offense to Coercive Strategy," in *In the Eyes of the Dragon*, ed. Deng and Wang, 232.

151. Chas. W. Freeman Jr., "Preventing War in the Taiwan Strait: Restraining Taiwan—and Beijing," *Foreign Affairs*, vol. 77, no. 4 (July–August 1998): 6–11.

152. See Zhao, "Taiwan," in *In the Eyes of the Dragon*, ed. Deng and Wang, 231, and Gurtov and Hwang, *China's Security*, 275–76.

153. For a typical view, which portrays TMD as an offensive as well as defensive system, see Hong Yuan (Institute of World Economics & Politics, Chinese Academy of Social Sciences), "The Implication of TMD System in Japan to China's Security" (paper

presented at the Sixth ISODARCO Beijing Seminar on Arms Control, October 29–November 1, 1998, Shanghai), online at www.nyu.edu/globalbeat/asia/Yuan0899.html.

154. Xie Wenqing, "US TMD and Taiwan," *International Strategic Studies* (Beijing), no. 3 (2000): 25–30. For similar PRC views on TMD, see Monterey Institute, *U.S.–China Conference on Arms Control*, 15–16.

155. Actually, the most persuasive reason for scratching ballistic missile defense is the faulty strategic and technological thinking that underlies it. The program has experienced repeated failures and rigged tests that raise serious questions about its technological feasibility no less than about its political wisdom. Among many critiques, see Robert L. Park, "Another 'Star Wars' Sequel," *New York Times*, February 15, 1999, A21; Joseph Cirincione, "Missile Defense Failures Offer Lessons," *Proliferation Brief*, vol. 2, no. 7 (March 30, 1999), online at the Carnegie Endowment for International Peace web site, www.ceip.org; and, on rigged tests, the *New York Times*, June 9, 2000, 1.

156. Michael O'Hanlon, "Why China Cannot Conquer Taiwan," *International Security*, vol. 25, no. 2 (Fall 2000): 51–86.

157. The February 14, 1999, issue of the PLA organ, *Liberation Army Daily*, warned that "since the United States can diffuse missile technology to Northeast Asia, other countries can naturally also diffuse missile technology to the Middle East, South Asia, and even to America's backyard." A senior PRC diplomat in Washington, He Yafei, said that TMD "will cause a new arms race. This is very destabilizing." (Bob Drogin, "Defense Project Strains U.S.-China Ties," *Los Angeles Times*, March 22, 1999, online ed.) Leading members of the PRC arms control community have pointedly stated that a decision to join the MTCR hinges on U.S. policy toward Taiwan with respect to military aid as well as TMD. Monterey Institute, *U.S.–China Conference on Arms Control*, 19.

158. See Richard D. Fisher, Jr., "China Rockets Into Military Space," *The Asian Wall Street Journal*, December 28, 1998, 6.

159. See the Jeremiah committee's report, cited in n. 136.

160. See David E. Sanger and Erik Eckholm, "Will Beijing's Nuclear Arsenal Stay Small or Will It Mushroom?" *New York Times*, March 15, 1999, online ed.; Michael R. Gordon and Steven Lee Myers, "Risk of Arms Race Seen in U.S. Design of Missile Defense," *New York Times*, May 27, 2000, online ed.

161. David E. Sanger and Erik Eckholm, "Will Beijing's Nuclear Arsenal Stay Small or Will It Mushroom?" *New York Times*, March 15, 1999, online ed.

162. *New York Times*, February 7, 1999, online, based on an Associated Press report that cited a story in the Taipei *United Daily News*.

163. See the April 14, 1999, testimony on the Taiwan Relations Act of the Deputy Assistant Secretary of State for East Asian and Pacific Affairs, Susan Shirk, and the Deputy Assistant Secretary of Defense for International Security Affairs, Kurt Campbell, online from NAPSNet, April 16, 1999. Campbell's testimony included the statement that "we have helped Taiwan achieve a formidable capacity to defend itself and to maintain a strong defense posture." The same message was given by the principal U.S. representative in Taiwan, Raymond F. Burghardt, "The U.S. Role in Asia-Pacific Security."

164. Shirley A. Kan, "Taiwan: Major U.S. Arms Sales Since 1990," CRS Report RS20483, June 20, 2000, 2. The report also mentions unlisted additional military transfers, such as commercial sales, "leases of naval vessels and other equipment," and training of Taiwan military personnel.

165. Michael D. Swaine, *Taiwan's National Security, Defense Policy, and Weapons Procurement Processes* (Santa Monica, Calif.: RAND Corporation, 1999), 70–71.

166. David A. Shlapak, David T. Orletsky, and Barry A. Wilson, *Dire Strait? Military Aspects of the China-Taiwan Confrontation and Options for U.S. Policy* (Santa Monica, Calif.: RAND Corp., 2000).

167. The sales package included four *Kidd*-class destroyers, which were in mothballs; eight diesel-powered submarines that the United States no longer manufactured; anti-submarine patrol aircraft; and minesweeping helicopters. The most controversial weapon not offered for sale was the *Aegis* combat radar system. *New York Times*, April 24, 2001, online ed.

168. Chen pledged "four no's": that he would not declare independence, would not hold a plebiscite on Taiwan's status, would not change the country's name, and would not revise the constitution.

169. This was the Taiwan Security Enhancement Act of 2000, which the House of Representatives approved by a large margin. Voting in the Senate was delayed until sometime after Chen Shui-bian assumed office. Though a U.S. President can ignore some of the act's requirements, he cannot so easily ignore the constant Congressional pressure to provide Taiwan with advanced defensive weapons, such as its own guided-missile destroyers.

170. See, for example, Steven Mufson, "China Puts Forth Persistent, Caustic Anti-U.S. Themes," *Washington Post*, August 13, 1996. A taste of PLA strategic thinking and pessimistic views of PRC–U.S. relations is provided by Michael Pillsbury, ed., *China Debates the Future Security Environment*, published in 2000 for the Pentagon's Office of Net Assessment. On nationalism among Chinese youth, in this case in response to the spy plane incident, see Craig S. Smith, "Chinese Youths Adopt Darkening Image of U.S.," *New York Times*, April 22, 2001, online ed.

171. Author interviews in China, summer 1999.

172. Ming Zhang, "Public Images of the United States," in *In the Eyes of the Dragon*, ed. Deng and Wang, 141–57. On the critical views of some young Chinese concerning globalization, see Susan V. Lawrence, "The Say No Club," *Far Eastern Economic Review* (January 13, 2000): 16–18, discussing the book, *China's Road: Under the Shadow of Globalization*, by Fang Ning et al. Some of these same opponents of economic globalization, it should be noted, favor political reform and admire U.S. principles such as freedom of the press.

173. Freeman, "Preventing War," 10.

174. As 2000 ended, Taiwan did inaugurate "mini-links" to the mainland by authorizing direct trade, travel, and mail between its outer islands, Jinmen (Quemoy) and Matsu, and China's Fujian province. Beijing, which has been pushing for unhindered direct ties, made statements on the decision that indicated its grudging acceptance.

175. For example, Chang King-yuh, chairman of Taiwan's cabinet-level Mainland Affairs Council, proposed ending military exercises directed against either side, agricultural cooperation, and assistance with China's troubled state-owned enterprises. Central News Agency (Taipei), "Beijing Urged to Build Up Military Trust Mechanism with Taipei," December 31, 1998; NAPSNet, January 6, 1999.

176. See *Renmin ribao*, February 8, 2001, and Erik Eckholm, "China Plans to Divert Rivers to Thirsty North," *New York Times*, October 17, 2000, A13 concerning ambitious, and politically as well as environmentally sensitive decisions of the Chinese government

to divert the waters of major rivers so as to meet the needs of Beijing and other major northern cities.

177. The revelation of the involvement of Chinese Communist Party politburo member Jia Qinglin and his wife in one such smuggling case brought to light numerous other instances in which the city of Xiamen has been a gateway for corruption, with public officials at all levels involved. See *New York Times* and *Washington Post*, January 22, 2000,1.

178. An excellent source that covers all these issues is U.S. Congress, Joint Economic Committee, *China's Economic Future*. See especially the contributions of Michael Swaine on military modernization and Kenneth Lieberthal and Hang-Sheng Cheng on the economy.

179. Minxin Pei, "Future Shock: The WTO and Political Change in China," *Policy Brief* (Carnegie Foundation), vol. 1, no. 3 (February 2001), online at www.ceip.org/files/PDF/dem.PolBrief3.pdf. Pei predicts that WTO will further complicate U.S.–PRC relations because the destabilizing consequences of compliance will force the Chinese authorities either to impose order or to find ways around the WTO regulations.

180. As Chen Jian points out, these domestic concerns about the course of China's modernization preoccupy younger PRC intellectuals and much of society as a whole, and are therefore better addressed in terms of the "China challenge" than the "China threat." See his *The China Challenge in the Twenty-First Century: Implications for U.S. Foreign Policy*, Peaceworks no. 21 (Washington, D.C.: U.S. Institute of Peace, June 1998), 9.

181. Quoted by Michael Richardson, "U.S. Commander Urges Security Role for China," *International Herald Tribune*, May 24, 1999.

*Chapter Five*

# Japan: Dependent Nationalism

## FOREIGN POLICY UNDER RESTRAINTS

The U.S.–Japan alliance has been a fixture of East Asian politics for over fifty years. Surprisingly little has happened to alter the alliance's fundamental characteristics. The subordinate role of Japan in the alliance is recognized and accepted by leaders on both sides as being mutually beneficial: good for the United States, because Japan provides numerous military bases and facilities, is a loyal ally, and keeps the American "cork in the bottle"[1] to prevent the reemergence of Japanese militarism; good for Japan, because the United States subsidizes and takes responsibility for its defense and enables it to focus on being an economic power; and good for the two economies, which do over $200 billion a year in trade and have sizable business investments in each other—though in both cases with a large edge to Japan. The bottom line of this peculiarly unbalanced alliance is that Japan has rarely departed from its "followership" of the United States, raising the question whether or not Japan *has* a foreign policy— a reasonably coherent, self-defined vision of Japan's place in the world.

Instead of self-determined principles and practices, the cornerstones of Japanese national security policy are prohibitions and restrictions: the constitution's provision (Article 9) against war and maintaining military forces; the "three no's" (possessing, producing, or introducing) governing nuclear weapons; the ban on arms exports; restrictions governing the Self-Defense Forces (SDF) when they are assigned to UN peacekeeping missions; and the limitation on military spending to 1 percent of GNP. In fact, Japan has breached nearly all of these restrictions at one time or another, usually in response to U.S. preferences.[2] Japan has the world's second-largest military budget (about $45 billion), 236,000 soldiers, and a technologically sophisticated arsenal, enough to make it an important second-rank military power and potential nuclear weapon state. The contradictions between Japan's potential and its performance can be maddening to those inside and outside Japan who want it to "do more" in behalf of international security.

The U.S.–Japan relationship rests on national interests, not common values. And interests do change. Washington has not only wanted Japan to "do more," it has also wanted it to pay more when it comes to collective security. But it has been like pulling teeth. The Americans perceive Japan as cooperating, but only under persistent pressure and then only for the minimum necessary to placate them. The Peacekeeping Operations Bill of 1992, for instance, was Japan's answer to widespread criticism of its "checkbook diplomacy" during the Gulf War, when Tokyo paid $13 billion to support the U.S. war effort but could only muster a few minesweepers to send to the region. But that bill, while breaking the taboo on overseas deployment of troops, keeps Japanese soldiers out of harm's way, thus exposing Japan to renewed criticism of its timidity and even deceptiveness in arguing that the peace constitution prevents Japan from making a stronger contribution.[3] In the area of defense technology, Japan has followed a course of "technonationalism," limiting its sharing of military technology with the United States.[4] Or take the 1997 "Guidelines for U.S.-Japan Defense Cooperation," which grew out of an April 1996 summit meeting between President Clinton and Prime Minister Hashimoto Ryutaro. The new document revised the guidelines of 1978. But though the new guidelines were supposed to tease a stronger commitment to East Asian security out of the Japanese, they accomplished something well short of that.[5] Japan's obligations in support of U.S. policy are limited to logistical backup in unspecified "situations in the area surrounding Japan," and even then subject to mutual agreement and parliamentary processes. Japan's commitment, in short, does not amount to a blanket, predetermined support of U.S. military operations in East Asia.

From a Japanese viewpoint, however, their country does not deserve the epithet of free rider; it has made considerable sacrifices when one keeps in mind its pacifist culture. During the Cold War, for example, Japan had to go along with U.S. containment of China and support of Taiwan. It thus not only postponed normalization of relations with China (until 1971); Japan also made itself an easy target in case of war. Japan's Liberal Democratic Party (LDP) had to endure years of derision from the leftist opposition and demonstrations by a pacifist public because of its endorsement of U.S. Cold War policies and basing of U.S. forces. Dependence on the United States facilitated the creation of a one-party democracy and inward-looking leaders. Japanese governments repeatedly violated the non-nuclear principles to accommodate U.S. strategic planning. At times, Japan could not follow through on its own interests when they differed from Washington's, such as during the oil crisis in the early 1970s, when Japan's reliance on Middle East oil called for an independent approach to the oil-exporting states. Since the Cold War's end, Japanese have had to endure several ugly incidents involving U.S. soldiers in Okinawa and elsewhere. Japan has increased its financial support of U.S. bases to around 75 percent (over $5 billion a year) of the total;[6] been a strong proponent of the WTO and other elements of economic globalization; been the only Asian country so far to subscribe to U.S. plans to construct a TMD system, despite China's energetic protests; contributed substantial amounts of rice and money in support of South Korean and U.S. efforts to contain North Korea's missile and nuclear weapon programs; and has embraced APEC rather than to accept approaches from some Asian countries that would like to see Japan head up an East Asian trading bloc.

Moreover, in the view of younger Japanese at least, the United States has just about worn out its welcome. With the Cold War over, the question can be asked aloud: Why must Japan continue to pay so much money—in fact, far more than other countries that host U.S. forces—to "contain" itself? It is a legitimate question inasmuch as the American argument for the last fifty years has been that U.S. forces are in Japan to prevent Japanese militarism from reasserting itself, and thus to calm Japan's neighbors who were once militarism's victims. If the answer is that the United States cannot afford to stay in Japan and needs Tokyo to step forward and pay for its defense, lest Congress pull the plug, the argument for a continued U.S. presence moves from the strategic to the purely financial. But in fact, that presence has always been self-interested; it has continued not only in order to contain Japan, but also to contain China, deter North Korea, and provide "strategic reassurance" to countries concerned about China and/or Japan. Whether or not, in the post–Cold War era, those reasons are sufficient to justify the costs, financial or political, is the real unanswered question.

## JAPAN'S OPTIONS

There is no lack of critical characterizations of Japan's foreign policy, among them "odd man out," "inward-looking exceptionalism," "one country pacifism," "economic giant and military dwarf," "GNP-ism," and "10 percent [of global GNP] nation."[7] Dissatisfaction outside Japan, and increasingly inside it, has mounted concerning its international role—not only because of what Japan has not done, but also because its contributions have never been fully appreciated, so that Japan has not "gotten its money's worth." Yet to date, as Yoichi Funabashi says, Japan still has a "psychological block against defining Japanese priorities in foreign policy." Despite an "apparent obsession with its status in the world," it lacks the "will in defining its own self-image and world role."[8]

Economic diplomacy (*keizai gaiko*) has been postwar Japan's substitute for foreign and national security policy. As Prime Minister Obuchi Keizo said in 1999, "currently it is impossible to revise" Article 9, and despite "a growing awareness that Japan should play its role in military efforts to resolve international conflicts . . . rather than a military role, I believe it is important that we are playing an economic role."[9] That role is to make the world safe for Japanese exports and investments, and therefore to keep policy making in the hands of bureaucrats and interest groups with ties to *keiretsu*. Unlike the United

States, which has traditionally gone overboard in seeking to universalize its values and interests—from Woodrow Wilson's call to make the world safe for democracy, to Bill Clinton's "engagement and enlargement" doctrine—Japan has no pretensions to global or even regional leadership. Its foreign policy is notable for its constraints, not its capacities, the first of which is the Japanese exceptionalism mentioned by Funabashi: the idea that Japan of course has the right of collective self-defense, but chooses not to exercise it.

Whatever ultimately accounts for the consequent foreign policy reactiveness—bureaucratic intransigence, U.S. pressure, or the asymmetry in U.S.–Japan trade and security relations[10]—Japan's leaders have found over many years that dependence pays. Even its economic diplomacy—strategically linking trade, aid, and overseas investment—has not sought ends larger than making money and expanding markets for *keiretsu*. Leadership incurs responsibilities, and Japan is loath to take them on. It is highly questionable, for example, whether Japan has the political will, the regional support, or the economic capacity to create or lead a separate regional, yen-based economic bloc. Not only does Japan exhibit weaknesses as the core economy; the Japanese market for Asian products is substantial but not overly large,[11] and the dollar, not the yen, holds the top position in most transactions.[12] Certainly, the Japanese government supports economic globalization, just as it supports human rights, nonproliferation of WMD, and sustainable development. But these policies and goals are defined and pushed mainly by the United States; in practice, the Japanese government and *keiretsu* may not always follow them.[13]

Even if a consensus could be built in Japan for doing things differently, what should its international role be? Since the Gulf War, variations of three foreign policy options have dominated discussion in Japan.[14] The first, from which Japan has never strayed far since the first post war administration of Yoshida Shigeru (1946–1954, with one brief interruption), is "dual identity": its role as both a constrained and a potentially independent security actor. The function of the U.S.–Japan alliance has been to mesh those identities, by encouraging Japanese burden-sharing while also discouraging Japan's security independence.[15] But the model of a passive, lightly-armed Japan selfishly pursuing economic gain is losing favor now that Cold War tensions have subsided. The second option, "global civilian power," calls for Japan to remain lightly armed and pacifist, but to identify national purpose with global needs.[16] This approach (elaborated below) would have Japan use its abundant technological, financial, and other resources for human and environmental benefit, including peaceful conflict resolution. The third option is a Japan that adopts an activist, independent security role, either within or outside the U.S. alliance, and makes the necessary constitutional changes to legitimate that new role.

Debates about these options reflect differences over whether or not, or to what extent, Japan is already becoming more independent-minded and less "self-absorbed," is behaving in ways consistent with its past passivism, or is simply "hedging its bets."[17]

Japan's dual identity has been under attack for years in the United States, where a number of critics believe that Japan should be brought much more fully into burden-sharing and "normalcy." All that is lacking is the will to act—to adopt policies in Japan's best interest. These critics remind us of the small size of Japan's military establishment and military spending (second in the world but well below Japan's capacity); its obfuscations concerning what Article 9 forbids; and its refusal to clarify its obligations even in a supporting role of the United States under the Treaty for Mutual Security. A normal Japan, critics contend, would revise its constitution, fully participate in collective (as opposed to unilateral) security (including combat responsibilities within UN PKOs), work to change APEC's structure to accommodate security issues, and make the Security Treaty an equal partnership.[18]

U.S. policy in the mid-1990s, however, disappointed the critics by failing to shift defense burdens onto American allies. Instead, the traditional forward-deployment policies were continued within the usual framework of bilateral alliances. This news was a source of great relief in Tokyo to "diehard Japanese adherents to the Yoshida strategy," Kenneth Pyle wrote, p. 120.[19] He warned, however, that such a U.S. policy was unsustainable: It would require overcoming Congressional opposition to subsidizing Japan's, and other allies' defenses—against China, clearly—without compensation.[20] The usual compensation would have to be in trade and investment concessions. But as the Clinton-Hashimoto summit in 1996 made clear, another form of compensation might have been the new U.S.–Japan security guidelines, which in oblique fashion suggested some new degree of Japanese support for U.S. forces in the event of a security crisis in East Asia.

The option of foreign policy autonomy stems from two concerns: first, that the post–Cold War regional security picture remains threatening to Japan, topped by Chinese assertiveness, North Korean missiles, and the Taiwan problem; second, that the American commitment to regional security is not as reliable as before due to domestic political constraints. Thus, Japan must act on behalf of its security interests: It should become a full-fledged military power, though without nuclear weapons, and undertake a variety of collective security obligations in close coordination with the United States. Such a Japan would shed its World War II guilt and its dual identity. It would begin to look and act like a traditional power, running the risk that its actions would not arouse hostility in China or South Korea (which could develop nuclear weapons in response) or alienate the ASEAN states.

There doubtless are circumstances under which Japan would seriously debate becoming a military great power, such as vulnerability to a credible nuclear threat from North Korea, closure of access to Middle East oil, or perception of a serious threat from China—coupled, in each instance, with loss of confidence in the U.S. security umbrella. Even then, Japan would have to make revolutionary changes in its foreign, economic, and national security policies to become a power willing and able to stand on its own.[21] A more probable course, as Chalmers Johnson has argued, is to sustain "technonationalism and the creation of American military dependencies on Japanese high-tech products."[22]

"Global civilian power" is an alternative to continued foreign policy dependence and the option of foreign policy autonomy. It is an option well suited to Japan's strengths. Despite years of recession, Japan's economic assets remain enormous, and constitute one basis for playing an independent international role *without becoming a major military power*. Nor is money Japan's only asset: It has the pacifism of its people, and its technological edge. Funabashi therefore urges that Japan "pursue two sometimes contradictory strategies: active engagement for world peace and military self-restraint." Behind both should be a new set of values and foreign policy goals: assistance to poor countries for economic development, and vigorous support of international peacekeeping, human rights, and environmental protection.[23] In response to critics who urge a new era of U.S.–Japan partnership, Funabashi sees no need for Japan to share leadership with the United States or modify the alliance. Instead, Japan should be concerned with achieving better balance in its international relations, especially in Asia, and with democratizing itself, "so that Japan may serve as an example to developing nations and make its institutions and practices more compatible with like-minded democracies."[24]

Funabashi was a member of a distinguished internationalist-minded panel appointed by Prime Minister Obuchi that submitted a wide-ranging report in January 2000 on revitalizing Japan inside and outside.[25] The essential argument of *Japan's Goals in the 21st Century* was that Japan needed to become a civil society, with a sense of national purpose, if it was going to rise above its "apathy and ennui" and regain international respect. The alternative, the report said, was a Japan "heading for decline." Its proposed foreign policy remedies closely followed Funabashi's earlier recommendations, including embracing the objective of becoming a global civilian power and pursuing an "enlightened national interest." "Global civilian power" was redefined so as to go beyond nonmilitary approaches, which the authors criticized as over-concentrating on economic success; and "enlightened national interest" meant "taking a long-term, indirect approach to satisfying a country's own needs by increasing the number of friendly countries and improving the international environment on the basis of 'mutuality.'"[26] The report thus urged that Japan transform the U.S.–Japan alliance into one of equals, put Japanese lives at risk in international peacekeeping such as humanitarian interventions, become a much more forceful and involved advocate of global common security measures (such as the CTBT and the population problem), and take an active role in revitalizing the international financial system so that the IMF is no longer the only recourse for faltering economies.

Japan's role as a global civilian power does not, however, satisfy critics such as Pyle. He argues that while Japan "would be happy to accept" such a role, it does not suit either party:

> In the longer term, it is not realistic to expect that the continued operation of American bases on Japanese soil in their present form and status will be acceptable to a

Japan inclined to return to orthodox nationhood. Nor is it realistic to perpetuate indefinitely a situation in which the United States alone is responsible for security and stability in the Asia-Pacific region.[27]

But "orthodox nationhood" does not have to mean a complete divorce with the United States and a resurgence of Japanese militarism. Much depends on the political and strategic context in which a new Japanese international outlook emerges. At the turn of the new century, for instance, a number of Japanese scholars and politicians talked about the emergence of a conservative "neo-nationalism" in security affairs as Japan looked for a "stronger" posture.[28] The outgoing Japanese ambassador to the United States took the unusual step of warning that continued harsh American criticism of Japan, specifically on trade issues, might create a nationalist backlash. "Memories of the 1930s and 40s are still fresh in our minds," he said.[29] Such a brand of nationalism might take Japan in the direction of ending security ties with the United States, developing nuclear weapons, cutting back on ODA and technology transfers, and geographically and politically widening the role of the military. But there is nothing inevitable about such a drastic outcome, as argued below. As to Pyle's second point, he may be right to be concerned about how long the United States can bear sole responsibility for Asia's security. But a "normal," *civilian-power* Japan might well question the Americans' expansive notion of regional security and think twice before giving the Americans a blank check to impose it.

## A NEW NATIONALISM

The new Japan clearly needs, for the first time since the Occupation, a positive outlet for nationalism. Thus far Japanese nationalism has found expression in "soft" ways, among them pride in economic achievements, a reassertion of traditional values (reflected, for instance, in Prime Minister Mori Yoshiro's reference to Japan in 2000 as "a divine nation centered on the Emperor"), one-nation pacifism, revival of the flag and national anthem, and a certain racial superiority.[30] Then there are Japan's plutonium imports, considered by many foreign experts to be in excess of energy needs, and continued toleration of World War II era militarism in school textbooks,[31] matters that give some observers the impression of a Japan with a hidden agenda. These forms of nationalism and national purpose are as yet a far cry from aggressive xenophobia; but, as Pyle comments, the continued U.S. containment of Japanese nationalism is capable of changing Japanese thinking:

> To assign the Mutual Security Treaty the purpose of containing Japanese power and influence in the Pacific will not square with the prevailing nationalist mood in Japan. The day is likely to arrive when Japan will reject the anomaly of financing foreign bases that are there in large part to "contain" Japan, particularly when this situation contributes to a politically deferential and dependent foreign policy. If

incrementalism at best, or drift at worst, continues to characterize the anomalous situation in U.S.-Japan relations, the alliance will continue to weaken in a way that is tantamount to its termination—with all the consequences of destabilizing the region and great power relations in the post–Cold War world.[32]

Though Japanese elite and mass opinion still supports the Security Treaty, close observers of Japan report rising resentment of America's unipolar arrogance and sentiment in favor of distancing Japan from the United States. Recommendations that address the new situation by calling for the U.S.–Japan partnership to be made more equal by tightening Japan's military cooperation with the United States miss the point, and move the relationship in precisely the wrong direction.[33] Rather, the challenge is to redefine Japan's identity in ways that are consistent with national normalcy, an end to Japan's second-class status, and the peace constitution. Barring a major disruption of East Asian security, U.S. forces and bases in Japan, particularly those clustered on Okinawa—where roughly three-fourths of all U.S. forces and bases in Japan are located—should gradually be reduced and closed down.[34] Some steps in that direction to pare down the Okinawa bases have been discussed, but they do not go far enough.[35] The protection afforded Japan under the Security Treaty, however, should be retained;[36] but Japan would have to "re-engage" the United States, probably in a revised treaty that would allow for U.S. access to Japanese bases in emergencies and with prior consultation. Revision of Japan's constitution would no doubt also be necessary to legitimize greater Japanese contributions to collective security, such as joint intelligence-sharing and military exercises with the United States, and SDF involvement in combat roles in UN humanitarian peacekeeping operations.

As the Obuchi report urged, Japan should greatly strengthen efforts to promote friendly ties with its key neighbors, China and South Korea, including not just economic and technological cooperation but also language and cultural learning and research. It should contribute more to multilateral cooperation in East Asia, thereby fulfilling the potential international security role that is part of its current dual identity. One way is to be more generous in providing ODA. As *Japan's Goals* noted, Japan actually ranks low among the major industrialized countries in terms of ODA as a proportion of gross domestic product, and ranks too high in the proportion of aid that is tied to the purchase of Japanese goods. Also in line with the report, Japan should promote a Northeast Asia multilateral security dialogue, which it officially favors, and a regional free trade agreement in cooperation with the United States.

Left untouched in the report on *Japan's Goals* is the ever-present issue of an official apology for Japan's aggressions and the inhumane conduct of certain military units in World War II. Expressions of atonement for colonial rule and imperialism have become more frequent since 1995, when Prime Minister Hosokawa offered "apologies and remorse." The Japanese government has thus far refused to make official compensation for the human tragedies inflicted by the wartime regime, however, such as the forced recruitment of Korean "comfort women" to serve the Imperial Army's sexual needs, the enslavement of millions of Chinese to work in the mines and factories of Manchuria and Japan, and the biological warfare experimentation of Unit 731 on villagers in China's Northeast region. Japanese courts have finally begun hearing the stories of survivors, and some compensation has been made through nonofficial sources, though in tiny sums compared with the billions of dollars awarded to Jewish victims of the Holocaust.[37] But the real issue is not money, it is the failure at many levels of society, including government, big business, and educational circles, to come to grips with the illegitimacy, immorality, and even the very fact of Japan's international crimes against its neighbors. So long as this circumstance continues, Japan's re-Asianization will be undermined by the appearance of racism and indifference to human tragedy.

## "Hedging Bets"?

In recent years Japanese leaders have been more active than in the past in taking initiatives that give shape to Japan's international role. For one thing, there is now a clear public and Diet consensus in Japan for constitutional revision, probably reflecting insecurities about China and North Korea. Also influencing public attitudes is the mounting hostility in Okinawa to the U.S. presence, prompted by a variety of incidents involving U.S. forces.[38]

Among the recent actions are two laws passed in 1999 that provide a framework for Japanese assistance to the United States, including local-level support, under the new security guidelines.[39] Japan is now more engaged than before in multilateral security cooperation with the United States—in the form of the Trilateral Coordination and Oversight Group (TCOG), which also includes the ROK, and in TMD, to which it has so far committed $10 million a year for research—as well as in bilateral security consultation with China and South Korea.[40] Japan also plans to develop air refueling capability for the SDF air force and to deploy an antimissile satellite warning system to supplement, or perhaps substitute for, TMD. Japan's aid commitments to sub-Saharan Africa made by Obuchi's successor, Mori Yoshiro, now seem to show a clear sense of purpose.[41] In early 2001 the unpopular Mori's successor, Koizumi Junichiro, pushed for constitutional revision that would enable Japan to act in collective self-defense in spite of Article 9.

Some of Japan's initiatives have gone against U.S. preferences.[42] Examples include the AMF proposal of 1997, which responded to perceived inequities in the IMF's response to the Asian financial crisis; the Obuchi government's support of China's membership in WTO, well before the United States gave its support; and Tokyo's large-scale commitment to financial relief in Southeast Asia (which also benefits to Japanese firms there). While Washington has carried the diplomatic load in dealing with North Korea, Japan has held back, insisting (among other things) on assurances from Pyongyang of no more missile tests before stepping up food aid and setting a timetable for normalizing relations.

The question is how to interpret these developments. Some observers see Japan "hedging its bets," in the event the alliance comes apart and China proves truculent. Hedging bets can, however, mislead: The term implies what does not appear to be true, namely, that Japan has active options, within a hidden agenda, so that if its security picture turns cloudy, it can swiftly change course to an independent foreign policy posture.[43] Specifically, Japan's involvement in East Asian multilateral groups is considered one example of hedging; but the history of that involvement shows that it came about as part of re-Asianization and is typically Japanese—promoting the Asian way to security without taking leadership of it.[44] Or consider TMD: Contrary to the hedging thesis, following North Korea's missile test over Japan, Tokyo looked to develop a satellite reconnaissance program and, in August 1999, agreed with U.S. Defense Department officials on a joint R&D program to develop a ballistic missile for defense against missile attack. Press reports in Japan quoted some observers who saw supporters of TMD playing politics with North Korea's missile test, using it to exaggerate the threat and strengthen the case for TMD and constitutional revision.[45] The Chinese would hardly call these developments hedging.

If Japan's international outlook is indeed changing, it is not in ways that amount to a sense of "enlightened national interest" as called for in *Japan's Goals* and elsewhere. Policies continue to be sporadic, often defensive responses to issues of the moment that Tokyo cannot avoid. The world awaits a Japanese government capable of setting a direction that merges its immense capabilities with its recognition of global citizenship.

## THE U.S.–CHINA–JAPAN TRIANGLE

Independent Japanese policy making can certainly move international politics in East Asia away from the Cold War paradigm. But the most important factor, recognized as such by all three countries, is China–U.S. relations. Ever since the Cold War began, China–U.S. relations have crucially influenced the relationship between China and Japan. For roughly thirty years the United States pressed Japan into service in support of the containment strategy. Japan's constitution was stretched and an antagonistic relationship with China was assured. But U.S. policy was double-edged: It also sought to restrain Japan from being an independent player in East Asian affairs, as the dual-identity thesis maintains. There was an unspoken but real mistrust of Japan's potential to move out from under U.S. leadership: burden-sharing was not to be confused with equality. For that reason, a certain kind of China-Japan balance became essential to U.S. policy— neither an assertive China *nor* an assertive Japan. As has been true of U.S. foreign policy generally, the essential enemy is nationalism, Chinese *or* Japanese. *Both* nationalisms have needed to be contained: China's, by U.S. forward deployments of military forces, including bases in Japan; Japan's, by U.S. bases in Japan and constant pressure to provide active support of U.S. policy in East Asia.

Thus, *U.S. policy's fixation on the China threat, and its obstruction of a positive evolution of Japanese nationalism, not only keeps the Cold War alive; it also ensures that Japan–China rivalry will remain a fixture in East Asia.* Despite the strong elements of economic interdependence between them—Japan ranks at or near the top in trade, investment, and technology transfers with China—it is not a sufficient condition of harmonious relations. Only positive U.S. relations with China can dispel Chinese mistrust of Tokyo; for so long as the PRC views the United States as using Japan to contain it, China–Japan relations are certain to be tension-filled. It thus makes sense for U.S. policy to focus on two things: improving relations with China on the basis, as previously suggested, of common security concerns and defusion of the Taiwan issue; and supporting Japanese initiatives to become a global civilian power, which would promote a more cooperative Sino-Japanese relationship. The worst U.S. course, which is the one that has long been pursued, and which the George W. Bush administration has promised to continue, is to throw its weight behind one or the other country, demonstrating a higher priority either to PRC or Japanese interests. Such a course constitutes alignment on behalf of crude balance-of-power calculations, and inevitably leads the abandoned party (China up until now) to take countermeasures that heighten regional tensions.

China has limited leverage in this situation. It can attempt to separate Japan from the United States, such as by giving preference to Japanese over U.S. trade and investment contracts. Or it can use its "strategic partnership" with Russia to "balance" against the U.S.–Japan alliance and help delay the day when Russia returns some or all of the so-called Northern Islands to Japan.[46] Or, thirdly, China can play a spoiler's role in Korean peninsula affairs, supporting a hard line in North Korea that makes life threatening for Japan. But these steps are either unlikely to have much impact on Japanese policy making, or they will have consequences (the strengthening of U.S.–Japan–ROK military ties after North Korea's missile test is an example) that are worse than the supposed benefits.[47] Triangular gamesmanship such as was practiced in U.S.–Soviet–PRC relations in the 1970s should have no place in post–Cold War East Asia. A more sensible direction to try could yield benefits for all three countries: *reducing* Japanese security responsibilities on the Americans' behalf in East Asia while *retaining* a revised U.S.–Japan alliance, *strengthening* Japan's capacity for regional economic and technological leadership (i.e., as a market for Asian products), *promoting* a "soft landing" in North Korea and, as noted earlier, *building confidence* through Japanese participation in multilateral dialogue on Northeast Asia security as well as through bilateral Japan–PRC dialogue.[48]

Until such directions are chosen, we can expect that Chinese analysts will continue to offer a generally harsh assessment of Japan's intentions. For instance, one analyst has argued that Japan's implementing legislation for the new Japan–U.S. defense guidelines "gives the green light to Japanese comprehensive support to U.S. military activities and wars and to the exercise of the SDF overseas." It could be the prelude to amending Article 9, thus regularizing Japanese military forces;

to making Japan "a giant war base" in support of U.S. actions; to carrying out military actions "without the Diet's approval"; and to acquiring the components of a major naval power. As for Japan's objectives, the analyst said they are "to obtain the status of a political and military power" (as various PRC commentators have been saying throughout the 1990s and in some cases even before); to lay the basis for a more equal partnership with the United States; and "to contain and attack China, North Korea and Russia by exploiting the U.S. [alliance] and build up strong military capability to become the hegemon of East Asia."[49]

The key point for Beijing is not that Japan should abandon the alliance, but that it should have a more balanced relationship with China and the United States. As one writer associated with a PLA think tank said:

> The character of Sino-U.S. relations directly affects the conditions of Sino-Japanese relations, even the whole framework of the three nations' relationship. If Sino-U.S. relations develop normally, Sino-Japanese relations will develop smoothly. On the contrary, the deterioration of Sino-U.S. relations would impose great pressure on Sino-Japanese relations, for under such circumstances Japan would be faced with a dilemma for choice. If Japan supports or assists the U.S. to confront China, it will risk worsening Sino-Japanese relations. . . . However, if Japan becomes too close to China or even tries to make use of the closeness to show the Americans its independence from and balancing capability against the U.S., it will arouse suspicion or pressure by the U.S., hence causing damage to U.S.-Japanese relations.[50]

Beijing does not expect Japan to lean toward it; but neither can it accept Japan's joining the United States in "containing" China. Beijing's preferred world seems to be a stable triangular relationship based on common interests—such as "economic complementarity" and tension reduction—and acceptance of the principle that bilateral relations do not develop at the expense of the third country.[51]

The other message to Tokyo in these Chinese analyses is that it should avoid having to face off with China in a decisive "test" of its intentions. The Taiwan issue poses more than one such test. If there were a military crisis over Taiwan, Japan would be forced to choose between destroying its alliance with the United States by not contributing to the common cause, or supporting the United States militarily and thus bringing about a confrontation with a nuclear China.[52] Another test would occur once Japan actually participates in the U.S. TMD deployment. China regards the TMD system as broadening in several ways Japan's military support of the U.S. containment strategy in East Asia and in the process undercutting China's missile deterrent.[53] The Japanese defense establishment seems to regard TMD as the most effective way to deter the growing ballistic-missile threat of both China and North Korea.[54] How deeply Japan associates with TMD will be closely watched by China.

A normal Japan, sensitive to its delicate position between the United States and China, would want to give highest priority to improving relations with Beijing, as called for in the "good neighbor" policy recommended in *Japan's Goals*. Tokyo's priority would be to demonstrate friendly intentions, an independent foreign policy, and reliability as a partner in China's economic reforms. But pleasing China will not be easy. For one thing, interpretation in Japan of the meaning of China's military modernization reveals a division of opinion similar to that in the United States. The consensus in Japan is said to be that while China is not an immediate military threat, China's "nuclear development programs, arms and technology transfer from Russia, and the military pressure towards Taiwan, all pose potential threats to Japanese security."[55]

Second, ever since the Richard Nixon–Sato Eisaku communiqué of 1969, Tokyo has claimed a direct interest in the security of Taiwan.[56] Japanese leaders have periodically reassured Beijing that Japan will not interfere in the Taiwan issue and rejects the idea of Taiwanese independence. But how Japan would behave in a crisis over Taiwan is far from clear, considering the new security guidelines and TMD. Third, the matter of a clear Japanese apology still hangs in the air. When Jiang Zemin made the first-ever visit to Japan by a Chinese head of state in November 1998, all he got was another Japanese statement (from Obuchi) of "acute responsibility" and "deep remorse" for Japan's aggression. This was well short of what Kim Dae Jung received just one month earlier ("remorseful repentance and heartfelt apology"). The difference clearly upset the Chinese side, since the wording had been a subject of intense negotiations for months beforehand.[57]

Fourth, Japan has had to re-think its China aid program. In a way this is hardly news; concerns about China's military ambitions have prompted cuts in ODA to China before, and even a freeze on some grant aid when China resumed nuclear testing in 1995.[58] These days, there is a general political leaning in the Japanese government toward cutting ODA, not only because of economic woes, but also because China's economic successes and its increasing military spending make it a less appealing recipient. Japan has certainly given generously to China: a total of ¥2.68 trillion (roughly $26 billion at late 1990s exchange rates) since ODA began in 1979, and ¥390 billion ($3.9 billion) for 1999–2000. ODA to China will surely remain a cornerstone of Japan's aid-giving, since Tokyo views aid to China as a means of positively influencing economic and political reforms; but the amounts, basis, and objectives will probably change.[59]

Lastly, the Russian factor must be considered. Japanese leaders will have a hard time rationalizing continued loans and investments in Russia—over $6 billion in the past decade—while Russia refuses to budge on the territorial dispute. And so long as the dispute simmers, a peace treaty that will finally put World War II behind them cannot be concluded.[60] Yet if Japan shows its displeasure by reducing economic and aid ties to Russia, Sino-Russian ties are likely to benefit— a situation Tokyo would obviously prefer to avoid. Like its China policy, Japan's Russia policy first and foremost needs to contribute to the country's economic well-being and democratization. Moreover, Russian leaders need to feel included in Asian affairs, not marginalized as they frequently have been (such as in ARF and the Four Party Talks on Korea). A downturn in relations with Russia

would not help and might worsen the security situation on the Korean peninsula. As mentioned before, domestic politics in both countries immensely complicates the problem, constricting what the diplomats can propose.[61]

## THE FUTURE

Japan as a global civilian power that rejects militarization "defies international
relations theory, and particularly the neorealist perspective."[62] Whether or not
Japan can stay the course will depend above all on societal changes—the public's participation in the policy making process, the bureaucracy's accession to
democratic norms, Japan's acceptance of a less homogeneous society, and the
economy's restructuring.[63] To put the matter that way is, to be sure, controversial. It accords with the views of those scholars who contend that Japan's pacifist culture is the overriding constraint on its security perspective—an *Asahi
Shimbun* poll in the spring of 2001 confirmed anew the public's overwhelming
support of Article 9—hence that global civilian power and activism in multilateral settings can endure, perhaps *even if the alliance with the United States
were downgraded.* But such views are, of course, disputed by scholars who emphasize the crucial influence of the alliance and international events.[64]

In a democracy, said *Japan's Goals,* "it is not in the people's interest to have
almost no idea where they are headed."[65] The report took special note of conditions in Okinawa since the rape of a local girl by three U.S. servicemen in
1995. The "heavy burden" borne by Okinawans, which includes low wages
and noise and other forms of pollution, should require consolidating the bases
and "promot[ing] Okinawa's long-term development." Cultivation of and attentiveness to public opinion implies a considerable diminution of bureaucratic power, strong prime ministerial leadership, and stability of tenure in that
office, developments that will require an extraordinary shakeup of Japan's
postwar political structure. Yet only dramatic structural change can disrupt
Japan's essentially tribal decision making process, put the prime minister's office and people with foreign policy expertise in charge of international affairs,
greatly increase Japanese staffing of multinational organizations, and thus end
the domination of Japan's foreign relations by economics-first bureaucrats.[66]
Prime Minister Koizumi came into office in 2001 on the wings of strong public
support for structural reform, but he faced the daunting task of overcoming resistance among the powerful LDP factions.

Next, Japan will have to become a truly international society if it is to have
credibility as a global civilian power. That means its citizens and public leaders
will have to change their thinking on many things: migrant workers from Asia
and beyond, who are often shabbily treated despite taking the lowest-paid jobs;
foreign professionals stationed in Japan, who typically have second-class status;
and Japanese students, especially women, who go abroad for training, only to
return and face discrimination precisely because they have not stayed home. As

Japanese society ages, it will need more and more foreign workers to perform basic services, and women to assume leadership positions.[67] Since Japan's elite is unlikely to take the lead in changing public attitudes and public policies on these matters, it is up to citizens' movements to do the job. Otherwise, Japan will continue to have the image of a selfish, insular country.

Economic restructuring is necessary in order for Japan to *afford* to be regionally and globally responsible. In 1999, Japan had to cut foreign aid and quarrel with the United States over a reduction of base support because of its economic doldrums. By the spring of 2001 Finance Minister Miyazawa Kiichi was saying that Japan's economy was "near a state of collapse" and heading into a recession. Public debt reached $5.6 trillion, corporate and bank debt were enormous,[68] economic growth had slowed, unemployment was high (5 percent in mid-2001), and consumer spending was low. Japan is unlikely to be able to sustain its generosity with regard to UN peacekeeping and development assistance to indebted countries if its own debt and other economic problems are not resolved.[69] The Japanese economy will eventually recover, but that could easily mean business as usual, including continuation of "Japan, Inc.," the incestuous triangle of LDP–big business–bureaucratic power, limited openness to foreign investors, and resistance to becoming a bigger market for Asian and other products. Since, in Japan, politics *is* economics, it is incumbent for Japan to change the political structure in order to change the terms of economic engagement with the world.

These changes will determine international responses to Japan's new role. Japan deserves to be a permanent member, with Germany, of the UN Security Council.[70] Opponents often point out that Japan with veto power might take actions contrary to U.S. positions, and that Japan as one of the "Perm-7" will be called upon to contribute combat troops to peacekeeping missions. But neither of those objections should stand in the way of Japan as a global civilian power. Of course Japan will take positions opposite the United States; that is to be expected of a nonmilitary great power. And so long as combat troops are for humanitarian interventions, and not the prosecution of wars (like the Gulf War), it is reasonable that Japan, along with the other permanent members, be obliged to send them. What really stands in Japan's way is Japan itself.

## NOTES

1. The phrase belongs to the U.S. Marine commander in Japan, Major General Henry Stackpole, who once undiplomatically allowed that bottling up Japan to prevent "a rearmed, resurgent Japan" was the real purpose of U.S. forces there. *Washington Post*, March 27, 1990; quoted in Bello, *People and Power in the Pacific*, 29.

2. Chalmers Johnson, "Japan in Search of a 'Normal' Role," *Daedalus*, vol. 14 (February 1992): 19–20. Specifically on the "three no's," Japan during the Cold War permitted the transit and basing of U.S. nuclear warheads and nuclear weapons components on its territory. See Robert S. Norris, William M. Arkin, and William Burr, "How Much Did Japan

Know?" *The Bulletin of the Atomic Scientists*, vol. 56, no. 1 (January–February 2000), on-line ed.

3. A good example of such criticism is Kenneth B. Pyle, "Japan and the Future of Collective Security," in *Japan's Emerging Global Role*, ed. Danny Unger and Paul Blackburn (Boulder, Colo.: Lynne Rienner, 1993), 99–117.

4. Johnson, "Japan in Search of a 'Normal' Role."

5. Text at www.defenselink.mil/cgi-bin/dlprint. Two principles stated at the outset of the guidelines qualify Japan's commitment. One is that Japan's conduct will occur "within the limitations of its Constitution and in accordance with such basic positions as the maintenance of its exclusively defense-oriented policy and its three non-nuclear principles." The other is that the guidelines "will not obligate either Government to take legislative, budgetary or administrative measures."

6. The total does not include the salaries of U.S. forces. Japan's financial support of U.S. forces increased from ¥6.1 billion in 1978 to ¥28.19 billion in 1997 and ¥26.03 billion in fiscal year 2000, according to the Japanese press. See *Asahi Shimbun* (Tokyo) and *Yomiuri Shimbun* (Tokyo), January 6, 2000; NAPSNet, January 7, 2000.

7. See, for instance, Yoichi Funabashi, "Japan and the New World Order," *Foreign Affairs*, vol. 70, no. 5 (Winter 1991–92): 60.

8. Funabashi, "Japan and the New World Order."

9. Reuters, May 1, 1999; NAPSNet, May 4, 1999.

10. Akitoshi Miyashita, "*Gaiatsu* and Japan's Foreign Aid: Rethinking the Reactive-Proactive Debate," *International Studies Quarterly*, vol. 43, no. 4 (December 1999): 695–731.

11. For example, in the early 1990s Japan imported only 14 percent of China's exports and 11 percent of exports from the Asian NICs. Soogil Young, "Globalism and Regionalism: Complements or Competitors?" in *Pacific Dynamism and the International Economic System*, ed. C. Fred Bergsten and Marcus Noland (Washington, D.C.: Institute for International Economics, 1993), 125.

12. Takatoshi Ito, "The Yen and the International Monetary System," in *Pacific Dynamism*, ed. Bargsten and Noland, 299–322. Though Japanese leaders, most recently Prime Minister Obuchi Keizo, have called for internationalization of the yen, two realities stand in the way. The only category in which the yen predominates is in debt held by countries that owe Japan money. Japan's own exports and especially imports are mostly denominated in dollars. Even in Asia, not to mention worldwide, yen-based trade by Japan accounts for only 27 percent of its imports and 48 percent of its exports. Second, in a yen bloc Japan would have to be lender of last resort and be certain to keep its value up. See Eriko Amaha, "Slowly but Surely," *Far Eastern Economic Review* (April 8, 1999): 42.

13. A few examples are Japan's friendly relations with Burma's military regime and the destruction of Southeast Asia's tropical forests by hardwood importers such as Mitsubishi.

14. For background, see Eugene Brown, "Japanese Security Policy in the Post–Cold War World: Threat Perceptions and Strategic Options," *Journal of Northeast Asian Studies*, vol. 8, no. 2 (Summer–Fall 1994): 327–62; and Young-Sun Song, "Prospects for U.S.-Japan Security Cooperation," *Asian Survey*, vol. 35, no. 12 (December 1995): 1087–101.

15. See Yoshihide Soeya, "Japan's Dual Identity and the U.S.-Japan Alliance," Institute for International Studies, Asia/Pacific Research Center, Stanford University, May 1998.

16. See Takashi Inoguchi, *Japan's Foreign Policy in an Era of Global Change* (New York: St. Martin's Press, 1993), and Inoguchi, "Japan in Search of a Normal Role," Adelphi Paper No. 275 (March 1993), 58–68.

17. For an outstanding review of the literature on these debates, see Michael J. Green, "State of the Field Report: Research on Japanese Security Policy," National Bureau of Asian Research, 1998; online at www.accessasia.org/products/aareview/vol2no1/essay1.html.

18. For instance, Sam Jameson has argued for "a new [U.S.] willingness to consult Japan both for its approval of military actions taken from bases in Japan as well as for its ideas and proposals on joint security actions. . . . Most of all, the government in Washington should eliminate the thinking that Japan needs to be put on a leash and that one of the values of the U.S.-Japan Security Treaty is to muzzle Japan. Like Japan itself, the United States also needs to take action to build up trust in its alliance with Japan." Jameson, "Japan's Security Problems and Challenges to the U.S.-Japan Alliance," speech at Japan Defense Research Institute, September 9, 1997 (text provided by author).

19. Kenneth B. Pyle, "The Context of APEC: U.S.-Japan Relations," in *From APEC to Xanadu*, ed. Hellmann and Pyle, 119–21.

20. As President Clinton warned at Seattle in November 1993, the United States "do[es] not intend to bear the cost of our military presence in Asia and the burdens of regional leadership only to be shut out of the benefits of growth that stability brings." Quoted in Pyle, "The context of APEC," (Boulder, Colo.: Lynne Reinner, 1993), 121.

21. For an excellent collection of expert opinion that comes down in support of this view, see *Japan in the Posthegemonic World*, ed. Tsuneo Akaha and Frank Langdon, especially the essay by Langdon, "The Posthegemonic Japanese-U.S. Relationship," 84–88.

22. Johnson, "Japan in Search of a 'Normal' Role," 17.

23. Funabashi, "Japan and the New World Order," 66.

24. Funabashi, "Japan and the New World Order," 67.

25. Prime Minister's Commission on Japan's Goals in the 21st Century, *Japan's Goals in the 21st Century* (Tokyo: January 2000), online at www.kantei.go.jp/jp/21century/report/pdfs/index.html.

26. See Prime Minister's Commission on Japan's Goals in the 21st Century, *Japan's Goals in the 21st Century*, ch. 6.

27. Pyle, "The Context of APEC," in *From APEC to Xanadu*, ed. Hellmann and Pyle, 123.

28. Cameron W. Barr, "Japan Moves Toward a New Assertiveness," *Christian Science Monitor*, July 8, 1999.

29. Ambassador Saito Kunihiko's speech to the Foreign Correspondents Club on March 16, 1999, was reported in "Japan Warns U.S. to Back Off or Face Revival of Nationalism" STRATFOR's Global Intelligence Update, March 19, 1999.

30. Brian J. McVeigh, "Postwar Japan's 'Hard' and 'Soft' Nationalism," Japan Policy Research Institute, Working Paper no. 73 (January 2001), 1–6.

31. See Ienaga Saburō, "The Glorification of War in Japanese Education," *International Security*, vol. 18, no. 3 (Winter 1993–94): 113–33. Ienaga Saburō fought for years in the Japanese courts to publish a textbook that correctly recorded Japanese war crimes during World War II, and eventually won a partial victory.

32. Pyle, "Japan and the Future of Collective Security," in *Japan's Emerging Global Role*, ed. Unger and Blackburn, 108.

33. See, for example, Robert A. Manning, "Futureshock or Renewed Partnership? The U.S.-Japan Alliance Facing the Millennium," *The Washington Quarterly*, vol. 18, no. 4 (Autumn 1995): 87–98.

34. The U.S. ambassador to Japan, Thomas J. Foley, even said as much in November 2000: "Maybe we ought to drastically reduce the whole presence of the Marines in

Okinawa." Symposium on "Security in the Midst of Change: A Japan-U.S. Alliance for the 21st Century," text online at www.asahi.com/english/symposium/main.html.

35. Based on recommendations developed by a special committee in 1996, the United States plans to turn over a number of military-controlled lands that amount to 21 percent of the total occupied by American facilities. Among them, the Marine Corps Air Station at Futenma is the most important; it functions as the air component of the III Marine Expeditionary Force. But to relocate that facility requires building a new offshore base, particularly for helicopter operations; and that requirement may take some time to implement. See U.S. General Accounting Office, *Overseas Presence: Issue Involved in Reducing the Impact of the U.S. Military Presence on Okinawa*, Report GAO/NSIAD-98-66 (Washington, D.C.: G.P.O., March 1998).

36. Hosokawa Morihiro, prime minister from 1992–1993, made just such a suggestion. See "Are U.S. Troops in Japan Needed?" *Foreign Affairs*, vol. 77, no. 4 (July–August 1998): 2–5.

37. For instance, the Kajima Corporation established a fund equal to about $4.6 million to compensate survivors and families from among the approximately 1,000 Chinese workers (of a total of about 50,000 Chinese) who were brought to Japan to work in a copper mine. The fund will be administered by the Chinese Red Cross. This action could enable other forced laborers from around Asia to press their own cases with the Japanese companies, such as Mitsubishi and Mitsui, that abused them during World War II. See Stephanie Strom, "Fund for Wartime Slaves Set Up in Japan," *New York Times*, November 30, 2000, A14. The "comfort women" have yet to accept a Japanese proposal for compensation via a semi-private foundation.

38. Governors of Okinawa prefecture have led the criticism. The current governor, Inamine Keiichi, told Japan's foreign minister: "In a way, we had been reserved about demanding a reduction of the Marines and other U.S. military forces. But we can no longer bear it." (*Japan Times*, February 26, 2001; in NAPSNet, March 2, 2001.) On conditions in Okinawa and the efforts to remove or reduce the U.S. presence, see Chalmers Johnson, ed., *Okinawa: Cold War Island* (San Diego, Calif.: Japan Policy Research Institute, 1999); Doug Bandow, "Okinawa: Liberating Washington's East Asian Military Colony," *Policy Analysis*, no. 314 (September 1, 1998), 1–27; and Chester Dawson, "Coming Undone in Okinawa," *Far Eastern Economic Review* (April 27, 2000): 22–23. Aside from Okinawa, other incidents have rankled many Japanese, such as the accidental sinking of the fisheries training vessel *Ehime Maru* by a U.S. submarine in Honolulu harbor. Nine Japanese, including several students, died in the accident; and though the submarine commander was tried and forced to leave the service, the punishment was widely considered insufficient. See, for example, "Waddle Penalty a Mockery of Civil Society's Common Sense," *Asahi Shimbun* (Tokyo), April 26, 2001, online English ed., which ended by saying: "U.S. forces will continue to encounter deep antipathy unless they change their attitude."

39. The Self-Defense Forces Law allows the use of guns, ships, and helicopters for search and rescue of Japanese civilians overseas. The Contingency Law allows mobilization of the SDF and specifies types of cooperation from local governments and the use of private facilities. Neither law, however, seeks to define the geographical scope of the security guidelines. See *Asahi Shimbun*, August 25, 1999; NAPSNet, August 27, 1999.

40. South Korean–Japanese security cooperation also includes joint naval exercises, the first of which was held in mid-1999 off the southern coast of South Korea. The exercise was limited to search-and-rescue so as not to offend North Korea—though of

course it drew protests anyway. See Don Kirk, "Seoul and Tokyo Hold Joint Naval Exercise," *International Herald Tribune*, August 6, 1999.

41. At the Group of Eight economic summit in July 2000, Japan pledged $15 billion for information technology projects in that region and $3 billion to combat AIDS and other diseases. The Mori government also spoke of allocating funds for NGOs doing refugee relief work and to African regional groups involved in conflict prevention. These commitments were said to be part of Japan's new "global diplomacy" designed to identify Japan with interests beyond East Asia and the U.S. relationship. See Junko Takahashi, "Mori to Embark on African Trip," *Japan Times*, January 6, 2001.

42. See Michael Green, "Why Tokyo Will Be a Larger Player in Asia," Global Beat (www.nyu.edu/globalbeat/asia/napsnet073100.html).

43. See Jim Mann, "Japan Taking Steps to Ensure Its Independence," *Los Angeles Times*, August 25, 1999.

44. See Tsuyoshi Kawasaki, "Between Realism and Idealism in Japanese Security Policy: The Case of the ASEAN Regional Forum," *Asian Survey, Pacific Review*, vol. 10, no. 4 (1997): 480–530.

45. Elaine Lies, "Politics Seen in Japan's N. Korea Furore," Reuters (Tokyo), January 6, 1999; NAPSNet, same date.

46. The four island groups north of Hokkaido have been in dispute since the end of World War II, and have been the subject of negotiations for their return since a 1956 Japan-Soviet Joint Declaration. In 1997 Russia and Japan agreed to conclude a peace treaty that would resolve the dispute; but that did not occur. As of 2001, the two sides could not even agree on whether all four islands or initially only two (Habomai and Shikotan) should be subject to negotiation for return to Japan.

47. Marcus Noland, *Avoiding the Apocalypse: The Future of the Two Koreas* (Washington, D.C.: Institute for International Economics, 2000), 163.

48. See the United States Institute of Peace report, "'Trialogue': U.S.-Japan-China Relations and Asian-Pacific Stability," September 1998. On the bilateral side, Japan and China did agree in 1999 to resume security dialogue, which had begun in 1994 and was suspended in 1997 because of differences over the U.S.–Japan security guidelines.

49. Lu Guangye, "The Impact of Reinforcement of Japan-U.S. Military Alliance on the Asia-Pacific Security and World Peace," *International Strategic Studies* (China Institute for International Strategic Studies), no. 3 (1999): 21–23.

50. Chen Wei, "The Sino-U.S.-Japan Relations at the Turn of the Century," *International Strategic Studies*, no. 4 (2000): 12.

51. Chen Wei, "The Sino-U.S.-Japan Relations, 13. The author identifies (p. 14) divergent strategic goals as the chief source of division among the three countries. The United States seeks hegemony, and use of Japan to further that ambition. Japan wants to become a major regional power and eventually a world power. It must rely on the United States, but ultimately seeks an independent role and a "break away from [U.S.] control." China wants to establish a "just and fair world and regional orders that are not controlled by the U.S."

52. Shinn, "Testing," 430.

53. Among other things, Chinese specialists worry that TMD would move Japan toward acquiring a long-range missile force of its own, would involve Japan in defense of Taiwan, and would give Japan a defense against Chinese ballistic missiles. See Monterey Institute, *U.S.–China Conference on Arms Control*, 16.

54. See, for instance, the paper by Ogawa Shinichi of the Japan National Institute for Defense Studies, "TMD and Northeast Asian Security," Nautilus Institute, September 28,

2000, NAPSNet, October 19, 2000. The arguments pro and con on Japan's involvement in TMD are summarized by Green, "State of the Field Report," 24–27.

55. Satoshi Morimoto, "Chinese Military Power in Asia: A Japanese Perspective," in *In China's Shadow: Regional Perspectives on Chinese Foreign Policy and Military Development*, ed. Jonathan D. Pollack and Richard H. Yang (Santa Monica, Calif.: RAND Corporation, 1998), 44–47.

56. The Nixon-Sato joint communiqué stated: "The Prime Minister also said that the maintenance of peace and security in the Taiwan area was also [in addition to Korea's security] a most important factor for the security of Japan."

57. See Nicholas D. Kristof, "China Gets an Apology from Japan," *New York Times*, November 27, 1998, A12.

58. See Peggy Falkenheim Meyer, "Sino-Japanese Relations: The Economic Security Nexus," in *Politics and Economics in Northeast Asia: Nationalism and Regionalism in Contention*, ed. Tsuneo Akaha (New York: St. Martin's Press, 1999), 144, for further discussion.

59. *Japan Times*, "Switch China's ODA Terms to Projects Basis, Panel Urges," December 19, 2000; NAPSNet, December 22, 2000.

60. For some Russian news reports that present attitudes on both sides, see NAPSNet, November 14, 2000, at a time when Japanese foreign minister Kono Yohei visited Moscow.

61. One positive development was the Japanese-Russian decision in 1999 to set up a hot line. Reportedly, the intrusion of a North Korean vessel into Japanese waters earlier in the year, and Japan's unprecedented pursuit of that vessel, prompted the hot line. Consideration was also being given to prior notice by both sides of naval maneuvers in the Sea of Japan. *Yomiuri Shimbun* (Tokyo), August 19, 1999 and *Daily Yomiuri* (Tokyo), August 20, 1999; NAPSNet, August 20, 1999.

62. Green, "State of the Field Report," 7.

63. On these and other current Japanese issues, see the collection of critical essays, *Dysfunctional Japan: At Home and in the World*, ed. Chalmers Johnson in *Asian Perspective*, vol. 24, no. 4 (2000).

64. See the discussion in Green, "State of the Field Report," 7–12.

65. *Japan's Goals*, ch. 6, 6.

66. See Kent E. Calder, "Japan's Changing Political Economy," in *Japan's Emerging Global Role*, ed. Unger and Blackburn, 127–29.

67. In a nutshell, Japan faces the problem that roughly one in five persons is 65 or older, whereas the birth rate is below the replacement rate, such that by the end of the century, the population will be about 67 million instead of the current 127 million. See Howard French, "In Stagnant Japan, Economic and Social Ills Match," *New York Times*, February 6, 2001, online ed.

68. Among the negative indicators is corporate debt: According to a private Japanese research firm, bankrupt corporations hold ¥23.99 trillion ($205 billion) in debts (*New York Times*, January 20, 2001). For banks, Japan's Financial Services Agency reported that as of mid-2000, they held ¥31.8 trillion ($274 billion) in bad loans. *Asian Wall Street Journal*, February 21, 2001.

69. See Aurelia George Mulgan, "Japan: A Setting Sun?" *Foreign Affairs*, vol. 79, no. 4 (July–August 2000): 51.

70. In actuality, Japan has frequently served as a nonpermanent member of the Security Council—nearly one-third of its years as a UN member, far more than Germany. See "Japan Determined to Win U.N. Security Council Role," *Asahi Evening News*, December 19, 1996, online ed.

# Chapter Six

# The Two Koreas: Uneasy Coexistence

## RECOVERING AUTONOMY

The Republic of Korea represents one of the great success stories in post–World War II international politics. In the space of about forty years, it rose from a divided, impoverished country that was nearly overrun by communist forces in the North to become an economic dynamo, the eleventh-largest economy in the world and the first Third World country to sit at the table with the leading ("First World") industrialized states. In 1993, South Korea's economic achievements began to be matched politically as the country's first civilian president in thirty-two years, Kim Young Sam, took office. Two former dictatorial presidents were tried and jailed during 1996. In 1997, the two Koreas, along with China and the United States, finally sat down to Four Party Talks designed to convert the Korean War armistice of 1953 into a permanent peace treaty. The same year, Kim Dae Jung, who had spent nearly half his life in exile or in jail, became the first person not from the ruling party to be elected president.

But in Korea as elsewhere in Asia, successes do not amount to full control of the country's present or future. There are limitations, as there are for all small countries. One such limitation is set by history and geography. Long before World War II, unified Korea was the "cockpit of Asia," always vulnerable to the interests of its principal neighbors: China, with which Korea had for centuries had a tributary state relationship but with relative autonomy; and a predatory Japan. After World War II, the United States and the Soviet Union divided Korea, laying the basis for a half century of Cold War hostilities: North Korea (the DPRK) aligned with China and the Soviet Union, and South Korea with the United States; war from 1950 to 1953 devastated both countries; and mutual propaganda attacks, armed incidents, and heavy spending on national defense became the norm thereafter. South Korea's lack of natural resources and capital created a dependence on other countries, and in the 1950s the United States, prompted by the Cold War and Japan's strategic importance

161

vis-à-vis China, hoped to make South Korea "another Japan."[1] The North, similarly, had to deal with the increasingly conflicting policies of its patrons. In the mid-1950s, its "Great Leader," Kim Il Sung, devised an economic development approach based on a philosophy of *juche* (self-reliance).

Out of this history came vulnerabilities and determinations that continue to the present, North and South: nationalism, which prompts a sensitivity to foreign pressures and influences, and great pride in Korea's cultural homogeneity and common sense of nationhood;[2] an authoritarian political culture strongly influenced by concerns about external threat; the strong or developmental state whose economic achievements have always been deemed critical to national security; the military's political prominence; difficult relations with Japan; and a greater affinity for China. As the oft-used metaphor of Korea as a "shrimp among whales" suggests, its autonomy in international affairs, including strategies for achieving national unification, has always been circumscribed by more powerful neighbors. But shrimps have ways to get around whales.

A second set of limits involves the closed circle of economic and political power in South Korea (and all the more so in North Korea's dictatorship). South Korea's economic prominence was not only achieved through hard work and investment in education. Repression of the democratic impulses of students, intellectuals, workers, the press, and other groups was also important. Democratization was stunted by personalism, factionalism, and the "Korean disease" of corruption, all of which contributed to the concentration of political power in the presidency and the ruling party, and to the dominant position of *chaebol* (ruling party) in the economy. Such concentrated power propelled Korea's growth in GNP and rising personal income, but it also carried risks. These became evident in 1997, when South Korea nearly had to default on its international obligations, which came to around $150 billion. Bank and corporate debt amounted to over $80 billion short-term and over $70 billion long-term. The bailout of Korea's economy was the largest in the IMF's history—around $58 billion—a great shock to a country that had prided itself on its accomplishments and the durability of its own approach to capitalist development. The crisis exposed the underside of the "miracle on the Han River," including excessive reliance on exports for growth; the cozy relationship among the *chaebol* and the banks; the degree to which personal relationships were allowed to dominate economic decision making; the poor regulation of the banking industry; and the favoritism shown to chaebol at the expense of smaller firms, organized labor, and foreign investors.

## NEW DIRECTIONS IN KOREAN FOREIGN POLICY

### Breaking with the Past

From the early Cold War years into the late 1980s, the foreign policies of the two Koreas were similarly motivated and followed similar patterns.[3] The primary motivating forces were a self-perception of victimization by outside powers, and thus a fierce nationalism; loss of control of the nation's fate; low international standing, due largely to dependence on one or the other superpower in the Cold War competition; and domestic insecurity. Both Koreas therefore sought legitimacy, national security, and state-centered paths to economic development. Their foreign policies were dominated by competition for international recognition, military alliances, and a search for economic self-reliance as the key to modernization, internal security, policy autonomy, and international respectability.[4] Politically, however, achievement of these objectives was undermined by harsh authoritarian rule, which both Korean governments justified in the name of national security.

National unification was actually only a secondary objective in the competition between the two Koreas. Although state leaders in Seoul and Pyongyang engaged in a constant war of words about unification, and from time to time offered proposals to the other side for bringing unification about, the reality is that unification was only acceptable to either one by conquest or absorption—"hegemonic unification," as Koh Byung Chul called it.[5] More decisive to both sides was preserving and extending state power, for which they devoted enormous resources. Strong-armed rule was the watchword: in North Korea, under Kim Il Sung and, upon his death in 1994, his son Kim Jong Il known as the "Dear Leader"; and in South Korea, under a succession of generals, notably Pak Chung Hee (1961–1979), Chun Doo Hwan (1980–1987), and Roh Tae Woo (1988–1993).[6] Anti-Communism in the South and anti-imperialism in the North became the new nationalisms.

Both Koreas pursued rapid industrialization, but in opposite ways.[7] North Korea turned inward. With access to far less foreign aid than the ROK, mainly from China, North Korea's economy performed remarkably well into the early 1980s, with per capita GNP roughly on a par with that of the South.[8] (In fact, by some estimates—since North Korea provides precious few hard figures—North Korea was abreast of South Korea in human development indicators such as life expectancy and literacy until around 1990.[9]) But Pyongyang's insularity, disastrous agricultural policies, natural disasters, and the military's huge drain on resources[10] eventually caught up with it, leading to technological backwardness, trade deficits, and unpayable external debts. By the early 1990s, the economy started to shrink: exports, which had been over $3 billion in 1988, began a precipitous decline (reaching $811 million in 1996); GDP "fell by nearly half between 1992 and 1996";[11] and arms exports assumed a key role in earning foreign exchange, accounting for about 15 percent of total exports in 1993.[12] In the mid-1990s, food shortages led to rationing; famine set in, requiring massive international food assistance that continues to the present. The human costs are staggering, and may take generations to overcome.[13]

South Korea, meanwhile, maintained substantial armed forces, but devoted capital accumulation to export-led growth from the early 1960s onward. Its successes gradually established the ROK's international legitimacy, not merely as a trading state but, by virtue of the diversification of its economic partners and its ability to grow with manageable international debt, as an autonomous actor. GNP, propelled by trade growth, surpassed $200 billion in 1989 and was close to $300 billion by 1991. GNP per capita reached $5,000 in 1990, passed $7,000 in 1994, and by 1997 was above $10,000. By 1990 the South's GNP was already ten times larger than the North's, and its per capita GNP was five times larger.[14] (The per capita income gap may now be over twenty times.[15]) Having become a richer country, Korea was able to join the twenty-five-member Organization for Economic Cooperation and Development (OECD) in 1996, become an affiliate of the G-7, and thus become the first third world country to graduate into the "first world."

In the 1980s clientalism in Korean foreign policy gave way to self-confidence, including a search for greater independence from U.S. interests. The Korean quality of life leaped forward, a highly competitive presidential election was held in 1987 (after Chun Doo Hwan's efforts to preserve his rule brought the middle class and other people into the streets in protest), and the Seoul Olympics were held (1988). Under President Roh Tae Woo, a new approach was adopted to North Korea and the socialist world. Dubbed the "Northern Policy," it opened the door to commercial and diplomatic relations with Eastern Europe and achieved substantive and wide-ranging agreements between the two Koreas.[16] As previously mentioned, in December 1991 North and South Korean leaders signed two accords that laid out conditions for denuclearization of the peninsula, coexistence, and confidence-building measures. North Korea, clearly prodded by Russia and China's decisions to establish diplomatic relations with the ROK (in 1990 and 1992), abandoned its long-standing opposition to dual Korean membership in the United Nations. And President Bush ordered the withdrawal of U.S. tactical nuclear weapons worldwide, which included several hundred based in South Korea.

## From "New Diplomacy" to "Sunshine" Policy

When Kim Young Sam assumed the presidency of South Korea, "New Diplomacy" was intended to signify a shift in foreign policy from traditional bilateralism (based squarely on the U.S.–ROK alliance) to increased reliance on multilateral diplomacy. The fundamental idea was to reposition South Korea in the post–Cold War world order of multipolar economic power, Asia-Pacific regional institutions (especially APEC), and a multitude of global issues (such as economic and environmental interdependence, and third world development) that would affect Korea's future. Kim, for example, said that Korea's foreign policy would no longer be "a hostage of inter-Korean competition" or narrowly focused on Northeast Asia. He spoke of national reconciliation along with national unification, sought to bring about a summit meeting with Kim Il Sung, and increased South Korea's involvement in regional and international security cooperation, such as by helping "resolv[e] global problems such as poverty."[17] South Korea contributed money and personnel to various UN peacekeeping operations (for example, in Somalia and Angola), established special funds for third world development assistance (total development aid reached about $170 million in 1993), and entered into talks with Japan, China, and other neighbors on cooperative approaches to transnational environmental problems such as fisheries and acid rain. Kim's administration also assigned a high priority to establishment of a multilateral mechanism, which would have to include North Korea, for dialogue on Northeast Asia security. Chaebol were encouraged by easy credit to expand their overseas operations. Korean FDI tripled between 1990 and 1995; but by 1997 chaebol overextension would become one of the ingredients of Korea's financial pain.

South Korea's quest for improved security and international standing was nearly derailed during 1993 and 1994 when the International Atomic Energy Agency (IAEA) and the United States found evidence that North Korea had diverted plutonium from its nuclear power plants to manufacture bombs. How far along Pyongyang actually got, and how many bombs it may have produced—President Clinton said two—may never be known. After arduous diplomacy amidst considerable saber-rattling, the United States and the DPRK concluded an "Agreed Framework" on October 21, 1994. The agreement in essence traded a North Korean freeze and the promise of an eventual opening up of all its nuclear facilities to international inspection for nuclear energy and oil assistance. If the step-by-step procedures in the agreement were followed, it would lead to full diplomatic relations. Following on the agreement, the KEDO was established to construct nuclear reactors in North Korea—an agreement between KEDO and the DPRK in December 1995 permits South Korean nuclear engineers access to power plant sites—and deliver oil. South Korea is KEDO's principal donor (around 60 percent of the costs, which may run to $4 billion); Japan, with over $1 billion, and the United States are the next-leading contributors.[18]

Though the handling of the nuclear issue avoided the use of force, the outcome left much to be desired from South Korea's perspective.[19] First, it showed that the road ahead to unification would be long indeed. In fact, unification took a back seat to U.S. nonproliferation objectives. Second, Seoul was an outside party to the formal negotiating sessions, leaving many Koreans suspicious of U.S. diplomacy, critical of American brinkmanship,[20] and upset that Pyongyang had exploited its nuclear potential to get U.S. aid and a leg up on diplomatic ties. Third, the nuclear standoff showed that the Korean peninsula was still a dangerous place in need of cooperative strategies to reduce the risks of conventional and nuclear war.[21] Even when small openings were attempted afterwards, such as business contacts, military incidents (the most serious of which involved a North Korean spy mission in 1996 that relied on a submarine landing in South Korea) intervened to stall or derail them.[22]

By the time he assumed the presidency, Kim Dae Jung had said and written a great deal concerning North Korea and reunification. He had always stressed the need to treat the North Korean leaders with respect, not to demonize them, and to calm their fears of absorption by the South. At various times he proposed summit meetings and conversion of the no-man's land that divides Korea at the 38th parallel into a "zone of peace." His reunification plan favored a gradual, multistage process. Starting with confederation (one Korean country, but separate states and social systems), the two Korean states would work toward federation, a merger into a single "socio-economic community." Only later would full-fledged unification occur: one Korean nation and government based on "democracy and prosperity."[23]

Starting out his administration amidst economic turmoil and in a political culture resistant to treating an opponent respectfully did not lend itself to attempting a new approach to North Korea. But Kim handled both the IMF crisis and Pyongyang with great finesse. His so-called Sunshine policy (later renamed engagement) followed through on earlier pronouncements: no use of force by either side; unification without absorption; feasible actions for inter-Korean reconciliation and cooperation; direct North-South dialogue; separation of economics from politics so as to promote South Korean aid and investment in the DPRK without conditions; and continuation of the Four Party Talks and the nuclear energy assistance called for under the Agreed Framework. In sum, Kim's goal was nothing less than to end the Cold War on the peninsula.[24] From all reports, it appears that the leadership in Pyongyang appreciated the breakthrough in thinking that Kim Dae Jung's policy represented.[25]

The culmination of Sunshine diplomacy was the June 2000 summit meeting between Kim Dae Jung and Kim Jong Il. It produced several agreements to expand contacts,[26] and one surprise:

> I said to Chairman Kim [Jong Il], "The Korean Peninsula is surrounded by the four powers of the United States, Japan, China and Russia. Given the unique geopolitical location not to be found any other time or place, the continued U.S. military presence on the Korean Peninsula is indispensable to our security and peace, not just for now, but even after unification."
>
> To this explanation of mine, Chairman Kim, to my surprise, had a very positive response. It was a bold switch from North Korea's longstanding demand [for U.S. withdrawal from South Korea], and a very significant move for peace.[27]

Kim Dae Jung's belief was that the summit had eliminated the possibility of war on the peninsula, though only a year later Kim Jong Il's promise seemed doubtful.

The summit was notable in other ways as well. First, it was a Korean initiative to break the deadlock. As the final statement said: "The South and North, as masters of national unification, will join hands in efforts to resolve the issue of national unification independently."[28] Perhaps of greatest importance was that the security of each was acknowledged as being important to the other. As Victor Cha wrote afterwards, unification was not brought closer, but mutual security was promoted: "the unification formulas referred to in the joint declaration are both premised less on integration and more on self-preservation, privileging one nation, two systems as the primary point of reference."[29] Second,

North Korea's leader showed his human side, deflating years of stereotypic reporting about his reclusiveness and lack of competence in foreign affairs. Third, South Korea's leader reestablished direct dialogue, an unrealized goal in the nuclear crisis. Fourth, the purpose of the U.S. presence in South Korea was put in doubt: Polls in South Korea showed most people no longer believed North Korea was a threat. Fifth, the summit was generally regarded as a triumph of Chinese diplomacy. Kim Jong Il visited China just prior to the summit, probably to coordinate strategy and obtain Beijing's blessing. But that provided China with an opportunity to demonstrate its importance to diplomacy on the peninsula, as well as with a chance to show Kim firsthand the successes of China's reforms.

## KOREA AND THE MAJOR POWERS

Today, it may safely be said that all four of the major powers concerned with Korean affairs—China, Japan, the United States, and Russia—share at least three interests. They want to avoid another war on the Korean peninsula, they want to keep the peninsula free of nuclear weapons, and they do not attach a high priority to Korea's unification (though all probably regard it as inevitable, and under Seoul's aegis). In this section, South Korea's evolving relationship with the four powers is explored.

### China

Since the establishment of relations with the ROK, China's official policy toward the Korean peninsula has been based on "peace and stability." PRC leaders welcomed the 1991 North-South accords, made economic partnership with South Korea a high priority, counseled North Korea to pursue economic reforms along Chinese lines, backed a nuclear-free Korea, and supported Korean unification through peaceful means.[30] During the nuclear standoff, China consistently urged resolution of the nuclear issue through dialogue. Beijing was helpful in counseling Pyongyang to avoid playing with fire, but it refused to play a mediator's role that might have put China in the position of imposing a solution on its longtime ally. Beijing's intention evidently was (and is) to maintain positive relations with both Koreas for as long as possible, essentially by separating its security interest in North Korea from its booming economic relationship with South Korea; and to position China to continue to have influence over Korean affairs after unification.

The paramount PRC interest in the Korean peninsula is to prevent destabilizing developments next-door that would jeopardize its own stability and security. A unified Korea with the South's open social system, capable of "infecting" ethnically Korean portions of north China;[31] a civil war and refugee crisis in North Korea; or a unified Korea that decided to "go nuclear" independently of the United States would be the kinds of developments that Beijing would probably considering threatening. Unified Korea might become the object of Sino-Japanese competition yet again; it might remain tied to the U.S. security system (present thinking in Seoul and Washington is that it will); or, as a nuclear state, it might be a competitor and potential threat.[32] If Korean unification under Seoul's authority is inevitable, China would probably prefer that it occur gradually, without open conflict or a sudden exodus of refugees. Thus, in the short-to-medium term, it is important to Beijing that North Korea be kept afloat, which it is attempting to do by providing food and energy assistance, maintaining close diplomatic ties, and accepting a deficit in trade with the North.[33] The Chinese preference clearly is that North Korea follow their lead on opening the economy; and Kim Jong Il's unexpected endorsement of China's reforms as "correct" during an early 2001 trip to Shanghai may signal important modifications of the juche strategy. China's probable long-term goal is to have a friendly Korea on its doorstep, one that might align with China on issues such as opposing the extension of Japanese military or economic power. As argued later, much of China's reaction to developments on the peninsula depends on the state of China–U.S. relations.

Kim Dae Jung's engagement policy promoted the kinds of tension-reducing benefits that Beijing appreciated.[34] It also gave China the space to have a two-Korea policy. The PRC's diplomatic relations with the ROK have involved numerous high-level exchanges of visits and regular defense consultations. In August 1999, for instance, an ROK defense minister visited China for the first time; China's defense minister reciprocated in January 2000; and the ROK's army chief of staff made a first-ever visit to China in February 2001. These are not just matters of protocol. The defense minister's trip was an attempt to head off another North Korean missile test and promote direct North-South Korean talks.[35] When Kim Dae Jung rejected participation in TMD, it won applause from Beijing, which thanked him by pressuring North Korea not to launch a new missile test in mid-1999.[36] At the same time, the PRC's contacts with the North, including military-to-military, remain cordial. Unlike Russia, China has not revised its mutual defense treaty with North Korea, though Beijing apparently stopped supplying arms to Pyongyang in the early 1990s.[37] China's overt diplomatic support of North Korea remains firm, such as on North Korea's right to retain a missile program and the necessity of U.S.–DPRK normalization of relations.[38]

Close PRC–ROK commercial relations represent an ideal marriage of economic, geographic, and strategic factors in promoting Chinese interests. By 1995 China and South Korea were each other's fourth most important trade partners, with a total trade of nearly $12 billion. The trade volume was double that amount in 1997 and 1999, by which time each country had moved up to number-three trade partner. Korean businesses made China their top choice, investing around $1 billion by 1994 and nearly $6 billion by 1998, mostly (about 44 percent) in the three northern provinces.[39] Today, bilateral trade and Korean FDI both exceed $30 billion. For China, the politics of the economic partnership was one reason for establishing diplomatic relations: It gave the PRC an alternative to excessive reliance on the U.S. market.[40] For South Korea, however, commerce with China has two drawbacks to go along with the obvious advantages: dependence on the China market (around 10 percent of exports) at a time of economic slump, and South Korea's loss of markets (especially the U.S. market) to cheaper, good-quality Chinese and Southeast Asian exports. There, exporters take advantage of lower labor costs, insufficient productivity gains among Korean chaebol, and (in Southeast Asia) Japanese investors. Hence, a central challenge to South Korean government and business will be how to reverse the pattern of declining competitiveness with and a certain dependence on China as an importer and investment host.

## Japan

The Korea–Japan relationship has repeatedly been buffeted by contending nationalisms, historical grievances, and Korean feelings of victimization and junior status in trade and political relations. Not until 1965, twenty years after World War II, did the two countries agree on appropriate Japanese compensation in the form of trade credits, loans, and aid, and thereby establish diplomatic relations. The Cold War linkage between Korea's defense and Japan's security helped to keep a lid on tensions, often (it seems) when confidence in the United States waned;[41] but suspicions of Japan's Korea policies have always been rife in Seoul, even in the best of times and no matter what Japanese officials may say publicly. When Roh Tae Woo inaugurated his "Northern policy" in 1988 and encouraged Japan and the United States to normalize relations with North Korea, Korean fears of a separate Japanese deal nearly came to pass, and Roh had to obtain Japan's agreement to consult Seoul before again attempting normalization.[42] As many Korean specialists see it, Japan's consistent intention has been to prolong Korea's division and profit from it, even though a reasonable argument can be made that Japan would benefit just as much from a unified, prosperous Korea. Obviously, in that case Japan would no longer have to contend with North Korean missiles; but a unified Korea might also be an even more difficult partner for Japan, and a greater trade and technology competitor than at present.

Prospects for a new level of understanding between South Korea and Japan seemed good when Prime Minister Hosakawa Morihiro and Kim Young Sam held a summit meeting at Kyongju in November 1993. Hosakawa made the most forthright apology any Japanese leader had ever given for his country's conduct before 1945, to which Kim responded that relations should henceforth be more "future-oriented."[43] In 1997 the two countries agreed to open a security dialogue to cover a host of bilateral issues. But, emblematic of the mistrust between them, the ROK military apparently oriented its weapons acquisitions toward a future Japanese threat rather than, to Washington's displeasure, toward North Korea.[44]

Not until Kim Dae Jung took office did Korean relations with Japan take a turn for the better. He explicitly buried the hatchet on the dark past when he received Japan's apologies during a 1998 state visit. In June 2000, South Korea lifted restrictions on imports of Japanese films and most television programming. (A more timid relaxation of controls on "cultural imports" from Japan had begun in 1988.) The two countries agreed to co-host the World Cup soccer tournament in 2002; the Japanese emperor was invited to visit Seoul; and Japanese tourists made Korea their favorite stopover—and in the process received an education in past oppressive Japanese conduct in Korea.[45] Kim Dae Jung said he favored normalization of Japan–DPRK relations as part of the engagement policy. Nevertheless, Japan was made to look out of step when the Korean summit took place. How could the LDP leadership explain its painfully slow diplomacy with North Korea to normalize relations, its support of TMD, or its continued hosting of so many U.S. forces on Okinawa and elsewhere? It appears that Japanese policy is, after all, to keep Korea divided as long as possible, "hoping to contain tensions and foster cordial ties with South Korea . . . promot[ing] a gradual reconciliation."[46]

History and economics still weigh heavily in the Japan–ROK relationship. Disputes continue over ownership of the Tokdo/Takeshima islands, fisheries, periodic insensitive remarks by Japanese officials about Japan's colonial rule of Korea (1910–1945), and compensation for the "comfort women." A typical run-in occurred in the spring of 2001, when South Korea withdrew its ambassador from Tokyo to protest historical inaccuracies and omissions in Japanese school textbooks. A long list of alleged errors was then presented to the Japanese foreign ministry with a demand for corrections. Few changes were made leading Kim Dae Jung to wonder aloud if Japan could ever be trusted. (These issues rankle North Korea even more. In numerous rounds of talks with Japanese officials since 1990, Pyongyang has typically demanded that Japan pay a substantial price for its past misdeeds if it wants diplomatic relations. Japan has rejected anything that looks like reparations, and has raised issues of its own, thus keeping normalization in limbo.[47]) Trade is also a major bilateral issue. The key issue is Korea's trade deficit with Japan, its second-most important trade partner after the United States. "While South Korea's cumulative trade deficits with Japan for 27 years between 1965 and 1991 totaled $66.1 billion, the figure for the five years between 1992 and 1996 was $59.42 billion."[48] The structural nature of the deficit is the fact that Korean automotive, electronics, and other high tech exports use very high percentages of Japanese components.[49] Even the more favorable yen-to-won exchange rate in the mid-1990s did not alter this structure, since higher Korean exports were offset by the dependence on Japanese imports, which has long hovered around 25 percent of import share. Nor has Korea been able dramatically to increase exports to Japan. In the mid-1980s Japan took 15 percent of Korean exports, but only 9.3 percent in 1998.[50]

One obvious way to alter this pattern is for Japan to significantly increase capital and technology flows into Korea, specifically in the development of key Korean industries.[51] But that is not likely to happen any time soon as Japan faces its own economic doldrums. In fact, Tokyo's halting response to Korea's financial woes in 1997 became another unpleasant factor in Korean–Japanese relations. A more practical way for Korea to ease its technology dependence is to allow, or entice, more foreign investment in high technology areas, and greatly to increase Korean government funding of research and development. These steps also require important changes in the way "Korea, Inc." does business.

## The United States

The Korea–U.S. relationship is surely the most complicated of Korea's external ties. On the surface it would appear to be otherwise, given U.S. sacrifices in the Korean War, its military presence in Korea ever since (around 37,000 soldiers today), its deep involvement in Korean politics and economy in the name of promoting stability and democracy, and its strong cultural impact on Korean society. But there are usually costs that come from such close attachments, particularly as a country like South Korea emerges from under the patron's shadow. The pervasiveness of American influence has long been a lightning rod for Korean nationalism.[52] Many Korean intellectuals, including students, look upon the U.S. military presence as an obstacle to national unification: Without it, they argue, South Korea would probably have been forced to engage the North long ago.

Though the United States played a positive role in Korea's break with authoritarianism beginning in the late 1980s, it had consistently supported military rule until then. When Korean special forces under Major General Chun Doo Hwan cracked down on dissenters in Kwangju in May 1980, causing anywhere from several hundred to a few thousand deaths, senior U.S. officials knew of Chun's intentions in advance and chose to do nothing to stop him.[53] They put Korean "stability" and friendliness with the military ahead of democracy and the rule of law. And for all the U.S. economic assistance that flowed to South Korea during the Cold War years, the United States is still regarded in some quarters as being (like Japan) a selfish power out to benefit its own trading interests. U.S. pressure on Korea to open its markets has long been a sore point in the relationship. In the unfolding bailout of Korea in 1997, anti-Americanism again came to the surface as Washington sought to force a restructuring of the Korean economy to the advantage of U.S. corporations and banks as a condition of loans.

Nevertheless, the fundamental elements of the Korea–U.S. relationship remain in place. As Kim Dae Jung's report of his conversation with Kim Jong Il showed, Korean leaders regard the U.S. presence as providing strategic stability on the peninsula now and after unification. South Korean thinking evidently is that unification will bring not only numerous demands for reconstructing the North, but also uncertainties about again being the cockpit of Asia, caught between a powerful China and a more nationalistic Japan.[54] Such ideas suit the Americans just fine. With no other basing options in East Asia, with a longstanding concern about Japan's reaction to a Korea left on its own, and with American reliability in Asia likely to be questioned, the United States is in no hurry to leave South Korea. Its East Asia strategy studies in the Clinton years consistently stated the U.S. intention to keep military forces in the ROK after unification, and one suspects an additional reason—keeping Korea, unified or not, under control.[55]

## Russia

A decade after Russia's tilt toward South Korea that began with Gorbachev's new diplomacy in 1990, the honeymoon is long over. A combination of unrealized economic gains, lack of inclusion in international discussions of Korean security, and the instability of Russian politics transformed Russian policy to one of equidistance between North and South Korea.

At the time of the nuclear standoff, the tilt of Russia's Korea policy to the South was abundantly clear.[56] Following Boris Yeltsin's visit to Seoul in November 1992, which ended with a friendship treaty and agreement on regular consultations, Russia made several goodwill gestures, including delivery of the black box from the Korean Airlines flight that its jet fighters had shot down in 1983, and archival materials from the Korean War. Russia was evidently upset with the Pyongyang leadership's intransigent opposition to economic reform, and with its apparent pursuit of a nuclear weapon option. At considerable economic sacrifice, Moscow in 1993 canceled delivery to North Korea of three light water nuclear reactors valued at $4 billion that it had agreed to sell in 1991.[57] Yeltsin's government also vowed to end (and did end) mutual defense commitments with North Korea under a 1961 treaty. The treaty was replaced with a friendship treaty, not finalized until early in 2000, that is similar to the one signed with South Korea.[58] In 1994, Yeltsin is said to have assured the South Korean government that Russia no longer considered that it had a defense obligation to North Korea and that it would stop providing weapons to the DPRK. Even more boldly, Moscow reached agreement with South Korea to repay not quite one-half of its $3 billion debt to South Korea, incurred at the time relations were established, with weapons—tanks and small arms at first, ground-to-air and anti-aircraft missiles later.[59]

These moves incurred North Korea's wrath but did not spell the end of its relations with Russia. When the Agreed Framework was put together in late 1994, Russian policy fully embraced an "equidistant diplomacy."[60] Moscow decided to show its dissatisfaction with what were regarded as U.S. efforts to ease it out of a role in Korean security or in the nuclear issue. That dissatisfaction continues to the present, fueled by the Yugoslav crisis and a wide range of Russia–U.S. policy differences as well as by sympathy among some senior Russian policy makers with North Korea's weakened situation.[61] A proposed six-power international conference is one means (though an old one, dating back to the late 1980s) by which Russia has tried to regain entry in the Korea game; but Pyongyang's preference for dealing with the United States on more immediate security matters precludes that approach for now. As Russia looks ahead, its chief concern may be that a strong Korea, unified under Seoul, will possess nuclear weapons. Only when Russian leaders feel assured that a unified Korea will not be a nuclear weapon state, and will subscribe to all the treaties that limit WMD and missile development, are they likely fully to support Korean unification.[62]

On the economic side there are other disappointments for Moscow. It has long been unhappy with the slow pace of economic relations with South Korea as total trade has declined and Korean business has seemed to lose its enthusiasm for the Russian market, at least until the Russians pay their debts.[63] Korean participation in natural gas and oil exploration in Siberia and Sakhalin Island is the one potential bright spot.[64] In 1995 the Russian defense ministry openly questioned the value of tilting too far toward the ROK, and in early 2001 Russia signed an agreement with North Korea to upgrade some weapons systems.[65] That development still leaves much to be resolved between the Russians and the North Koreans. Their trade with Russia is small (under $100 million in 1997) and in deficit, they owe Russia about $3.5 billion (but seem to believe that Russia's abandonment of them also incurred a debt), and they have some 20,000 people working under apparently terrible conditions in the mines and forests of the Russian Far East.[66]

## KOREA'S FUTURE

The keys to a future of economic stability and military security for South Korea would seem to lie in further democratization and economic restructuring, continuation of the security- and confidence-building process that the 2000 summit opened up, and U.S. policies that support the engagement strategy. National unification is still a number of years away, and carries a high price tag (estimated in the several hundreds of billions of dollars to reconstruct the North). The South's engagement policy hopes to provide for a "soft landing" in the North when the day of unification dawns. By dealing forthrightly with its own problems, South Korea can make the soft landing affordable.

### Political and Economic Security

Globalization was a severe test for a Korean president who always believed in the importance of economic security, protection of the working class, and opening of the economy to international forces. The financial crisis forced Kim Dae Jung to make some unpleasant choices in order to ensure access to IMF bailout funds. He had to accept substantial layoffs and unprecedented levels of unemployment, on one hand; but on the other, the crisis gave him the chance to push for consolidation of *chaebol* as part of his long-range plan to break from the developmental state model. The IMF program of structural adjustment opened the way to foreign investors as bankrupt companies (including ten of the top thirty chaebol) and banks folded or were absorbed by others. FDI in South Korea, which was $2.3 billion in 1996, topped $5.4 billion in 1998.[67] This meant that FDI now accounted for about 20 percent of foreign capital inflows, a historic high.[68] Union leaders and chaebol executives found something in common after all: resisting foreign takeovers of Korean assets.[69]

Although Seoul paid off its debt to the IMF in August 2001, and despite several positive signs that Korea's economy in 2001 had rebounded, it continues to have serious weaknesses. Unemployment is still over 4 percent (a bit under one million workers); GNP per person is down to $8,500; the banking system is saddled with enormous debt due to bad loans, which the government (in defiance of market forces) has spent huge sums to cover;[70] and export growth is flagging. The top chaebol have retained much of their power despite having to whittle down the number of their subsidiaries.[71] While chaebol sit under a mountain of debt, the government's intervention in the economy to fix the problem is inconsistent, perhaps showing that the largest chaebol still are considered "too big to fail."[72] When the dust settles and the various mergers, bankruptcies, reorganizations, and foreign takeovers have ended, the structure of the South Korean economy—that is, the government–big business–bank triangle that is "Korea, Inc."—may look different from before the financial crisis; but big business may emerge with as much economic power as before.[73]

The other face of globalization is political: the opportunity Kim Dae Jung saw on taking office to perfect democratic institutions and social justice. Here, South Korea's recent record is mixed. On one hand, the military as a political force was silenced due to the firing by Kim Dae Jung of key generals and the banning of private military groups within the armed forces. The political system has become much more competitive with the expansion of local elections and greatly increased room for NGOs and other elements of civil society. Restrictions on contacts with North Korea have been greatly reduced. Yet, vestiges of the old order and the Cold War remain. Cases of official corruption are still commonplace. Party politics is as uncompromising and uncivil as ever. Kim Dae Jung is often accused, and not just by the opposition, of adhering to the old style of authoritarian, inner-circle governance. What happened is what two writers call "the inherent conflict between economic globalization and democratic consolidation": In order to push his economic reform agenda, Kim has had to strengthen the state's interventionist role.[74] The infamous National Security Law, long a target of North Korean propaganda, has been relaxed but not repealed, and Koreans continue to be arrested under its expansive antisubversion terms.[75] The state still exercises a forceful hand against untimely strikes by unions.

## Inter-Korean Relations

North Korea faces the problem of avoiding economic and environmental ruin and social collapse brought on by a food and health-care crisis that has sharply reduced individual well-being.[76] Numerous reports from aid agencies and even from North Korean officials[77] indicate the grim reality of life in one of the last Stalinist systems. Thus far, except for allowing foreign investment in an isolated corner of the country—the Rajin-Sonbong free trade and economic zone, established late in 1991—Pyongyang has clung to juche and resisted globalization.[78] Foreign trade is strictly limited and has been in deficit since 1985. The food crisis forced the DPRK to rely on international assistance; from 1996 to 1999 it received over $1 billion, mostly from the United States, China, and South Korea.[79] Nevertheless, the DPRK's leaders fear—not unrealistically—that to go the way of China and "marketize" socialism will eventuate in absorption by the South and domination by Japanese capital. Yet failure to follow the Chinese example is likely to condemn the country to a crisis of basic needs, more economic refugees, and defections by the political and military elite. Even civil war is within the realm of possibility.

Caught in this vise, and perhaps in the throes of a leadership debate about its future direction, North Korea's response to the engagement strategy has been inconsistent. Which is the real North Korea? analysts ask. Realists in Seoul and Washington point to North Korea's ongoing production of missiles and WMD, its arms exports, its maintenance of large military forces and weapons within range of the DMZ, the involvement of North Korean officials in drug smuggling, counterfeiting, and other crimes,[80] and the usual difficulties in pinning down North Korean diplomats on concrete steps to facilitate North-South contacts. Supporters of the engagement policy can cite just as many positive developments: North Korea's apparent adherence to the Agreed Framework; its declining arms sales, which are considerably less than South Korea's;[81] Kim Jong Il's seeming acceptance of a U.S. military presence in Korea after unification;[82] his support of the idea of turning the 38th parallel into an economic development zone;[83] North Korea's moratorium on long-range missile tests in September 1999, renewed in October 2000 and again in May 2001 for two years;[84] successful diplomacy on family reunions and restoration of rail links; and the march together of the two Korean teams under one flag at the Sydney 2000 Olympic Games. Additionally, the optimistic view notes that the balance of military forces has favored South Korea for over a decade, and never more so than today.[85] Still, North Korean behavior and intentions remain as difficult to read as ever.

One thing is certain, however: In a hostile world, Kim Jong Il will do whatever it takes for North Korea's social system to survive. The North Koreans' commitment to four different processes—the Agreed Framework, the Four Party Talks, KEDO, and direct North-South talks—naturally reflects their belief that these processes promote survival. At the same time, though, the four processes have created a web of confidence-building steps that enhance strategic stability on the peninsula. Over time, North Korea may have to take further steps if it wants to continue receiving international assistance, such as rejoining the IAEA (which it left in 1994) and opening all its nuclear facilities to the agency's full inspection. If the confidence-building process works, it could lead to a peace agreement between the two Koreas, with the peace guaranteed by the United States, China, Russia, and Japan—a "2-plus-4" or six-sided arrangement currently favored by all the parties except China and North Korea.[86]

The peace process is a delicate one, and showing generosity toward North Korea will be important to its continued success. Reflecting that view, the Kim Dae Jung government urged acceptance of the DPRK in ARF (which it was) and eventually in APEC, normalization of U.S. and Japan ties with Pyongyang, and continued high-level direct dialogue with Pyongyang. In response to North Korea's economic crisis, Kim pushed for increased South Korean investments in North Korea and expanded trade.[87] The ROK is now the DPRK's second-largest trade partner, with total North-South trade of around $425 million in 2000. Its economic aid to the North, both directly in food and indirectly via KEDO, is already substantial in spite of the obstructionism of the old-line political opposition in the ROK National Assembly. Increased security for North Korea is actually in South Korea's long-term best interest, Kim Dae Jung is evidently saying, since the end game is a *nonviolent* transfer of power. Kim also is wary of a resurgence of Japanese nationalism. The greater North Korean *in*security becomes, the more likely is Japan's move toward a more assertive defense program. That would put great pressure on a South Korean government to abandon the engagement policy.

Thus, rather than focus, as Washington does, on North Korea's arms exports and nuclear capability, which justify a deterrence strategy, Kim has sought to provide North Korea with alternatives to its dependence on weapons for profit and security. Whether becoming partner to North Korea's quest for economic and political survival is a winning strategy remains to be seen.[88] The military is the most powerful institution in North Korea; its views on engagement are not clear. And in the South, Kim is under constant pressure from the opposition party and academic critics to slow down the peace process. There is a demand for more concrete results, such as in more and larger family reunions and force reductions by North Korea in areas near the demilitarized zone. By late 2001, with the economy and Kim's popularity slipping badly, the greatest threat to the Sunshine policy lay not in the North but in the South. Instead of national consensus, Kim is faced with political rancor, regional rivalry, and lack of public faith in officials, all of which made further progress on unification policy extremely difficult.

Meanwhile, debate goes on in Washington about North Korea's missile and WMD programs. In the last days of the Clinton administration, a U.S.–DPRK deal that would essentially have stopped North Korea's missile exports and production was apparently within reach.[89] When Kim Jong Il said in May 2001 that North Korea would continue its suspension of missile tests, he made clear that missile production and sales would go on (because they earn money, he said). He thus challenged the Washington to resume exploration of an aid-for-missiles deal. Key figures in the Bush administration are convinced, however, that the potential for DPRK missiles capable of reaching the United States is only a matter of time (2005 by some estimates) and thus justify moving ahead on ballistic missile defense. That is usual worst-case hypothesizing, however; it makes no allowance for normal diplomacy to search for a solution, either in bilateral relations or through KEDO. Nor does the hardline view assign sufficient weight to the fact that North Korea's medium-range missiles (capable of reaching Japan) are primitive (the 1998 multistage rocket test over Japan was a failure), or that U.S. intelligence on secret North Korean weapons programs has often been dead wrong.[90]

In 2000 and 2001, North Korea established relations with nearly all the major industrialized countries, and with the European Union. Only the United States, Japan, and France remained off the list. The DPRK's outreach was reminiscent of South Korea's "Northern policy" under Roh Tae Woo, a diplomatic offensive in the socialist world that began with establishing trade and official relations in Eastern Europe and ended in the early 1990s with diplomatic recognition from the Soviet Union and China. Unlike the Northern policy, which also aimed to weaken North Korea, the DPRK's new diplomacy has South Korea's full support. Gaining new international acceptance may provide Pyongyang with the additional leverage it needs to offset American pressure.

### U.S. Policy—and the China Factor

Future U.S. policy must deal with the prospects for change in both Koreas and not just in the North. Even though the welcome mat is still out to U.S. bases in the ROK, the South Koreans' welcome might wear thin. The 2000 inter-Korean summit planted in many Koreans' minds the idea that Koreans are capable of reaching a peaceful settlement by themselves, and that perhaps U.S. forces are no longer needed. That idea was punctuated by disagreements between Washington and Seoul that were eventually resolved, but may return.[91] The two Koreas might sign a peace treaty, which would make it hard for either Seoul or Washington to justify keeping U.S. forces in South Korea.[92] Meanwhile, South Korea has been strengthening its defense autonomy. The purchase of Russian weapons has already been mentioned. Another sign may be found in the now-resolved dispute with the United States over increasing the range of South Korean missiles. Their effect is to remove the need to be under TMD, which (as noted above) Kim Dae Jung rejected, and instead to enable the ROK to have its own answer for North Korea's medium-range ballistic missiles.[93]

Should an increasingly self-confident South Korea reduce or eliminate the U.S. presence, before or after unification, that probably would influence Japan to do the same. The United States would then be left without permanent air or naval bases in East Asia. As argued in the previous chapter, that may be a blessing in disguise. But it does not have to mean an end to U.S. extended deterrence under the bilateral defense treaty. Indeed, given opinion polls that show strong support among South Koreans for possessing nuclear weapons if Japan or North Korea goes nuclear, or if the alliance with the United States collapses, maintaining the defense treaty makes sense.[94] Still another option, though highly unlikely at this time, cannot be dismissed: *Korean neutrality*, with security guaranteed by the major powers.

In its relations with the DPRK, the United States has a fundamental choice to make. It can either confront North Korea and actively seek its demise; or it can nourish the seeds planted by Kim Dae Jung's policies and engage the North— accepting, as it does in its China policy, that communist rule is not going to disappear right away, that normal diplomatic relations simply make good sense and are not a reward for proper behavior, and that a relationship burdened by history, ideology, and uncommon interests is bound to have many ups and downs. The first course is highly unlikely to succeed and "would risk destructive war and would not win the support of U.S. allies in the region."[95] Clinton considered and rejected it. The latter course, engagement, is more difficult but also more promising, since it accords with the North's preferred path to security, which is through Washington. As William J. Perry said in an interview at the time he presented his report to Clinton urging a reciprocal strategy designed to "reduce pressures on the DPRK that it perceives as threatening":

> I do not condone or admire the [North Korean] regime, but I do recognize that it is very much in control in that country. And I think it would be imprudent on our part to assume that this regime is going to collapse. We have to deal with the North Korean government not as we wish they would be, but as in fact they are. . . . We do not think of ourselves as a threat to North Korea, but I fully believe that they consider us a threat to them and, therefore, they see this missile [program] as a means of deterrence.[96]

It is therefore appropriate, even if ironic, that the United States is North Korea's principal source of foreign aid—in fact, the largest recipient of U.S. aid in East Asia.[97] Easing trade and investment sanctions, which occurred in mid-2000 as part of Perry's recommended response to North Korea's suspension of long-range missile tests, is also sensible. It should be taken further, despite the inevitable slow pace of actual business.[98] Diplomatic relations should be culminated quickly rather than await a deal on North Korea's missile deployments and sales. Extending international legitimacy to North Korea enhances opportunities for promoting inter-Korean dialogue and diplomatic relations; for reducing Korean military spending and deployments on both sides of the DMZ; for reducing the U.S. military presence in South Korea and Japan; and ultimately for creating a security mechanism in Northeast Asia.

Unfortunately, the Perry report rejected any change in U.S. military deployments in Northeast Asia. U.S. forces and bases in South Korea, regional conventional and nuclear war capabilities, and plans for TMD stayed in place. Nor did the report urge accelerating the timetable for establishing diplomatic relations with North Korea, though the Joint U.S.–DPRK Communiqué of October 2000 did contain positive language about prospects for normalizing relations.[99] Perhaps the existence of other, hardline proposals for dealing with North Korea limited the scope of what the Perry group could propose.[100] Even so, the report's effort to craft a roadmap to normal relations with North Korea is unlikely to be followed in the George W. Bush administration, where the perspective is generally hostile to the Clinton engagement model represented in the Agreed Framework. If there were any doubts about that, Bush's meeting with Kim Dae Jung in March 2001 put them to rest—the differences in the two countries' approaches to North Korea were clear for all to see. The meeting starkly revealed how dependent the Sunshine policy is on U.S. decisions.

Though PRC policy toward the Korean peninsula ultimately is dictated by its strategic interests, the state of U.S.–China relations will have an important bearing on that policy.[101] To the extent their differences narrow, and PRC insecurities over "American hegemonism" are reduced, China is more likely to let North-South Korean relations take their natural course. Beijing might restore its "1.5 Koreas" policy, tilting to the ROK; might be amenable to expanding the agenda of the Four Party Talks to embrace the idea of a Northeast Asia dialogue forum on mutual security issues; and might be more cooperative with South Korea on the matter of North Korean economic refugees who have fled into northern China (if caught they are forced to return to an uncertain fate in North Korea).[102] Korean unification, and even a (small) U.S. military presence in southern Korea thereafter, may be considered less threatening and more conducive to Chinese interests (i.e., blocking Japanese influence) if U.S.–PRC relations are positive. Where U.S.–PRC differences widen, on the other hand, they propel Chinese "nationalism cum ideology" forward, as Xiaoxiong Yi has clearly shown.[103] In such circumstances, we can expect that prospects for successful dialogue on mutual security in and around the Korean peninsula will decline, whereas Chinese support of North Korea will stiffen and common cause with Russia will strengthen.[104] Indeed, the key to North Korea's long-term survival these days may hinge on Chinese and Russian support, not because Beijing and Moscow have any great affection for Kim Jong Il's regime, but out of their antagonism toward "American hegemony" in world affairs.

The best course for U.S. (and Japanese) policy is to continue supporting Kim Dae Jung's engagement policy and avoid straying into self-interested approaches that may undermine that policy. The danger exists that, as happened during the nuclear crisis, U.S. diplomacy with North Korea will overshadow inter-Korean dialogue and subordinate South Korean interests to those of Washington. Military issues would displace Korean concerns about increasing inter-Korean contacts and reforming North Korea's economy, which are steps toward eventual unification. Japan's hesitancy to provide food assistance until various bilateral issues with North Korea are resolved, and Pyongyang's insistence on Japanese reparations for damages incurred during colonial rule also hinder the engagement policy. It would be far more productive for Japan to follow the lead of the EU in 2001, when it established diplomatic relations with North Korea and promised to provide food and other assistance. In Japan's case, a substantial dose of ODA would be beneficial—a "development assistance plan for the Korean Peninsula like the U.S. Marshall Plan for Europe after World War II," as a former South Korean minister recommended.[105] Kim would clearly prefer that Washington and Tokyo normalize relations with Pyongyang in advance of dealing with bilateral issues that keep the parties apart. But U.S. and Japanese domestic political pressures stand in the way of that schedule, with a substantial number of legislators in both countries insisting that North Korea reciprocate for the benefits it has been received before being given full diplomatic recognition or the aid it wants.[106]

# NOTES

1. Bruce Cumings, *Korea's Place in the Sun: A Modern History* (New York: W.W. Norton, 1997), 305–8. Washington saw little prospect that South Korea would ever have a strong economy, and thus supported President Syngman Rhee's import substitution policy with enormous amounts of military and economic aid.

2. See Han-Kyo Kim, "Korean Unification in Historical Perspective," in *Korea and the World: Beyond the Cold War*, ed. Young Whan Kihl (Boulder, Colo.: Westview, 1994), 23–24.

3. See, for example, Edward A. Olsen, "The Diplomatic Dimensions of the Korean Confrontation," in *East Asian Security in the Post–Cold War Era*, ed. Simon W. Sheldon (Armonk, N.Y.: M.E. Sharpe), 89–96; Youngnok Koo and Sung-joo Han, eds., *The Foreign Policy of the Republic of Korea* (New York: Columbia University Press, 1985); Koh Byung Chul, *The Foreign Policy Systems of North and South Korea* (Berkeley, Calif.: University of California Press, 1984).

4. Koh, *Foreign Policy Systems*, ch. 2.

5. Byung Chul Koh, "A Comparison of Unification Policies," in *Korea and the World*, ed. Kihl, 155.

6. The essential source is Sung Chul Yang, *The North and South Korean Political Systems: A Comparative Analysis* (Boulder, Colo.: Westview, 1994).

7. A finely detailed account is by Marcus Noland, *Avoiding the Apocalypse: The Future of the Two Koreas* (Washington, D.C.: Institute for International Economics, 2000), chs. 2–3.

8. Cumings, *Korea's Place in the Sun*, 424.

9. Noland, *Avoiding the Apocalypse*, 76–77.

10. The ROK's estimate is that in 1999 North Korea's actual military spending consumed 52 percent of its total budget, or about $4.7 billion. Most other categories of spending dropped substantially. (Unification Ministry report in *Joongang Ilbo* [Seoul], January 9, 2000; NAPSNet, January 10, 2000.) Noland discusses the North Korean military's "parallel economy" and observes that its over one million soldiers are equivalent to "one-fifth of men of working age . . . North Korea appears to devote a higher share of national income to the military than any other country in the world" (*Avoiding the Apocalypse*, 71–72).

11. Noland, *Avoiding the Apocalypse*, 81.

12. Anthony H. Cordesman, "A Comparative Summary of Military Expenditures; Manpower; Land, Air, Naval, and Nuclear Forces; and Arms Sales," Center for International and Strategic Studies (January 2000), 68, www.csis.org/military/asianchinese_milbal.pdf.

13. A very rough estimate is that about 2 million people perished between 1994 and 1998, in a total population of around 22 million. Some observers, and the North Koreans themselves, put the figure at between 200,000 and 300,000. Whatever the actual count, most visitors to North Korea agreed that the famine would have generational consequences due to stunted mental and physical growth of children. The famine also revealed

the desperate situation of health care and other living conditions of people outside Pyongyang. For a concise review and analysis of the famine, see Andrew Natsios, "The Politics of Famine in North Korea," U.S. Institute of Peace Special Report, August 2, 1999.

14. Il SaKong, *Korea in the World Economy* (Washington, D.C.: Institute for International Economics, 1993), 178; tables A.4 and A.5, 226–29.

15. See the 1996 estimate of a 20:1 income gap in Noland, *Avoiding the Apocalypse*, 79.

16. Dan C. Sanford, "ROK's *Nordpolitik*: Revisited," *The Journal of East Asian Affairs*, vol. 7, no. 1 (Winter/Spring 1993): 1–31; Tae Dong Chung, "Korea's Nordpolitik: Achievements and Prospects," *Asian Perspective*, vol. 15, no. 2 (Fall–Winter 1991): 149–78.

17. See in particular the speeches of Foreign Minister Han Sung-joo, *Korean Diplomacy in an Era of Globalization: Speeches of Foreign Minister Han Sung-Joo, March 1993–December 1994* (Seoul: Chisik Publishing House, 1995), 73–103 and 112–123.

18. More than a dozen other countries have helped finance and administer KEDO. For a listing of contributions to KEDO between 1995 and mid-1999, see Noland, *Avoiding the Apocalypse*, table 4.1, 155–56.

19. I have explored these in "South Korea's Foreign Policy and Future Security: Implications of the Nuclear Standoff," *Pacific Affairs*, vol. 69, no. 1 (Spring 1996): 8–31.

20. Years later, Kim Young Sam told of his anger over the Clinton administration's preparedness to "stage a war with the North on our land" in June 1994 by bombing the main North Korean nuclear site at Yongbyon. Kim said he refused to cooperate with such a step. Former President Carter's visit to Pyongyang shortly afterward for talks with Kim Il Sung defused the situation. Interview of Kim in *Hankyoreh Daily*, Agence France Presse report, May 24, 2000; NAPSNet, May 24, 2000.

21. Leon V. Sigal's *Disarming Strangers* (Princeton, N.J.: Princeton University Press, 1999) shows just how close the crisis came to a collision. He lays the principal responsibility on hawkish U.S. officials who were viscerally opposed to a cooperative strategy in dealing with North Korea. To Sigal, one of the chief lessons of the crisis is that "inducements work, [and] cooperation is far less costly than coercion" (see especially pp. 251–52).

22. Kim Young Sam's government gave initial approval for some thirty companies to explore business opportunities in North Korea, but only one, Daewoo Business Group, actually began operations (a garment and bag factory in Nampo). *Korea Herald* (Seoul), September 30, 1996; NAPSNet online, same date.

23. Kim Dae Jung, speech of August 15, 1994, "Three-Phase Unification Formula for Building Korean National Community," in *Korea Focus*, vol. II, no. 4 (July–August 1994): 174.

24. Kim said: "I want to emphasize that during the remaining three years of my term, I do not think that reunification will take place and this is not my goal now, my goal is to end the Cold War and bring about peaceful exchanges. I do believe that if we stay with the [engagement] policy with consistency . . . we will be able to end the Cold War on the Korean peninsula during my term." Agence France Presse, "N. Korea Urged to Abandon Nuclear, Missile Ambitions to Save Economy," Seoul, February 10, 2000; NAPSNet, February 10, 2000.

25. See articles in the Seoul newspapers, *Korea Times*, December 20, 1999 and *Korea Herald*, December 21, 1999, in NAPSNet, December 21, 1999.

26. The agreements were to reunite a small number of separated families, establish a hot line, restore the inter-Korean railway to facilitate trade, exchange prisoners, step up the level of South Korean investment, and arrange for a return visit to Seoul by Kim Jong Il.

27. Speech on accepting the 2000 Nobel Peace Prize; text in *New York Times*, December 12, 2000, A8.

28. Text in *New York Times*, June 14, 2000, online.

29. Victor Cha, "Let's Not Get Summit Slap-Happy in Korea," Nautilus Forum contribution, www.nautilus.org/fora."

30. Tian Zhongqing, "China-ROK Relations in the New Asian-Pacific Context," *Korean Journal of International Studies*, vol. 25, no. 1 (1994): 65–74; *Korea and China in a New World: Beyond Normalization*, ed. Ilpyong J. Kim and Hong Pyo Lee (Seoul: Sejong Institute, 1993).

31. From time to time Chinese authorities have complained about the efforts of Korean visitors to stir up nationalistic feelings among ethnic Koreans. (See, for example, *Korea Herald*, June 4, 1995 and *Korea Times*, June 5, 1995, in NAPSNet, June 6, 1995.) According to one Korean source, 39 percent of all overseas Koreans, nearly two million people, live in China. That would make Korean Chinese the single largest grouping of overseas Koreans anywhere. (See Lee Goo-hong, "Overseas Koreans: Invaluable Asset," *Korea Focus*, vol. 4, no. 1 [January–February 1996]: 24–33.) Add to that a few hundred thousand North Koreans who have escaped into China and a cause of concern for PRC authorities is apparent.

32. Bonnie S. Glaser, "China's Security Perceptions: Interests and Ambitions," *Asian Survey*, vol. 33, no. 3 (March 1993): 261–62. Glaser's conversations with PRC specialists also brought out reasons why a unified Korea *would* be in China's interests. These included assisting the development of Northeast China and providing a buffer against Japan.

33. In 1997, China was North Korea's number-one trade partner, supporting the DPRK economy by running a deficit of $489 million, which was more than one-half of North Korea's total trade deficit. Noland, *Avoiding the Apocalypse*, table 3.11, 91.

34. A typical example of the praise China has lavished on Kim's policies comes from a military think tank (the China Institute for International Strategic Studies): see Zhang Jinbao, "Changes in the Situation on the Korean Peninsula and their Impacts on the Strategic Pattern in Northeast Asia," *International Strategic Studies*, no. 1 (2001): 35–44.

35. Yi, "Dynamics of China's South Korea Policy," 79–82.

36. The official reasons for South Korean nonparticipation are TMD's costs and technological commitment, and skepticism about its effectiveness against North Korean missiles. *Korea Herald*, May 4, 1999; NAPSNet, May 4, 1999.

37. See Daniel L. Byman and Roger Cliff, *China's Arms Sales: Motivations and Implications* (Santa Monica, Calif.: RAND Corporation, 1999), 17–18.

38. See Duan Hong (China Institute for International Studies), "Korea and Regional Security in Northeast Asia," Nautilus Institute Nuclear Policy Project, April 20, 2000, online at npp@nautilus.org.

39. *Korea Herald*, March 27, 1994 (supplement) and March 30, 1994; Yi, "Dynamics of China's South Korea Policy," 77–78.

40. See Samuel S. Kim, "The Future of China and Sino-ROK Relations," in *The Future of China and Northeast Asia*, ed. Tae-Hwan Kwak and Melvin Gurtov (Seoul: Institute for Far Eastern Studies, Kyungnam University Press, 1997), 273–74.

41. This is the thesis of Victor D. Cha's book, *Alignment Despite Antagonism: The United States–Korea–Japan Security Triangle* (Stanford, Calif.: Stanford University Press, 1999).

42. One incident in particular aroused South Korean suspicions. It occurred in 1990, when a Japanese Diet delegation led by the LDP kingmaker Kanemaru Shin visited Py-

ongyang and held private talks with Kim Il Sung. The ensuing negotiations would have led to diplomatic relations in exchange for Japanese reparations and a formal apology for colonialism and occupation of Korea; but the uproar that followed the trip, including South Korean and U.S. protests, terminated the deal. For the full story and background, see Hong Nack Kim, "Japan and North Korea: Normalization Talks Between Pyongyang and Tokyo," in *Korea and the World*, ed. Kihl, especially 116–18.

43. See Hong Nack Kim, "Japanese-Korean Relations in the 1990s," Woodrow Wilson Center Occasional Paper no. 59 (March 29, 1994), 12.

44. See Steve Glain, "U.S. Officials Question South Korea Readiness to Fight Off the North," *Wall Street Journal*, January 17, 1995, 1; *Hankyoreh Shinmun* (Seoul), November 28, 1996, based on a *Defense News* report, in NAPSNet, December 2, 1996; Paul Richter, "S. Korea's Defense Efforts Fail to Pass U.S. Muster," *Los Angeles Times*, April 12, 1997; Barbara Opall, "South Korean Arms Buys Raise Japanese Ire," *Defense News*, November 25–December 1, 1996. I also heard this view expressed in 2001 by a member of the U.S. military in South Korea who is in a position to know.

45. Howard W. French, "Travel Boom Pulls Japan and South Korea Closer," *New York Times*, July 13, 2000, online ed.

46. Kenneth B. Pyle, "North Korea in U.S.-Japan Relations," Occasional Paper no. 80, The Woodrow Wilson International Center for Scholars, Washington, D.C., January 1999, 3.

47. Japan will probably have to pay several times the amount it compensated South Korea in 1965, which was around $800 million. See Noland, *Avoiding the Apocalypse*, 106–7. The Japanese, meanwhile, demand to know the whereabouts of several nationals kidnapped in Japan by North Korean agents.

48. Chung-in Moon and Dae-Won Ko, "Korea's Perspective on Economic and Security Cooperation in Northeast Asia," in *Politics and Economics in Northeast Asia*, ed. Akaha, 187.

49. On the "structural squeeze" and technological dependence, see Walden Bello and Stephanie Rosenfeld, *Dragons in Distress: Asia's Miracle Economics in Crisis* (San Francisco: Institute for Food and Development Policy, 1990), 6, 114; SaKong, *Korea in the World Economy*, 190–91; and Gi-Wook Shin and Jeong-Sik Ko, "A Troubled Little Dragon: Competition and Dependence in Korea's International Economic Relations," n.p., n.d.

50. *Asian Development Outlook 2000*, table A12, 253.

51. Kak-Soo Shin "A New Paradigm for Changing Korea-Japan Relations: A Regional Partnership," *IFANS Review*, vol. 2, no. 5 (July 1994): 14. Shin was director of Northeast Asia Division I in the Ministry of Foreign Affairs.

52. See Kim Kyong-Dong, "Korean Perceptions of America," and Donald N. Clark, "American Attitudes Toward Korea," both in *Korea Briefing 1993*, ed. Donald N. Clark (Boulder, Colo.: Westview, 1993), 163–84 and 185–200, respectively.

53. See Tim Shorrock, "The U.S. Role in Korea in 1979 and 1980," based on the so-called Cherokee files of the decision group in the administration of Jimmy Carter that dealt with the Kwangju affair. Online at www.kimsoft.com/korea/kwangju3.htm.

54. Kim Dae Jung reportedly said: "Even when the two Koreas are unified, the U.S. troops are needed here to maintain stability in Northeast Asia. If there is a power vacuum, Russia, China and Japan would exercise their influence upon the peninsula." *Korea Times*, August 17, 2000; NAPSNet, August 17, 2000.

55. Two scholars close to the U.S. policy making community have implied as much by observing that if Seoul were not under the U.S. umbrella, it "might well feel compelled to establish security links with one of its larger neighbors." They also note how

a North-South Korea peace treaty might bring about pressure to end the U.S.–ROK security treaty, clearly a development the authors resist. Ralph A. Cossa and Alan Oxley, "The U.S.-Korea Alliance," in *America's Asian Alliances*, ed. Robert D. Blackwill and Paul Dibb, (Cambridge, Mass.: MIT Press, 2000) 71, 85.

56. See Peggy Falkenheim Meyer, "Russia's Post-Cold War Security Policy in Northeast Asia," *Pacific Affairs*, vol. 67, no. 4 (Winter 1994–95): 506–8.

57. Shim Jae Hoon, "Silent Partner," *Far Eastern Economic Review* (December 29, 1994–January 5, 1995): 14–15.

58. See Agence France Presse report, Seoul, February 9, 2000; in NAPSNet, same date.

59. The Russian debt stands at around $1.7 billion. See, for example, *Chosun Ilbo*, March 9, 1999; NAPSNet, March 9, 1999.

60. Alexander Zhebin, "Russia and Korean Unification," *Asian Perspective*, vol. 19, no. 2 (Fall–Winter 1995): 175–90.

61. "A common belief in Russia is that the DPRK is a militarily weak state that faces overwhelmingly powerful opponents and must fear for own survival. All its efforts are viewed as defensive in nature and not adequate to the threats it faces. Indeed, some Russians hold the view that Washington and its allies pose a real threat to the DPRK and that 'it is only a matter of time before they attack North Korea as they attacked Yugoslavia [in 1999].'" *The DPRK Report*, No. 20 (September–October 1999); in NAPSNet, November 1, 1999.

62. Vladimir A. Orlov, "Russia's Policy Perspective toward the Korean Peninsula: Security Aspect," *KNDU Review*, vol. 5, no. 2 (December 2000): 155. Russia and South Korea did find common ground on arms control. An official visit to Seoul by President Vladimir Putin in February 2001 led to a joint statement with Kim Dae Jung opposing TMD, supporting the ABM Treaty, and calling (in obvious criticism of the United States) for speedy ratification of the CTBT and START II. See *New York Times*, February 28, 2001, online ed.

63. In 1994 total ROK–Russia trade was only $2.19 billion, and Korean direct investment in Russia was $37 million. (Choong Yong Ahn, "Search for New Approaches and Methods for Economic Cooperation in Northeast Asia," *Korean Journal of International Studies*, vol. 24, no. 3 [Autumn 1993]: table 4, 351, 354.) By 1999 trade was still only $2.2 billion (it had been as high as $3.2 billion) and direct Korean investment in Russia (in 1996) was a merely $130 million. Ko Jae-nam, "Ten Years of Korea-Russia Diplomatic Relations," *Korea Focus*, vol. 8, no. 6 (November–December 2000): 67.

64. That possibility was a primary topic when Putin visited Seoul in February 2001. At that time he and Kim Dae Jung also agreed to construction of South Korean links to the Trans-Siberian Railway and the Far East region's economy. The rail projects would also benefit North Korean commerce.

65. During an official visit to Seoul by the Russian defense minister, a ministry official is quoted as having said: "The Russian leadership's sentiment is that it has gained no particular advantages by opening ties with South Korea at a cost of distancing itself from its erstwhile staunch ally in the North." (*Korea Times*, May 20, 1995; NAPSNet, May 22, 1995.) The Russian decision to resume military assistance was reported in the *Washington Post*, April 28, 2001, online ed.

66. Noland, *Avoiding the Apocalypse*, 91 (table 3.11) and 98.

67. *Asian Development Outlook 2000*, table A17, 258.

68. From 1982 to 1992, FDI had only constituted just under 10 percent of foreign capital inflows. Peter M. Beck, "Foreign Direct Investment in Korea: From Exclusion to Inducement," *Joint U.S.-Korea Academic Studies*, vol. 9 (1999): 224.

69. On Kim Dae Jung's plan for structural change, see Barry K. Gills and Dong-Sook S. Gills, "South Korea and Globalization: The Rise to Globalism?" *Asian Perspective*, vol. 23, no. 4 (1999): 203–4. For a look at union and chaebol responses, see John Larkin, "Korea's Winter of Discontent," *Far Eastern Economic Review* (December 7, 2000): 16–20.

70. As 2000 ended, South Korean banks held about $64 billion in bad loans, equal to 12.3 percent of all loans; the government, which already had spent about $100 billion since the financial crisis to help out troubled banks, committed another $5.8 billion to support six of them; and several thousand bank employees were striking to protest a bank merger. *New York Times*, December 26, 2000, C3.

71. As Noland mentions (*Avoiding the Apocalypse*, 229–32), management control of *chaebol* by families through cross-shareholding actually increased, chaebol investment in non-banking financial institutions rose, and consolidation of certain businesses such as automobiles probably will increase the market shares of the most powerful chaebol.

72. See "Korea's 'Too-Big-To-Fail' Myth Continues, Uncertainty Remains," *Korea Times*, November 3, 2000, online ed., and *Korea Times*, July 2, 2001, online ed.

73. For a detailed review of the "chaebol problem," see Yoo Seong Min, "Corporate Restructuring in Korea: Policy Issues Before and During the Crisis," in "Korea and the Asian Economic Crisis," *Joint U.S.-Korea Academic Studies*, vol. 9 (1999), 131–99.

74. Gills and Gills, "South Korea and Globalization," 210–11, 225. See also Sunhyuk Kim, "The Politics of Reform in South Korea: The First Year of the Kim Dae Jung Government, 1998–1999," *Asian Perspective*, vol. 24, no. 1 (2000): 163–86.

75. *Korea Herald*, December 27, 1999 (NAPSNet, January 5, 2000), citing a report of the ROK Bar Association.

76. On the environmental problems, which are of the sort typically experienced by underdeveloped countries, see David F. Von Hippel and Peter Hayes, "Environmental Problems and the Energy Sector in the Democratic People's Republic of Korea," *Asian Perspective*, vol. 22, no. 2 (1998): 51–77. Concerning health care, see Elisabeth Rosenthal, "Collapse of Health System Adds to North Korea's Crisis," *New York Times*, February 20, 2001, online ed., and the following note.

77. A deputy foreign minister, in a rare statement concerning the effects of the famine, reported to a UNICEF conference that between 1993 and 1999 average life expectancy fell from 73.2 years to 66.8; the mortality rate for children under five rose from twenty-seven deaths per 1,000 to forty-eight per 1,000; and infant mortality rose from fourteen to over twenty-two per 1,000 births. Per capita GNP, meanwhile, dropped from $991 a year to $457. *New York Times*, May 16, 2001, online ed.

78. As of March 1998 the Rajin-Sonbong FTEZ had only attracted about $35 million in actual committed funds. (NAPSNet online, *The DPRK Report*, No. 11 [January–February, 1998], 2.) In fact, only 149 foreign companies, 131 of them Japanese, had invested in all of North Korea between 1984, when the first joint venture law was announced, and 1995. *Korea Times*, September 26, 1995; NAPSNet, September 27, 1995.

79. In 1999 the United States donated $207 million, or 53 percent of the total, followed by the PRC ($78.6 million), the ROK ($46.8 million), and the EU ($37.4 million). About 90 percent of all aid was food. Report of the ROK Ministry of Unification, reported in various Seoul newspapers; see NAPSNet, March 31, 2000.

80. For specific incidents, see David E. Kaplan, "The Wiseguy Regime," *US World Today*, World Report, February 15, 1999, 1–8.

81. According to South Korean sources, North Korea earned only about $50 million in arms sales in 1998, about ten percent of its total exports, and around half as much as it earned through drug trafficking. (*Korea Times*, September 28, 1999; NAPSNet, September 29, 1999.) The *Korea Times* (September 29, 1999; NAPS, October 1, 1999) reported that the ROK's arms exports reached $171 million in the first six months of 1999, up from $147 million for all of 1998, $58 million in 1997 and $45 million in 1996.

82. Kim Jong Il's motives here must be a matter of speculation. Besides his agreement with Kim Dae Jung that a U.S. presence would offset the power of the other large countries, he may also think it would keep South Korea from absorbing the North and would draw the South Korean public's attention to the continuing U.S. "occupation" of the ROK. In the latter sense, the North might hope to use the U.S. presence as a lightning rod for Korean nationalism in hopes of driving a wedge between the two allies, or at least keeping them at bay. Indeed, there were demonstrations in South Korea against U.S. forces in the months after the summit.

83. *Asahi Shimbun* (Tokyo), reported on December 14, 2000 (NAPSNet, December 15, 2000) that PRC Foreign Minister Tang Jiaxuan had told a visiting Japanese opposition party leader that at talks in May between Kim Jong Il and PRC Prime Minister Zhu Rongji in Beijing, Kim had stated: "For the North and the South to develop economically, it would be good to establish an economic development area." Zhu's response was: "It would be also good if such an area were established on the 38th parallel line. Such economic development would be better off if established in such a tense place." To which Kim replied: "That is very good."

84. The first renewal of the promise came in a joint communiqué of October 12, 2000, during the visit to Washington of Kim Jong Il's special envoy, Vice Marshal Jo Myong-rok, First Vice Chairman of the DPRK National Defense Commission. (Text in U.S. State Department, "U.S.-DPRK Joint Communiqué," NAPSNet, special report of the same date.) The second renewal occurred when an EU delegation visited North Korea to promote the peace process. Kim Jong Il promised to maintain the testing moratorium until he could ascertain what George W. Bush's Korea policies would be.

85. See Taik-young Hamm, *Arming the Two Koreas: State, Capital and Military Power* (New York: Routledge, 1999).

86. "2-plus-4" would presumably evolve from the Four Party Talks. South Korea's interest goes back to 1988 and Roh Tae Woo's proposal for a "consultative conference for peace" that would bring the two Koreas together with the four outside powers. The Japanese version of "2-plus-4," proclaimed when Kim Dae Jung and Obuchi Keizo conferred in Japan in October 1998, is actually "4-plus-2": expanding the Four Party Talks to include Japan and Russia. Russian policy has more generally been to support multi-party talks on Korean security that include the RF.

87. The government reported in 1999 that fifteen South Korean firms had been approved for business deals in North Korea worth about $170 million, and that ROK products worth $80 million were being processed in the DPRK. Kyodo News International, April 21, 1999; NAPSNet, April 21, 1999.

88. For a skeptical view that raises important questions about the challenges to South Korean democracy that would occur if North Korea actually were taken over, see Alvin Magid, "Contemplating Survivalist North Korea," *Asian Perspective*, vol. 24, no. 1 (2000): 103–32.

89. Michael R. Gordon, "How Politics Sank Accord on Missiles with North Korea," *New York Times*, March 6, 2001, online ed. According to Gordon's account, Pyongyang would have agreed to terminate its entire long-range missile program (with the question

of its existing missile arsenal left for future discussions) in exchange for a visit by Clinton and food and energy assistance. The deal was never consummated, Clinton's aides said, because of his preoccupation with the contested presidential election results in Florida.

90. See Cordesman, "Comparative Summary," 41–42. The U.S. Defense Intelligence Agency has made various accusations of North Korean secret sites for nuclear-weapons production that, on inspection, have proven wrong. Its biggest mistake came in 1999 when Washington accused North Korea of having an underground site (at Kumchangri) for nuclear-weapon research or production. It demanded the right to inspect the site, eventually was granted it, and found it empty. Philip Shenon, "Suspected North Korea Atom Site is Empty, U.S. Finds," *New York Times*, May 28, 1999, online ed.

91. Two of the disagreements were resolved in January 2001. The first concerned changes in the Status of Forces Agreement (SOFA) that deals with the always-touchy issue of jurisdiction over rapes, fights, and other incidents involving U.S. soldiers. The new SOFA broadens ROK authority for treating and trying suspects. The second conflict was over South Korea's desire to increase the range and payload of its missiles in response to North Korea's missile program. The United States agreed to the new limits, but also insisted that South Korea join the MTCR (it did, in late March 2001) and comply with its limits on missile range (187 miles) and payload (1,100 pounds). Another dispute concerned U.S. refusal to apologize for or compensate victims of the Korean War-era No Gun Ri incident in July 1950, in which U.S. soldiers fired on Korean civilians who were fleeing advancing North Korean troops. President Clinton did make a statement of regret at the time the Defense Department released a joint U.S.–ROK "Statement of Mutual Understanding" on the incident, which acknowledged that civilians had been fired upon and killed but left unresolved the question whether or not an order to fire had been given by superior officers. An excerpt from the report is in *New York Times*, January 12, 2001, online ed.

92. See Cossa and Oxley, "The U.S.-Korea Alliance," in Blackwill and Dibb. eds., 71.

93. In November 1999 it was revealed that the United States for years had been aware of South Korean ballistic missile research that was being hidden from U.S. view. The Koreans clearly were seeking to offset North Korean *Nodong* medium-range missiles, which can already travel 600 miles. James Risen, "South Korea Seen Trying to Extend Range of Missiles," *New York Times*, November 14, 1999, online ed.

94. *Joongang Ilbo* editorial, March 11, 1999, in *Korea Focus*, vol. 7, no. 2 (March–April, 1999): 117–19. The poll found support of over 80 percent for nuclear arms in all three circumstances, the highest (86.9 percent) in the case of Japanese acquisition of nuclear weapons.

95. This is the language of the Perry Report—"Review of United States Policy toward North Korea: Findings and Recommendations"—written October 12, 1999, by a special policy review team headed by William J. Perry, former U.S. Secretary of Defense and, under Clinton, Policy Coordinator and Special Advisor to the President and the Secretary of State. Text of the unclassified version in NAPSNet special report, October 13, 1999.

96. Interview on the Public Broadcasting System, Washington, D.C., September 17, 1999; NAPSNet, September 20, 1999.

97. From 1995 to 1999 the United States granted about $750 million in aid to the DPRK, a figure that "will grow to over $1 billion in the year 2000." Speech of U.S. Congressman Benjamin A. Gilman to the Asia Society, October 21, 1999; in NAPSNet special report, same date.

98. Associated Press, June 19, 2000. Among the steps taken were to allow North Korea to export raw materials and goods to the United States; open air and shipping routes; and allow U.S. investments in various sectors, such as agriculture. U.S. representatives to the World Bank and other international lending institutions are barred from supporting aid to North Korea under present legislation. On the practical difficulties of doing business with North Korea, see Samuel Len, "Western Business Tempers Its New Enthusiasm for North Korea," *New York Times*, July 6, 2000, online.

99. For example, the two countries "confirmed the commitment of both governments to make every effort in the future to build a new relationship free from past enmity," and "work to remove mistrust, build mutual confidence, and maintain an atmosphere in which they can deal constructively with issues of central concern." It was in that communiqué that North Korea renewed its pledge concerning long-range missile tests and that the United States agreed to explore trade and commercial possibilities. U.S. State Department, "Joint U.S.-DPRK Communiqué."

100. One such hardline alternative was put together by group chaired by former U.S. Assistant Secretary of Defense Richard L. Armitage. He is now a senior defense official in the George W. Bush administration. See Armitage, "A Comprehensive Approach to North Korea," *Strategic Forum* (National Defense University), no. 159 (March 1999): 1–6.

101. Three excellent presentations on this point are made by Yi, "Dynamics of China's South Korea Policy," 84–85; Taeho Kim, "Korean Perspectives on PLA Modernization and the Future East Asian Security Environment," in *In China's Shadow*, ed. Pollack and Yang, 59–62; and Jia Qingguo, "China's Policy Perspective Toward the Korean Peninsula," *KNDU Review*, vol. 5, no. 2 (December 2000): 118.

102. Seoul has made only quiet protests to Beijing about its treatment of North Korean defectors, so as not to provoke a rift; but its anguish over the issue is clear enough. See Mary Jordan, "Fearing Deluge, Political Fallout, China Spurns Fleeing N. Koreans, *Washington Post*, April 14, 1997.

103. Yi, "Dynamics of China's South Korea Policy."

104. The trip of Kim Young Nam, head of the DPRK National Assembly and thus head of state, to China following on the Belgrade embassy bombing in May 1999; CMC vice-chairman Zhang Wannian's meetings in Moscow in June 1999; and the Yeltsin-Jiang summit in late 1999 to enlarge the "strategic partnership," may have been just such events. Sino-Russian cooperation by early 2000 seemed to be extending beyond "cash-and-carry" deals to a vigorous partnership that provides China with important additions to its deterrent capabilities that it could not have readily developed on its own. Craig S. Smith, "New Chinese Guided-Missile Ship Heightens Tension," *The New York Times*, February 9, 2000, 1.

105. Interview with Kim Young-ho, former Minister of Commerce, Industry and Energy, in *Nikkei Weekly*, December 25, 2000–January 1, 2001, 3.

106. Japan's foreign minister, Kono Yohei, revealed the salience of domestic politics when he described the lack of diplomatic relations with North Korea as "abnormal" and said normalization "is an issue of morality as well as an inevitable historical one." But he also said: "To get people's trust and understanding, we have to be seen to be making progress in humanitarian issues such as kidnaping." Agence France Presse, Tokyo, January 23, 2001; NAPSNet, January 23, 2001.

## Chapter Seven

# The United States and East Asia

As the Asian way evolved, it became a model of regional economic and security interdependence based on "open regionalism" and step-by-step confidence building. It sought to take East Asia beyond the Cold War, relying on multilateral processes but also on improvements in bilateral relations. The keys to the success of any security model, however, have always been in the hands of leaders in the United States, China, and Japan. There, as we have seen, interest in multilateral initiatives exists to different degrees; but in all three countries, bilateral relationships and preoccupation with the balance of power predominate. And because they do, patterns of Cold War thinking and foreign policy behavior remain very much alive in East Asia.

Given its alliance system and military presence in East Asia, and a long history of entanglement in the internal as well as international politics of the region, it is hardly surprising that the United States adheres so strongly to traditional ways of conducting foreign policy. This chapter critically examines U.S. policy, mainly the presumptions behind it, in order to introduce discussion of conceptual and policy alternatives.

## BALANCING POWER?
## A CRITICAL APPRAISAL OF U.S. POLICY

### "Realism" in Asia?

If the Asian way represents the optimistic view of East Asia's future, Realism represents the pessimistic view. Two arguments frame the Realists' agenda. The first is that Asia has a conflict-ridden future—resurgent nationalism, ethnic conflicts, divided states, territorial disputes, unregulated arms buildups, several states with nuclear weapons or the potential to possess them, concerns about

Chinese and/or Japanese militarism—the list is long indeed. The second argument is that Asia lacks offsetting sources of regional cohesion: the slow pace of East Asian integration and development of security institutions (compared with Europe), the absence of one or more regional leaders, and the contradiction between the fear of outside domination and the fear of exclusion from outsiders' arrangements (such as NAFTA and the EU). For American Realists in particular, what remains is almost axiomatic: The danger exists of a power vacuum that will be filled either by an expansionist country or by an unselfish peacekeeper.

As noted earlier, Realists still assess power in Cold War terms, as though only military bases, arsenals, and deployments count. Their security concepts remain governed by geopolitics and relative national capabilities. Strategies for extending national power and satisfying specific national interests still rely on defense of territory, control of resources, and deterrence of rival powers; on identifying major and minor poles of power, and how these can be "balanced"; and on weighing the threat potential of neighboring states in a presumptively hostile, "worst case" environment. Critical factors that have redefined security in the post–Cold War world, such as multilateral cooperation, human and technological resources, and the many sources of human, environmental, and financial insecurity discussed in previous chapters, are either omitted or barely noted in Realist accounts. While most East Asian states (not to mention most of the rest of the world) struggle with issues of economic and political development, Realists persist in focusing on external threats and internal conflicts, both of which (in their view) require that states remain heavily armed or closely protected. The large, unmatched U.S. military presence in East Asia is the result.[1]

In terms of traditional sources of insecurity, East Asia has plenty of them: divided Korea, the Taiwan Strait, the South China Sea, separatism in Indonesia, disputed fisheries and boundaries, and instability around China's rim. As a leading advocate of an Asian balance of power and the creation of an Asian security organization admits, however, none of these disputes threatens the balance. What they do threaten is the lives of many innocent people and the achievements of economic interdependence over the last twenty years or so.[2] Even then, common to all these disputes is competing nationalisms, which make their strategic implications much less dire than in the days of East-West military and ideological competition. Whereas Realists still tend to analyze regional security in ways that stress defense and deterrence capabilities, there are strong grounds for questioning such an approach. The foremost need today seems to be for invigorated cooperative ventures at many levels—multilateral and bilateral, governmental and nongovernmental, commercial and military—that provide the disputing parties with common reason to talk past their differences.

## "Indispensable Nation"?

Analysts who seek to define a post–Cold War grand strategy for U.S. policy in East Asia from a Realist perspective continue to operate from old premises. As a consequence, their realism simply lends support to policies that at most merely update those of the Cold War. Realist perspectives are not monolithic; but they do embrace common themes and policy objectives while dismissing promising alternatives made possible by the end of the Cold War. Among those alternatives, examined here and in the concluding chapter, are reductions of the U.S. military presence around Asia, a consultative approach to security building, and greater reliance on multilateral mechanisms.

Virtually all analysts of U.S. policy mark East Asia as a region of turmoil and "strategic uncertainty." For Realists, the tools for assessing the implications of uncertainty are the same ones that served them so well during the Cold War: geopolitical power shifts, power vacuums, worst case planning, and threat analysis.[3] The prescribed antidotes are almost axiomatic—American primacy, bilateral alliances, and of course "maintenance" of the balance of power. As they emphasized during the Cold War, U.S. national security interests are transcendent; threats that may seem remote from American concerns have spillover consequences. In fact, to listen to Realists, regional stability in East Asia is threatened in more ways today than yesterday; the only pertinent questions for U.S. leaders concern which threats should receive priority and how direct a role the United States should take in handling them, since the money and domestic political will are not as reliably available as they once were.

A problem that was occasionally identified by Realist thinkers during the Cold War but never eliminated was the seemingly endless growth of national interests and therefore of national commitments to protect them. The Cold War's end has not curtailed the list of U.S. interests or commitments in East Asia, which include: constraining Japan; containing (while engaging) China; preventing the emergence of a rival hegemon; providing a stable political environment for corporate investors; sustaining the confidence of bilateral treaty partners and other friendly countries; and deterring "rogue states" such as North Korea. Nor has the end of the Cold War transformed the domestic political environment that shapes strategic interests and enables commitments: the ideological crusaders against communism, terrorists, nationalist leaders, and protectionist economies; the global corporations, arms exporters, and supporters of higher defense spending; the opponents of development assistance and environmental NGOs; and the military services, which seek to uphold and where possible expand roles and mission, keep weapons flowing to allies, and talk up *actual or potential threats* to regional order.[4]

In fact, in response to General Colin Powell's famous lament at the time of the Gulf War that the United States was "running out of enemies," a new and expanded menu of international threats has been concocted. The Realists' threat agenda consists of rogues, terrorists, biological weapons, and "global peer competitors" (China and Russia). After September 11, 2001, terrorists were elevated to the top spot, with President Bush saying (in a speech to the U.S. Congress on September 20) that "our war on terror . . . will not end until every terrorist group of global reach has been found, stopped, and defeated." Bush called the war not just America's fight but "civilization's fight."[5] He received plenty of international support; but among the supporters were states that themselves had been accused of terrorism: Russia in Chechnya, China in Tibet, Pakistan in Kashmir, and Indonesia in East Timor.

Globalists also have new enemies: WMD proliferation, drug trafficking, information warfare, economic nationalists, (non-Western) religious fundamentalists, ethnic separatists. To be sure, the Globalism of the Clinton years was supposed to represent an alternative to thinking only of enemies, and to excessive reliance on the military. But it did not. Clinton's national security policy fully embraced the staples of power politics, such as being able to fight two major wars simultaneously, deter a great diversity of threats, and "act with others when we can, but alone when we must."[6] Military power under George W. Bush essentially embraced these same objectives.

U.S. interventions abroad under Clinton and Bush succeeded at keeping down the cost in U.S. lives; but they could not deliver on the promise of fewer and more "selective" involvements, as the military actions in Somalia, Iraq, Haiti, Bosnia, Kosovo and Afghanistan showed. In the last of these, in fact, the United States deployed a vast array of air and naval power against one of the world's poorest countries. Rejecting negotiations with the ruling Taliban, Bush vowed to "pursue nations that provide aid or safe haven to terrorism."[7] Thus did an overseas conflict become yet another worldwide crusade.

Powell, now secretary of state, hailed the international cooperation in prosecuting the war as marking the end of the "post–cold war period"[8] The reality was somewhat different, however. The "war against terrorism" was no more carried out by a genuine coalition than the Gulf War had been. Like the Gulf War, the new war was led and mainly fought by the United States; neither supporting countries nor the United Nations determined the war's contours or objectives. The war in Afghanistan also revealed the usual blending of Realism and Globalism in American foreign policy thinking—the common focus on maintaining world order: "the pre-condition for economic interdependence is the geo-political stability and reassurance that flow from America's security commitments."[9] As Clinton said, "Our extraordinary diplomatic leverage to reshape existing security and economic structures and create new ones ultimately relies upon American power."[10] Specifically, it is the power to create order out of chaos, which makes *disorder* in general the central enemy of U.S. foreign policy—the kind of disorder that inhibits capital flows or otherwise undermines the "Washington consensus." Hence, the Defense Department's strategic papers on East Asia of recent years never fail to mention military power divorced from American business interests (around $500 billion in trade and $150 billion in investments in 1998) and dependents (400,000) who live there.[11]

Once threats to regional order are accepted as America's central concern about East Asia, worst-case hypothesizing takes over. China's military budget and deployments probably reveal expansionist ambitions, North Korea's missiles threaten Japan and even the United States,[12] Japan must be kept on a tight leash lest it become a danger to its neighbors, ASEAN is too weak to be reliable—all of which leads policy prescriptions in predictable directions. One is that U.S. forces and bases in East Asia must stay put. A second direction is that the U.S. bilateral alliances cannot be altered or abandoned. Third is that the array of "challenges" to U.S. interests requires additional military capabilities (and therefore more money). Fourth is that only the United States can undertake the awesome task of leadership to keep East Asia from coming apart—the kind of missionary zeal that Secretary of State Madeleine Albright evidently had in mind when she spoke in 1998 of the United States as the "indispensable nation."[13]

These are justifications for maintaining U.S. primacy. "Staying engaged" in Asia is the mantra; debate is limited to the means of engagement. While all but the most militant Cold Warriors reject full-out containment, its replacement, often called "selective engagement," hardly represents a strategic revolution. To the contrary, it risks a repetition of the mistaken alignments, overweening ambition, and major foreign policy crises that characterized the Vietnam War era.[14] There are several variations on the theme of "selective engagement," but all of them use balance-of-power strategies and rely primarily on military power (including nuclear weapons) to promote security.

Realists share with Globalists the perspective mentioned in chapter 2—treating Asia as object rather than subject. APEC can be supported so long as it subscribes to the rules of the global trading system (WTO); and ARF can be supported so long as it in effect backstops the U.S. security system. Independent Asian initiatives are unlikely to receive U.S. endorsement, as Malaysia and Japan have found out when they tried to take trade and financial actions that were contrary to U.S. preferences. Or, consider U.S. policy toward China: Even the most sensitive China watchers persist in framing policy issues in terms of China's playing a "constructive role," "seek[ing] only gradual change" in the international system, and abiding by "global norms."[15] How can any Chinese leader accept such rules, which are made in and refereed by America? The issue in truth is *control*; and because U.S. leaders have always had a very hard time yielding control, least of all now that the United States is the only superpower, they are open to the charge (made by its friends, and not only by China) of bullying and arrogance.

Underlying this U.S. strategic consensus are two traditionally American assumptions: indispensability and exceptionalism. Asia needs "a force for stability, reducing the need for arms buildups and deterring the rise of hegemonic forces."[16] But Asia is too diverse, it is said, has too many disputes, and has no history of formal security cooperation that would enable it to monitor its own affairs. Nationalism in Asia is seen as a source of vulnerability in U.S. analyses—not surprisingly in a country that was an expansionist power in the Pacific at the end of the nineteenth century, and that during the Cold War sought to contain nationalism rather than identify with it. Yet the United States is said to be in the best position to ensure Asia's stability, since it is the least commonly disliked power in Asia. In the words of two prominent U.S. analysts, the United States must be "the sheriff in the posse."[17] This implied dismissal of Asian nationalism (not to mention the cowboy imagery) is troubling, since it fails to take seriously the norm of noninterference and the sensitivity to external pressure that is widely shared in the region.

Most countries in Asia-Pacific do value the U.S. security role, but not all in the same way or for the same reasons. Within some of the ASEAN countries, for instance, the United States is viewed as the *necessary* balancer—as a Singapore scholar puts it, a "benign hegemon"[18]—by which is meant the provider of strategic reassurance, usually against a rising China but also against a future "normal" (assertive) Japan. That kind of U.S. balancing role is not thought of as being a permanent feature of the political landscape, however. It is a temporary (though important) convenience, an aspect of burden-sharing that for now serves all sides well—not just the East Asian countries, since keeping the "balance" lowers the cost and uncertainty of regional security, but also the Americans, for whom regional stability promotes economic opportunity, military access, and political support. Consequently, from an Asian perspective, maintaining the balance of power is a U.S. "service," but not one that gives Washington carte blanche to meddle in East Asia's domestic affairs, demand trade concessions in exchange for a U.S. military presence (as Clinton once did with reference to APEC), or use economic globalization as a wedge that opens the door for American TNCs and banks.

A core issue separating Asian from American notions about the felicity of the balance of power rests on the relationship between military power and economic security. Granted that during the Cold War it was widely perceived that U.S. power in Europe and in East Asia played some part in promoting economic openness,[19] the case for *how much* of a part remains at issue. After all, U.S. military power clearly also helped to destabilize and militarize the region, thus undermining economic openness. (It need hardly be added that U.S. alliances and interventions also distorted political development, enabling oppressive regimes backed by the military to gain and keep power for decades.) Since the end of the Cold War, military power has greatly receded in importance, and cannot be considered the primary reason behind Asia's economic successes. While U.S. leaders continue to believe in the efficacy of military power to promote economic growth, as well as democracy,[20] that is not a cardinal rule among most East Asian leaders. Most of them now accept the necessity of "comprehensive" security. They probably—and if so, accurately—interpret U.S. policy as wanting to preserve military preponderance in East Asia as a means of leveraging economic and political influence.

## Balance of Power, or Predominance?

Further weakening the East Asian–U.S. consensus on Pacific security is the looseness of the balance-of-power concept when it comes to policy making. "Balance of power" is subject to important differences of interpretation—*how and when* a balancer role should be maintained. Even East Asian governments that favor a U.S. presence in the region do not agree on how a balance of power should operate or might come into play at moments of feared imbalance. No East Asian country other than South Korea stood by the United States during its standoff with North Korea in 1993–1994, nor later when North Korea tested a missile over Japan. When PRC–Taiwan tensions rose in 1996 and again in 1999, the ASEAN states were quick to issue statements in support of the "one China" principle, not of U.S. military action to deter China or strengthen Taiwan's capabilities to defend itself. As a practical matter, moreover, most Asian governments that support a U.S. balancer role probably reason, logically, that it is cheaper and wiser to have the United States assume the chief regional security burden than for them to do so. While Washington tries simultaneously to engage and contain China, Asians are free to focus on engagement and economic development, all the while hoping that containment will not lead to war.

At the conceptual level, balance of power is terribly ambiguous. It may be a theory of state behavior based on the structure of the international system, a policy prescription for particular states, a description of actual strategic circumstances, or a perceived circumstance of balance. The concept may refer to the way power is distributed—a relatively equal distribution of national capabilities, or any distribution of power. As policy, the balance of power may specify actions that would *create* it or actions that would *maintain* it. In some balance-of-power systems, one state's power position is crucial, whereas in other systems, no state dominates, either because of roughly equal national capabilities or because of state policies (such as deterrence, intervention, and coalition) that seek to sustain or re-create a balance.[21] Thus we find quite an array of balance-of-power ideas in the literature on East Asian security, including a U.S.–Japan alliance to balance explicitly against China;[22] the United States as the balancer power between China and Japan;[23] and the United States as a distant (extra-regional or offshore) balancer.[24]

All too often, balance of power is simply a misnomer or even a deception. It describes neither strategic circumstances nor possibilities, but is rather a stand-in for U.S. predominance. Developments that run contrary to U.S. interests are ipso facto threats to the "balance" and need to be "deterred." The U.S. alliance system, the cornerstone of deterrence and balancing, is often presented as though it is universally accepted.[25] But, again, that is not the common view among America's friends in East Asia, where talking about the U.S. role in keeping the balance of power is not the same thing as agreeing with the United States on how and when to act on behalf of the balance. One wonders, for instance, how Asian allies of the United States react to continued American resistance to major cutbacks in nuclear forces in Asia. The American argument is that nuclear weapons promote regional stability and reassure allies, hence denuclearization proposals are beyond the horizon.[26] Are nuclear weapons the kind of strategic reassurance most Asian governments are looking for? Or is preservation of America's nuclear preponderance, with its presumed advantages of nuclear threats, the actual end game?

Placing the United States in the role of balancer is a position that is ambiguous enough to be dangerous and, in a crisis, isolating. Is there a consensus in the United States, in government let alone among the public, that supports possible kinds of "balancing" acts such as against China over Taiwan or in between the Sino-Japanese rivalry? Are the rules of the game of balancing well understood and accepted by all the players? Is a balance of power really the appropriate response when we consider, for example, that China is a rapidly developing but still underdeveloped economy and military power, while Japan is an economic and technological superpower whose armed forces are technically advanced but small? If the answers to these questions is "no" or "not clear," the concept of balance of power needs to be replaced by a framework more appropriate to the complexities of post–Cold War East Asia.

As various U.S. officials have commonly used the term, balance of power refers to the role of forward-deployed U.S. forces in East Asia, where they serve as "honest broker" (James A. Baker), "security guarantor and regional balancer" (William S. Cohen), or "sheriff of the posse" (Joseph Nye). As a current senior official on East Asia once wrote, "the entire U.S. strategic mind-set is conditioned by forward deployments. The frontiers of the United States are not at its continental coastline, but far to its east or west."[27] All these officials stress a multitude of post–Cold War threats and advocate that the United States manage the strategic environment in Asia by relying mainly on deterrent power rather than diplomacy or multilateral institutions.[28] In Nye's summation, the U.S. presence simply works: It is desired by all the region's governments, is cheap, anchors U.S. treaty commitments in Asia, deters the North Koreans and other potential troublemakers, and in general promotes political and economic stability.[29]

Left unsaid is that forward deployment keeps the strategic situation in Asia as *unbalanced* as possible in the Americans' favor. In fact, as Richard Betts observes, it is hard to imagine that the United States, so accustomed to operating unilaterally throughout the Cold War, is actually capable of "playing the game of agile external balancer, tilting one way then another, rather than faithful ally."[30] Indeed, to the extent that the United States might actually play the role of external balancing power, it would risk casting adrift its alliance partners, South Korea and Japan and, contrary to U.S. policy, seeing them become independent military powers.[31] Such an outcome has always been unacceptable to American leaders.

Actually, a case can be made that in the post–Cold War era, aggression has become improbable not only because of fear of countervailing U.S. power but also, perhaps even more so, because an aggressor would have to act alone. North Korea no longer can count on help from China or Russia should it attack South Korea or Japan. That fact and the strength of South Korea's economy and political system, *not* U.S. power, is probably what deters North Korea. China's "strategic partnership" with Russia is far from being a mutual security alliance. Beijing would be instantly isolated from its major markets and sources of capital and technology should it unilaterally seek to absorb the South China Sea islands or attack Taiwan (assuming Taiwan did not formally declare its independence). If an autonomous Japan should become a major military power again, what would it threaten? Would not all of Asia unite against it? And so on. There simply is no reason to believe that aggression pays: When the stakes are commonly shared, the penalties for engaging in aggression or any other large-scale use of force are going to be very high, balance of power or not.

## Balance of Threat?

A "balance-of-threat" strategy is sometimes proposed in place of a balance-of-power strategy. States will act, in other words, not only to balance against the power (capabilities) of other states, but also in response to their perceived intentions.[32] Presumably, a benign foreign policy will lessen other states' sense of threat and thus reduce the chances of a balance of power being formed against it. But such a formulation, though properly drawing attention to intentions, also has many drawbacks. Because intentions are so much a matter of perception, they are inevitably colored by ideology, history, mixed signals (as in U.S.–PRC relations), and worst-case planning, among other factors. Thus, correctly divining intentions is problematic for all states, not just the dominant one (i.e., the United States). Even if a state's intentions are perceived by others as being mischievous, that does not mean East Asian states will align against it. In East Asia, at least four states—the United States, China, Japan, and North Korea—are perceived by some other states as having threatening intentions. Lacking a consensus about the threat itself, the region as a whole is not going to seek to "balance" against it.

A final consideration about balance of threat is that communicating intentions in a complex environment such as East Asia is often prone to failure. Our discussion of the U.S.–Japan alliance provided an example. A long-standing objective of the alliance has been to reassure Japan's neighbors that Japanese militarism will never again be a problem. But another prong of U.S. policy has been to get Japan to contribute more to the American regional deterrence strategy, which conveys just the opposite of reassurance, at least to China. One clear consequence is closer Sino-Russian relations which, like U.S.–Japan security ties, is justified on the grounds of contributing to "regional stability" and in response to the threat of hegemony.[33]

Some writers who recognize the foibles of balance-of-power logic applied to East Asia, such as Richard Betts, fall back on the negative goal for the United States of *preventing dominance* by a hostile great power. "A China, Japan, or Russia that grows strong enough to overturn a regional balance of power would necessarily also be a global power that could reestablish bipolarity on the highest level."[34] But the reference to balance of power is far too loose, since by Betts's own definition it is nothing more than a "distribution of national capabilities that is not obviously hierarchical."[35] That leaves room for interpreting numerous political disputes in Asia—such as over the Spratlys, North Korea, or Taiwan—as having strategic importance. Betts's discussion also reveals that "preventing dominance" should make an exception for "a genuinely democratic government." While he excludes "American hegemony," it seems that only the United States can qualify for hegemony in Asia, since "the principal U.S. strategic aim should be to prevent the emergence of a hierarchical regional system under any dominant power other than the United States."[36]

## AMERICAN HEGEMONY

The U.S. "game" is hegemony, not balancing. To be sure, the end of the Cold War raises the question whether or not U.S. thinking and behavior in world politics can still be called "hegemonic" in the face of advancing globalization of capital, the oft-claimed decline in the role of the state in international affairs, and the absence of a strategic vision that might replace anti-communism. But the definition of Cold War era U.S. hegemony provided by Wallerstein and others still seems to fit with post–Cold War U.S. practices in the crucial respects that the United States exerts a uniquely powerful influence in world politics generally, seeks to preserve its preeminent position in both global military and economic affairs against all comers, and justifies its predominance in moral no less than strategic terms.[37] This robust notion of national security, equivalent to the self-conception of empire, was present throughout the Cold War but has become magnified now that the competition with the Soviet Union is over. It is well understood outside the United States if not often acknowledged inside.[38]

Consider, to begin with, that no other country takes as its mandate the active shaping of a world order to make it hospitable to its own interests and values. All countries seek to achieve their interests; but none besides the United States regards its leadership as so indispensable, its power as so disinterested and vital, and its values as so universally applicable. Nor does any country involve itself as deeply or widely in the domestic affairs of other countries as does the United States. For instance, only the United States:

- sets the limits of other countries' sovereignty, and uses sanctions and military force to impose those limits—as in the Yugoslavia-Kosovo conflict and Iraq;
- publicly and persistently criticizes other countries' political shortcomings and pronounces on their need of reforms (e.g. China, Indonesia, Burma, Japan, and Russia) while rejecting criticism of American institutions and human rights conditions;
- is the central player in decisions about mobilizing global finance to bail out economies, as in the Mexico peso crisis and the financial crises in Asia, Russia, Turkey, and Latin America;
- seeks to dictate when and whether other countries should make investments in unfriendly countries, as in U.S. laws to limit trade with Iran and Cuba;
- finds no contradiction between playing a lead role in global nonproliferation while standing alone atop the list of countries when it comes to nuclear weapons, arms exports, and military spending;
- defines "rogue states," "international terrorism," and other international public enemies, and then takes unilateral actions to punish them;
- has as basic military doctrine the ability to simultaneously fight and win wars of various sizes that may be continents apart;
- is usually first to speak in favor of human rights, international law, and international peacekeeping, yet makes those considerations secondary when they go

against self-interest—as in U.S. policies on China, Chechnya, East Timor (while under Indonesian rule), and Turkey (in its repression of the Kurds); the failure to respond to genocide in Rwanda; the forced repatriation of Haitian and other refugees; and the refusal to sign or ratify major international agreements such as the CTBT, the Rome treaty establishing an international criminal court, the Kyoto Protocol on global warming, and the Ottawa treaty banning land mines;[39]

* is the essential actor in attempting to resolve intractable conflicts, such as in Northern Ireland and the Arab-Israeli conflict;
* dominates international media and all other information outlets, thus essentially defining global "news" and culture.

Hegemony means control for its own sake, and therefore the ability and willingness to act unilaterally when necessary, as the United States has been prone to do in East Asia.[40] Hegemony has been the heartbeat of U.S. policy since the end of World War II. The U.S. mission was to make the world safe for the American way of life—Henry Luce's "American century." In the broadest sense, U.S. policy encompassed the *"suspension of international politics through hegemony,"* that is, keeping other countries from pursuing their self-interest in order to secure a favorable global (capitalist) order.[41] The United States sought not merely to contain ideological adversaries, the Soviet Union and China; just as crucial was the objective, supported by friendly countries (and even some adversaries) in Europe and Asia, to contain and manage its new partners, Germany and Japan. Now that the Cold War has been won, it is understandable why many influential Americans believe the United States has that same unique opportunity to exercise primacy, and should unhesitatingly seize it.

That imperial temptation goes back to the post–World War II years in another respect: the desire to universalize U.S. institutions, values, and security preferences. Triumphalism was at its height after the Soviet demise and the Gulf War, as expressed in the writings of Frances Fukuyama and Charles Krauthammer.[42] And precisely because the United States was the only country that could, at either of those historic junctures, *afford* globalism and sustain an appetite for it, the choice to pursue globalism was all the more natural. In some respects NAFTA, APEC, and WTO are the post–Cold War equivalents of the Marshall Plan: Alike, they are intended not merely to preserve the century-old American goal of an Open Door—the liberal economic order—but also, and as importantly, to strengthen or bring to power governments committed to support that order. George W. Bush thus repeated the mantra that free trade will transform rival states when he said:

> Open trade is not just an economic opportunity, it is a moral imperative. Trade creates jobs for the unemployed. When we negotiate for open markets, we're providing new hope for the world's poor. And when we promote open trade, we are promoting political freedom. . . . Look at our friends in Mexico and the political reforms there. Look at Taiwan. Look at South Korea. And someday soon I hope that an American president will end that list by adding, Look at China.[43]

The notion is therefore unsupportable that U.S. policy in Asia has been limited to preventing any *other* state from gaining hegemony or blocking an aggressively nationalistic power. In East Asia (and even in Europe) no state or combination of states has been a serious contender for hegemony. The argument of some academic Neorealists that in the post–Cold War era, Japan and China will inevitably seek great power status in order to balance American power—for example, because a one-superpower world will prove intolerable and unstable[44]—is consistent with Realist theory but does not jibe with Japanese or Chinese realities as discussed in chapters 4 and 5. Japan has been snugly under the U.S. umbrella, with no indication of any interest in a militarily independent foreign policy. Only abrupt abandonment by the United States would force Japan to consider that alternative; otherwise, Japan's wisest independent course would be as a global civilian power. China, though certainly unhappy with many aspects of U.S. policy, needs American and Japanese investments, aid, and technology to push ahead with modernization. It also needs the Security Treaty that contains Japan. China's ambitions for great power status must be measured against its military weakness and preoccupation with domestic order.

Nor does the explanation of U.S. policy as seeking merely to provide reassurance against the (re-)emergence of aggressive nationalism ring true. That explanation, applied to Japan, may have been persuasive for a brief time after World War II, but not after fifty years. Japan is a mature, if distorted democracy, with a tiny military, a consistently strong pacifism among the public, and a sometimes unnerving focus on making money. There is no excuse for barring its exercise of sovereignty and letting it make its own choices. China's economic and military modernization is also a search for normalcy. It should not be confused with expansionist ambitions or a long-term strategic plan to supplant, as opposed to becoming a competitor of, the United States. Besides, the choices these governments make are going to be determined by many factors, among the most important of which will be whether or not the United States treats them as equal partners or hegemonic rivals.

The real conflict within the U.S. policy making elite has been over hegemony's costs and tactics: What mix of Realism and Globalism will preserve a favorable global order? History in the 1990s, contrary to Fukuyama, was not yet over. It was being extended by internal wars, economic conflicts, fundamentalist movements, and other destabilizing forces—far more than the United States could afford to confront. Clinton's alternative was captured in the twinned notions of engagement (in East Asia) and enlargement (in Eastern Europe). In the name of promoting democratization (which was no more the *objective* of policy than it had been in Cold War days), the United States would rely in the first instance on the powerful inducements of capitalism to create dependence on global trade and finance, and ultimately to transform the political and social systems of nationalistic governments. Carrots and sticks: So long as China and other recalcitrant states toed the line, they could expect the benefits of globalization—hence, the U.S.–China agreement of 1999 on market-opening measures that was expected to pave the way for China's entry in WTO, and the U.S.–DPRK agreement on suspension of missile testing that opened the door to U.S. trade with North Korea. If these states chose to assert their independent interests, however, "the [U.S.] foreign policy community looks to American military power to impose harmony so that free trade can take place"[45]—which is what happened in response to North Korea's nuclear weapons program in 1993 and China's missile tests in 1996.

The Asian financial crisis was important to U.S. leaders because it was viewed as a threat to regional and global security on a par with the Soviet threat of Cold War days. The "Washington consensus" trembled at the possibility of large-scale economic turmoil that would undermine investor confidence, lead to long-term economic decline, and precipitate social and political collapse. The crisis was therefore treated as a *strategic* problem and not merely an economic one.[46] In leading the bailout operation, the United States acted defensively, to stave off disaster; but it also acted opportunistically, pronouncing the Asian development model dead and pressuring the Koreans and others to restructure their economies. Trouble is, prying open doors to foreign investors and insisting on reductions in work forces caused new frictions. There was considerable resentment in South Korea and Indonesia of the IMF and the "vulture capitalists" who swooped down to pick the carcasses of bankrupt companies.[47]

## "HEDGING BETS" UNDER BILATERALISM

Actually, the best argument for not tinkering with U.S. policy in Asia is the simplest one: It is unwise to change horses in midstream. This is Robert Art's reason for favoring a policy of "hedging bets": A sudden pullout from South Korea, transfer of authority over U.S. bases to Japan, or withdrawal of security commitments to Taiwan might have highly negative and unpredictable consequences. So why upset the apple cart?[48] Unfortunately, the argument also provides a convenient pretext for never changing policy. And while the argument rests on the belief that hedging bets is less risky than any other alternatives, the truth of the matter may be just the opposite. Hanging on carries risks too, in Korea, Japan, and Taiwan—resurgent nationalism from a Japan that finally "says no," resentment in Korea over the seeming permanence of the U.S. presence, or constant U.S. upgrading of Taiwan's defenses to the point of being trapped into defending Taiwan's pro-independence forces.

Hedging bets might still be a useful policy option, however. For example, as indicated in chapters 5 and 6, one can imagine the withdrawal of U.S. forces from South Korea and Japan, but *retention* of security guarantees and access to military facilities in the (highly unlikely) event of overt aggression. Given the demonstrably long reach of U.S. power, a government with aggressive intentions toward a U.S. ally could hardly fail to consider a forceful U.S. response. Why, then, the necessity of forward bases in an era in which there is no single-minded large-scale threat, in which preventing a terrorist attack is largely a matter of intelligence rather than troop deployments, and in which growing nationalism and local anger sooner or later will make U.S. bases liabilities, as has already happened in Okinawa?

Besides, no other country has anything in Asia like the military access, mobility, diversity, technology, and firepower of the United States. Quite apart from the 175 military installations in South Korea and Japan—though in mid-2001, U.S.-ROK agreement was close on turning over fifteen bases to Korea—the United States has numerous military partnerships all over East Asia. The plaint of official sources that U.S. military access to East Asia is woefully inadequate is simply disinformation—and is contradicted by the Defense Department's own reports.[49] Following the loss of U.S. bases in the Philippines in 1992, "a new plan known as 'places, not bases' was quietly put into effect in Indonesia, Singapore, and Malaysia . . . to maintain fleet and aircraft mobility and training."[50] New agreements were reached on ship visits, combined exercises, and port access. Among the extensive kinds of systematic, annual U.S. military contacts with East Asian countries are four series of joint major military exercises (and hundreds of smaller ones), several hundred port visits, and numerous disaster and humanitarian projects.[51] A Visiting Forces Agreement was concluded with the Philippines in 1999 that permits joint military exercises to continue; military exercises and training programs with Indonesia resumed eight months after the East Timor massacres, which elements of the Indonesian army incited;[52] Singapore has made available a new pier to accommodate an American aircraft carrier; and Brunei is used for jungle training.

Among its other treaty partners, the United States retains access to bases in Thailand and Australia. With Thailand, it conducts the largest annual training exercise (*Cobra Gold*) in Southeast Asia; with Australia, the United States has developed an expanded menu of joint war games and intelligence gathering at the Pine Gap spy satellite base.[53] The quest for military partnerships has even extended to Vietnam, where the first military-to-military contacts since the war ended were made in 1997.[54] Thus, the actual situation with respect to the U.S. presence in Asia goes beyond "strategic reassurance"; it is overextension, and makes no strategic sense. But neither does the alternative policy reportedly being considered by the new Bush administration, which includes intensified security dialogue with Australia, Japan, and possibly South Korea (because of dissatisfaction with the ARF), and emphasis on long-range power projection in order to reduce reliance on U.S. bases in the belief they will become too vulnerable to Chinese missiles.[55]

The concern about unduly destabilizing long-standing U.S. relationships in East Asia is understandable. But it fails to give due weight to the transforming effects of economic integration on regional cooperation and domestic politics. The positive, sometimes (like the North-South Korea summit) unanticipated events that reduce tensions merit just as much consideration as worst cases. Still more seriously, concern about allies glosses over the diverse reasons why governments in Asia say they want a continuing U.S. presence. Their purposes differ, and may not be consistent with those of the United States.[56] In the past, governments have manipulated U.S. security commitments to make the United States a co-conspirator in repression of human rights and a party to internal political as well as foreign policy disputes. There is no reason to think that will not happen again.

## RETHINKING U.S. SECURITY STRATEGY

The United States needs most of all to be a partner with Asia-Pacific states, not a balancer or military ally. Though there are many sources of friction in the region, partnership is more plausible now than ever before inasmuch as most of the region's governments subscribe to the idea of using regional dialogue to resolve disputes and promote collaboration, cooperating on sustainable development, preventing the use of force to alter political boundaries, and preventing nuclear proliferation. In an increasing number of countries, furthermore, the movement is growing (thanks especially to pressure from NGOs) to create more accountable economic and political institutions, improve human rights conditions across the board (which means attention to human development and not merely growth indicators), and strengthen environmental protection.[57] There is, consequently, reason for optimism, of the kind recently expressed by the Commander-in-Chief of the U.S. Pacific Command, Admiral Dennis C. Blair:

> The fundamental security challenge in the Asia-Pacific region is to transform the balance of power approach proposed by those who advocate a multi-polar global power structure into one that instead aims to produce security communities where there is a dependable expectation of peaceful change and thought of using armed force to resolve disputes does not arise.[58]

Multilateral problem solving to promote common and comprehensive forms of security does not require that the United States maintain 100,000 forward-deployed military personnel (which are actually only one-third of the total forces under the U.S. Pacific Command), rely for deterrence on nuclear weapons, or be the leader in arms transfers to the region. Washington's decision in 1995 to reverse its intended further reduction of those 100,000 soldiers was a mistake, one that has been compounded by the "places, not bases" strategy. "Empire is the problem," as Chalmers Johnson has written.[59] Long-term mutual security would be better served by the United States setting an example of restraint and assistance to countries and parties that have a serious interest in addressing their real security needs.[60] These goals could be accomplished by reducing military sales and training programs in areas of tension (Taiwan and Indonesia), abandoning TMD, drawing down forces and bases in Japan and South Korea, and focusing assistance programs on reducing social inequalities instead of on cultivating military ties.[61] The United States, in partnership with Japan, which has been far more generous in foreign aid to Asian and other developing economies, could dramatically increase assistance to the least developed Asian countries.[62] Human development assistance, relying for its distribution much more than is currently the case (around 15 percent of ODA) on NGOs, debt relief, and AIDS should be the chief targets of the aid. It could increase environmental aid to governments (such as China's) that face serious water, deforestation, and public health problems as a consequence of rapid economic development and reliance on fossil fuels. And the United States could put far more diplomatic weight than is currently the case into multilateral security cooperation, following the path set by a number of Track II NGOs in convening regional dialogues in Northeast and Southeast Asia.

It is fairly obvious why the U.S. government has shown little interest in common security ideas. They pose a direct challenge to all the key elements of the American-centered security system in East Asia: extended deterrence based on bilateral alliances, forward deployments, U.S. military primacy, and the dependence of U.S. allies. Common security measures, moreover, would detract from U.S. nuclear weapon and naval superiority, and thus the American ability to confront adversaries with overwhelming force or deny them access to strategic resources. As Admiral Blair's comment above indicates, U.S. policy will have to rise above old thinking about national security and leadership if it is to accommodate common security ideas. In the post–Cold War era, demonstrations of "resolve" and desire to "shape" Asia's future (the latter a favorite Pentagon word these days) may reassure some friendly countries; but they may also turn disputes into crises that will isolate the United States from its Asian friends. Acting in multilateral settings and on behalf of informal regional integration has broad support in East Asia, and has the potential, especially if backed by the United States, to enhance security across the board and at far less cost than in the past.

## NOTES

1. U.S. forces stationed in East Asia include 47,000 personnel ashore and 12,000 afloat at ninety locations in Japan; and 37,500 personnel at eighty-five installations in South Korea. The *Washington Post* (May 26, 2000) also lists "U.S. forces dedicated to the Pacific region" as follows:

- U.S. Army Pacific: 60,000 soldiers and civilians (two divisions and one brigade);
- U.S. Pacific Fleet: 130,000 sailors and civilians (170 ships);
- Pacific Air Forces: 40,000 airmen and civilians (380 aircraft in nine wings);
- Marine Forces Pacific: 70,000 Marines and civilians(two expeditionary forces).

2. Paul Dibb, *Towards a New Balance of Power in Asia* (London: Adelphi Paper No. 295, Oxford University Press, 1995), 41.

3. This has been true of U.S. policy and security planning for the Asia-Pacific as well as of a good deal of academic writing, especially by Western analysts. On the official side, see James A. Baker III, "America in Asia: Emerging Architecture for a Pacific Community," *Foreign Affairs*, vol. 70, no. 5 (Winter 1991–92): 1–18; and Joseph S. Nye Jr.,

"East Asian Security: The Case for Deep Engagement," *Foreign Affairs*, vol. 74, no. 4 (July–August 1995): 91. On the academic side, see for example, Jonathan D. Pollack, "The United States in East Asia: Holding the Ring," Adelphi Paper no. 275 (March 1993), 69–82; Richard K. Betts, "Wealth, Power, and Instability: East Asia and the United States After the Cold War," *International Security*, vol. 18, no. 3 (Winter 1993–94): 34–77; Robert J. Art, "A Defensible Defense: America's Grand Strategy after the Cold War," in *America's Strategic Choices*, ed. Michael E. Brown et al. (Cambridge, Mass.: MIT Press, 1997), 78–80; and Dibb, *Towards a New Balance of Power*.

4. Among many examples is the U.S. military's role in promoting ROK military spending, not only to increase the Korean share of the costs of maintaining U.S. forces in South Korea, but also to ensure their purchases of advanced American weapons. In 1996, for instance, total ROK weapons procurements from the United States came to $1 billion, thus linking U.S. military interests with those of the defense industry in the name of improved "interoperability" of weapons. See "Statement of General John H. Tilelli Jr., Commander in Chief United Nations Command/Combined Forces Command & Commander United States Forces Korea, Before the House National Security Committee," March 6, 1997, mimeo., 7–8.

5. Text in *New York Times*, September 21, 2001, B4.

6. William J. Clinton, *A National Security Strategy of Engagement and Enlargement* (Washington, D.C.: The White House, February 1996), ii–iii, 11.

7. Speech to a joint session of the U.S. Congress, September 20, 2001; *New York Times*, September 21, 2001, B4.

8. "Not only is the cold war over," Powell told Russian foreign minister, "the post–cold war period is also over." *New York Times*, October 19, 2001, 1.

9. Christopher Layne and Benjamin Schwarz, "American Hegemony—Without an Enemy," *Foreign Policy*, no. 92 (1993): 3 (online ed.).

10. Clinton, *Engagement and Enlargement*, ii.

11. William S. Cohen, *Report of the Quadrennial Defense Review 1997*, May 1997; see also U.S. Department of Defense, *The United States Security Strategy for the East Asia-Pacific Region 1998* (www.defenselink.mil/pubs/easr98); hereafter, *USSS 1998*.

12. Official interpretations of North Korea's missile capabilities are a perfect example of how worst-case assumptions drive security thinking and the weapons business. The surprising launch of the *Taepodong-1* led to a CIA projection that "during the next 15 years the United States will most likely face ICBM threats" from North Korea, among other countries. But the report is laced with numerous actions North Korea "could" take; it deliberately stopped short of assessing North Korea's ability actually to create a usable long-range missile, or examine why it would attack the United States and thus ensure its total destruction. (See National Intelligence Council, "Foreign Missile Developments and the Ballistic Missile Threat to the United States Through 2015" (September, 1999); online at www.cia.gov/cia/publications/nie/nie99msl.html.) Subsequently (*New York Times*, July 5, 2000, online ed.), internal disputes over such worst-case projections were reported, with the State Department cited as a strongly dissenting voice.

13. These themes dominate the U.S. Defense Department's and the CIA's strategic perspective, for example. See *USSS 1998*, 9; William S. Cohen, *Annual Report to the President and the Congress*, February 2000 (www.dtic.mil/execsec/adr2000/); and Director of Central Intelligence George J. Tenet, "The Worldwide Threat in 2000: Global Realities of Our National Security," statement before the Senate Select Committee on Intelligence, February 2, 2000 (www.nyu.edu/globalbeat/usdefense/Tenet020200.html).

14. Christopher Layne, "From Preponderance to Offshore Balancing: America's Future Grand Strategy," in *America's Strategic Choices*, ed. Brown et al., 244–82.

15. David M. Lampton, "A Growing China in a Shrinking World: Beijing and the Global Order," in *Living With China: U.S./China Relations in the Twenty-first Century*, ed. Ezra F. Vogel (New York: W.W. Norton, 1997), 121–22.

16. Nye, "The Case for Deep Engagement," 91.

17. The "sheriff in the posse" metaphor is used by Richard N. Haass, "Beyond Containment: Competing American Foreign Policy Doctrines for the New Era," in *The Future of American Foreign Policy*, ed. Eugene R. Wittkopf and Christopher M. Jones (New York: St. Martin's/Worth, 1999), 3d ed., 22–38; and by Joseph S. Nye Jr., "Conflicts After the Cold War: Realism, Liberalism, and U.S. Interests," in *The Future of American Foreign Policy*, ed. Wittkopf and Jones, 68–82. Nye defines the fundamental U.S. security role as not "that of a lone global policeman; rather, the United States can frequently serve as the sheriff of the posse," operating within coalitions such as Desert Storm. Haass concludes: "For now and for the immediate future, the real question hanging over the promise of posses is not so much their utility as it is the willingness and ability of the United States to saddle up and to lead."

18. Private conversation. Among numerous examples of how U.S. scholars see America as the exceptional power, see Donald C. Hellmann, "America, APEC, and the Road Not Taken: International Leadership in the Post–Cold War Interregnum in the Asia-Pacific," in *From APEC to Xanadu*, ed. Pyle and Hellmann, 70–97.

19. For an exceptional critique along these lines, see Chalmers Johnson, *Blowback: The Costs and Consequences of American Empire* (New York: Metropolitan Books, 2000).

20. Under Clinton, "security, open markets, and democracy go hand in hand" in East Asia policy, with security, based above all on bilateral alliances, "the first pillar." That was merely a continuation of U.S. policy. See Clinton, *Engagement and Enlargement*, 39.

21. For example, strengthening the U.S.–South Korea–Japan coalition as against a coalition of China, Russia, and India.

22. Richard Bernstein and Ross H. Munro, *The Coming Conflict with China* (New York: Knopf, 1997).

23. For example, the view of the South Korean foreign ministry's think tank—the Institute of Foreign Affairs and National Security (IFANS). In a study of future security in Northeast Asia, the IFANS said that the United States must remain as a "stabilizing force," playing the "role of a balancer in which the United States maintains a power balance between China and Japan." As reported in *Korea Herald*, July 28, 1999.

24. Layne, "From Preponderance to Offshore Balancing," in *America's Strategic Choices*, ed. Brown et al.

25. See *USSS 1998*, 10: "U.S. alliances in the region . . . are not directed at any third power but serve the interests of all who benefit from regional stability and security. . . . [They are] evidence of our continued confidence that an integrated network of security relations is in the mutual interest of all Asia-Pacific nations."

26. Barbara Opall, "Denuclearization Drive May Imperil East Asian Security," *Defense News*, January 6–12, 1997.

27. James A. Kelly, "U.S. Security Policies in East Asia: Fighting Erosion and Finding a Balance," *The Washington Quarterly*, vol. 18, no. 3 (Summer 1995): 31. Kelly is now the Assistant Secretary of State for Asia and the Pacific in the George W. Bush administration.

28. *USSS 1998*, 2–6; Nye, "Conflicts After the Cold War" and Haass, "Beyond Containment," both in *The Future of American Foreign Policy*, ed. Wittkopf and Jones. Douglas

Paal ("China and the East Asian Security Environment: Complementarity and Competition," in *Living With China*, ed. Vogel, ch. 2) explicitly favors a balance of power directed at "managing" China—"to serve as a hedge or an insurance policy against the possibility that China might become confrontational" (p. 98). Here again is the managerial approach by the self-appointed Asia-Pacific "supervisor," in which China is placed under obligation either to play by U.S.-prescribed rules—phrased as "dissuad[ing] China and others from counter-productive paths" (118)—or be subject to punishment of one kind or another. Paal too now serves in the George W. Bush administration.

29. See the debate between Joseph Nye, "The Case for Deep Engagement," 90–102, and Chalmers Johnson and E. B. Keehn, "The Pentagon's Ossified Strategy," *Foreign affairs*, vol. 74, no. 4 (July–August 1995): 103–14.

30. Betts, "Wealth, Power, and Instability," 63.

31. Betts, "Wealth, Power, and Instability," 64.

32. See John A. Vasquez, "The Realist Paradigm and Degenerative versus Progressive Research Programs: An Appraisal of Waltz's Balancing Proposition," *American Political Science Review*, vol. 91, no. 4 (December 1997: 899–912), and Michael Mastanduno's discussion of Stephen Walt's balance-of-threat theory, in "Preserving the Unipolar Moment: Realist Theories and U.S. Grand Strategy after the Cold War," in *America's Strategic Choices*, ed. Brown et al., 133–39.

33. See the final statements made by Boris Yeltsin and Jiang Zemin following their meeting in August 1999, in NAPSNet, August 25, 1999.

34. Betts, "Wealth, Power, and Instability," 74.

35. Betts, "Wealth, Power, and Instability," 35.

36. Betts, "Wealth, Power, and Instability," 74.

37. Wallerstein's understanding of hegemony is adapted in Thomas McCormick, "Hegemony and World System," in *Major Problems in American Foreign Policy*, vol. 2, 3d ed., ed. Thomas G. Patterson (Lexington, Mass: D.C. Health, 1989): 25–28. Its six conditions are: a dominant center; an international division of labor among center, periphery, and semi-periphery; clear advantages in technology, products, management, and banking; a dominant position in world trade; military superiority; and ideological superiority. Some of the economic conditions no longer pertain; yet it remains indisputable that the U.S. dollar still reigns supreme, the United States still is the dominant influence in international financial and economic organizations, and the U.S. economy still is the key to international economic order.

38. See the trenchant essay of William Pfaff, "The Question of Hegemony," *Foreign Affairs*, vol. 80, no. 1 (January–February 2001): 221–32. On the rising criticism of the United States for becoming the "lonely superpower," see Samuel Huntington, "The Lonely Superpower," *Foreign Affairs*, vol. 78, no. 2 (March–April 1999): 35–49. French, Chinese, and Russian criticism (France's expressed in disagreement over policy toward Iraq, China's over Taiwan, and Russia's during Yeltsin's visit to Beijing in fall 1999, over Chechnya) has been especially vocal. Yet among American academics, there remains an inability to come to grips with hegemony—instead, "the grand strategy of preserving primacy" realism. See Michael Mastanduno, "Preserving the Unipolar Moment: Realist Theories and U.S. Grand Strategy after the Cold War," in *America's Strategic Choices*, ed. Brown et al., 125.

39. These and other contradictions are fully explored by Johnson, *Blowback*, ch. 3.

40. See Scalapino, "The United States and Asia."

41. Benjamin Schwarz, "Why America Thinks It Has to Run the World," *The Atlantic*, June 1966, 92–102, emphasis mine.

42. Fukuyama, "The End of History," *The National Interest*, no. 16 (Summer 1989): 3–18; Charles Krauthammer, "The Unipolar Moment," *Foreign Affairs*, vol. 70, no. 1 (Winter 1990–91): 23–33.

43. *New York Times*, May 8, 2001, online ed.

44. See, for instance, Kenneth N. Waltz, "Structural Realism after the Cold War," *International Security*, vol. 29, no. 1 (Summer 2000): 5–41.

45. Layne and Schwarz, "American Hegemony," 4.

46. David E. Sanger, "Asian Crisis May Take a Painful Step," *New York Times*, December 29, 1997, online ed., and a revealing speech on January 21, 1998 by Robert Rubin, treasury secretary under Clinton, on "The Asian Flu," excerpted in *The Politics of United States Foreign Policy*, 2d ed., ed. Jarel A. Rusati (Ft. Worth, Tex.: Harcourt Brace, 1999): 58–62.

47. See Johnson, *Blowback*, 226–27.

48. Robert J. Art, "Defense Policy," in *U.S. Foreign Policy: The Search for a New Role*, ed. Robert J. Art and Seyom Brown (New York: Macmillan, 1993), 112–13.

49. See *USSS 1998*.

50. Paal, "China and the East Asian Security Environment," in *Living with China*, ed. Vogel, 111. The original military agreement with Malaysia on Bilateral Training and Educational Cooperation was signed in January 1984, but was kept secret at Prime Minister Mahathir's request. See Nayan Chanda, "U.S. Maintains Broad Asian Military Pacts," *Asia Wall Street Journal*, April 8, 1992.

51. The major exercises are *Cobra Gold* (with Thailand and Singapore), *Foal Eagle* (with South Korea), *Crocodile* (with Australia), and *Rim of the Pacific* (with Australia, Japan and South Korea). *Washington Post*, May 26, 2000, based on U.S. Pacific Command information. See also Kenneth W. Allen and Eric A. McVadon, *China's Foreign Military Relations*, 76. The authors compare U.S. military exchanges with those of China, and of course find that there *is* no comparison. PLA military exchanges continue to increase, but are minuscule compared with those of the U.S. Pacific Command.

52. Johnson, *Blowback*, 78; Elizabeth Becker, "United States and Indonesia Quietly Resume Military Cooperation," *New York Times*, May 24, 2000, A8.

53. *USSS 1998*, 6; Reuters and Associated Press (Sydney) reports, July 26, 1996; NAPSNet, same date.

54. See *Defense News*, March 3–9, 1997.

55. The security dialogue was an Australian initiative; see excerpts from the Australian press in NAPSNet, August 8, 2001. On power projection see Michael R. Gordon, "Pentagon Review Puts Emphasis on Long-Range Arms in Pacific," *New York Times*, May 17, 2001, online ed. The review in question, by a long-time civilian consultant to Secretary of Defense Donald Rumsfeld, is being challenged by Admiral Blair, who is said to believe that China's hostile intentions are not proven, and its capabilities to endanger U.S. forces are exaggerated.

56. For example, the 1999 Visiting Forces Agreement with the Philippines, with which the United States still has a mutual defense treaty (1951), provides some incentive for Manila to contribute to regional peacekeeping, such as the 750 troops it provided to the East Timor PKO. But the agreement could also lead to increased U.S. military aid to the Philippines armed forces. (See U.S. Senate, Foreign Relations Committee, Subcommittee on East Asian and Pacific Affairs, testimony of Thomas Hubbard, Acting Assistant Secretary of State for East Asian and Pacific Affairs, March 6, 2001 [mimeo.].) That increased military closeness might, in turn, influence American decision making should contention between the Philippines and China over the

Spratlys turn violent. Up to now, the United States has wisely avoided committing itself to defend the Spratlys or the Paracels from Chinese attack, basing its interest in the SCS area on freedom of the seas.

57. The CIA's director under Clinton, George Tenet, recognized this trend—"the continuing pressure in East Asia for more open and accountable political systems"—but, in typical fashion, concluded that it represented just another potential source of political instability. Tenet, "The World Threat in 2000."

58. Excerpts from address of Admiral Blair, in Carnegie Endowment for International Peace, *Issue Brief*, vol. 3, no. 7 (March 23, 2000). Blair defined security communities as incorporating states that do not intend to fight one another and are willing to contribute military forces to collective security activities in support of diplomatic solutions, whether or not the states are treaty signatories. Clearly, such a definition leaves room for China and Japan to cohabit.

59. Johnson, *Blowback*, 223.

60. The approach being suggested here should be distinguished from the "pivotal states" strategy advocated by Robert S. Chase, Emily B. Hill, and Paul Kennedy (*The Pivotal States: A New Framework for U.S. Policy in the Developing World* [New York: Norton, 1999]). While correctly focusing on the internal problems of developing countries, that strategy reinvents the myth of states as "falling dominoes," upholds the objective of U.S. primacy, and presumes the ability of the United States to save "pivotal" countries from "chaos and instability." These are not the ingredients of a new foreign policy.

61. Just one of many examples of misplaced assistance was U.S. military aid to Thailand in 1997 at a time when it knew quite well that elements of the Thai military were colluding with the Khmer Rouge in illegal logging operations that were denuding Cambodia's forests. Such corrupt practices had been going on for some years, and under U.S. law required that the Clinton administration cut off aid to Thailand. But the administration refused to make a finding of ongoing illegality, and thus the military aid continued. See Thomas W. Lippman, "U.S. Clearance of Thailand in Logging Dispute is Questioned by Some Experts," *Washington Post*, February 16, 1997.

62. In 1998, total Japanese ODA (disbursed) worldwide came to $10.6 billion, equal to 0.28 percent of GNP, or $82 for every Japanese citizen. Total American ODA was $8.7 billion, or 0.10 percent of GNP and $29 per American citizen. (UNDP, *Human Development Report 2000*, table 17, 218.) For Asian countries, U.S. aid went steadily downward from 1991, when it was about $1.5 billion, to 1997, when it was just over $500 million. Japanese development loans and grants to Asia were larger than those of the United States in the case of every country. See U.S. Congress, House, Committee on International Relations, Subcommittee on Asia and the Pacific, *Hearing: U.S. Foreign Assistance in Asia* (Washington, D.C.: U.S. GPO, 1996), charts at 85 and 87.

## Chapter Eight

# Toward a More Pacific Asia

## IDENTIFYING WAYS TO COOPERATE

The preceding chapters tried to do two things. First, they portrayed the rapidly changing international relations of East Asia in a more optimistic light than one usually finds in the literature. While taking account, as all observers must, of the variety of conflicts and policy differences that divide the region, I discarded worst-case scenarios in favor of a more balanced, Asia-sensitive picture. There are many positive post–Cold War developments that have greatly reduced the chances of major conflict, and the Asian way of consultative problem solving has contributed to reducing tensions between states. Nationalism is again at center stage in East Asia, as it is everywhere else; but that has not meant, and does not have to mean, arms races and other manifestations of incessant rivalry. On a variety of issues, such as the China–Taiwan–U.S. imbroglio, the South China Sea controversy, Japan's future security role, and divided Korea, previous chapters pointed to courses of action that can channel nationalism in a positive direction. By "positive," I mean equitable, mutually beneficial, and of course peaceful. Stable, mutually accommodating U.S.–China relations holds the key to successfully managing most of those disputes.

Second, the chapters argued on behalf of a common-security approach to defining security in East Asia. Within that approach, attention was drawn to many dimensions of an unfolding human and environmental crisis across the region. Poverty, inadequate and unsafe water, exploited migrant workers, oppressive conditions for women and children, deforestation, rapid urbanization—the kinds of insecurities reflected in these issues affect huge numbers of people. Neither power-political nor economic globalization strategies provide remedies for crises of such proportions; and in some ways their cures are worse than the disease. Relief is urgent, as a matter of global ethics as well as good politics, but it will take a combination of preventive measures, redirection of state and international financial, human, and technological resources, and perhaps most of all popular social change movements. To say that is to underscore the importance of domestic no less than international political institutions and structures in obstructing needed changes.

Our remaining task is to consider the implications of these two general findings—a cautious optimism about the prospects for resolving state disputes and an urgency about the need to resolve nonmilitary security issues—for international cooperation. The Asian way of conflict resolution offers a useful though incomplete guide: Effective inter-state cooperation in nonmilitary areas can help manage dangerous disputes. But issues involving the threat or use of force must also be addressed directly. Below, I note some existing and possible projects that are promising in both respects.

## TOWARD ENVIRONMENTAL AND ENERGY SECURITY

Equitable and sustainable development may be the most important contribution international cooperation can make to real security. The consequences of rapid, unregulated growth should be anticipated, and sustainability and equity should systematically be built into the trade, production, foreign investment, and social policies of governments, regional organizations, and transnational corporations.[1] Farsighted policies would take into account, for example, the effects of trade practices on local environments and labor, the impact of production decisions on worker health and safety, and the environmental costs no less than the employment benefits of FDI. Immigration reform is especially important, in at least two basic respects. First, foreign workers in East Asia need to be accorded basic civil and cultural liberties in recognition of the contributions they make to their country of employment. Second, with the information revolution the need for information technology (IT) specialists is expected to be very large throughout Asia-Pacific. Some countries, such as Malaysia, are reluctant to rely too much on foreign-born specialists; but most countries, starting with Thailand and Singapore, see immigration of skilled labor as a key to future economic growth.[2] Asian countries will have to compete with the EU and the United States to attract IT specialists, which will require re-examining visa requirements and, beyond that, abandoning narrow-minded notions of citizenry such as those that exist in Japan.

Energy and environmental security seem to be the most promising and critical areas for future multilateral and bilateral cooperation. The reasons are clear enough. Energy use, particularly dependence on imported oil but also on imported coal, is climbing rapidly wherever economic growth is rising. The capital requirements to produce power will be huge, as will surely be the transnational and global environmental consequences. Natural environments, meanwhile, are fast disappearing, and urban environments are under assault. The insecurities these trends breed, in threats to resources (such as agricultural land) and finances as well as to impoverished communities, is palpable. On the other hand, recognition is growing around East Asia that huge gains can be made in development from investments in water management, alternative energy use, and energy conservation. The real problem is fundamentally political: Underdeveloped countries are not going to put conservationist strategies ahead of production targets unless they are paid to do so by the industrialized countries and the global bankers. Since their argument, though justified in many ways, is unlikely to persuade, only one other recourse would seem to be available—reliance on NGOs to do the painstaking grassroots work that demonstrates the cost-effectiveness of alternative energy sources and environmental protection.

As Calder observes, resource issues provide opportunities as well as present security problems in East Asian international relations.[3] Conca makes a complementary point: The very fact that environmental problems are "low politics" and promise a significant payoff for relatively small investments make interstate cooperation compelling.[4] Because of their technology, capital, and experience, the United States and Japan can play significant roles in assisting with China's oil exploration, Indonesia's and China's energy conservation, natural gas exploration and delivery, and joint resource development in the commons (such as the SCS). Here is where Japanese leadership can make a significant impact, such as in assistance to promote environmental protection research (of the kind already given to Thailand and China) and in introducing environmental technologies through foreign investments.[5]

It is well to remember, from the discussion in chapter 2, that a foundation for environmental and energy cooperation is already in place, and that it includes significant multilateral and NGO activity as well as state-to-state agreements. Thus, there is no lack of meetings or good ideas, only of the political will and foresight that will put serious money and technology behind a new understanding of security. For instance, wide use of alternative sources of energy, such as biomass, solar energy, and wind power, needs to be encouraged, particularly to give poor villagers access to cheaper energy. An example is being provided by a team from the Nautilus Institute in California, which is installing small wind turbines in North Korean villages.[6] Providing assistance with clean technologies for coal-fired plants is a short-term necessity (e.g., North Korea). When the leaders of North and South Korea held their first summit meeting, they pledged environmental cooperation. Acid rain is one of North Korea's many serious environmental problems, and South Korean assistance would be an important contribution to the peninsula's and the region's environmental security.[7]

In China, a variety of American governmental and nongovernmental organizations have been actively assisting China on water issues for twenty years.[8] The two countries have also established joint groups for research on global warming.[9] Additional cooperative arrangements on common environmental problems are needed that pool scientific and management skills, as well as have citizen input—for instance on air and marine pollution.[10] China, South Korea, and Japan have set a good example: They agreed to establish an environmental monitoring network that reportedly involves province governments and private groups as well as environmental officials.[11] Identifying new energy sources and ways to conserve energy could also benefit from regional networks—one such exists within ASEAN, and includes attention to energy management training and research.

Nuclear energy presents special problems. As a power source, it can help move an economy away from dependence on Middle East oil and polluting coal. But the drawbacks of nuclear energy are overriding. Foremost, as a leading Japanese specialist has emphasized, is the plutonium problem: Its use as a fuel cannot be separated from its reprocessing for use in bomb manufacturing. Nuclear disarmament and nuclear energy are thus part of the same problem, much as the United States and Japan would like to have it otherwise.[12] A second unresolved issue is nuclear plant safety. Accidents continue to happen, even in the most technologically advanced and supposedly safety-conscious countries such as Japan.[13] As China, South Korea, and Taiwan build more reactors to meet electricity demand, the chances increase of a catastrophic accident. By definition, such an accident would be regionwide—an Asian Chernobyl. Third is plutonium theft, or at least unaccounted-for plutonium. A fourth concern is the problem of storage and disposal of radioactive waste, high-level waste in particular. Here, South Korea, with eleven reactors; Taiwan, with six (and two others being built); and North Korea, with two (and two others to be constructed under the Agreed Framework), face serious challenges: They seem to have no options for burying their high-level nuclear waste. Dumping the waste in someone else's backyard, as Taiwan tried to do with its low-level waste in North Korea and now seems to be doing on the China mainland, merely shifts the burden. It is clearly not a solution so far as high-level waste is concerned.[14]

The situation cries out for a cooperative strategy dedicated to *ending* reliance on the nuclear option while enhancing energy security in the interim. Some Asia experts have recommended formation of a "PACATOM" or "Asiatom" organization to promote regional cooperation on plant safety, waste storage, and tougher safeguards (beyond those of the IAEA) against plutonium diversion or theft. PACATOM would be a project that Japan could lead.[15] As a mechanism of functional cooperation that can help prevent accidents, focus expert attention on the disposal problem, and allay suspicions about a country's (notably Japan's) plutonium acquisitions, it is a fine idea. PACATOM is already the subject of a CSCAP working group, and as a CBM, it might give a boost to security cooperation in Northeast Asia. But it is also important that PACATOM not become a vehicle to prolong reliance on nuclear energy.

## Overcoming Obstacles to Cooperative Ventures

Of the many obstacles to regional cooperation in the above areas, three stand out: opposition to civic participation in decision making, resistance in the major global lending institutions to giving priority to human and environmental security, and structural dependence in the regional economy.

National and international NGOs working in East Asia are vital to the achievement of social justice and environmental protection. Their research, activism, and networking sometimes spell the difference between outside indifference and involvement. These are the groups, for instance, that are documenting environmental abuses in Indonesia (Walhi), the fitness of candidates for public office in South Korea (Citizens' Coalition for General Election 2000 and Citizens' Coalition for Economic Justice), crimes of war against women in East Timor (Fokupers), the military dictatorship's oppressiveness in Burma (Free Burma Network), social injustice in East Asia (Focus on the Global South), violations of labor rights in Asia (Global Exchange), and political and religious oppression and legal abuses in China and elsewhere (Human Rights Watch, Human Rights in China, Lawyers Committee for Human Rights). Without these groups, not only would East Asia's oppressed and marginalized people have no voice—the propaganda machinery of governments, global corporations, and international governmental organizations would continue to speak for them.

The support of the United States is crucial in prodding groups such as APEC to give serious attention to sustainable development (SD) and to the NGOs that represent SD interests. Washington's focus on trade liberalization has pushed SD into the background, thus dovetailing with Asian governments' pattern of ignoring environmental, human rights, and civil society NGOs that want (and should have) a seat at the table. Instead of gaining acceptance as participants in APEC summit meetings, NGOs are finding that as time passes, the opposite is true.[16] If the United States has a serious interest in Asia-Pacific stability, it ought to do at least two things: first, acknowledge the legitimate role of government in meeting citizen's basic needs, especially in times of new social challenges being presented by globalization; second, press for greater inclusiveness in the APEC process. Sustainable development is a weak concept unless accompanied by social justice, but up to now that way of thinking has not penetrated either the U.S. government or the corporate community. Yet unless governments, NGOs, and community groups, in the United States and around Asia-Pacific, energetically cooperate to address the environmental and economic sources of social unrest, it seems likely to lead to widespread violence.

A second set of obstacles is the IMF's and World Bank's reliance on private capital to promote economic growth. For one thing, private investment does not typically go to the poorest countries. They must rely on development assistance at a time when it is not politically popular in the richest countries, which give the most money but are among the stingiest in terms of their overall wealth. While Japan has sometimes gone beyond ODA in its aid to Asia and targeted empowerment of communities rather than state institutions— launching a new facility, the Japan Social Development Fund, within the World Bank to provide grants ($95 million) to the poorest victims of the financial crisis and pledging the largest sum of any government ($16 million) to support the Bank's Trust Fund for East Timor development—these are stopgap forms of assistance. People in underdeveloped countries need systematic, dependable grassroots level help that will promote self-reliant, long-term, environmentally friendly development.

Furthermore, private investment is not usually devoted to addressing fundamental sources of insecurity such as land erosion, inadequate education and health care, overfishing, and other consequences of poverty. Nor do proven methods of self-reliant development, such as micro-loans to women to start small businesses, have a high priority among investors and official aid agencies. Most likely, investment will, as in the past, flow into sectors that have high profit-making opportunities, such as real estate, banking, power, telecommunications, and high technology. The IMF, while acknowledging criticism of its insistence on fast structural reform by Asian governments that took its loans, still rejects the idea that government has a key role to play in regulating economic development.[17] That promises no social safety net for people at the bottom of the income scale.

To be sure, the rate of poverty has been reduced in some parts of Asia, dramatically in some East Asian countries. But the numbers of people still living in poverty are astounding—recall the ADB's figure of two billion people living on less than $2 a day, as well as the 213 million Chinese and two million Mongolians living on less than $1 a day (17 percent and 80 percent, respectively, of their populations in 1998). Furthermore, poverty rates among certain groups (namely women, children, and rural dwellers) are well above average. In fact, a firm relationship between improving income and gains in human development has yet to be established.[18] Likewise when it comes to economic growth: Though the ADB maintains that "when economic growth rates rise, poverty falls,"[19] it is referring to the poverty rate (percentage of people living in poverty) and not to the number of poverty-stricken people. The real answer to poverty lies (as the ADB clarifies subsequently) in how "inclusive" economic growth is, which in turn is a matter of good governance and human decency. It seems clear that neither globalization of finance nor of trade can possibly lift millions of people out of poverty. To the contrary, speculative finance and the export by the richest economies of low wage jobs under health-threatening conditions most likely will exacerbate poverty. Only a few boats are actually lifted by the rising tide of GNP.

## Northeast Asia's Special Problems

The discussion in chapter 2 of the East Asian political economy highlighted the prominence of regional production networks, Japanese predominance in trade and overseas investment, and the continuing technological dependence on Japan by South Korean and Taiwanese companies. These trends are not likely to change anytime soon, and thus have important implications for international relations and economic development in East Asia.

One implication is that so long as Japan limits entry into its market and keeps a tight hold on technology transfers, it will incur the resentment or criticism of other Asian countries. Second, so long as Japan's market remains relatively closed, reliance on the U.S. market will continue to be intense, sustaining the basis for trade disputes. Third, a high degree of dependence on Japanese technology and capital goods for export-led development is not in the best interest of other Asian economies or of Japanese workers. Being part of the regional production chain will mean higher figures for Thai exports and Korean FDI, but the main beneficiary of both will be Japanese corporations. Countries need to invest much more in their own research and development, which is to say in human resources, and they need to provide the higher wages and skilled work forces that will widen their own consumers' buying power.

With respect to Northeast Asia, the problem of dependence on Japanese capital and technology is particularly acute—and will deepen if North Korea's economy opens up. The prospect of Japanese–South Korean competition in North Korea is worrisome. Perhaps the answer lies in reorienting trade and investment patterns in Northeast Asia away from Japan and toward Russia and China. Greater economic involvement by the EU would be important, considering significant outside help will be necessary—for example, to develop the Russian Far East or to create a Northeast Asia Development Bank.

## TOWARD COMMON SECURITY

### Redefining Security

The Cold War's end represents an opportunity *fundamentally* to change strategic thinking. *Common* security needs to replace threat analysis and the quest for unilateral economic or military advantage. In broad outline, the concept involves a search by states for common ground that will avoid spiraling crises and will instead establish the basis for predictability, trust building, and in the end possibly conflict resolution. Common security strategies consequently emphasize transparency, multilateral dialogue, "cooperative-security" approaches to conflict prevention, and CBMs.[20] These are strategies that usually apply to the military aspects of security, however. As the discussion throughout this book has emphasized, we need to consider how these and other concepts can be used to address the nonmilitary sources of instability in East Asia.

Two ideas are central to constructing such a broad-gauged common security agenda. One is a *redefinition of security*; the other is a shift from confrontation to *strategies of collaboration.*

Over the last decade or so, "comprehensive security" has become a fixture in regional dialogue. The notion is now embraced in most of East Asia that a sound economy and social advances (especially in education and technology) are critical elements of real national security. Two reasons may account for the term's appeal: first, economic strength and an intelligent society provide the foundation for domestic legitimacy and political stability; second, comprehensive security is the essential ingredient of international legitimacy and successful diplomacy (including a peaceful resolution of national division). Of course, there is a difference between theory and practice, between promise and performance; no one would say that comprehensive security means the end of military force modernization or policies devoted to peace and sustainable development. But experiences such as the Asian financial crisis have reinforced this noteworthy attentiveness to the *fundamentally domestic* sources of security and insecurity.[21]

The second basic idea behind common security is represented in the Asian way. One aspect is the consultative, dialogue-based process. The other is economic development on the pattern of "open regionalism," which provides a powerful incentive for states to avoid armed conflict—and, in the case of unstable, highly underdeveloped states such as North Korea and Burma, an incentive to partake of the benefits of economic association and dialogue with critics. The Asian way has thus introduced both a new process and new interests in the strategic calculus of states, not only within ASEAN, but more specifically in relations between formerly hostile or suspicious neighbors: China and Taiwan, South Korea and China, South Korea and Japan, and Japan and the ASEAN states. To be sure, increased dialogue does not ensure problem solving, and intensified economic interdependence produces its own set of problems. Nevertheless, conflicts in East Asia are now far more amenable to discussion and compromise than were the ideologically laden conflicts of the Cold War era.

A common security approach to security can pay large dividends at far less cost than would policies of confrontation. North Korea provides an excellent example. The KEDO, the Four Party Talks, and the Perry Mission's recommendations for a threat-reduction strategy toward North Korea all showed that acceptance of the other side's security legitimacy, patient diplomacy without threats, and linkage of reward to performance can enhance the security interests of all sides.[22] These efforts, complemented by bilateral initiatives taken under President Kim Dae Jung's Sunshine policy, produced concrete results: increased contacts and high-level political dialogue between the two Koreas, North Korea's suspension of missile tests and military threats, an opening for DPRK–U.S. trade, and North Korean membership in ARF. Greater security for North Korea improved prospects of further trust- and security-building steps, such as normalization of South-North relations, U.S. and Japanese diplomatic recognition of Pyongyang, and an improved energy picture for North Korea. The possibility also emerged of North Korea's gradual embrace of economic reforms.

Common security and cooperative security strategies do not, of course, guarantee against aggressive behavior between states or widespread repression within states any more than forces deployed for deterrence. But in East Asia, cooperative strategies have at least two distinct advantages over threat-based strategies. One is their focus on the region's most pressing mutual security need—conflict *prevention* and *management*. Overt aggression is the least likely kind of crisis; should it occur, the United Nations and the Asian community's refusal to cooperate with the aggressor are the first lines of defense. Much more probable than aggression are disputes between states over territory, trade, resources, and military intentions; and within states, conflicts over ethnic and religious autonomy, widespread denial of human rights, official corruption, and other issues that generate government repression or at least political instability. Resolving these kinds of disputes requires finding ways to *avoid resorting to force*—opening lines of communication, building trust, implementing CBMs, and stopping external arms assistance.

Our examination has revealed plenty of examples of multilateral as well as bilateral approaches to conflict prevention and conflict management that have had varying degrees of success. They include codes of conduct pertaining to the Spratly Islands, border security cooperation among China, Russia, and some of the Central Asian states, ARF security dialogues and workshops, increased transparency in reporting on conventional arms deals and military budgets, regional peacekeeping under the UN in East Timor, bilateral and trilateral security consultations among the Northeast Asian countries, and NGO leadership in Track II political and military dialogues and environmental cooperation projects.

The second advantage of a common security strategy is its suitability for addressing the most pressing underlying sources of insecurity in East Asia: poverty, social injustice, and official corruption. The financial crisis of 1997 made some ASEAN leaders and intellectuals acutely aware of the constraints on regional cooperation that are imposed by the noninterference principle in the face of human and environmental crises and weak governance within member countries. ASEAN and APEC need to turn that experience to their advantage and use their networking framework to focus official attention and resources (including international assistance) on common domestic problems. This means taking steps to ensure that states and global corporations invest in sustainable, human- and environment-centered development, social safety nets are strengthened, military spending is reduced, and principles of good governance (political and corporate) are adopted and implemented. The potential security payoffs are huge: increased social stability and sense of national belonging, due (for example) to higher incomes and narrowing income disparities; better educational and health-care systems, empowerment of women; more widespread access to information technology; cleaner air and water; and improvements in social justice for minorities, migrant workers, and the elderly. The alternatives, judging by current trends, are clear. East Asian societies are changing rapidly, becoming more ethnically and culturally mixed, more affected by global (read: Western) values and trends, more aged, more urban, more polluted, more energy deficient, and more politically corrupt.

## Building Common Security the Asian Way

East Asia does not have regimes for interposition (such as mandatory dispute resolution), rule-making, or even dialogue. Yet its security-promoting assets are substantial. The array of existing governmental and nongovernmental groups in East Asia provide many points of contact for discussing security issues. ASEAN's strategy is to involve the major powers in the dialogue process; as they do so, they become vested in the process and enhance its capacity to work.[23] What the Asian way has thus far meant is an increasingly complex network of nonmilitary relationships—inter-state, inter-firm, and inter- as well as intra-regional.

With specific respect to inter-state relations, there are several ways to build on the ASEAN model in East Asia, especially in Northeast Asia. One way is to universalize membership in the various Asia Pacific organizations. North Korea is on its way to being a formal participant in all of them. Gaining China's agreement to full Taiwanese membership, under whatever name, in security-related dialogue groups such as ARF and CSCAP would be a major step forward. But Northeast Asia needs its own group at the moment—first, because ARF is widely regarded as being more suited to and concerned with Southeast Asian issues; second, because the more ambitious idea of a security organization in Northeast Asia is premature. A looser framework for dialogue, based on the concept of open regionalism, seems to coincide with the status of Northeast Asian international relations today.[24] Provided the outcome of North–South Korean interactions is positive and terms of the Agreed Framework and KEDO's mission are fulfilled, enough confidence might be generated to create a six-party multilateral dialogue mechanism for Northeast Asia. The agenda of such a group could range from cooperative projects on energy and the environment, as discussed above, to political disputes. But from the standpoint of confidence building, its most significant initial contribution would be the increased trust that would hopefully come from the regularity of its meetings and the high level of governmental representation.

Confidence building often occurs by means of modest functional cooperation. KEDO is one example; PACATOM could be another. A third example is the agreement between China, South Korea, and Japan as a spinoff of the ASEAN-+3 process. The agreement pledges cooperation on environment, information technology, and economy. Dialogue among the three countries will take place annually.[25] A fourth example, already well along, is provided by the Shanghai Accord of 1996 between China, Russia, Kazakhstan, Krygyzstan, and Tajikistan. Though that agreement began as an effort to certify borders, it evolved into a policy dialogue group now called the Shanghai Forum. Other countries may join the process as the member governments discuss common security issues as well as economic cooperation.[26]

A third security-building approach is nonintrusive forms of transparency when formal arms control agreements are not yet attainable. This is not meant to minimize the importance, even urgency, of reaching regionwide agreement on specific weapons issues, such as a ban on nuclear weapon deployments. As Ball suggests, however, the immediate and common need in Asia Pacific is for "discussion and sharing of information on security perceptions and threat assessments (including intelligence assessments of general regional security developments as well as particular issues such as refugee movements, piracy and terrorism); major weapons acquisition programs; military exercises and forward deployments; and defense doctrines and operational concepts."[27] ARF would seem to be the obvious setting for implementing these ideas. However, with the wide range of military capabilities and regional security objectives of the countries involved, the lack of restraint among sellers as well as buyers of arms, and the difficulties of limiting military technology transfers and coproduction arrangements, improved transparency has been slow to take root. Nevertheless, East Asian governments do seem more willing now than previously to divulge some kinds of military information.[28] Most of them, including China, belong to the UN Register of Conventional Weapons, which happens to omit important categories of arms transfers.[29]

Fourth, governments can devise new structures and missions that promote dialogue. The EU did just that in 2001 when it sent a mission to North and South Korea to show its support for the peace process and see that none of the parties, inferentially including the United States, backtracked.[30] This was a welcomed intervention in light of the Bush administration's lack of enthusiasm for the Sunshine policy. In the case of the Spratly Islands dispute, one analyst has suggested establishing a "Spratly Development Authority" to administer the most contested areas and guarantee China and Taiwan a combined 51 percent share of the proceeds. This authority would be similar to the International Seabed Authority under UNCLOS, and would essentially place joint development for mutual benefit ahead of the question of sovereignty.[31] ARF has finally expanded its purview in preventive diplomacy by authorizing its chair to provide good offices in inter-state disputes. This facilitating role should extend to disputes *within* states. ASEAN should follow suit and make use of its inter-state dispute resolution mechanism (the High Council under the Treaty of Amity and Cooperation). Yet another idea, originally put forward by the Russian Ministry of Foreign Affairs in the early 1990s, is to create a regional crisis prevention center. Depending on the parties' level of commitment, the center's activities might range from data collection (e.g., on countries' armaments and arms transfers) to dispute resolution capacities.[32] Such an idea could be folded into ARF or a Northeast Asia dialogue group.

Fifth, nongovernmental forces have an important part to play in promoting international security, starting with international and local NGOs. They can provide the kind of informal setting and off-the-record communication that is essential to successful dialogue. In some cases they may be the only way for disputing parties and different kinds of official and unofficial individuals to meet. NGOs are a particularly important channel because of the longstanding tendency in the conduct of American foreign policy to go it alone. U.S. resistance to a consultative model for doing business, even with allies, puts a particular burden on unofficial groups and individuals to open up new diplomatic tracks.

## Beyond the Asian Way?

The preceding discussion suggests that "Asian" approaches to security cooperation have considerable unexplored potential. To make a real imprint on regional security, they will need to become bolder and more flexible in adopting CBMs, linking up with NGOs, and establishing methods of (if not mechanisms for) conflict management within as well as between states. Even then, the resulting security network will be febrile. One cannot claim it will prevent another Cambodia, reduce nuclear arms in Northeast Asia, or stop the clear-cutting of Indonesia's forests. And while the Asian way may prove the key to resolving the South China Sea disputes, it is unlikely to be consulted when it comes to the major bilateral territorial disagreements, such as China-Taiwan and Russia-Japan. The best that can be said of the Asian way is that in an era of uncertainty, it goes some of the way toward meeting the need for reassurances of intentions rather than reliance on a provocative show of strength.

Politics as a science is still very weak when it comes to identifying why states choose conflict over negotiations and threats over a common security strategy. There is no assurance, therefore, that the policies supported here, such as a deepening of the Asian dialogue process and a regionwide effort to strengthen the environmental and human underpinnings of national and regional security, will work better than either a balance-of-power approach or reliance exclusively on economic forces. What I do contend is that such a combination of policies will lower the risks of open conflict, and might even prevent some from happening.[33] They will deeply enmesh states and societies, including outside powers, in mutually beneficial enterprises—meaning not merely trade and investment but also protection of the society and region's natural resource base and promotion of social justice. The end result will be widening and deepening democracy, political and economic, which should make for a stronger, shared commitment to regional peace.

There are many multilateral projects one might like to see Asia Pacific states pursuing in common for the sake of peace and stability. For example, they might establish a regional peacekeeping center (for conducting humanitarian missions), reach agreement to demilitarize borders or common sea areas, include regional security discussions in APEC, or create a development bank for Northeast Asia. These and many other ideas have been proposed before and will be again. One future project has particular urgency—establishment of a nuclear weapon-free zone in Northeast Asia (NEA-NWFZ). The reasons are worth reiterating: the concentration of actual and potential nuclear weapon states in that region, Japan's plutonium buildup, China's modernization of its nuclear forces, an American history of nuclear weapons deployments in and through Northeast Asian territory, and the continuing importance of nuclear weapons in the strategic doctrines of the states that possess them. In addition, some specific events add to the case for a NEA-NWFZ: the unique circumstance of use of atomic bombs against a Northeast Asian country; the interest at various times in South

Korea, Taiwan, North Korea, and Japan[34] in acquiring a nuclear weapon capability; the rapid development of ballistic missiles by several countries and the American concept of ballistic missile defense in Northeast Asia; the widely accepted view that should any more states go nuclear, it would be difficult if not impossible to stop the others from doing so; and the failure of the international community to prevent or effectively sanction India and Pakistan when they conducted nuclear weapon tests in 1998.

Since all the major powers are publicly committed to keeping the Korean peninsula denuclearized, and since the two Koreas agreed in their 1991 accord to far-reaching restrictions on nuclear weapons, Korea provides a convenient starting point for a NEA-NWFZ.[35] But various specialists have proposed that given the many difficulties of negotiating an agreement that is acceptable to all the parties in Northeast Asia, it would be more practical to start instead with a limited NWFZ and build from there.[36] Putting these specialists' ideas together to illustrate the possibilities, the zone might be applied initially to the Korean peninsula, Japan, Taiwan, and Mongolia (which declared itself a nuclear weapon-free state in 1992). Those governments and the PRC, Russia, and the United States would agree to ban nuclear threats, nuclear weapons use against states in the zone, nuclear testing, and storage and possession of nuclear weapons. At a second stage, the parties might further agree to ban the manufacture, acquisition, deployment, and transit of nuclear weapons within the zone. As a final step, with the zone expanded to include China, Russia, and perhaps part of the United States, the parties would agree to forbid nuclear weapon research, the dumping of nuclear materials, the possession of "facilities for nuclear reprocessing or uranium enrichment" (per the inter-Korean accord), and the production of fissile materials.

Africa, Latin America, the South Pacific island states, ASEAN, and five Central Asian states have established NWFZs with differing conditions.[37] As Andrew Mack has written, "Nuclear-free zones strengthen the taboo against nuclear weapons; they enhance 'the nuclear allergy.' They are, above all, about creating norms that delegitimize reliance on weapons of mass destruction to preserve security."[38] NWFZs, Mack further observes, go much more directly to the heart of the problem—states' *demand* for nuclear weapons—rather than, as in the NPT regime, being satisfied with supply-side approaches such as technical limitations and sanctions on nuclear weapons that are already possessed.

What would a NEA-NWFZ accomplish? The treaty would add immeasurably to regional security in Northeast Asia, since it would directly address concerns about a Japan, Taiwan, and unified Korea with nuclear weapons. The NWFZ would strengthen and potentially go well beyond the NPT. It would enable security guarantees to remain in place, thus providing the reassurances that the non-nuclear states would want to have. If the zone were not the result of a Northeast Asia dialogue group's agreement, it would surely lend itself to creation of one. At the global level, the zone would give impetus to the creation of other zones in regions of intense international competition and where the nuclear weapon danger is real, namely, the Middle East and South Asia. In the long view, the zone would boost the case for a global agreement to abolish nuclear weapons altogether by demonstrating that there is a different, cooperative path to security.

## SOME FINAL THOUGHTS

Force of habit is one of the enemies of clear thinking. So far as East Asia's security is concerned, habit moves dialogue along familiar lines: the balance of power, power vacuums, geopolitics, and even the inevitability of globalization. Analytically, the impact of such habitual thinking is that countries, leaders, and decisions become frozen in time; old stereotypes smother new possibilities. A deep pessimism tends to be the winner in such exercises; worst-case thinking is usually assumed to work best.

Planning for the worst in today's East Asia seems very likely to result in wasted effort and missed opportunities. If China is assumed to be aggressive, if North Korea is projected to be eternally disingenuous, or if Japan is dismissed as unchanging, it is quite likely that the Cold War will continue, and perhaps become even more dangerous than during the Soviet era. But what if one approaches matters with a cautious optimism about the future? What if China does not have to be contained because its highest priority really *is* economic development, and because it really would prefer to coexist with Taiwan based on preservation of the one-China principle? What if North Korea's leaders *are* genuinely interested in rapprochement with South Korea? What if Kim Dae Jung is right to say that "for North Korea change is not a matter of choice but of survival"[39]—and therefore needs the assurances that continued engagement with it would provide? Finally, what if Japanese security thinking *is* open to change, and needs to be prodded toward a healthy independence rather than leashed tighter to the United States?

Should optimistic scenarios prove faulty, of course, they will need to be replaced. But there is plenty of time for that; few if any critical assessments, including this one, argue for U.S. abandonment of East Asia. The kinds of alternatives discussed here and in many other writings seek to set in motion a process of change in concepts and actions, based on the enormously increased possibilities for peace that the end of the Cold War has created. Realism and Globalism have proven incapable of addressing the deep-rooted insecurities of nations and peoples; those schools of thought are too attached to power and markets to notice the suffering and inequalities that lie beneath statistics on arms and trade. There must be room for new thinking that can seize the moment and make a serious attempt to identify and work with the forces of engagement, equity, and demilitarization, in East Asia and beyond.

Change of the magnitude called for in this study is actually in the long-term best interests of states and corporations. But they are highly unlikely to see things that way. The role of ordinary citizens and foreign affairs professionals, especially educators, is therefore crucial to move public dialogue and decision making in humane, globally responsible directions. Strengthening that role is important above all in the United States, given its singular and hegemonic position in world affairs. Hegemony is not in the best interest of working people, whereas policies that envision and promote a new sense of global community are. It is the task of citizens everywhere to demonstrate that reality, within their own countries and in transnational alliance.

## NOTES

1. As the Foreign Secretary of the Philippines, Domingo Siazon, said at the Manila APEC summit meeting in November 1996: "APEC must remain a catalyst for harmonizing economic and equitable and sustainable development. If growth does not result in development that is both fair and sustainable, then APEC will lose its relevance and its future." *Japan Times* (Tokyo), November 23, 1966, 1.

2. See Nayan Chanda, "The Tug of War for Asia's Best Brains," *Far Eastern Economic Review* (November 9, 2000): 38–43.

3. Kent E. Calder, "Asia's Empty Tank," *Foreign Affairs*, vol. 75, no. 2 (March–April 1996): 65–68.

4. Ken Conca, "Environmental Confidence Building and Regional Security in Northeast Asia," *Ecological Security in Northeast Asia*, ed. Miranda A. Schreurs and Dennis Pirages (Seoul: Yonsei University Press, 1998).

5. See Elizabeth Economy, "The Environment and Development in the Asia-Pacific Region," in *Fire Across the Water*, ed. James Shinn (New York: Council on Foreign Relations, 1998), 61, 65.

6. "Building a Political Bridge with Wind," *Windpower Monthly* (May 1999), online at www.nautilus.org/dprkrenew/wpowerarticle.html. The project was preceded by North Korean tours of U.S. alternative energy facilities.

7. See David F. Von Hippel and Peter Hayes, "Environmental Problems and the Energy Sector in the Democratic People's Republic of Korea," *Asian Perspective*, vol. 22, no. 2 (1998): 51–77.

8. Woodrow Wilson Center, *China Environment Series*, no. 2 (Summer 1998).

9. Jeffrey Logan et al., *Climate Action in the United States and China* (Princeton, N.J.: Woodrow Wilson Environmental Change and Security Project, May 1999).

10. See, for example, Tomohiro Shishime (Environment Agency of Japan), "Promoting a Plan for a Marine Environment Monitoring Network in the North Pacific" (paper presented at the ESENA Workshop on Energy-Related Marine Issues in the Sea of Japan, Tokyo, July 11–12, 1998).

11. *Chosun Ilbo*, January 13, 1999; NAPSNet, January 13, 1999. Areas of cooperation will include air pollution, marine environment, and global warming mitigation.

12. Ryukichi Imai, "Energy Issues in Asia: Nuclear Energy and Nuclear Disarmament Must Be Solved Simultaneously," Institute for International Policy Studies, Paper 182E (June 1997).

13. The main accident in Japan, which has fifty-three nuclear reactors, occurred in December 1995 at the Monju fast-breeder reactor; but there have been others of varying

severity, and in a number of cases authorities attempted to cover up radiation leaks. See, for example, Peter Landers, "Nuclear Bombshells," *Far Eastern Economic Review* (May 8, 1997): 19–20.

14. See the comments of Peter Hayes, "Much Ado About Little Radiation," NAPSNet special report, March 4, 1997.

15. Robert A. Manning, "PACATOM: Nuclear Cooperation in Asia," *The Washington Quarterly*, vol. 20, no. 2 (Spring 1997): 217–32. See also Hiroyoshi Kurihara, "Regional Approaches to Increase Nuclear Transparency," *Disarmament*, vol. 18, no. 2 (1995): 25–40.

16. See John Gershman, "Asia Pacific Economic Cooperation (APEC)," *Foreign Policy In Focus*, vol. 5, no. 39 (November 2000): 1–7, online at www.foreignpolicy-infocus. org/briefs/vol5/v5n39apec.html.

17. Stanley Fischer (First Deputy Managing Director of the IMF), "The Financial Crisis in Emerging Markets: Lessons for Eastern Europe and Asia," Speech at the EastWest Institute, New York City, April 23, 1999 (www.imf.org).

18. *Asian Development Outlook 2000*, 179, 187–193.

19. *Asian Development Outlook 2000*, 192.

20. Mack and Kerr, "The Evolving Security Discourse," 123–40, provide an excellent discussion of common-security strategies.

21. In Southeast Asia, recognition of the critical relationship between domestic and international security has been strongly preached by the countries that are most advanced democratically, Thailand and Philippines. See, for example, the commentary by the Thai foreign minister, Surin Pitsuwan, "Heeding Asean's Legacy," *Far Eastern Economic Review* (February 17, 2000): 29.

22. The preventive approach to conflict was behind the Perry Mission's approach. See Ashton B. Carter, William J. Perry, and John D. Steinbruner, *A New Concept of Cooperative Security* (Washington, D.C.: Brookings Institution, 1992). Preventing conflicts from arising already has a large literature, a principal contributor to which is the Harvard Negotiation Project. See, for example, Roger Fisher et al., *Beyond Machiavelli* (New York: Penguin, 1996).

23. Pengiran Osman Bin Penigran Haji Patra, "The Future Course of the ASEAN Regional Forum: Openness and Regional Approach to Disarmament," *Disarmament*, vol. 18, no. 2 (1995): 145–57. Paul Dibb, *Towards a New Balance of Power in Asia*, (London: Adelphi Paper No. 295, Oxford University Press, 1995) 44, 56.

24. See Chung-In Moon, "Economic Interdependence and the Implications for Security in Northeast Asia," *Asian Perspective*, vol. 19, no. 2 (Fall–Winter 1995): 29–52.

25. Victor D. Cha, "Ending 2000 with a Whimper, Not a Bang," *Comparative Connections*, www.csis.org/pacfor/cc/004Qjapan_skorea.html.

26. See Gregory Gleason, "Policy Dimensions of West Asian Borders after the Shanghai Accord," *Asian Perspective*, vol. 25, no. 1 (2001): 107–31.

27. Ball, "The Most Promising CBMs," 72.

28. See Peggy Mason, "The Role of Confidence-Building in the Asia Pacific Region: The United Nations Guidelines for Regional Approaches to Disarmament," *Disarmament*, vol. 18, no. 2 (1995): 55–57.

29. See Herbert Wulf, "The United Nations Register of Conventional Arms," in *SIPRI Yearbook 1993*, 535–36. As Wulf emphasizes, "The Register is not a 'transfer' register but, as its name clearly indicates, a 'Register of Conventional Arms.'" Thus, it does not include all weapons transfers as a matter of course, nor arms production and procure-

ments, but only certain categories of arms imports and exports that governments *voluntarily* report.

30. The delegation was led by the Swedish prime minister, Goran Persson, whose government stated at the time of the trip that the EU's purpose was to "help to make this [peace] process irreversible," and to confirm from Kim Jong Il that "the missile freeze will stay." NAPSNet, May 1, 2001.

31. Mark J. Valencia, "A Spratly Solution," *Far Eastern Economic Review* (March 31, 1994): 30. A Chinese analyst has proposed a similar solution by China, Japan, and Taiwan in the case of the disputed Diaoyutai (Senkaku) islands; see Ji Guoxing, "The Diaoyudao (Senkaku) Disputes and Prospects for Settlement," *Korean Journal of Defense Analysis*, vol. 6, no. 2 (Winter 1994): 285–311.

32. See Vassili Dobrovolski, "A Crisis Prevention Center and Center for Strategic Studies," Northeast Asia Cooperation Dialogue II, IGCC Policy Paper no. 9 (April 22, 1996); online at gopher://irpsserv26.ucsd.edu:70/0F-1%3A18592%3A06-Dobrovolski.

33. Though not discussed here, an additional element that is consistent with the other policy directions is pursuit of *nonprovocative defense strategies and arsenals*, that is, military programs sufficient to provide a credible defense but insufficient to pose a threat to other states. For elaboration, see Mack and Kerr, "The Evolving Security Discourse," 132–34.

34. From time to time Japanese policy makers on the right have spoken of the need for Japan to have its own nuclear weapons. The most recent was Nishimura Shingo, vice-defense minister in 1998 (at the time of the India and Pakistan nuclear tests and North Korea's missile test over Japan), who said Japan "ought to have aircraft carriers, long-range missiles, long-range bombers. We should even have the atomic bomb." Even though Nishimura was forced out of office, he doubtless spoke for others. Todd Sechser, "The Asian Nuclear Reaction Chain," *Proliferation Brief*, vol. 3, no. 3 (February 2, 2000), in NAPSNet, March 2, 2000.

35. The Joint Declaration of the Denuclearization of the Korean Peninsula states that the two Koreas "shall not test, manufacture, produce, receive, possess, store, deploy or use nuclear weapons"; "shall use nuclear energy solely for peaceful purposes"; and "shall not possess nuclear reprocessing and uranium enrichment facilities." See appendix C of Kihl, ed., *Korea and the World*, 347.

36. See Andrew Mack, "Proliferation in Northeast Asia," Occasional Paper no. 28, The Henry L. Stimson Center (Washington, D.C.: July 1996), 55–56; John E. Endicott, "A Limited Nuclear-Weapons-Free Zone in Northeast Asia: A Track-II Initiative," *Disarmament Diplomacy*, no. 35; online at www.inta.gatech/cistp. (Endicott has led this multinational project of about ten years' duration, sponsored by the Center for International Strategy, Technology and Policy at Georgia Tech University in Atlanta.) And see Morton H. Halperin, "The Nuclear Dimension of the U.S.-Japan Alliance," 1999, online from the Nautilus Institute at www.nautilus.org/nukepolicy/Halperin/index.html.

37. The best review and comparison is by Jozef Goldblat, "Nuclear-Weapon-Free Zones: A History and Assessment," *The Nonproliferation Review*, vol. 4, no. 3 (Spring–Summer 1997): 18–32.

38. Mack, "Proliferation in Northeast Asia," 58.

39. Quoted in the *New York Times*, March 11, 2001, online ed.

# Bibliography

## BOOKS

Aggarwal, Vinod K., and Charles E. Morrison, eds. *Asia-Pacific Crossroads: Regime Creation and the Future of APEC.* New York: St. Martin's Press, 1998.

Akaha, Tsuneo, ed. *Politics and Economics in Northeast Asia: Nationalism and Regionalism in Contention.* New York: St. Martin's Press, 1999.

Akaha, Tsuneo, and Frank Langdon, eds. *Japan in the Posthegemonic World.* Boulder, Colo.: Lynne Rienner, 1993.

Art, Robert J., and Seyom Brown, eds. *U.S. Foreign Policy: The Search for a New Role.* New York: Macmillan, 1993.

*The Asian Crisis and Human Security: An Intellectual Dialogue on Building Asia's Tomorrow.* Tokyo: Japan Center for International Exchange, 1999.

Ayoob, Mohammed, ed. *Regional Security in the Third World: Case studies from Southeast Asia and the Middle East.* London: Croom Helm, 1986.

Bello, Walden. *People and Power in the Pacific: The Struggle for the Post-Cold War Order.* London: Pluto Press, 1992.

Bello, Walden, and Stephanie Rosenfeld. *Dragons in Distress: Asia's Miracle Economies in Crisis.* San Francisco: Institute for Food and Development Policy, 1990.

Bergsten, C. Fred, and Marcus Noland, eds. *Pacific Dynamism and the International Economic System.* Washington, D.C.: Institute for International Economics, 1993.

Bernstein, Richard, and Ross H. Munro. *The Coming Conflict with China.* New York: Knopf, 1997.

Blackwill, Robert D., and Paul Dibb, eds. *America's Asian Alliances.* Cambridge, Mass.: MIT Press, 2000.

Brown, Michael E. et al., eds. *America's Strategic Choices.* Cambridge, Mass.: MIT Press, 1997.

Burnett, Alan. *The Western Pacific: The Challenge of Sustainable Growth.* Sydney: Allen and Unwin, 1993.

Byman, Daniel L., and Roger Cliff. *China's Arms Sales: Motivations and Implications.* Santa Monica, Calif.: RAND Corporation, 1999.

Calder, Kent E. *Pacific Defense: Arms, Energy, and America's Future in Asia.* New York: William Morrow, 1996.

Carter, Ashton B., William J. Perry, and John D. Steinbruner. *A New Concept of Cooperative Security.* Washington, D.C.: Brookings Institution, 1992.

Cha, Victor D. *Alignment Despite Antagonism: The United States–Korea–Japan Security Triangle.* Stanford, Calif.: Stanford University Press, 1999.

Chalmers, Malcolm. *Confidence-Building in South-East Asia.* Boulder, Colo.: Westview Press, for the University of Bradford, 1996, 61–199.

Chase, Robert S., Emily B. Hill, and Paul Kennedy. *The Pivotal States: A New Framework for U.S. Policy in the Developing World.* New York: W.W. Norton, 1999.

Chia Siow Yue, and Marcello Pacini, eds. *ASEAN in the New Asia: Issues and Trends.* Singapore: Institute of Southeast Asian Studies, 1997.

Clark, Donald N., ed., *Korea Briefing, 1993.* Boulder, Colo.: Westview, 1993.

Crocker, Chester et al., eds. *Herding Cats: Multiparty Mediation in a Complex World.* Washington, D.C.: U.S. Institute of Peace, 1999.

Cumings, Bruce. *Korea's Place in the Sun: A Modern History.* New York: W.W. Norton, 1997.

da Cunha, Derek, ed. *Southeast Asian Perspectives on Security.* Singapore: Institute of Southeast Asian Studies, 2000.

Deng, Yong, and Fei-Ling Wang, eds. *In the Eyes of the Dragon: China Views the World.* Lanham, Md.: Rowman & Littlefield, 1999.

Dirlik, Arif, ed. *What's in a Rim? Critical Perspectives on the Pacific Region Idea.* Boulder, Colo.: Westview, 1993.

Economy, Elizabeth. *Reforms and Resources: The Implications for State Capacity in the PRC.* Cambridge, Mass.: American Academy of Arts and Sciences, 1997.

Eder, Norman R. *Poisoned Prosperity: Development, Modernization, and the Environment in South Korea.* New York: M.E. Sharpe, 1996.

Everett, Michael W., and Mary A. Sommerville, eds., *Multilateral Activities in South East Asia: Pacific Symposium.* Washington, D.C.: National Defense University Press, 1995, 166–70.

Fisher, Roger et al. *Beyond Machiavelli.* New York: Penguin, 1996.

Fukuyama, Frances, and Kongdan Oh. *The U.S.–Japan Security Relationship after the Cold War.* Santa Monica, Calif.: RAND National Defense Research Institute, 1993.

Funabashi, Yoichi. *Asia-Pacific Fusion: Japan's Role in APEC.* Washington, D.C.: Institute for International Economics, 1995, 55–66.

Gill, Bates, and Lonnie Henley. *China and the Revolution in Military Affairs.* Carlisle Barracks, Penna.: U.S. Army War College, 1996.

Gill, Bates, and Taeho Kim. *China's Arms Acquisitions from Abroad: A Quest for "Superb and Secret Weapons,"* SIPRI Research Report no.11. Oxford, U.K.: Oxford University Press, 1995.

Greider, William. *One World, Ready or Not: The Manic Logic of Global Capitalism.* New York: Simon & Schuster, 1997.

Grimmett, Richard F. *Conventional Arms Transfers to Developing Nations, 1987-1994,* Congressional Research Service Report no. 95-862F2, August 4, 1995 (www.fas.org).

Gurtov, Mel. *Global Politics in the Human Interest,* 4th ed. Boulder, Colo.: Lynne Rienner, 1999.

Gurtov, Melvin, and Byong-Moo Hwang, *China's Security: The New Roles of the Military.* Boulder, Colo.: Lynne Rienner, 1999.

Hamm, Taik-young. *Arming the Two Koreas: State, Capital and Military Power.* New York: Routledge, 1999.

Han Sung-joo. *Korean Diplomacy in an Era of Globalization: Speeches of Foreign Minister Han Sung-Joo, March 1993–December 1994.* Seoul: Chisik Publishing House, 1995.

Harding, Harry. *A Fragile Relationship: The United States and China since 1972.* Washington, D.C.: Brookings Institution, 1992.

Hellmann, Donald C., and Kenneth B. Pyle, eds. *From APEC to Xanadu: Creating a Viable Community in the Post–Cold War Pacific.* Armonk, N.Y.: M.E. Sharpe, 1997.

Inoguchi, Takashi. *Japan's Foreign Policy in an Era of Global Change.* New York: St. Martin's Press, 1993.

Johnson, Chalmers. *Blowback: The Costs and Consequences of American Empire.* New York: Metropolitan Books, 2000.

——, ed. *Okinawa: Cold War Island.* San Diego, Calif.: Japan Policy Research Institute, 1999.

Kihl, Young Whan, ed. *Korea and the World: Beyond the Cold War.* Boulder, Colo.: Westview, 1994.

Kim, Dalchoong, and N. Sopiee, eds. *Regional Cooperation in the Pacific Era.* Seoul: Yonsei University, 1991.

Kim, Ilpyong J., and Hong Pyo Lee, eds., *Korea and China in a New World: Beyond Normalization.* Seoul: Sejong Institute, 1993.

Kim, Samuel S., ed. *East Asia and Globalization.* Lanham, Md.: Rowman & Littlefield, 2000.

Koh Byung Chul, *The Foreign Policy Systems of North and South Korea.* Berkeley, Calif.: University of California Press, 1984.

Koo, Youngnok, and Sung-joo Han, eds. *The Foreign Policy of the Republic of Korea.* New York: Columbia University Press, 1985.

Kwak, Tae-Hwan, and Melvin Gurtov, eds. *The Future of China and Northeast Asia.* Seoul: Institute for Far Eastern Studies, Kyungnam University Press, 1997.

Lewis, John, and Xue Litai. *China Builds the Bomb.* Stanford, Calif.: Stanford University Press, 1988.

——. *China's Strategic Seapower: The Politics of Force Modernization in the Nuclear Age.* Stanford, Calif., Stanford University Press, 1994.

Logan, Jeffrey et al. *Climate Action in the United States and China.* Princeton, N.J.: Woodrow Wilson Environmental Change and Security Project, May 1999.

McGrew, Anthony, and Christopher Brook, eds. *Asia-Pacific in the New World Order.* London: Routledge, 1998.

Medeiros, Evan S., and Bates Gill. *Chinese Arms Exports: Policy, Players, and Process.* Carlisle, Penn.: U.S. Army, Strategic Studies Institute, August 2000.

Morrison, Charles E., Akira Kojima, and Hanns W. Maull. *Community-Building with Pacific Asia: A Report to the Trilateral Commission.* New York: Trilateral Commission, 1997.

Noland, Marcus. *Avoiding the Apocalypse: The Future of the Two Koreas.* Washington, D.C.: Institute for International Economics, 2000.

Park, Choon-ho et al., eds. *The Regime of the Yellow Sea: Issues and Policy Options in the Changing Environment.* Seoul: Yonsei University Institute of East and West Studies, 1990.

Paterson, Thomas G., ed. *Major Problems in American Foreign Policy,* vol. 2: *Since 1914,* 3d ed. Lexington, Mass.: D.C. Heath, 1989.

Pollack, Jonathan D., and Richard H. Yang, eds. *In China's Shadow: Regional Perspectives on Chinese Foreign Policy and Military Development*. Santa Monica, Calif.: RAND Corporation, 1998.

Puska, Susan M. *New Century, Old Thinking: The Dangers of the Perceptual Gap in U.S.–China Relations*. Carlisle Barracks, Penn.: Strategic Studies Institute, U.S. Army War College, 1998.

Rosati, Jerel A., ed. *The Politics of United States Foreign Policy*, 2d ed. Fort Worth, Tex.: Harcourt Brace, 1999.

Rotberg, Robert I., ed. *Burma: Prospects for a Democratic Future*. Washington, D.C.: Brookings Institution Press, 1998.

SaKong, Il. *Korea in the World Economy*. Washington, D.C.: Institute for International Economics, 1993.

Schreurs, Miranda A., and Dennis Pirages, eds. *Ecological Security in Northeast Asia*. Seoul: Yonsei University Press, 1998.

Shinn, James, ed. *Fire Across the Water: Transnational Problems in Asia*. New York: Council on Foreign Relations, 1998.

Shirk, Susan L., and Christopher P. Twomey, eds. *Power and Prosperity: Economics and Security Linkages in Asia-Pacific*. New Brunswick, N.J.: Transaction Publishers, 1996.

Shlapak, David A., David T. Orletsky, and Barry A. Wilson. *Dire Strait? Military Aspects of the China-Taiwan Confrontation and Options for U.S. Policy*. Santa Monica, Calif.: RAND Corp., 2000.

Sigal, Leon V. *Disarming Strangers*. Princeton, N.J.: Princeton University Press, 1999.

Simon, Sheldon W., ed. *East Asian Security in the Post–Cold War Era*. Armonk, N.Y.: M.E. Sharpe, 1993.

Smil, Vaclav. *China's Environmental Crisis: An Inquiry into the Limits of National Development*. Armonk, N.Y.: M.E. Sharpe, 1993.

So, Alvin Y., and Yok-Shiu Lee, eds. *Asia's Environmental Movements*. Armonk, N.Y.: M.E. Sharpe, 1999.

Soesastro, Hadi, ed. *Indonesian Perspectives on APEC and Regional Cooperation in Asia Pacific*. Jakarta: Centre for Strategic and International Studies, 1994.

Sutter, Robert G. *The China Quandary: Domestic Determinants of U.S. China Policy, 1972–1982*. Boulder, Colo.: Westview, 1983.

Swaine, Michael D. *The Role of the Chinese Military in National Security Policymaking*. Santa Monica. Calif.: RAND Corp., 1996.

———. *Taiwan's National Security, Defense Policy, and Weapons Procurement Processes*. Santa Monica, Calif.: RAND Corporation, 1999.

Thompson, W. Scott, and Kenneth M. Jensen, eds. *Rapid Economic Growth, Conflict, and Peace in Southeast Asia*. Washington, D.C.: United States Institute of Peace, 1997.

Tow, William T. *Encountering the Dominant Player: U.S. Extended Deterrence Strategy in the Asia-Pacific*. New York: Columbia University Press, 1991.

Unger, Danny, and Paul Blackburn, eds. *Japan's Emerging Global Role*. Boulder, Colo.: Lynne Rienner, 1993.

Vogel, Ezra F., ed. *Living with China: U.S./China Relations in the Twenty-first Century*. New York: W.W. Norton, 1997.

Wittkopf, Eugene R., and Christopher M. Jones, eds. *The Future of American Foreign Policy*, 3d ed. New York: St. Martin's/Worth, 1999.

Woods, Lawrence T. *Asia Pacific Diplomacy: Nongovernmental Organizations and International Relations*. Vancouver: University of British Columbia Press, 1993.

Wortzel, Larry M. *The ASEAN Regional Forum: Asian Security without an American Umbrella*. Carlisle Barracks, Penn.: U.S. Army War College, 1996.

*Xinshiqi Mao Zedong junshi sixiang di fazhan* (Development of Mao Zedong's Military Thought in the New Period). Beijing: PLA Press, 1991.

Yang, Sung Chul. *The North and South Korean Political Systems: A Comparative Analysis*. Boulder, Colo.: Westview, 1994.

Zhao, Quansheng. *Interpreting Chinese Foreign Policy: The Micro-Macro Linkage Approach*. Hong Kong: Oxford University Press, 1996.

## ARTICLES AND PAPERS

Acharya, Amitav. "Transnational Production and Security: Southeast Asia's 'Growth Triangles.'" *Contemporary Southeast Asia*, vol. 17, no. 2 (Spring 1995), 173–85.

Ahn, Choong Yong. "Search for New Approaches and Methods for Economic Cooperation in Northeast Asia." *Korean Journal of International Studies*, vol. 24, no. 3 (Autumn 1993), 345–63.

Alagappa, Muthiah. "Regionalism and the Quest for Security: ASEAN and the Cambodian Conflict." *Journal of International Affairs*, vol. 46, no. 2 (Winter 1993), 439–67.

Antolik, Michael. "The ASEAN Regional Forum: The Spirit of Constructive Engagement." *Contemporary Southeast Asia*, vol. 16, no. 2 (September 1994), 117–36.

Armitage, Richard L. "A Comprehensive Approach to North Korea." *Strategic Forum* (National Defense University), no. 159 (March 1999), 1–6.

Austin, Greg. "The Strategic Implications of China's Public Order Crisis." *Survival*, vol. 37, no. 2 (Summer 1995), 7–23.

Baker, James A., III. "America in Asia: Emerging Architecture for a Pacific Community." *Foreign Affairs*, vol. 70, no. 5 (Winter 1991–92), 1–18.

Ball, Desmond. "Arms and Affluence: Military Acquisitions in the Asia-Pacific Region." *International Security*, vol. 18, no. 3 (Winter 1993–94), 79–95.

———. "The Most Promising CSBMs in the Asia/Pacific Region." Paper prepared for the conference on "The Asia-Pacific Region: Links Between Economic and Security Relations," Institute on Global Conflict and Cooperation, University of California, San Diego, May 13–15, 1993.

Bandow, Doug. "Okinawa: Liberating Washington's East Asian Military Colony." *Policy Analysis*, no. 314 (September 1, 1998), 1–27

Beck, Peter M. "Foreign Direct Investment in Korea: From Exclusion to Inducement." *Joint U.S.-Korea Academic Studies*, vol. 9 (1999), 221–46.

Bernard, Mitchell, and John Ravenhill. "Beyond Product Cycles and Flying Geese: Regionalization, Hierarchy, and the Industrialization of East Asia." *World Politics*, vol. 47, no. 2 (January 1995), 171–209.

Bernstein, Richard, and Ross H. Munro. "The Coming Conflict with America." *Foreign Affairs*, vol. 76, no. 2 (March–April, 1997), 18–32.

Betts, Richard K. "Wealth, Power, and Instability: East Asia and the United States after the Cold War." *International Security*, vol. 18, no. 3 (Winter 1993–94), 34–77.

Bickford, Thomas J. "The Business Operations of the Chinese People's Liberation Army." *Problems of Post-Communism*, vol. 46, no. 6 (November–December 1999), 28–36.

Bin Pengiran Haji Patra, Penigran Osman, "The Future Course of the ASEAN Regional Forum: Openness and the Regional Approach to Disarmament," *Disarmament*, vol. 18, no. 2 (1995), 145–57.

Bitzinger, Richard A. *Chinese Arms Production and Sales to the Third World*. RAND Note N-3334-USDP, RAND Corporation, Santa Monica, Calif., 1991.

Brown, David. "Dialogue in Neutral: Private Sector in Gear." *Comparative Connections* (www.csis.org/pacfor/cc/004Qchina_taiwan.html).

Brown, Eugene. "Japanese Security Policy in the Post–Cold War World: Threat Perceptions and Strategic Options." *Journal of Northeast Asian Studies*, vol. 8, no. 2 (Summer–Fall 1994), 327–62.

"Building a Political Bridge with Wind." *Windpower Monthly*, May 1999, at www.nautilus.org/dprkrenew/wpowerarticle.html.

Buszynski, Leszek. "ASEAN Security Dilemmas." *Survival*, vol. 34, no. 4 (Winter 1992–93), 90–107.

Buzan, Barry, and Gerald Segal. "Rethinking East Asian Security." *Survival*, vol. 36, no. 2 (1994), 3–21.

Calder, Kent E. "Asia's Empty Tank." *Foreign Affairs*, vol. 75, no. 2 (March–April, 1996), 55–69.

Cao Jiaxiang. "China's Desertification Problem." *World Press Review*, August 2000, 44–45.

Cha, Victor D. "Ending 2000 with a Whimper, Not a Bang." *Comparative Connections* (www.csis.org/pacfor/cc/004Qjapan_skorea.html).

Chen Wei. "The Sino-U.S.-Japan Relations at the Turn of the Century." *International Strategic Studies*, no. 4 (2000), 11–15.

Christoffersen, Gaye. "Economic Reforms in Northeast China: Domestic Determinants." *Asian Survey*, vol. 28, no. 12 (December 1988), 1245–63.

Chung, Tae Dong. "Korea's Nordpolitik: Achievements and Prospects." *Asian Perspective*, vol. 15, no. 2 (Fall–Winter 1991), 149–78.

Cirincione, Joseph. "Assessing the Ballistic Missile Threat." Testimony before the Subcommittee on International Security, Proliferation and Federal Services, Committee on Governmental Affairs, U.S. Senate, February 9, 2000 (www.ciep.org/programs/npp/bmtestimony.htm).

———. "Missile Defense Failures Offer Lessons." *Proliferation Brief*, vol. 2, no. 7 (March 30, 1999) (www.ceip.org).

Cordesman, Anthony H. "A Comparative Summary of Military Expenditures; Manpower; Land, Air, Naval, and Nuclear Forces; and Arms Sales," Center for International and Strategic Studies, January 2000 (www.csis.org/military/asianchinese_milbal.pdf).

Davis, Elizabeth Van Wie. "Global Conflicts in Marine Pollution: The Asian Pacific." *Journal of East Asian Studies*, vol. 10, no. 1 (Winter–Spring 1996), 192–222.

De Castro, Renato Cruz. "The Association of Southeast Asian Nations as an *Entente Cordiale*." *Asian Perspective*, vol. 24, no. 2 (2000), 59–85.

"Debating Asian Security: Michael Leifer Responds to Geoffrey Wiseman." *Pacific Review*, vol. 5, no. 2 (1992), 167–69.

Denoon, David B. H., and Evelyn Colbert. "Challenges for the Association of Southeast Asian Nations (ASEAN)." *Pacific Affairs*, vol. 71, no. 4 (Winter 1998–99), 505–23.

Ding, Arthur S. "Is China a Threat? A Defense Industry Analysis." *Issues & Studies*, vol. 36, no. 1 (January–February 2000), 49–75.

Dobrovolski, Vassili. "A Crisis Prevention Center and Center for Strategic Studies." Northeast Asia Cooperation Dialogue II, IGCC Policy Paper no. 9, April 22, 1996 (gopher:// irpsserv26.ucsd.edu:70/0F-1%3A18592%3A06-Dobrovolski).

Douglass, Mike. "Unbundling National Identity: Global Migration and the Advent of Multicultural Societies in East Asia." *Asian Perspective*, vol. 23, no. 3 (1999), 79–127.

Duan Hong. "Korea and Regional Security in Northeast Asia." Nautilus Institute Nuclear Policy Project, April 20, 2000 (npp@nautilus.org).

Elek, Andrew. "The Challenge of Asian-Pacific Economic Cooperation." *The Pacific Review*, vol. 4, no. 4 (1991), 322–32.

Endicott, John E. "A Limited Nuclear-Weapons-Free Zone in Northeast Asia: A Track-II Initiative." *Disarmament Diplomacy*, no. 35 (www.inta.gatech/cistp).

Evans, Paul M. "The Council for Security Cooperation in Asia Pacific: Context and Prospects." Paper prepared for the Conference on Economic and Security Cooperation in the Asia Pacific, Canberra, Australia, July 27–29, 1993.

Feigenbaum, Even A. "Who's Behind China's High Technology 'Revolution,'" *International Security*, vol. 24, no. 1 (Summer 1999), 95–113.

Foot, Rosemary. "China in the ASEAN Regional Forum: Organizational Processes and Domestic Modes of Thought." *Asian Survey*, vol. 38, no. 5 (May 1998), 425–40.

Frankenstein, John, and Bates Gill. "Current and Future Challenges Facing Chinese Defence Industry." *China Quarterly*, no. 146 (June 1996), 394–427.

Freeman, Chas W., Jr. "Preventing War in the Taiwan Strait: Restraining Taiwan and Beijing." *Foreign Affairs*, vol. 77, no. 4 (July–August 1998), 6–11.

Frieman, Wendy. "China's Defense Industries." *The Pacific Review*, vol. 6, no. 1 (1993), 51–62.

Fukuyama, Frances. "The End of History." *The National Interest*, no. 16 (Summer 1989), 3–18.

Funabashi, Yoichi. "Japan and the New World Order." *Foreign Affairs*, vol. 70, no. 5 (Winter 1991–92), 58–74.

Gallagher, Michael G. "China's Illusory Threat to the South China Sea." *International Security*, vol. 19, no. 1 (Summer 1994), 169–94.

Garver, John W. "China's Push through the South China Sea: The Interaction of Bureaucratic and National Interests." *The China Quarterly*, no. 132 (December 1992), 1999–1028.

Gershman, John. "Asia Pacific Economic Cooperation (APEC)." *Foreign Policy In Focus*, vol. 5, no. 39 (November 2000), 1–7 (www.foreignpolicy-infocus.org/briefs/vol5/ v5n39apec.html).

Gibney, Frank B. "Creating a Pacific Community: A Time to Bolster Economic Institutions." *Foreign Affairs*, vol. 72, no. 5 (November–December 1993), 20–25.

Gills, Barry K., and Dong-Sook S. Gills. "South Korea and Globalization: The Rise to Globalism?" *Asian Perspective*, vol. 23, no. 4 (1999), 199–228.

Glaser, Bonnie S. "China's Security Perceptions: Interests and Ambitions." *Asian Survey*, vol. 33, no. 3 (March 1993), 252–71.

Gleason, Gregory. "Policy Dimensions of West Asian Borders after the Shanghai Accord." *Asian Perspective*, vol. 25, no. 1 (2001), 107–31.

Goldblat, Jozef. "Nuclear-Weapon-Free Zones: A History and Assessment." *The Nonproliferation Review*, vol. 4, no. 3 (Spring–Summer 1997), 18–32.

Green, Michael J. "State of the Field Report: Research on Japanese Security Policy." National Bureau of Asian Research, 1998 (www.accessasia.org/products/ aareview/vol2no1/essay1.html).

———. "Why Tokyo Will Be a Larger Player in Asia." Global Beat (www.nyu.edu/ globalbeat/asia/napsnet073100.html).

Guo Bingqi. "Development of the Tumen River Area and Economic Cooperation in the Northeast Asia Region." *Xiboliya yanjiu* (Siberian Studies), no. 1 (1995), 7–11.

Gurtov, Melvin. "South Korea's Foreign Policy and Future Security: Implications of the Nuclear Standoff." *Pacific Affairs*, vol. 69, no. 1 (Spring 1996), 8–31.

Halperin, Morton H. "The Nuclear Dimension of the U.S.-Japan Alliance." Nautilus Institute, 1999 (www.nautilus.org/nukepolicy/Halperin/index.html).

Hart-Landsberg, Martin. "The Asian Crisis: Causes and Consequences." *Against the Current*, no. 73 (March–April 1998), 26–29.

Hay, John E., Atsutoshi Oshima, and Gillian D. Lewis. "Capacity Building for Sustainable Development in Asia." *Asian Perspective*, vol. 23, no. 3 (1999), 7–32.

Hosokawa Morihiro. "Are U.S. Troops in Japan Needed?" *Foreign Affairs*, vol. 77, no. 4 (July–August 1998), 2–5.

Hunter, Jason. "APEC: Promise or Peril in the Asia-Pacific?" Nautilus Institute paper, June 5, 1997 (www.nautilus.org/vforum.html).

———. "The Tumen River Area Development Program, Transboundary Water Pollution, and Environmental Security in Northeast Asia." Talk at the Woodrow Wilson Center, Environmental Change and Security Project, January 7, 1998, via Nautilus Institute (APRENet@nautilus.org).

Huntington, Samuel P. "The Clash of Civilizations?" *Foreign Affairs*, vol. 72, no. 3 (Summer 1993), 22–49.

———. "The Lonely Superpower." *Foreign Affairs*, vol. 78, no. 2 (March-April 1999), 35–49.

Imai, Ryukichi. "Energy Issues in Asia: Nuclear Energy and Nuclear Disarmament Must be Solved Simultaneously." Institute for International Policy Studies, Paper 182E, June 1997.

Inoguchi, Takashi. "Japan in Search of a Normal Role." Adelphi Paper no. 275, March 1993.

Jameson, Sam. "Japan's Security Problems and Challenges to the U.S.-Japan Alliance." Speech at Japan Defense Research Institute, September 9, 1997.

Jia Qingguo. "China's Policy Perspective Toward the Korean Peninsula." *KNDU Review*, vol. 5, no. 2 (December 2000), 103–19.

Ji Guoxing. "The Diaoyudao (Senkaku) Disputes and Prospects for Settlement." *Korean Journal of Defense Analysis*, vol. 6, no. 2 (Winter 1994), 285–311.

Johnson, Chalmers. "Japan in Search of a 'Normal' Role." *Daedalus*, vol. 14 (February 1992), 1–33.

Johnson, Chalmers, ed. "Dysfunctional Japan: At Home and in the World." *Asian Perspective*, vol. 24, no. 4 (2000).

Johnson, Chalmers, and E. B. Keehn. "The Pentagon's Ossified Strategy." *Foreign Affairs*, vol. 74, no. 4 (July–August 1995), 103–14.

Johnston, Alastair Iain. "But Is It Socialization? International Institutional Effects on Chinese Arms Control Policy." MIT Security Studies Program Seminar, May 13, 1998.

Kahler, Miles. *Institution-Building in the Pacific*, Research Report 93-03 (San Diego, Calif.: Graduate School of International Relations and Pacific Studies, 1993).

Kamal, Nazir. "China's Arms Export Policy and Responses to Multilateral Restraints." *Contemporary Southeast Asia*, vol. 14, no. 2 (September 1992), 112–41.

Kang, Jung Mo. "The Economic Necessity of the Northeast Asia Economic Sphere." *Global Economic Review*, vol. 27, no. 1 (Spring 1998), 63–87.

Kaplan, David E. "The Wiseguy Regime." *US World Today*, World Report, February 15, 1999, 1–8.

Kawasaki, Tsuyoshi. "Between Realism and Idealism in Japanese Security Policy: The Case of the ASEAN Regional Forum," *Pacific Review*, vol. 10, no. 4 (1997), 480–503.

Kelly, James A. "U.S. Security Policies in East Asia: Fighting Erosion and Finding a Balance." *The Washington Quarterly*, vol. 18, no. 3 (Summer 1995), 21–35.

Kennedy, Scott, and Michael O'Hanlon. "Time to Shift Gears on China Policy." *Journal of East Asian Affairs*, Winter–Spring 1996 (Nautilus Institute, www.nautilus.org).

Kim, Chungsoo. *Regional Economic Cooperation Bodies in the Asia-Pacific: Working Mechanism and Linkages*, Working Paper no. 90-01 (August 1990), Korea Institute for International Economic Policy, Seoul.

Kim Dae Jung. "Is Culture Destiny? The Myth of Asia's Anti-Democratic Values." *Foreign Affairs*, vol. 73, no. 6 (November–December 1994), 189–94.

————. "Three-Phase Unification Formula for Building Korean National Community." *Korea Focus*, vol. II, no. 4 (July–August 1994), 170–75.

Kim, Hong Nack. "Japanese-Korean Relations in the 1990s." Woodrow Wilson Center Occasional Paper no. 59, March 29, 1994.

Kim, Icksoo. "Tumen River Area Development Program and the Prospects for Northeast Asian Economic Cooperation." *Asian Perspective*, vol. 19, no. 2 (Fall–Winter 1995), 75–102.

Kim, Samuel S. "China As a Great Power." *Current History*, vol. 96, no. 611 (September 1997), 246–51.

Kim, Sunhyuk. "The Politics of Reform in South Korea: The First Year of the Kim Dae Jung Government, 1998–1999." *Asian Perspective*, vol. 24, no. 1 (2000), 163–86.

Klare, Michael T. "The Next Great Arms Race." *Foreign Affairs*, vol. 72, no. 3 (Summer 1993), 136–52.

Ko Jae-nam. "Ten Years of Korea-Russia Diplomatic Relations." *Korea Focus*, vol. 8, no. 6 (November–December 2000), 55–70.

Koppel, Bruce. "Fixing the Other Asia." *Foreign Affairs*, vol. 77, no. 1 (January–February 1998), 98–110.

Krauthammer, Charles. "The Unipolar Moment." *Foreign Affairs*, vol. 70, no. 1 (Winter 1990–91), 23–33.

Kurihara, Hiroyoshi. "Regional Approaches to Increase Nuclear Transparency." *Disarmament*, vol. 18, no. 2 (1995), 25–40.

Layne, Christopher, and Benjamin Schwarz. "American Hegemony—Without an Enemy." *Foreign Policy*, no. 92 (1993), online ed.

Lee Goo-hong. "Overseas Koreans: Invaluable Asset." *Korea Focus*, vol. 4, no. 1 (January–February 1996), 24–33.

Leifer, Michael. "Chinese Economic Reform and Security Policy: The South China Sea Connection." *Survival*, vol. 37, no. 2 (Summer 1995), 44–59.

Li Qiang et al. "China's Comparative Gap Between Rich and Poor." *Xinhua wenzhai* (New China Digest, Beijing), no. 2 (1996), trans. *Inside China Mainland*, vol. 18, no. 6 (June 1996), 70–74.

Lindsay, Jonathan M. "Overlaps and Tradeoffs: Coordinating Policies for Sustainable Development in Asia and the Pacific." *The Journal of Developing Areas*, no. 28 (October 1993), 20–31.

Lu Guangye. "The Impact of Reinforcement of Japan-U.S. Military Alliance on the Asia-Pacific Security and World Peace." *International Strategic Studies* (China Institute for International Strategic Studies), no. 3 (1999), 21–24.

Mack, Andrew. "Naval Arms Control and Confidence Building for Northeast Asian Waters." *The Korean Journal of Defense Analysis*, vol. 5, no. 2 (Winter 1993), 135–64.

———. "Proliferation in Northeast Asia." Occasional Paper no. 28, The Henry L. Stimson Center. Washington, D.C.: July 1996.

Mack, Andrew, and Desmond Ball, "The Military Build-up in Asia-Pacific." *The Pacific Review*, vol. 4, no. 3 (1992), 202–14.

Mack, Andrew, and Pauline Kerr. "The Evolving Security Discourse in the Asia-Pacific." *The Washington Quarterly*, vol. 18, no. 1 (Winter 1995), 123–40.

Maehara, Yasuhiro. "The Role of Foreign Direct Investment in the Economies of East Asia." *Joint U.S.–Korea Academic Studies*, vol. V (1995), 75–95.

Magid, Alvin. "Contemplating Survivalist North Korea." *Asian Perspective*, vol. 24, no. 1 (2000), 103–32.

Mahbubani, Kishore. "The Pacific Way." *Foreign Affairs*, vol. 74, no. 1 (January–February 1995), 100–112.

Manning, Robert A. "Futureshock or Renewed Partnership? The U.S.-Japan Alliance Facing the Millennium." *The Washington Quarterly*, vol. 18, no. 4 (Autumn 1995), 87–98.

———. "PACATOM: Nuclear Cooperation in Asia." *The Washington Quarterly*, vol. 20, no. 2 (Spring 1997), 217–32.

Marton, Andrew et al. "Northeast Asian Economic Cooperation and the Tumen River Area Development Project." *Pacific Affairs*, vol. 68, no. 1 (Spring 1995), 9-33.

Mason, Peggy. "The Role of Confidence-Building in the Asia-Pacific Region: The United Nations Guidelines for Regional Approaches to Disarmament." *Disarmament*, vol. 18, no. 2 (1995), 49–71.

McVeigh, Brian J. "Postwar Japan's 'Hard' and 'Soft' Nationalism." Japan Policy Research Institute, Working Paper no. 73 (January 2001), 1–6.

Meyer, Peggy Falkenheim. "Russia's Post–Cold War Security Policy in Northeast Asia." *Pacific Affairs*, vol. 67, no. 4 (Winter 1994–95), 495–512.

Miller, Steven E. "Arms and East Asia: Supplier Motivations and Arms Transfer Control." *The Korean Journal of International Studies*, vol. 24, no. 4 (Winter 1993), 405–30.

Miyashita, Akitoshi. "*Gaiatsu* and Japan's Foreign Aid: Rethinking the Reactive-Proactive Debate." *International Studies Quarterly*, vol. 43, no. 4 (December 1999), 695–731.

Mochizuki, Mike M. "Security and Economic Interdependence in Northeast Asia." Asia/Pacific Research Center, Stanford University, May 1998.

Montaperto, Ronald N., and Hans Binnendijk, "PLA Views on Asia Pacific Security in the 21st Century." *Strategic Forum*, no. 114 (June 1997), 1–4.

Moon, Chung-In. "Economic Interdependence and the Implications for Security in Northeast Asia." *Asian Perspective*, vol. 19, no. 2 (Fall–Winter 1995), 29–52.

Moore, Thomas G. "China and Globalization." *Asian Perspective*, vol. 23, no. 4 (1999), 65–95.

Morgan, Patrick M. "Comparing European and East Asian Regional Security Systems." Paper prepared for the annual meeting of the International Studies Association, Acapulco, Mexico, March 1993.

Mulgan, Aurelia George. "Japan: A Setting Sun?" *Foreign Affairs*, vol. 79, no. 4 (July–August 2000), 40–52.

Mulvenon, James. *Chinese Military Commerce and U.S. National Security*, RAND Paper DAR-1626-CAPP, June 1997.

Natsios, Andrew. "The Politics of Famine in North Korea." U.S. Institute of Peace Special Report, August 2, 1999.

Norris, Robert S., William M. Arkin, and William Burr, "How Much Did Japan Know?" *The Bulletin of the Atomic Scientists*, vol. 56, no. 1 (January–February 2000), online ed.

Nye, Joseph S., Jr. "East Asian Security: The Case for Deep Engagement." *Foreign Affairs*, vol. 74, no. 4 (July–August 1995), 90–102

———. "What New World Order?" *Foreign Affairs*, vol. 71, no. 2 (Spring 1992), 83–96.

Ogawa Shinichi. "TMD and Northeast Asian Security." Paper for Nautilus Institute, September 28, 2000 (NAPSNet@nautilus.org, October 19, 2000).

O'Hanlon, Michael. "Why China Cannot Conquer Taiwan." *International Security*, vol. 25, no. 2 (Fall 2000), 51–86.

Olsen, Edward A. "The Tumen Project CBM: An American Strategic Critique." *Asian Perspective*, vol. 19, no. 2 (Fall–Winter 1995), 53–74.

Orlov, Vladimir A. "Russia's Policy Perspective toward the Korean Peninsula: Security Aspect." *KNDU Review*, vol. 5, no. 2 (December 2000), 121–56.

Park Chin Keun. "The ASEAN Free Trade Area: Concepts, Problems and Prospects" in *AFTA after NAFTA*, Joint Korea-U.S. Academic Symposium, vol. 4, (1994), 127–42.

Pei, Minxin. "Future Shock: The WTO and Political Change in China." *Policy Brief* (Carnegie Foundation), vol. 1, no. 3 (February 2001), (www.ceip.org/files/PDF/dem.PolBrief3.pdf).

Pengiran Osman Bin Pengiran Haji Patra, "The Future Course of the ASEAN Regional Forum: Openness and the Regional Approach to Disarmament." *Disarmament*, vol. 18, no. 2 (1995), 145–57.

Pfaff, William. "The Question of Hegemony." *Foreign Affairs*, vol. 80, no. 1 (January–February 2001), 221–32.

Pollack, Jonathan D. "The United States in East Asia: Holding the Ring." Adelphi Paper no. 275, March 1993.

Porter, Gareth. "The Environmental Hazards of Asia Pacific Development: The Southeast Asian Rainforests." *Current History*, vol. 93, no. 587 (December 1994), 430–34.

Pu Chenghao. "The Future of Strategy and Cooperation in the Regional Economic Development of Northeast Asia." *Shehui kexue jikan* (The Social Sciences), no. 6 (1993), 67–71.

Pyle, Kenneth B. "North Korea in U.S.-Japan Relations." Occasional Paper no. 80, The Woodrow Wilson International Center for Scholars, Washington, D.C., January 1999.

Ross, Robert S. "Beijing as a Conservative Power." *Foreign Affairs*, vol. 76, no. 2 (March–April 1997), 33–44.

Saburo, Ienaga. "The Glorification of War in Japanese Education." *International Security*, vol. 18, no. 3 (Winter 1993–94), 113–33.

Salameh, Mamdouh G. "China, Oil and the Risk of Regional Conflict." *Survival*, vol. 37, no. 4 (Winter 1995–96), 133–46.

Sanford, Dan C. "ROK's *Nordpolitik*: Revisited." *The Journal of East Asian Affairs*, vol. 7, no. 1 (Winter–Spring 1993), 1–31.

Scalapino, Robert A. "The United States and Asia: Future Prospects." *Foreign Affairs*, vol. 70, no. 5 (Winter 1991–1992), 20–40.

Scheer, Robert. "No Defense: How the *New York Times* Convicted Wen Ho Lee." *The Nation*, October 23, 2000, 11–20.

Schwarz, Benjamin. "Why America Thinks It Has to Run the World." *The Atlantic*, June 1966, 92–102.

Scobell, Andrew. "Playing to Win: Chinese Army Building in the Era of Jiang Zemin." *Asian Perspective*, vol. 25, no. 1 (2001), 73–105.

Sechser, Todd. "The Asian Nuclear Reaction Chain." *Proliferation Brief*, vol. 3, no. 3 (February 2, 2000); NAPSNet, March 2, 2000.

Segal, Gerald. "'Asianism' and Asian Security." *The National Interest*, no. 42 (Winter 1995–96), 58–65.

———. *China Changes Shape*, Adelphi Paper no. 287, London: IISS, 1994.

———. "East Asia and the 'Constrainment' of China." *International Security*, vol. 20, no. 4 (Spring 1996), 107–135.

———. "Tying China Into the International System." *Survival*, vol. 37, no. 2 (Summer 1995), 60–73.

Sen, Amartya. "Human Rights and Asian Values." *The New Republic*, July 14–21, 1997, 33–36.

Shambaugh, David. "China's Military: Real or Paper Tiger?" *Washington Quarterly*, vol. 19, no. 2 (Spring 1996), 19–36.

Shin, Kak-Soo. "A New Paradigm for Changing Korea-Japan Relations: A Regional Partnership." *IFANS Review*, vol. 2, no. 5 (July 1994), 10–16.

———. "Japan's Regional Role in Asia: A Korean Perspective." *Korea and World Affairs*, vol. 17, no. 2 (Summer 1993), 276–97.

Shin, Gi-Wook, and Jeong-Sik Ko. "A Troubled Little Dragon: Competition and Dependence in Korea's International Economic Relations." n.p., n.d., 27 pp.

Shishime, Tomohiro. "Promoting a Plan for a Marine Environment Monitoring Network in the North Pacific." Paper presented at the ESENA Workshop on Energy-Related Marine Issues in the Sea of Japan, Tokyo, July 11–12, 1998.

Shorrock, Tim. "The U.S. Role in Korea in 1979 and 1980" (www.kimsoft.com/korea/kwangju3.htm).

Simon, Sheldon W. "Arms Control, the Economic Crisis, and Southeast Asian Security." Paper prepared for the International Studies Association annual meeting, Washington, D.C., February 16–20, 1999.

Soeya, Yoshihide. "Japan's Dual Identity and the U.S.-Japan Alliance." Institute for International Studies, Asia/Pacific Research Center, Stanford University, May 1998.

———. "Japan's Multilateral Diplomacy in the Asia-Pacific and Its Implications for the Korean Peninsula." *Asian Perspective*, vol. 19, no. 2 (Fall–Winter 1995), 223–41.

Song, Young-Sun. "Prospects for U.S.-Japan Security Cooperation." *Asian Survey*, vol. 35, no. 12 (December 1995), 1087–101.

Spence, Jonathan. "A Flood of Troubles." *New York Times Magazine*, January 5, 1997, 34–39.

Stubbs, Richard. "Asia-Pacific Regionalization and the Global Economy." *Asian Survey*, vol. 35, no. 9 (September 1995), 785–97.

Sukma, Rizal. "ASEAN and the ASEAN Regional Forum: Should the 'Driver' Be Replaced?" Unpublished paper, Center for Strategic and International Studies, Jakarta, July 1999.

Suttmeier, Richard P. "Does 'Globalization' Matter? Technology and the Changing Context of U.S.–China Relations." *In Depth*, vol. 4, no. 3 (Fall 1994), 65–83.

———. "The Technological Emergence of the Pacific Rim: Threat or Opportunity to the US?" Unpublished paper, February 1992.

Suttmeier, Richard P., and Peter C. Evans. "China Goes Nuclear." *The China Business Review*, September–October 1996, 16–21.

Thayer, Carlyle A. "China's 'New Security Concept' and ASEAN." *Pacific Forum*, (www.csis.org/pacfor/cc/003Qchina_asean.html).

Tian Zhongqing, "China-ROK Relations in the New Asian-Pacific Context." *Korean Journal of International Studies*, vol. 25, no. 1 (1994), 65–74.

Tyler, Patrick. "The (Ab)normalization of U.S.–Chinese Relations." *Foreign Affairs*, vol. 78, no. 5 (September–October, 1999), 93–122.

Vasquez, John A. "The Realist Paradigm and Degenerative versus Progressive Research Programs: An Appraisal of Neotraditional Research on Waltz's Balancing Proposition."*American Political Science Review*, vol. 91, no. 4 (December 1997), 899–912.

Von Hippel, David F., and Peter Hayes. "Environmental Problems and the Energy Sector in the Democratic People's Republic of Korea." *Asian Perspective*, vol. 22, no. 2 (1998), 51–77.

Wallace, Michael D., Brian L. Job, Jean Clermont, and André Laliberté. "Rethinking Arms Races: Asymmetry and Volatility in the Taiwan Strait Case." *Asian Perspective*, vol. 25, no. 1 (2001), 157–93.

Waltz, Kenneth N. "Structural Realism after the Cold War." *International Security*, vol. 29, no. 1 (Summer 2000), 5–41.

Wanandi, Jusuf. "ASEAN's Challenges for Its Future." *Global Beat* (www.nyu.edu/globalbeat/asia/Wanandi012399.html).

———. "ASEAN's China Strategy: Towards Deeper Engagement." *Survival*, vol. 38, no. 3 (Autumn 1996), 117–28.

Wang Jisi. "U.S. Policy Toward China: Containment or Engagement?" *American Studies in China*, vol. 2 (1995), 24–39.

Weidenbaum, Murray and Harvey Sicherman. "The Chinese Economy: A New Scenario." *Wire* (Foreign Policy Research Institute), vol. 7, no. 1 (January 1999), (fpri@aol.com).

Whiting, Allen S. "ASEAN Eyes China: The Security Dimension" *Asian Survey*, vol. 37, no. 4 (April 1997), 299–322.

———. "Chinese Nationalism and Foreign Policy After Deng." *China Quarterly*, no. 142 (Summer 1995), 295–316.

Wolfensohn, James, "Asia and the World Economy," address at Harvard University, June 12, 2000, (www.worldbank.org), 8.

Woodrow Wilson Center, *China Environment Series*, no. 2 (Summer 1998).

Woods, Lawrence T. "Non-governmental Organizations and Pacific Cooperation: Back to the Future." *Pacific Review*, vol. 4, no. 4 (1991), 312–21.

Xie Wenqing. "US TMD and Taiwan." *International Strategic Studies* (Beijing), no. 3 (2000), 25–30.

Yi, Xiaoxiong. "Dynamics of China's South Korea Policy: Assertive Nationalism, Beijing's Changing Strategic Evaluation of the United States, and the North Korea Factor." *Asian Perspective*, vol. 24, no. 1 (2000), 71–102.

Yoo Seong Min. "Corporate Restructuring in Korea: Policy Issues Before and During the Crisis." *Joint U.S.-Korea Academic Studies*, vol. 9 (1999), 131–99.

Yuan, Hong. "The Implication of TMD System in Japan to China's Security." Paper presented at the Sixth ISODARCO Beijing Seminar on Arms Control, Shanghai, October 29–November 1, 1998 (www.nyu.edu/globalbeat/asia/Yuan0899.html).

Zagorsky, Alexei V. "Confidence-Building Measures: An Alternative for Asian-Pacific Security?" *The Pacific Review*, vol. 4, no. 4 (1991), 345–57.

Zakaria, Fareed. "Culture is Destiny: A Conversation with Lee Kwan Yew, *Foreign Affairs*, vol. 73, no. 2 (March–April 1994), 109–26.

Zarsky, Lyuba. "APEC, Globalization, and the 'Sustainable Development' Agenda." *Asian Perspective*, vol. 22, no. 2 (1998), 133–68.

Zarsky, Lyuba, and Jason Hunter. "Environmental Cooperation at APEC: The First Five Years." *The Journal of Environment & Development*, vol. 6, no. 3 (September 1997), 222–51.

Zhang Jinbao. "Changes in the Situation on the Korean Peninsula and their Impacts on the Strategic Pattern in Northeast Asia." *International Strategic Studies*, no. 1 (2001), 35–44.

Zhao, Suisheng. "Asia-Pacific Regional Multipolarity: From Alliance to Alignment in the Post-Cold War Era." *World Affairs*, vol. 159, no. 4 (Spring 1997), 183–96.

Zhebin, Alexander. "Russia and Korean Unification." *Asian Perspective*, vol. 19, no. 2 (Fall–Winter 1995), 175–90.

## REPORTS AND DOCUMENTS

Allen, Kenneth W., and Eric A. McVadon, *China's Foreign Military Relations*, Report no. 32. Washington, D.C.: Henry L. Stimson Center, October 1999.

Asian Development Bank (ADB). *Asian Development Outlook 2000*. New York: Oxford University Press, 2001.

Blair, Admiral Dennis C. Address, in Carnegie Endowment for International Peace, *Issue Brief*, vol. 3, no. 7 (March 23, 2000).

Carnegie Commission. *Preventing Deadly Conflicts*. New York: Carnegie Commission, 1997.

*The China Challenge in the Twenty-First Century: Implications for U.S. Foreign Policy*, Peaceworks no. 21. Washington, D.C.: U.S. Institute of Peace, June 1998.

Clinton, William J. *A National Security Strategy of Engagement and Enlargement*. Washington, D.C.: The White House, February 1996.

Cohen, William S. *Annual Report to the President and the Congress*. February 2000 (www.dtic.mil/execsec/adr2000/).

———. *Report of the Quadrennial Defense Review 1997*. May 1997 (www.dtic.mil/defenselink).

Dibb, Paul. *Towards a New Balance of Power in Asia*. London: Adelphi Paper No. 295, Oxford University Press, 1995.

Environment Canada, "Fact and Figures: The Impact of Urbanization on APEC Economies." (www.ec.gc.ca/apecmeet/rtab5k_e.htm).

Fischer, Stanley. "The Financial Crisis in Emerging Markets: Lessons for Eastern Europe and Asia," Speech at the EastWest Institute, New York City, April 23, 1999 (www.imf.org).

Gill, Bates, "Arms Acquisitions in East Asia," in Stockholm International Peace Research Institute, *SIPRI Yearbook 1994: World Armaments and Disarmament* (London: Oxford University Press, 1994), 556.

Hubbard, Thomas. Testimony before U.S. Senate, Foreign Relations Committee, Subcommittee on East Asian and Pacific Affairs, March 6, 2001, mimeo.

International Institute for Strategic Studies. *The Military Balance 1992/93.* London: IISS, 1993.

International Labor Organization. *The Social Impact of the Asian Financial Crisis.* Bangkok: ILO Regional Office for Asia and the Pacific, April 1998 (www.ilo.org/public/english/bureau/intpol/bangkok/index.htm).

Monterey Institute of International Studies, Center for Nonproliferation Studies. "Chinese Participation and Positions Regarding Various Arms Control and Nonproliferation Agreements, Organizations, and Regimes." April 1999 (cns.miis.edu/cns/projects/eanp/fact/cregime.htm).

———. *Individuals, Institutions and Policies in the Chinese Nonproliferation and Arms Control Community.* Monterey, Calif., November 6–9, 1997.

———. *U.S.–China Conference on Arms Control, Disarmament and Nonproliferation.* Beijing, September 23–25, 1998.

Nautilus Institute and Center for Global Communications. "Energy, Environment and Security in Northeast Asia: Defining a U.S.–Japan Partnership for Regional Comprehensive Security." December 1999 (www.nautilus.org/papers/energyu/finalreport.html).

People's Republic of China, State Council, News Bureau. *2000 nian Zhongguo de guofang baipishu* (White Paper on China's National Defense in 2000). *Renmin ribao* (People's Daily, Beijing), November 6, 2000 (www.peopledaily.com.cn).

People's Republic of China, State Council, Taiwan Affairs Office and Information Office. *The Taiwan Question and Reunification of China,* August 1993.

Perry, William J. et al. "Review of United States Policy toward North Korea: Findings and Recommendations." October 12, 1999; NAPSNet special report, October 13, 1999.

Pillsbury, Michael, ed. *China Debates the Future Security Environment.* Washington, D.C.: Office of Net Assessment, U.S. Department of Defense, 2000.

———. *Dangerous Chinese Misperceptions: The Implications for DoD,* report. Washington, D.C.: Office of Net Assessment, 1998.

Prime Minister's Commission on Japan's Goals in the 21st Century. *Japan's Goals in the 21st Century.* Tokyo: January 2000 (www.kantei.go.jp/jp/21century/report/pdfs/index.html).

"Security in the Midst of Change: A Japan-U.S. Alliance for the 21st Century." Symposium (www.asahi.com/english/symposium/main.html).

Sha Zukang, Director-General of the Department of Arms Control and Disarmament, Ministry of Foreign Affairs. "Some Thoughts on Non-Proliferation." Speech to the 7th Annual Carnegie International Non-Proliferation Conference, Washington, D.C., January 11–12, 1999, mimeo.

"Statement of Admiral Joseph W. Prueher, U.S. Navy, Before the House National Security Committee, Posture Hearing," March 6, 1997, mimeo, 13.

"Statement of General John H. Tilelli, Jr., Commander in Chief United Nations Command/Combined Forces Command & Commander United States Forces Korea, Before the House National Security Committee." March 6, 1997, mimeo.

Stockholm International Peace Research Institute (SIPRI). Database (projects.sipri.se).

———. *SIPRI Yearbook 1992.* London: Oxford University Press, 1992.

———. *SIPRI Yearbook 1993: World Armaments and Disarmament.* London: Oxford University Press, 1993.

———. *SIPRI Yearbook 1995: Armaments, Disarmament and International Security.* London: Oxford University Press, 1995.

Roth, Stanley O. Testimony before the Senate Foreign Relations Committee. May 14, 1998, transcript.

Samore, Gary. Briefing at the Carnegie Endowment for International Peace. March 17, 1999 (www.ceip.org).

Slocombe, Walter B. "U.S. Security Interests in the Pacific." Statement before a hearing of the House Committee on International Relations, Subcommittee on Asia and the Pacific, May 11, 1998, via Internet.

Tasman Institute. "Environmental Priorities in Asia and Latin America." Report to the Monash Group, November 7, 1997 (www.arts.monash.edu.au/ausapec/epala8.htm).

Tenet, George J. "The Worldwide Threat in 2000: Global Realities of Our National Security." Statement before the Senate Select Committee on Intelligence, February 2, 2000 (www.nyu.edu/globalbeat/usdefense/Tenet020200.html).

United Nations Development Program. *Human Development Report 1998.* New Delhi: Oxford University Press, 1998.

———. *The China Human Development Report.* New York: Oxford University Press, 1999.

U.S. Central Intelligence Agency. "The Intelligence Community Damage Assessment on the Implications of China's Acquisition of U.S. Nuclear Weapons Information on the Development of Future Chinese Weapons." April 21, 1999, press release (www.odci.gov/cia/public_affairs/press_release/0421kf.html).

———. National Intelligence Council. "Foreign Missile Developments and the Ballistic Missile Threat to the United States Through 2015." September 1999 (www.cia.gov/cia/publications/nie/nie99msl.html#rtoc12).

———. Nonproliferation Center, "Unclassified Report to Congress on the Acquisition of Technology Relating to Weapons of Mass Destruction and Advanced Conventional Munitions, 1 January through 30 June 1999."

U.S. Congress, House Committee on International Relations, Subcommittee on Asia and the Pacific. *Hearing: Sino-American Relations and U.S. Policy Options.* 105th Cong., 1st Sess., April 23, 1997. Washington, D.C.: U.S. GPO, 1997.

———. *Hearing: U.S. Foreign Assistance in Asia.* Washington, D.C.: U.S. GPO, 1996.

U.S. Congress, Joint Economic Committee. *China's Economic Future: Challenges to U.S. Policy.* 104th Cong., 2d Sess., August. Washington, D.C.: U.S. GPO, 1996.

U.S. Congress, Senate, Select Committee on Intelligence, *Hearing on People's Republic of China,* 105th Cong., 1st Sess., September 18, 1997. Washington, D.C.: U.S. GPO, 1998.

U.S. Department of Defense, Office of International Security Affairs. *The United States Security Strategy for the East Asia-Pacific Region.* November 1998 (www.defenselink.mil/pubs/easr98).

U.S. Department of State. "China Country Report on Human Rights Practices for 1998." February 26, 1999 (www.state.gov).

U.S. General Accounting Office. *National Security: Impact of China's Military Modernization in the Pacific Region.* Report to Congressional Committees GAO/NSIAD-95-84, 1995.

———. National Security and International Affairs Division. *China: U.S. and European Union Arms Sales since the 1989 Embargoes.* Testimony before the U.S. Congress, Joint Economic Committee. GAOA/T-NSIAD-98-171, April 28, 1998.

———. *Overseas Presence: Issue Involved in Reducing the Impact of the U.S. Military Presence on Okinawa.* Report GAO/NSIAD-98-66. Washington, D.C.: U.S. GPO, March 1998.

United States Institute of Peace. "'Trialogue': U.S.-Japan-China Relations and Asian-Pacific Stability." Washington, D.C.: U.S. GPO, September 1998.

U.S. Senate, Select Committee on Intelligence. *Report on Impacts to U.S. National Security of Advanced Satellite Technology Exports to the People's Republic of China (PRC), and Report on the PRC's Efforts to Influence U.S. Policy.* 106th Cong., 1st Sess., May 1999 (www.apbonline.com/911/1999/05/06/report.html).

## PRINCIPAL NEWSPAPERS AND
## OTHER NEWS SOURCES CONSULTED

*Asahi Shimbun* (Tokyo)
*Asian Wall Street Journal* (Hong Kong)
*Beijing Review* (Beijing)
*Christian Science Monitor* (Boston)
*The Daily Yomiuri* (Tokyo)
*Defense News* (Washington, D.C.)
*Far Eastern Economic Review* (Hong Kong)
*International Herald Tribune* (Paris)
*Japan Times* (Tokyo)
*Korea Times* (Seoul)
*New York Times*
NAPSNet (Northeast Asia Peace and Security Network) Daily Reports
*Renmin ribao* (People's Daily, Beijing)
*Washington Post*

## WEB SITES OF RELEVANT ORGANIZATIONS

Asia-Pacific Economic Cooperation (APEC): www.apecsec.org.sg
Association of Southeast Asian Nations (ASEAN): www.asean.or.id
Carnegie Endowment for International Peace: www.ceip.org

Center for Defense Information: www.cdi.org
Monterey Institute (California), Center for Nonproliferation Studies: cns.miis.edu/
    cns/projects/eanp/pubs/chinaorg.html
Natural Resources Defense Council: www.nrdc.org/nuclear/nudb
Nautilus Institute: www.nautilus.org
Henry Stimson Center: www.stimson.org
RAND Corporation: www.rand.org
Stockholm International Peace Research Institute: www.sipri.se
U.S. Department of Defense: www.defenselink.mil
World Bank: www.worldbank.org

# Index

Afghanistan, 33, 192
Africa, 223
Agreed Framework, 214, 220
AIDS/H.I.V., 9, 13, 37, 39, 53n70, 204. *See also* Japan
Akaha, Tsuneo, 84n6
Albright, Madeleine, 193
Amnesty International, 71
Arab-Israeli conflict, 199
arms, 56n104, 57n119, 191, 198, 221, 226n29; assistance, 219; buildups, 60, 79, 189; control, 70, 76, 220–21; Europe and Asia, 76; and regional security, 43–48, 55n97, 55nn102–3. *See also* weapons of mass destruction (WMD)
Art, Robert, 201
ASEAN Post-Ministerial Conference (ASEAN-PMC), 67–68, 70, 73–75, 86n30, 87n54, 193
ASEAN Regional Forum (ARF), 86n30, 86n39, 87n54, 100, 134, 219–21; and the Asian way, 60, 64, 68–70, 72–77, 79–82; and North Korea, 176
Asia: cohesiveness, 77–78; identity, 2, 3–7, 19n1; regional issues, 10–14; relations between states, 8–10; "values," 6
Asia-Europe Meeting (ASEM), 65, 66, 75, 76
Asian Development Bank (ADB), 13, 22n39, 36, 65, 74–75, 88n69, 216

Asian Monetary Fund (AMF), 78, 149
"Asiatom," 214
Asian way, 2–3, 60–84, 189, 212, 218, 220–24
Asia-Pacific Economic Cooperation (APEC), 2, 6, 12, 105, 164; and the Asian way, 62–63, 65–67, 68, 71–72, 75–77, 83; and business, 27; and Cambodia, 19n3; and China, 71; development, 225n1; and economy, 29, 51n36; environment, 40, 41, 54n83; and Hong Kong, 19n3, 71, 87n54; and Japan, 72, 142, 145; members, 19n3; and North Korea, 19n3, 87n54, 176; and regional security, 219, 222; and Taiwan, 19n3, 71, 87n54; and United States, 72, 193, 199, 215; and Vietnam, 19n3
Asia Pacific identity, 2–4, 19n1
Asia Watch, 71
Association of Southeast Asian Nations (ASEAN), 2, 10, 12, 40, 97, 100, 218, 220–21; arms, 47, 223; and Burma, 13, 19n2, 69, 71, 77; and business, 27, 28, 34, 86n33; and Cambodia, 12, 19n2, 71, 72; and China, 55n92, 72, 81–82, 84n3, 88n64; and East Timor, 84; and economic relations, 29, 30; and environment, 89n104, 214; Free Trade Area (AFTA), 12, 68, 86n33; and human rights, 80, 84; and IMF, 89n86; and Japan, 69, 145; members, 19n2;

247

186n82; and National Security Law,
174; and nuclear power, 165; and
nuclear weapons, 164–65, 172–73,
177–78, 187n90, 187n94; and oil, 165;
and party politics, 174; and Russia,
164, 172–73, 179, 184nn63–65; and
security, 163, 165, 172; and Soviet
Union, 161; and Sunshine policy,
166–76; and UN, 164; and
unemployment, 174; and UNICEF,
185n77; unification, 161–80, 181n24,
182n32, 183n54; and United States,
161, 165, 169, 171–72, 176–78, 181n20.
*See also* North Korea; South Korea
Kosovo, 23n54, 59, 77, 192, 198
Krauthammer, Charles, 199
Kuril Islands. *See* Northern Islands
Kyoto Protocol, 41
Kyrgyzstan, 8, 220

labor issues, 10, 13, 15, 21n35, 36–37, 72,
76, 158n37, 215. *See also* children's
issues
Laos, 4, 9, 11, 19nn2–3, 61, 71–72
Latin America, 65, 223
Lawyers Committee for Human Rights,
215
Lee Kwan Yew, 6
Lee Teng-hui, 122
Li Xiannian, 110
literacy, 13, 51n44
London Convention of 1975, 54n77
Loral Space and Communications, 112,
133n108, 134n118
Lord, Winston, 76
Luce, Henry, 199

Macedonia, 59
Mack, Andrew, 223
Malaysia: and arms, 44, 55n103; and
ASEAN, 19n2; and business, 27–28, 34;
and diversity, 77; economy, 12, 51n36,
78; and environment, 10, 41, 72,
89n104; and ethnic minorities, 15; and
immigration, 212; migrant workers, 37;
military, 9; military spending, 56n115;
Muslim tensions, 77; nationalism, 5;

PKOs, 18; politics, 4, 9, 14; poverty,
21n27; regional security, 67; and
Singapore, 61; and United States, 193,
202, 208n50
Manila, 208n56
Mao Zedong, 102
McCormick, Thomas, 207n37
McDonnell Douglas Aircraft, 114,
134n120
Mexico, 19n3, 198–99
Middle East, 37, 45–46, 70, 142, 145, 224
migrant workers, 10, 15, 36–37. *See also*
immigration
military, 9–12, 42, 44, 46–47, 60, 190, 194,
224; spending, 43–44, 46, 48, 55n103,
56n104, 56n114–15. *See also*
Association of Southeast Asian Nations
(ASEAN); economic issues; *individual
countries*; security
minorities, ethnic, 15, 36. *See also*
immigration
Miyazawa Doctrine, 74–75
Miyazawa Kiichi, 74–75, 89n84, 155
Miyazawa Plan, 89n84
Mohamad, Mahathir bin, 19n5, 51n36, 72,
76, 78, 208n50
Mongolia: and ASEAN-PMC, 86n30; and
environment, 40; and Neorealism, 26;
nuclear weapons, 223; politics, 4, 9;
poverty, 216; and TRADP, 28
Montreal Protocol, 41
Mori Yoshiro, 149, 159n41
multilateralism, 6, 40, 217–22
Myanmar, 35

Nakayama Taro, 74
nationalism, 5–7, 60–62, 74, 77–78,
189–90, 193, 200–201, 202
Nautilus Institute for Security and
Sustainable Development, 40–41,
54n83, 71, 213
Neorealism, 25–27, 48
Nepal, 15
Netherlands, 47
New Zealand, 4, 67, 86n30
Nishimura Shingo, 227n34
Nixon, Richard M., 102, 109

# About the Author

Mel Gurtov is professor of political science and international studies at Portland State University, Oregon. Previously, he served with the RAND Corporation in Santa Monica, California, and as a professor at the University of Calfornia, Riverside. He is editor-in-chief of *Asian Perspective*, an international affairs quarterly journal. A frequent visitor to Asia, he has been a Senior Fulbright Scholar in South Korea (1994) and a Visiting Scholar at Waseda University (2001). Gurtov is the author of numerous books and articles on Asian and international politics, including *Global Politics in the Human Interest* (4th ed., 1999), which has been translated into Japanese, Spanish, and Chinese, and (with Byong-Moo Hwang) *China's Security: The New Roles of the Military* (1998), which has a Korean edition.